£3-50

This book is dedicated to my grandfather and my uncle,
two Englishmen who faithfully served their King and country
throughout two World Wars

HOWARD LEIGH SAMPSON

202796 PRIVATE, 1/4TH. BN.
THE QUEEN'S ROYAL
WEST SURREY REGIMENT
UK, INDIA, NW FRONTIER &
UK, 1914–1919

REGINALD HOWARD SAMPSON

T/62326 SERJEANT,
ROYAL ARMY SERVICE CORPS
UK, BEF (DUNKIRK), N AFRICA
(EIGHTH ARMY), ITALY,
FRANCE, BELGIUM, HOLLAND
(ARNHEM), GERMANY, POLAND
& UK, 1936–1946

British Army Uniforms & Insignia of World War Two

Brian L. Davis

ARMS AND
ARMOUR

"I will apparel them all in one livery that they may agree like brothers . . ."

William Shakespeare, Henry VI, Part 2, Act IV, Scene 2

Overleaf: Men of the Suffolk Regiment practise crossing barbed wire defences by means of ladders and mats.

Arms and Armour Press
A Cassell Imprint
Villiers House, 41-47 Strand, London WC2N 5JE.

Reprinted 1993

Distributed in the USA by Sterling Publishing Co. Inc., 387 Park Avenue South, New York, NY 10016-8810.

Distributed in Australia by Capricorn Link (Australia) Pty. Ltd, P.O. Box 665, Lane Cove, New South Wales 2066.
First published 1983; revised edition, with amendments and corrections 1992
© Brian L. Davis, 1983, 1992

British Library Cataloguing in Publication Data
Davis, Brian L. (Brian Leigh) 1935–
British Army uniforms and insignia of World War Two
1. Great Britain. Army. Uniforms, history
I. Title
355.1
ISBN 1-85409-159-X

Printed in Great Britain.

Acknowledgments
I wish to express my gratitude to the following establishments and individuals for their advice and assistance in the preparation of this book: the Director and staff of the Imperial War Museum, Lambeth, London, in particular the staffs of the Department of Printed Books and the Photographic Library; the Director and staff of the National Army Museum, Chelsea, London, in particular the staff of the Reading Room; the Directors and staff of Messrs Bermans & Nathans costumiers of Camden, London, in particular the General Manager and the staff of the Military Department and Library; the Keeper and staff of the Public Record Office, Kew; the Curators and Custodians of various regimental museums that I had the pleasure of visiting over the last eight years or so while gathering material for this book – alas, too many to acknowledge here individually; Ken Green, for allowing me to photograph certain items of insignia in his collection; Robert J. Marrion; Lieutenant-Commander W. Maitland Thornton, MBE, RD*, RNR for answering my occasional questions; and lastly Ray Westlake for sharing his knowledge of metal shoulder straps. The majority of the photographs are from my own collection; the remainder are from the Imperial War Museum, the collection of the late Lieutenant-Colonel Howard N. Cole, OBE, and other private sources.

Contents

Preface   7

Introduction: The British Army between the Wars   9

Part I: Ranks and Appointments   11

Part II: Badges and Insignia   16
1. Badges of Rank and Appointment   16
2. Shoulder Strap Titles (Metal)   37
3. Collar Badges, Gorget Patches and Buttons   41
4. Armlets   45
5. Good Conduct Badges   51
6. Tradesmen's, Instructors' and Skill-at-Arms Badges   52
7. Special Dress Distinctions   76
8. Slip-on Shoulder Strap Titles   81
9. Colour Section   85
10. Shoulder Designations   89
11. Formation and Unit Coloured Distinguishing Marks 1940–45   92
12. Wound Stripes and Service Chevrons   113
13. Officer Cadet Insignia   115
14. Cap Badges   116

Part III: Uniforms and Clothing   120
1. General Instructions   120
2. Head-dress   129
3. Officers' Service Dress   158
4. Trousers, Breeches, Pantaloons and Trews   161
5. Footwear and Handwear   163
6. Greatcoats, Trench Coats and Capes   170
7. Khaki Drill and Jungle Green Clothing   174
8. Service Dress for Other Ranks   178
9. Battle-Dress, Serge and Denim   181
10. Kilts and Kilt Covers   189
11. Personal Clothing   195
12. Personal Accoutrements   197

Part IV: Specialist and Protective Clothing   200
1. Airborne Forces   200
2. Physical Training Instructors   205
3. Hospital Clothing   205
4. Work Clothing   206
5. Tank Suits   208
6. Motor-Cyclists' Clothing   211
7. Protective Coats   212
8. Snow Camouflage and Cold Climate Clothing   213
9. Groundsheets and Waterproofs   217

Part V: Equipment   218
1. Protective Headwear   218
2. Web Equipment   229
3. Anti-Gas Equipment   238
4. Miscellaneous Equipment   246
5. Miscellaneous Personal Equipment   251
6. The Carrying of Arms and Ammunition   255

Part VI: Local Defence Volunteers and the Home Guard   256
1. Local Defence Volunteers   256
2. The Home Guard   258
3. Home Guard Ranks and Insignia   261
4. Uniforms and Personal Equipment   269
5. Home Guard Auxiliaries   270

Appendices   271
1. Glossary   271
2. The Army Council   272
3. Army Numbers   274

Bibliography   276

Preface

The ten years from 1935 to 1945 have proved to be an important period in the development of British Army uniforms of modern times: until 1939 it was a period of transition and experimentation, with the all-important introduction of the ubiquitous Battle-Dress; after 1939 it was a period of rapid development, with numerous innovations, many of which paved the way for items still in use with the Army today.

Regulations for the wearing of military uniforms by commissioned officers were contained in *Dress Regulations for the Army* (Dress Regulations) and those for warrant officers, non-commissioned officers and other ranks were governed by *Regulations for the Clothing of the Army* (Clothing Regulations). In June 1934 the War Office published a set of Dress Regulations together with three subsequent sets of amendments for 1937, 1938 and 1940. These proved to be the last of their kind to be issued, not only before the outbreak of the Second World War but for over 35 years. It was not until 1969 that a completely new series of Dress Regulations began to appear, although as an interim measure five pamphlets had been produced by the War Office between 1954 and 1956 entitled *Rules Relating to Dress.* These, however, did not constitute an authority for detailed dress regulations or for scales of issue.

May 1936 saw the publication of a set of Clothing Regulations which were followed by seven separate sets of amendments dating from January 1937 to October 1939. Unlike the Dress Regulations, these Clothing Regulations were upgraded during the 1939–45 war: they were republished as War Clothing Regulations in 1941 and 1943 with amendments added in 1947.

Because the Battle-Dress suit was introduced in 1939 after the final prewar Dress Regulations and Clothing Regulations had been published and because this style of uniform ceased to be used in the late 1960s before the publication of the first of the new, postwar Dress Regulations, detailed instructions regarding the wearing of Battle-Dress and everything associated with it were never properly dealt with, although limited information was published in War Clothing Regulations and in wartime Army Council Instructions (ACIs).

By drawing extensively on information published in prewar and wartime, and to some extent in postwar, publications, such as the already mentioned Dress, Clothing and War Clothing Regulations, and by gleaning information from ACIs, Army Orders and Special Army Orders, King's Regulations and Priced Vocabularies of Clothing and Necessaries as well as official handbooks of all sorts, supplemented with material available at the Public Record Office and regimental museums throughout the country, this book endeavours to bridge the gap between 1935 and 1945, covering all aspects of drab Army uniforms, insignia, clothing and equipment.

As shown by the contents listing, the book is divided into five main parts, a sixth being devoted to the Local Defence Volunteers and the Home Guard; this separate section in many ways mirrors the information contained in the preceding parts. A few words of comment on each main part would not go amiss at this point.

Part I deals with ranks and appointments. These include every known rank and appointment from Boy soldier to Field Marshal, and I have endeavoured to list them from the lowest to the most senior.

Part II is one of the most extensive and most complex sections of the book. It covers badges, patches, titles and flashes, not only describing their appearance, but also showing how, when and by whom they were worn and discussing their introduction, their development and, in some cases, their withdrawal from use. In many respects this is the most important section of the book. Without these individual marks—these badges, emblems of rank, signs, patches strips of coloured cloth, buttons, crests, flashes, titles and the like—no distinction could be made between individuals who were dressed alike or amongst units, battalions, regiments, divisions, corps or even armies. These were the outward signs of efficiency, proficiency, regimental pride, individual sacrifice, wounds and hurts, past military history, skills and trades of all sorts and a whole multitude of separate and individual or collective incidentals that went to make up the very stuff of the British Army. This part includes many lists, a number of which contain all the regiments and units of the British Army of the period in question, Regular, Territorial and Yeomanry. These lists have been compiled in such a way that they are in descending order of regimental precedence.

Parts III and IV constitute the bulk of the book. Practically every item of head-dress, footwear, handwear, clothing and uniform is dealt with in the third part; specialist and protective clothing is considered in the fourth. Together, these two parts deal with every aspect of the Army's drab or khaki coloured clothing. Full Dress, which was in abeyance between the two World Wars and was only worn by the Household Troops and by those senior officers who were already in possession of such attire, has been excluded from this work, as has Mess Dress. With the brief exception of the 'Blues' issued for the special occasion of the parade in 1936 for the coronation of King George VI, Full Dress in the British Army did not reappear until the 1950s.

Below: A Grenadier Guardsman wearing full kit while standing guard outside Chelsea Barracks, March 1942.

Many of the items of Full-Dress apparel and accoutrements included in Part III went a long way towards enlivening the drabness of the khaki uniforms. I have made a point of including in this section such things as coloured Field Service caps, lanyards, bugle cords, kilts and the like. Whilst these Full-Dress items were not part of the basic khaki Service Dress, Battle-Dress, Khaki Drill or jungle green clothing, they were permitted to be worn with these forms of dress. The kilt, for example, worn with Service Dress tunic, Glengarry, tartan hose tops and white spats, was the nearest thing many Scottish regiments had to Full Dress between the wars.

The equipment section, Part V, deals with a lot of the commonplace items of personal equipment. Most of the items of web equipment that went to make up the 1937 and 1944 patterns of web equipment are given here. Not included, however, are many of the 1908 pattern items that lingered on well into the 1930s, and 1940s, and in a limited way into the 1950s. These were usually worn mixed with other pattern items and normally used by second-line troops, Home Guard units or cadets. My experience of collecting and studying items of equipment has brought home to me that very many 'off-beat' items of webbing exist for which no reference can be found as to its purpose; unfortunately, this category of equipment has had to be excluded from the book.

The photographs have been specially selected to help illustrate many of the more interesting features of Army uniforms as well as items of insignia and equipment. I have also used line drawings to supplement the photographic selection.

Wherever possible I have tried to give known dates of the introduction of items, together with my source of reference. I feel that this is important, as it can be of assistance to those readers who feel inclined to research through the original material for themselves.

Throughout the book I have used the past tense, having chosen to do so for the sake of uniformity. (The obvious exception to this self-imposed general rule is where I have made direct quotations, and such are shown within inverted commas.) Having adopted this system, I should, however, point out that many of the subjects and objects so referred to still exist today.

The preparation for this book has very much been a labour of love. One of the most difficult aspects of the preparation was limiting the volume of information available to a manageable amount for the purposes of publication, but even after considerable pruning the work still runs to over 200,000 words.

I am also very much aware that my chosen subject is the domain of many acknowledged experts, some of whom specialize in the study of particular aspects of British Army uniforms and insignia. I have done my best to double-check my facts and I apologize in advance for any errors that may have crept in. Finally, I welcome constructive criticism, especially if it can usefully be used to correct future editions of this book.

Brian L. Davis, Sanderstead, 1983

Introduction
The British Army between the Wars

Following the Great War of 1914–18 the British Army was, to all intents and purposes, relegated to its pre-1914 basis and strength. In 1922 its establishment was reduced as a measure of economy, and with the setting up of the Irish Free State five Irish infantry regiments were disbanded. During the previous year sixteen cavalry regiments were merged, the new-style regiments being made up of two squadrons of the senior regiment and one of the junior. The Regular Army, which in 1914 had possessed six infantry divisions, found itself reduced to five; artillery batteries were reduced from six to four guns each.

The Territorial Force, which had been created in 1907, was reconstituted as the Territorial Army in 1922. Most Yeomanry regiments were unhorsed and either converted into artillery regiments or mechanized as armoured car units. In 1935 it was decided that the Territorial Army should assume the entire responsibility for anti-aircraft defence at home. At that time the strength of the air defence formations in the Territorial Army was under 2,000, but in January 1936 the first anti-aircraft division was formed, and by the end of April 1939 the establishment of the Territorial Army AA units was 96,000.

From 1925 to 1935 recruiting into the Army was poor. A remedy was sought by making the conditions of service more attractive, and special proficiency pay was granted on a graduated scale, in such a way that the rise became greater with increasing length of service. The experiment was also tried of making the Army a lifelong career for men in the ranks by allowing them to enlist for twelve years' service with the Colours, with the option of re-engaging to complete a total service of twenty-one years, when they became eligible for a pension, whilst short-term soldiers were given vocational training during their last six months of service to fit them for civilian life. Much greater attention was also paid to improving and modernizing barracks, the soldiers' menu was improved, and more opportunities were given for promotion.

Careful experimentation laid the foundation for progress in mechanization and reorganization, and as funds became available the effects began to be felt. Under the vigorous régime imposed by the Secretary of State for War, the Rt. Hon. Leslie Hore-Belisha PC, MP, and with the general and growing realization of approaching danger, the pace of this progress was greatly accelerated. Divisions, and also units, were reduced in size, while the ratio of firepower to manpower was greatly increased. Divisions were split into two classes, motorized divisions, based on the light machine gun, and mechanized armoured divisions, based on the tank, the former made up of nine battalions instead of twelve, each provided with fifty Bren guns.

Apart from the Household Cavalry (The Life Guards and the Royal Horse Guards, 'The Blues'), the Royal Scots Greys (2nd Dragoons) and the 1st The Royal Dragoons, all British Cavalry on the Home establishment were mechanized, light and fast tanks replacing horses. The role of the Cavalry remained the same, however, namely to provide the reconnaissance elements for the division. The battalion of Infantry consisted of headquarters, an HQ company and four other companies, each company having three platoons of three sections each. A battalion commander had one platoon per company fewer than hitherto, but although he had a smaller number of men to command his fire strength was much greater.

The most useful acquisition under the new organization was considered to be the carrier platoon, equipped with armoured carriers. These were speedy and afforded protection to the flanks, whilst they also acted as links between the tanks and the Infantry or as covering parties and provided mobile fire units for use in a counter-attack. The crews of these carriers were armed with Bren light machine-guns or 'Boys' anti-tank rifles.

The Artillery was again reorganized, this time into batteries of twelve guns each, and it also took over from the Infantry the 2pdr anti-tank gun. The basic artillery piece was the 25pdr gun, which had a far greater range than the former 18pdr, and the guns and their limbers were now towed by motor vehicles instead of horses.

Composition and Strength, 1939

Prior to 6 September 1939 the various units of the British Army comprised several different parts:

The Regular Army. This differed in many respects from the armies of the Continent: compared with them, for example, it was relatively small, since it depended on voluntary enlistment. Recruits to the Regular Army joined for long service periods, normally seven years, and thus made up a highly trained force.

The Army Reserve. Complementary to the Regular Army in time of war was the Army Reserve. This consisted of men who had returned to civilian life after having completed their service with the Colours but who still remained for a further period liable to recall in case of an emergency.

The Territorial Army. Behind the Regular Army stood the Territorial Army, composed of civilians who had volunteered for military training on a four-year engagement, with an option of extending it. These units were administered by the County Associations, thus retaining the old Yeoman spirit, but their training was organized by the military commands of the areas in which they were situated, under the direction of the War Office. TA training comprised an annual camp of a fortnight's duration and a certain number of obligatory drill parades during the course of each year. In 1938 the field force units of the TA were reorganized along modern lines and were provided with the latest equipment.

The Officers Training Corps. The Officers Training Corps (OTC), a self-explanatory term, was made up of a senior and junior division, whose units were formed by members of public schools and universities.

The Supplementary Reserve. This was composed mainly of technicians, formed to meet the emergency needs of the Regular Army.

The Militia. The units listed above would have, in themselves, provided a formidable field force, but a further augmentation of manpower was brought about by the introduction of conscription throughout the country in April 1939. Men who were conscripted under this scheme were allowed to state their preference as to the service they wished to join, the Army, the Royal Navy or the Royal Air Force. Those who chose the first were drafted into what was called the Militia.

Mobilization

In the House of Commons on 27 April 1939 Mr. Hore-Belisha stated that the strength of the Regular Army was 224,000, that of the Territorial Army Field Force 325,000 and that of the Anti-Aircraft Units (TA) 96,000; this gave a total of men under arms of 645,000. During the middle of July 1939 the first batch of militiamen, numbering 34,000, were called up by age group; additional recruiting for the Territorial Army between April and September 1939 brought in a further 36,000. To these were added the Army Reserve and the Supplementary Reserve, called up by proclamation on the outbreak of war and numbering 150,000 men. Thus on 3 September 1939 the British Army numbered about 865,000 men. Three days later, on 6 September 1939, by the passing of the Armed Forces (Conditions of Service) Act, all units of the Regular Army, the Territorial Army, the Militia and other auxiliary forces were merged into a single entity, the British Army.

Amendments

Author's note: *British Army Uniforms* first appeared in 1983. From about 1985 it has been out of print, new copies being virtually unobtainable. The publishers have agreed to re-issue the book while at the same time allowing me to correct those errors that, unfortunately, crept into the first edition. Since the book was first published I have received a considerable amount of correspondence from fellow enthusiasts, both in Great Britain and abroad. Much of this correspondence was taken up with expanding on aspects of various subjects dealt with in the book as well as adding valuable, and much of it new, information to what I had already written. Some of those persons who wrote to me took the trouble to point out those errors that I had made and sent me their corrections. It is this information that I have made full use of in preparing this corrected edition of the book. Unfortunately insufficient space precludes my including any of the additional information I received, much of which was based on personal experience and all of which makes fascinating reading.

Dedication page: The date on caption to photograph of Howard Leigh Sampson should read '1900–1919' and not '1914–1919'.

Page 4: Acknowledgements column. Fifth line up from bottom end of sentence should read 'shoulder strap title' and not 'shoulder straps'.
Page 12: Left hand column. The upper end of the page-deep bracket for appointments should start at 'Trumpeter' and should not include 'A boy holding any appointment'.
Page 15: Table showing commissioned officer ranks should be correctly subdivided thus:

Second Lieutenant	
Lieutenant	Junior officers
Captain	
Major	
Lieutenant-Colonel	Field officer ranks
Colonel[1]	
Brigadier[2]	
Major-General	
Lieutenant-General	General officers
General	
Field Marshal	

Page 25: Caption to photo, upper row *'Opposite, left'* should read 'CSM Reginald Bolland, MBE, DCM, of The Devonshire Regiment, 21 March 1944'.
Page 25: Caption to photo, lower row, *'Far left'* should read 'S.Sjt. H. Andrews, DFM, of the Glider Pilot Regiment, 3 May 1944'.

Page 26: Table 5. Rank or appointment column. Eleventh line down should read '1st King's Dragoon Guards'. Last line of footnote 2 should read '2/5ths-inch'.
Page 27: Photographic illustration of RSM Foot Guards Royal Arms arm badge, item 1, is of the incorrect pattern. Item shown has the modern, current pattern of crown and not the style in use during the 1939–45 period. Item 4. Caption should read 'SQMS, Middlesex Yeomanry, and 1st King's Dragoon Guards'. Item 5. The number '5' is missing from the caption to item 5, which should also read 'Staff Serjeant-Farrier, RHA'.
Page 30: Last line of description of arm badge for 25th Dragoons should read '. . . outwards, the whole within a laurel wreath surmounted by an Imperial Crown'. Photo caption. Last two lines should read 'SSM McHardy; see also the photograph top left on page 141'.
Page 31: Captions to line illustrations of rank badges for officers. Item 6 should read '6, Chaplain 1st Class (also Deputy Chaplain-General to the Forces);'.
Page 37: Caption to item 12 of metal shoulder strap titles should read '12, Royal Irish Fusiliers' and not '12, Royal Inniskilling Fusiliers'.
Page 41: Under the general heading of 'Gorget

Patches' the list of coloured gorget patches taken from the 1934 edition of *Dress Regulations for the Army*, after 'Field-Marshal[2]', the rank of 'General' and not 'eneral' should appear. Right hand column, seventh line down. The reference to the Dress Regulation Amendments of 1939 should read 'Amendments to 1940'.

Page 42: Part of caption to photo on page 42, top row, *Far right* should read 'Maj.-Gen. C. G. C. Nicholson, CBE, DSO and bar, MC and bar'.

Page 43: Part of caption to photo on page 43, top row, *'Right'* 'Brig. Geoffrey Harding DSO' should be corrected to read 'Brig. Geoffrey Harding, CBE, DSO, MC and bar in Service Dress'. Part of caption to button types and sizes should be corrected to read '7–9 are pocket and shoulder strap buttons'.

Page 48: Under heading 'Armlets for Other Ranks' and at the end of passage sub-headed *'Other ranks personnel employed as regimental police'*, the last sentence in this passage should have added 'See page 141'.

Page 53: Footnote 1 to Table 9 as shown should be replaced with the following: '1. As published in Clothing Regulations for 1936 and War Clothing Regulations for 1941 and 1943'.

Page 55: Caption to photo showing printed Ordnance issue Army Fire Service arm badge should be corrected so that the last three lines of caption read '(green and red) and his crown and rank chevrons (below); July 1942'.

Page 57: Right hand column. Fourth paragraph down, which starts 'An exception to the above rule was made in the case of Cavalry regiments'. Replace all words after 'regiments' with 'who wore the "crown and crossed swords", or "lances in wreath" and the "crown and crossed rifles" on the right sleeve of the jacket'. Also fifth paragraph, which incorrectly starts with repeated text should be replaced with 'NCOs who were employed as signallers but who were not in possession.', etc.

Page 67: The sentence in parentheses at the end of the caption column relates to the photo of Staff Sjt. Bill Brough, MM, and not to the reference to modern SAS operational wings.

Page 80: Personnel of the CMP(VP) were 'Vulnerable Points' personnel and not 'Vulnerability Points' personnel.

Page 82: It was incorrect to have included the black-on-khaki 'Royal Hampshire' shoulder strap slip-on (item 9) in this layout. This particular item is a post-war issue, the Hampshire Regiment having received the Royal prefix in 1946.

Page 89: Left hand column, fourth line down

should refer to '(Army Order 10 of 1902)' and not '1920'.

Page 94: Caption to photograph shows the GOC (General Officer Commanding) of the 6th Armoured Division and not the CO (Commanding Officer).

Page 102: Photographic illustration at the top of caption column features the '56th (London) Division' formation sign and not, as incorrectly captioned, the sign for the '5th (London) Division'.

Page 106: Caption to the photograph shown on this page contains a direction to refer to page 90 for a comparison of the form of Chaplains Department shoulder designation. This should refer to page 89.

Page 109: The tartan flash shown in the shape of a fusilier grenade (item 1) is of MacKenzie tartan. The tartan grenade flash worn by the Royal Scots Fusiliers was of Government or 42nd tartan. The diced flash (item 3) of the Argyll and Sutherland Highlanders is shown upside down.

Page 113: It has been pointed out to me that there is no reference made to the colour of the Service Chevrons illustrated as line drawings in the left hand caption column. For wear by Army personnel these were red on khaki cloth, either printed Ordnance issue or embroidered on cloth.

Page 119: Table 26, third column on right headed 'Worn by', fifth line down. Delete the two words 'except pipers' shown in parentheses.

Page 123: Right hand column. Under the heading 'Regimental Numbers', second line up from the bottom, 'Appendix 1' should read 'Appendix 3'.

Page 137: The first two lines of the right hand column of footnote 1 are incorrectly placed. These two lines should appear as the last two lines at the base of the footnote column on this page.

Page 138: Footnote 1 for Table 31 refers the reader to see footnote 1 on page 131. This page reference is incorrect. The footnote in question appears on page 137. This same error appears a further three times on page 140 under Tables 32, 33 and 34, and again on page 142 under Table 35.

Page 146: Items 1 and 7 shown as line drawings of pagri flashes have been incorrectly drawn. The Queen's Royal Regiment (West Surrey) flash (item 1) was in fact a large square patch of dark blue cloth worn on its point and having stitched across the centre a horizontal rectangle of scarlet cloth on which was embroidered the curved title 'QUEEN'S' in white worsted letters with serifs. Item 7, the pagri flash for the Suffolk Regiment, was in reality a more elaborate design than that shown in the book. The representation of the castle

had three prominent castellated towers, the centre one set higher than the two flanking towers. There was no door or archway in the wall of this castle. The yellow felt castle stitched to a khaki drill patch 2in × 2½in was worn up to 1941; after 1941 the castle was worn with a red felt backing of similar dimensions.

Page 151: The last line of the photo caption dealing with the 11th Hussar beret worn by Sjt. Hugh Lyon, MM, should read '(See also the photograph on page 30)'.

Page 152: Right hand column, sixth line of fifth paragraph down should read '(see page 153)'.

Page 154: Right hand column, second line of third paragraph down should refer to Table 38 on page 156 and not Table 28.

Page 186: Caption to photograph should refer to 'pocket pleats' and not 'pocket flaps'.

Page 199: Major Robert Cain was commissioned into the Royal Northumberland Fusiliers but won his Victoria Cross as a member of The South Staffordshire Regiment, a fact of which the present day Staffordshire Regiment is particularly proud. Major Cain immobilised the German Tiger tank; he did not demobilise it.

Page 200: Right hand column. The heading for the Jump Jacket should read 'The 1940 Pattern Gabardine Jump Jacket'.

Page 218ff: I have been informed that technically it is incorrect to refer to the Army Group that invaded Europe on 6 June 1944 as 21st Army Group. During the 1944–45 period it was correctly referred to as 21 Army Group, being made up of the 2nd British Army and the 1st Canadian Army. It was known as 'Two one Army Group' and not referred to as 'Twenty-first Army Group'.

Page 219: Right hand column, eighth line down of second paragraph, the word 'wherever' should be replaced by 'whenever'.

Page 237: Caption to photograph on right should commence 'A 1908 Pattern Large Pack worn by troops'.

Page 254: Right hand column, first line of third paragraph. The word 'advantages' should be replaced by 'disadvantages'.

Page 274: Right hand column, table and footnote. It has been pointed out to me that the General Service Corps was created in 1942. Footnote 16 refers to this Corps and four other formations as having been introduced from September 1943. The allocation of blocks of army numbers to all those formations shown in table 46 with the footnote number '16' was promulgated in Amendments No. 35 of King's Regulations dated 30 September 1943.

PART I
Ranks and Appointments

The ranks and appointments held by soldiers of the British Army are shown in the accompanying table, and the grant, under due authority, of any appointment therein detailed conferred on the holder the rank specified opposite that appointment in the table. Appointments made in a temporary capacity, when authorized by regulations or by special instructions of the Army Council, or under the provisions of the Pay Warrant, 1940, Article 793, conferred corresponding temporary rank; such temporary rank was relinquished from the date on which the soldier ceased to hold the temporary appointment. Appointments made in an acting capacity only conferred corresponding acting rank. The table does not purport to include the designations of all Army trades; for these see page 52 of this book or consult the Pay Warrant, 1940, Appendix IV.

Men, NCOs and warrant officers.

Warrant officers and NCOs of the RAPC, and also those whose appointment in the table is marked with an asterisk (*), were not entitled to assume any command on parade or duty, except over soldiers who may have been placed under their orders. In matters of discipline, however, they at all times exercised the full authority attached to their rank or appointment. All warrant officers and NCOs, other than those of the Royal Engineers, Royal Signals, RASC and RAOC (Store Section only), who were appointed in any trade mentioned in the Pay Warrant, 1940, Appendix IV, were subject to the same limitations in their power of command as those whose appointments are marked with an asterisk.

When the appointment was classified under more than one rank, the lowest rank was granted an appointment, unless the soldier already held a higher rank.

In January 1940 it was decided that all private soldiers of the Royal Armoured Corps would be given the rank of Trooper (ACI 7, 3 January 1940). For the sake of uniformity in the Royal Armoured Corps, and at the same time to facilitate cross postings between units of the RAC, it was decided on 25 May 1940 by ACI 505 that sub-units of regiments and battalions, including army tank battalions, would be designated 'squadrons' and 'troops' respectively. In consequence, the designations of certain warrant and non-commissioned officers became 'squadron serjeant-major', 'troop serjeant-major' and 'squadron quarter-master-serjeant'.

Precedence of men, NCOs and warrant officers.

The following was the order of precedence of NCOs and men.[1]

(5) Squadron quarter-master-corporal (Household Cavalry) or squadron, battery or company quarter-master-serjeant
Colour-serjeant
Staff-corporal (Household Cavalry) or staff-serjeant
(4) Corporal-of-horse (Household Cavalry) or serjeant
(3) Corporal or bombardier
(2) Trooper, gunner, sapper, signalman, driver, guardsman, rifleman, fusilier or private
(1) Boy

NCOs who held the appointment of farrier-staff-corporal (Household Cavalry) or farrier-staff-serjeant ranked regimentally next below the squadron quarter-master-corporal or the company, etc., quarter-master-serjeant, respectively. A lance-serjeant or acting lance-serjeant took precedence over all corporals, and a lance-bombardier, an acting lance-bombardier, a lance-corporal or an acting lance-corporal took precedence over all privates etc. NCOs of groups (5), (4) and (3) took precedence in these groups according to the date of their promotion to the rank covered by the particular group.

Warrant officers Class III ranked respectively with one another according to the date of their promotion to the rank.

The following was the order of precedence of warrant officers Class II.

(8) Master gunner, 3rd class
(7) Garrison quarter-master-serjeant, regimental quarter-master-corporal (Household Cavalry), regimental quarter-master-serjeant or any other warrant officer of Class II holding the appointment of quarter-master-serjeant
(6) Squadron corporal-major (Household Cavalry), or squadron, battery or company serjeant-major

[1] The numbers in parentheses in the following paragraphs refer to the categories of ranks and appointments indicated in Table 1 overleaf.

Table 1. Ranks and Appointments for Men, NCOs and Warrant Officers

Rank	Appointment	Rank	Appointment
Men and non-commissioned officers			
(1) Boy	A boy holding any appointment Trumpeter Signaller (other than Royal Signals) Pioneer Piper Musician	(5) Staff-Corporal (Household Cavalry) or Staff-Serjeant	Staff serjeant instructor in equitation Staff-serjeant instructor Mechanist staff-serjeant* Foreman of works staff-serjeant* Experimental staff-serjeant Engineer draughtsman staff-serjeant* Engineer clerk staff-serjeant* Artisan staff-serjeant* Armourer staff-serjeant* Armament staff-serjeant* Staff-serjeant artillery clerk* Company quarter-master-serjeant (technical)
(2) Trooper Gunner Sapper Signalman Driver Private Guardsman Fusilier Rifleman Craftsman Others[1]	Lance-corporal[2] Kettle-drummer Drummer Driver, RA Bugler Bandsman Armourer private (appointment ceased 1942) Armament private (appointment ceased 1942) Armourer craftsman (introduced 1942) Armourer lance-corporal* Engineer draughtsman lance-corporal* Engineer clerk lance-corporal* Band lance-bombardier Lance-bombardier artillery clerk* Lance-bombardier	(5) Colour-Serjeant	Staff colour-serjeant*[7] Orderly-room serjeant*[7] Company quarter-master-serjeant (Foot Guards, RTR (later dropped) and Infantry of the Line)[7]
	Band bombardier Bombardier signaller (RA) Bombardier-instructor in equitation Bombardier-cook* Bombardier artillery clerk* Armourer-corporal* Corporal-cook*	(5) Squadron Quarter-Master Corporal (Household Cavalry) or Squadron, Battery, or Company Quarter-Master-Serjeant (except RTR (later dropped), Foot Guards and Infantry of the Line)	
(3) Corporal Bombardier	Engineer draughtsman corporal* Engineer clerk corporal* Band corporal Provost corporal Transport corporal Armourer lance-serjeant* Band lance-serjeant Lance-serjeant[3] Signalling corporal Lance-serjeant artillery clerk* Engineer draughtsman lance-serjeant* Corporal orderly-room clerk*		Foreman of signals company quarter-master-serjeant[8] Orderly-room serjeant (Cavalry and RAC)*[8] Orderly-room corporal-of-horse (Household Cavalry)*[8] Battery quarter-master-serjeant instructor in gunnery[4,8]
		Warrant officers	
		Warrant Officer Class III[5]	Platoon serjeant-major (Foot Guards and Infantry of the Line) Section serjeant-major (R Signals and RTR) Troop serjeant-major, Cavalry of the Line and mechanized cavalry regiments of the RAC, RA and R Signals
(4) Corporal-of-Horse (Household Cavalry) or Serjeant	Armourer-serjeant* Trumpet-major Pipe-major Drum-major Bugle-major Signalling-serjeant Serjeant orderly-room clerk* Serjeant-instructor (RAC, Small Arms School and School of Signals) Serjeant-instructor in physical training Serjeant-instructor (education)* Serjeant-instructor-in-musketry (infantry depots) Serjeant-instructor in equitation Transport serjeant Provost serjeant Signalling corporal-of-horse (Household Cavalry) Provost-corporal-of-horse (Household Cavalry) Cook-corporal-of-horse (Household Cavalry) Band-corporal-of-horse (Household Cavalry) Corporal-of-horse riding instructor (Household Cavalry) Serjeant-cook* Band serjeant Serjeant of the band, RE Serjeant of the band, RA Serjeant artillery clerk* Pioneer-serjeant Orderly-room serjeant Orderly-room cpl-of-horse (Household Cavalry)[6] Engineer draughtsman serjeant* Engineer clerk serjeant*	(6) Warrant Officer Class II	Warrant officer instructor, Class II (education)* Squadron serjeant-major riding instructor Squadron serjeant-major-instructor in fencing and gymnastics Squadron serjeant-major-instructor in musketry Squadron corporal-major-instructor in fencing and gymnastics (Household Cavalry) Squadron corporal-major-instructor in musketry (Household Cavalry) Squadron corporal-major riding instructor (Household Cavalry) Squadron corporal-major (Household Cavalry) or squadron, battery or company serjeant-major (including RAC, Foot Guards, Infantry of the Line and CMP) Company serjeant-major instructor, RAC and RE Company serjeant-major instructor (Small Arms School and School of Signals) Company sergeant-major-instructor in musketry Company serjeant-major-instructor in physical training Battery serjeant-major (experimental) Battery serjeant-major-instructor in equitation Battery serjeant-major-instructor in gunnery

Rank	Appointment
	Quarter master serjeant (technical), RAC
	Regimental quarter-master-serjeant (technical)[4]
	Staff quarter-master-serjeant
	Quarter-master-serjeant
	Quarter-master-serjeant, RE
	Quarter-master-serjeant staff clerk*
	Quarter-master-serjeant instructor (Small Arms School and Army School of Physical Training)
	Quarter-master-serjeant instructor in gunnery
	Quarter-master serjeant instructor, RAC*
	Quarter-master-serjeant artillery clerk*
	Orderly-room serjeant*[9]
	Orderly-room cpl-of-horse (Household Cav.)*[9]
	Mechanist quarter-master-serjeant*
Warrant Officer Class II	Foreman of signals quarter-master-serjeant
	Clerk of works quarter-master-serjeant*
	Experimental quarter-master-serjeant*
	Engineer draughtsman quarter-master-serjeant*
	Engineer clerk quarter-master-serjeant*
	Company serjeant-major, drill serjeant (Foot Guards only)
	Artisan quarter-master-serjeant*
	Armourer quarter-master-serjeant*
	Armament quarter-master-serjeant*
	Regimental quarter-master-serjeant
	Regimental quarter-master-cpl (Household Cav.)
(7)	Garrison quarter-master-serjeant
(8)	Master gunner, 3rd class

Rank	Appointment
	Serjeant-major
	Superintending draughtsman*
	Superintending clerk*
	Sub-conductor, RAOC
	Staff serjeant-major
	Serjeant-major instructor in gunnery
	Serjeant-major-instructor*
	Serjeant-major (educational establishment)*
	Serjeant-major, artillery clerk*
	Warrant officer instructor, Class I (education)*
	Mechanist-serjeant-major*
	Foreman of signals, serjeant-major
	Clerk of works, serjeant-major*
	Experimental-serjeant-major*
(9) Warrant Officer Class I	Farrier-serjeant-major*
	Farrier-corporal-major (Household Cavalry)
	Bandmaster*
	Artificer-serjeant-major, RA*
	Artisan-serjeant-major*
	Armourer-serjeant-major*
	Armament-serjeant-major*
	Regimental serjeant-major
	Regimental corporal-major (Household Cavalry)
(10)	Garrison serjeant-major
(11)	Master gunner, 2nd class
(12)	Staff-serjeant-major, 1st class
	Master gunner, 1st class
	Conductor, RAOC

[1]Other terms were applied to rank and file members of certain Infantry of the Line regiments. 'Kingsman' was used in place of 'private' within The King's Regiment (Liverpool), whilst the term 'volunteer' was used instead of 'private' in the Prince of Wales's Volunteers (South Lancashire). The title 'guardsman' was approved and authorized by King George V on 22 November 1918 to be used in place of 'private' for all battalions that formed the Brigade of Guards. The King gave his assent for this change of title as a mark of His Majesty's appreciation of and pride in the splendid services rendered by the Guards Division during the Great War.

[2]As a point of interest, on 1 September 1961 the lance-corporal appointment was designated a rank. See Queen's Regulations, page 67.

[3]The appointment of lance-serjeant was abolished in 1946.

[4]This appointment was discontinued for the RAC with effect from 17 November 1934.

[5]The rank of Warrant Officer Class III was introduced in 1938–39.

[6]When below the rank of Colour-Serjeant.

[7]When ranking as Colour-Serjeant.

[8]When ranking as Squadron Quarter-Master-Sergeant or equivalent rank.

[9]When graded as Quarter-Master-Serjeant.

Right: The Colour Party and troops of The Essex Regiment marching out of Rheims railway station on their way home from duty with the International Army in the Saar, 20 February 1935.

Warrant officer instructor Class II (education)

Warrant officers Class II in groups (7) and (6) above ranked with others in the respective groups and took precedence within the particular group according to the date of promotion, except that (a) a garrison quarter-master-serjeant took precedence over all other quarter-master-serjeants; (b) a regimental quarter-master-corporal (Household Cavalry) or a regimental quarter-master-serjeant ranked regimentally above all other warrant officers Class II holding the appointment of quarter-master-serjeant; and (c) a company serjeant-major of the Foot Guards who was employed as a drill serjeant ranked regimentally above other company serjeant-majors.

The following was the order of precedence of warrant officers Class I.

(12) Conductor, RAOC
(12) Master gunner, 1st class
(12) Staff serjeant-major, 1st class
(11) Master gunner, 2nd class
(10) Garrison serjeant-major
(9) All other warrant officers Class I

Warrant officers Class I in groups (12) and (9) respectively ranked with one another in these groups according to the date of their promotion or appointment, except that a regimental corporal-major and a regimental serjeant-major ranked regimentally above the other members of group (9). The bandsmaster ranked next after the regimental serjeant-major and with the warrant officer instructor (education) if the latter was a warrant officer Class I, according to the date of promotion to that rank. The status of warrant officers was inferior to that of all commissioned officers, but superior to that of all NCOs.

Cavalry Troopers. All Cavalry regiments used the rank of Private until 1921, after which that of Trooper was adopted.

The rank of 'Gunner' in the Royal Artillery. In 1933 Standing Orders of the Royal Artillery for 1933 instructed that all personnel other than NCOs and tradesmen were to hold the rank of Gunner and were to be designated as such. Gunners holding the appointment of Driver RA, Driver IC, Musician, Signaller, etc. were designated as Gunner (Driver RA), Gunner (Driver IC), Gunner (Musician), etc. for the purposes of all orders, correspondence and returns.

The rank of Bombardier in the Royal Artillery. The rank of Bombardier in the Royal Artillery was that of a junior NCO. Bombardiers originally wore a single rank chevron, but when in 1920 (Army Order 142 of 1920) the rank of Corporal lapsed bombardiers were permitted to wear two rank chevrons.

Craftsmen in the REME. Tradesmen below NCO rank in the REME held the rank of Craftsman; REME non-tradesmen were Privates or Drivers, according to the duties they performed (ACI 1605, 1 August 1942).

Second Corporals. Up to 1920 there was a rank in certain corps, including the Royal Engineers and the Royal Army Ordnance Corps, known as Second Corporal. This was a full rank and the holder wore a single rank chevron. On promotion to Second Corporal, the lance-corporal who was entitled to wear good conduct badges had to take them down, the principle being that the holder of a full rank was not required to wear these chevrons to show that he had conducted himself properly. Until the end of the 1914–18 war there were no lance-serjeants; this being the case, it was the custom for second corporals and corporals in small units to be members of the serjeants' mess, although they were not privileged to visit serjeants' messes of other units. From 1920, by authority of Army Order 142 of 1920, the rank of Second Corporal (which was by then only used in the Royal Engineers and Royal Army Ordnance Corps) was abolished. NCOs who held this rank were appointed Lance-Serjeants, distinguished by wearing a three-bar chevron.

Corporals in the Royal Artillery. The rank of Corporal in the Royal Regiment of Artillery lapsed under the authority of Army Order 142 of 23 April 1920, and no further promotions were made to that rank after 1 May that year.

Local Serjeants and Local Corporals of the Grenadier Guards. It is a long established custom that the King's Guard (now the Queen's Guard) be required to be mounted by a serjeant. At one time there were so few serjeants in the Grenadier Guards that the responsibility of carrying out the guard duty meant that serjeants found themselves performing the duty all the time. To overcome this problem, corporals of the Grenadier Guards were made up to Local Serjeants, then called Unpaid Serjeants, in order to share in the duty of guard mounting; lance-corporals were similarly made up. Even when the rank of Lance-Sergeant was discarded in 1947, corporals in the Grenadier Guards continued to be called Local Serjeants and lance-corporals to be called Local Corporals.

The mythical rank of 'King's Corporal'. The term 'King's Corporal' probably had its origins in the early nineteenth century when soldiers were sometimes recommended for immediate promotion in the field. As a result they were sometimes given the honorary rank of Corporal within their own regiment, but neither rank nor promotion received official recognition. There is no such rank as 'King's Corporal', nor has there ever been.

Warrant officers Class III. On 1 October 1938 the War Office announced that about 1,000 non-commissioned officers were to be promoted. They were to form the first batch of selections for the new rank of Warrant Officer Class III. They were selected on the basis of being men of special character and ability and were to be promoted to hold command of platoons and equivalent sub-units hitherto commanded by subaltern officers. This reform was a corollary of the changes in the conditions of service and the promotion of officers being introduced into the British Army by the Secretary of State.

The warrant officers Class III were all to be commanders, to be trained in officers' duties in tactics, in the use of weapons and in administration. They were not only available for duty as commanders but were to carry out other officer employments, such as those with signals and transport. They were trained to be able to undertake duty as orderly officers on courts of inquiry and on regimental and garrison boards. They were also given financial powers so that the handling of money and the responsibility for accounts was delegated to them in the same way as was then done with subalterns.

In connection with the creation of this new rank steps were also taken which widened the powers of warrant officers of Class I, II, or III which enabled them to have financial powers to check stores, sign certificates, conduct drafts, supervise range practices and so forth.

Warrant officers Class III were introduced into the Cavalry of the Line, Royal Artillery, Foot Guards, Infantry of the Line and Royal Tank Corps in all units. In the Royal Signals they were introduced into certain units only, and searchlight units, which in 1938 were coming under the Royal Artillery, were also to have them.

These changes marked a definite innovation in Army organization. They considerably widened the prospects of promotion and the opportunities of high responsibility to the rank and file, which enabled advantage to be taken of the superior education and ability of the soldier and non-commissioned officer; simultaneously, the opening to NCOs of posts that had hitherto been held by commanding officers reduced the proportion of junior officers to senior officers in the Army and thereby also improved the prospect of promotion of commanding officers.

In 1940 it was announced by ACI 804 of 1940 that a decision had been made that no further promotions to Warrant Officer Class III were to take place and that as a consequence the rank was placed in suspension; holders of the rank were, however, allowed to retain their rank until they were promoted, were reduced or left the service. By 1947, the year when the first postwar alterations to the badges of warrant rank took place (ACI 991 of 1947), very few such warrant officers of Class III rank were left in the Army.

Commissioned officers ranks were as follows:
Second Lieutenant
Lieutenant
Captain
Major
Lieutenant-Colonel, the highest
  regimental rank
Colonel[1]
Brigadier[2]   Field
Major-General   Officers
Lieutenant-General
General
Field Marshal

[1] This is an Army rank as opposed to a regimental rank. The colonel of a regiment was usually a retired general. A colonel does not actually command a battalion or regiment, this task being left to a lieutenant-colonel, but devotes himself to administrative duties of various kinds.
[2] During the First World War a brigadier was correctly referred to as a Brigadier-General, and this rank was given to colonels commanding a brigade or to those

The Brevet Rank

This was suspended in 1939 when the wartime promotion code replaced the peacetime code. (Brevet ranks were reintroduced into the Army in January 1952.)

The prewar rank of Brevet Lieutenant-Colonel was a nominal rank given to majors and carried neither the pay nor the privilege of the higher rank. Promotion to the rank of Major was by time; above that rank it was by selection. Majors selected as lieutenant-colonels, if the establishment allowed, were given brevet rank, which meant that they held equal place on the roster with substantive or temporary lieutenant-colonels and could thus be considered for promotion to the rank of full Colonel.

Substantive majors who already held senior temporary rank (such as Temporary Brigadier) could also be made brevet lieutenant-colonels, whilst a major serving in a unit which was commanded by a lieutenant-colonel could be given brevet rank and was allowed to wear the badges of that rank. Thus it was possible for a company commander in a battalion to be made Brevet Lieutenant-Colonel and to wear the crown and star on his shoulder straps. He did not, however, draw extra pay.

The Use of Military Rank by Former Officers

A permanent Regular Army officer automatically retained his rank on retirement or on ceasing to belong to the Regular Army Reserve of Officers. He was entitled at all times to use his rank, or any higher honorary rank which may have been granted to him. An ex-Army officer (other than a permanent Regular Army officer) who was granted permission to retain his rank, or who was granted an honorary rank on retirement, resignation or relinquishment of commission, or on ceasing to belong to a reserve, was also entitled to use at all times the rank granted or retained. The use of such rank by a former officer was however left to his conscience and sense of propriety.

awaiting appointment to higher rank. After the war, with so many brigadier-generals, it was decided to drop the word 'general' and these officers became just 'brigadiers'. For a short period of time even the term 'brigadier' ceased to be used and in its place the term 'colonel commandant' was adopted, but owing to its somewhat cumbersome enunciation this was discontinued and 'brigadier' revived.

PART II
Badges and Insignia

1. BADGES OF RANK AND APPOINTMENT

The Wearing of Chevrons and Badges of Rank or Appointment

Before the 1939–45 war only one set of chevrons or badges of rank, other than metal ones, that were required on appointment by a soldier to lance rank, on promotion, on reduction or on transfer etc., was, when no other alterations in the pattern of clothing were necessary, issued free for each Service Dress, Battle-Dress and Khaki Drill jacket. Two sets of metal badges for wear with Service Dress, Battle-Dress and Khaki Drill clothing were supplied free on appointment or promotion only. Chevrons and badges of rank or appointment were worn on both arms of Tropical shirts, Khaki Drill jackets, Service Dress jackets, Battle-Dress blouses and the drab greatcoat; on other garments, such as the Airborne Forces gabardine smock, the Denison smock, PT smocks and working clothing, the chevrons or badges of rank or appointment were worn on the right arm only.

Chevrons and badges of rank or appointment were, unless otherwise stated, worn point down-

wards in the case of one, two or three-bar chevrons and point upwards in the case of four-bar chevrons. Except where otherwise stated, badges and chevrons of rank or appointment were worn in the following manner.

When worn on the forearm. The lower edge of a badge was positioned 6½in from the bottom of the sleeve. The uppermost point of a chevron was positioned 9in from the bottom of the sleeve, except in the case of the four-bar chevron that was worn on the greatcoat, when the uppermost point was 11in from the bottom of the sleeve. (On garments with pointed or braided cuffs, such as the Service Dress jackets worn by warrant officers Class I, the lower edge of the badge and the centre of the lower edge of the chevron was positioned ½in above the point of the cuff or braiding; on garments with gauntlet cuffs, such as the Service Dress jackets worn by warrant officers Class I of Scottish regiments, the lower edge of the badge or the lower points of chevrons were positioned ½in above the point of the cuff.

Table 2. Coloured Rank Badges worn on the Arm

Regiment or corps	Colour of badge or chevrons adopted
4th/7th Dragoon Guards	Gold lace
4th Queen's Own Hussars	Gold on red background
The Queen's Royal Regiment (West Surrey)	Mounted on blue cloth
The Royal Warwickshire Regiment[1]	White cloth on red background for 1st Bn only
The Cheshire Regiment[1]	Buff on cerise
The Cameronians (Scottish Rifles)	Black on green ground
The Gloucestershire Regiment	Scarlet cloth
The Duke of Cornwall's Light Infantry	Gold on red for serjeants and above; red on green for lance-serjeants and under
The Duke of Wellington's Regiment (West Riding)[1]	Scarlet on white ground
The Queen's Own Royal West Kent Regiment[1]	Drab, mounted on dark blue cloth
The King's Own Yorkshire Light Infantry	Green on white ground
The King's Shropshire Light Infantry	Mounted on dark green cloth
The Middlesex Regiment (Duke of Cambridge's Own)	Maroon on yellow background
The King's Royal Rifle Corps	Black on red ground
The Durham Light Infantry	Mounted on dark green cloth
The Royal Ulster Rifles	Black mounted on rifle green
The Royal Irish Fusiliers (Princess Victoria's)[2]	Black mounted on rifle green
The Argyll and Sutherland Highlanders (Princess Louise's)[2, 3]	Black mounted on rifle green

[1]It is of interest to note that with the exception of these regiments, all also appeared in the 1929 and the 1935 editions of *Clothing Regulations (India)*.
[2]These regiments appear only in the 1936 edition of the *Clothing Regulations (India)*.

[3]The inclusion of the Argyll and Sutherland Highlanders as wearing what were in effect rifle regiment chevrons may have been an error on the part of the compiler or printer of these Clothing Regulations.

When worn on the upper arm. The lower edge of the badge was positioned 9in from the top of the sleeve. The lower point of the one-bar chevron was placed 9in from the top of the sleeve, of the two-bar chevron 9½in and of the three-bar chevron 10½in from the top of the sleeve.

Badges of appointment and those of tradesmen and instructors were, unless otherwise provided, worn below the rank badge by warrant officers and above the rank chevrons by NCOs.

From 1943, when warrant officers and NCOs wore special cold climate clothing (see also page 214), their badges of rank were worn on the peak of the all-weather cap instead of the sleeves of garments. Miniature chevrons were worn by NCOs and the normal size arm badges by warrant officers.

Badges of rank or appointment and rank chevrons were provided in worsted for wear on the Service Dress jacket, the Battle-Dress blouse and the drab greatcoat. For wear on the Khaki Drill jacket,[1] the Tropical shirt, the PT smock and working clothing, badges were provided in worsted and chevrons were in cotton material. For use with clothing where the sleeves were either short or worn rolled up, warrant officers and occasionally NCOs wore wrist straps, either in cloth (usually KD cloth) or leather, on which were mounted their warrant officer badge of rank in brass or worsted or NCO miniature brass chevrons.

Rank badges, other than worsted on khaki, worn on the arm.

Published in *Regulations for the Clothing of the Army, 1936*, Appendix 8, page 179 under the heading 'Optional Articles – Articles which May be Worn provided that no expense to the Public is Incurred', is the statement that 'full dress chevrons, rank badges and good conduct badges' were permitted to be worn with Service Dress uniform by personnel of rifle regiments. Green chevrons on a white background were permitted to be worn by The King's Own Yorkshire Light Infantry, also with Service Dress uniform.[2]

[1] ACI 253 of May 1939 stated that cotton chevrons were to be worn as both rank and good conduct badges on KD clothing instead of worsted chevrons. These continued in use until worn out.

[2] This information also appears in the 1926 edition of the *Regulations for the Clothing of the Army.*

edging corresponding to the wearer's arm-of-service, as detailed below, was introduced by ACI 1193 dated 13 October 1945, and these badges were taken into wear by warrant officers Class I in all arms of the Service, including the ATS, except as indicated. The colours of the edging to these badges were identical to those used as backing colours for officers' rank badges first authorized in September 1940 by ACI 1118 (see page 98) and fully implemented by ACI 905 dated 12 June 1943 (see page 115), together with subsequent amendments. Listed particulars of the new badges are as shown in Table 3.

Table 3. Royal Arms and Royal Arms in Wreath Printed Arm Badges

Edging colour	Arm-of-service
Black	Army Physical Training Corps
Blue	Royal Engineers, Royal Signals
Cambridge blue	Army Air Corps, Army Educational Corps
Dull cherry	Royal Army Medical Corps
Green	Reconnaissance Corps, Army Dental Corps, Intelligence Corps
Red	Royal Artillery, Royal Army Ordnance Corps, Pioneer Corps, Corps of Military Police
Rifle green	Infantry, rifle regiments
Scarlet	Infantry, except rifle regiments
Yellow	Royal Armoured Corps, Royal Army Service Corps
Beech brown[1]	Auxiliary Territorial Service
Red[2]	Royal Artillery, Royal Army Ordnance Corps, Pioneer Corps, Corps of Military Police
Yellow[2]	Royal Armoured Corps, Royal Army Service Corps

[1]The ATS had only just been permitted to wear beech brown as rank badge backing for officers' badges of rank (ACI 1145 dated 3 October 1945).
[2]The only Royal Arms in Wreath badges listed as having a coloured edging.

No mention is made in this ACI of a 'Royal Arms, Warrant Officer Class I' arm badge with dark blue edging worn by WOIs of the Royal Army Pay Corps or the Royal Electrical and Mechanical Engineers. The colour of the backing to RAPC officers' badges of rank had been changed from yellow to dark blue by ACI 666 dated 6 June 1945.

Warrant officers Class I of the Army Catering Corps were so few in number at the time of this ACI that the requirements of that corps were met by the local conversion of the existing arm badges by the addition of grey cloth edging.

Warrant officers Class I of the Household Cavalry, the five regiments of Foot Guards and the Army Cadet Force were not affected by this introduction and continued to wear the existing plain edged Royal Arms badge.

The usual procedure applied for the issue and scale of issue of these new badges. Both old style and new pattern were permitted to be worn together in any one unit: no wholesale change-over merely for the sake of uniformity was allowed, and existing stocks of the former pattern had to be used up before the issue of the new style badge was permitted.

Right: A WO Class I of the Parachute Regiment.

Although the practice of wearing coloured, multi-coloured or full dress rank badges, chevrons or good conduct stripes was not widespread throughout the British Army, further details were published in *Clothing Regulations (India), 1939*, Appendix XX, under the heading 'Description of Optional Articles to be Worn on Occasions as Directed'. Table 2 is a description of those items to be worn by British troops in all orders of dress (which obviously included Service Dress) but not to be worn on field service.

Introduction of coloured edging to the Royal Arms and Royal Arms in Wreath arm badges as worn by warrant officers Class I.

In order to facilitate the recognition of warrant officers Class I, a badge of rank with coloured

Table 4. Badges and Chevrons of Rank and Appointment, 1936–45

Rank or appointment	Description of chevrons and badges, 1936[1]	Description of chevrons and badges, 1941/1944[2]
Warrant officers		
Conductor, RAOC[3]	Royal Arms in wreath worn on both forearms of jackets and greatcoats	Royal Arms in wreath
Staff serjeant-major, 1st class	Royal Arms in wreath worn on both forearms of jackets and greatcoats	Royal Arms in wreath
Master gunner, 1st class	Gun over Royal Arms in wreath worn on both forearms of jackets and greatcoats[4]	Royal Arms in wreath over gun
Master gunner, 2nd class	Gun over Royal Arms worn on both forearms of jackets and greatcoats[4]	Royal Arms over gun
Bandmaster	Bandmaster badge of crown over lyre on wreath worn on both forearms of jackets only	Bandmaster badge of crown over lyre on wreath
Regimental corporal-major, Household Cavalry	Royal Arms worn on both forearms of jackets and greatcoats	
Farrier-corporal-major, Household Cavalry	Royal Arms worn on both forearms of jackets and greatcoats	
Regimental serjeant-major, Foot Guards	Small Royal Arms worn on both forearms of jackets and on right forearm of greatcoats	
Superintending clerk, Foot Guards	Small Royal Arms worn on both forearms of jackets and on right forearm of greatcoats	
Other WOs Class I	Royal Arms worn on both forearms of jackets and greatcoats	Royal Arms
Master gunner, 3rd class	Gun over large crown in wreath worn on both forearms of jackets and greatcoats[4]	Crown in wreath over gun
Quarter-master-serjeant ranking as WO Class II	Large crown in wreath worn on both forearms of jackets and greatcoats[5]	
Regimental quarter-master corporal, Household Cavalry	Small crown in wreath worn on both forearms of jackets and greatcoats	
Regimental quarter-master-serjeant, Foot Guards	Crown in wreath worn on both forearms of jackets and on right forearm of greatcoats	
Squadron corporal-major and other WOs Class II, Household Cavalry	Large crown worn on both forearms of jackets and greatcoats	
Company serjeant-major, Foot Guards	Crown worn on both forearms of jackets and on right forearm of greatcoats	
Other WOs Class II, Foot Guards	Crown worn on both forearms of jackets and on right forearm of greatcoats	
Other WOs Class II	Large crown worn on both forearms of jackets and greatcoats	Crown in wreath
WO Class III[6]		Large crown
Non-commissioned officers and men		
Squadron quarter-master-corporal, Household Cavalry	Crown over 4-bar chevron with chevrons point uppermost worn on both forearms of jackets and greatcoats	
Squadron quarter-master-corporal, other regiments		Small crown worn over 4-bar chevron on jacket and Battle-Dress blouse only
Staff corporal, Household Cavalry	Small crown over 4-bar chevron worn on both forearms of jackets and 4-bar chevron only worn on both forearms of greatcoats, point uppermost	
Staff corporal		Small crown worn over 4-bar chevron on jacket and Battle-Dress blouse only
Trumpet-major, Household Cavalry	Crown over crossed trumpets over 4-bar chevron worn point uppermost on both forearms of jackets and greatcoats	Small crown over crossed trumpets worn on jacket and Battle-Dress blouse only over 4-bar chevron

Left: Badges and chevrons of rank and appointment, 1936–45. 1, Conductor, RAOC; 2, Master Gunner 1st Class c.1936; 3, Master Gunner 1st Class c.1941 and 1944; 4, Master Gunner 2nd Class c.1936; 5, Master Gunner 2nd Class c.1941 and 1944; 6, Band Master; 7, Regimental Corporal-Major, Household Cavalry etc; 8, Regimental Serjeant-Major, Foot Guards; 9, Master Gunner 3rd Class c.1936; 10, Master Gunner 3rd Class c.1941 and 1944; 11, QMS ranking as WO Class II; 12, SCM and other WOs Class II, Household Cavalry; 13, SQMC, Household Cavalry; 14, Trumpet-Major, Household Cavalry; 15, Trumpet-Major, RA and RE; 16, Trumpet-Major, other regimental bands; 17, Drum-Major, Foot Guards; 18, Drum-Major, other regiments; 19, Pipe-Major, Foot Guards; 20, Pipe-Major, other regiments; 21, Bugle-Major, other than RE; 22, Corporal-of-Horse, Household Cavalry; 23, Band Corporal-of-Horse, Household Cavalry; 24, Band Serjeant, Serjeant or Lance-Serjeant, Foot Guards; 25, Band Corporal, Corporal or Lance-Corporal, Foot Guards; 26, Corporal, Household Cavalry; 27, Bombardier, RA, and Band Corporal; 28, Bombardier, Corporal; 29, Lance-Corporal, Household Cavalry c.1936; 30, Lance-Corporal, Lance-Bombardier; 31, Trumpeter, Household Cavalry, c.1936; 32, Drummer; 33, Bugler.

Table 4 *(continued)*

Rank or appointment	Description of chevrons and badges, 1936[1]	Description of chevrons and badges, 1941/1944[2]
Trumpet-major, Royal Artillery	Crossed trumpets on 4-bar chevron worn point uppermost on both forearms of jackets and greatcoats	Crossed trumpets worn on 4-bar chevron
Trumpet-major, Royal Engineers	Crossed trumpets on 4-bar chevron worn point uppermost on both forearms of jackets and greatcoats	Crossed trumpets worn on 4-bar chevron
Trumpet-major, other regimental bands	Crossed trumpets over 4-bar chevron worn point uppermost on both forearms of jackets and greatcoats	Crossed trumpets worn over 4-bar chevron
Drum-major, Foot Guards	Drum over 4-bar chevron worn point downwards on both upper arms of jackets and drum over 4-bar chevron worn point uppermost on right forearm of greatcoats	Drum worn over 4-bar chevron worn point downwards, except on greatcoats
Drum-major, other regiments	Drum over 4-bar chevron worn point uppermost on both forearms of jackets and greatcoats	Drum worn over 4-bar chevron
Pipe-major, Foot Guards	Crown over 4-bar chevron worn point downwards on both upper arms of jackets and crown over 4-bar chevron worn point uppermost on right forearm of greatcoats	Small crown worn over 4-bar chevron worn point downwards; not worn on greatcoats
Pipe-major, other regiments	4-bar chevron worn point uppermost on both forearms of jackets and greatcoats	4-bar chevron
Bugle-major, Royal Engineers	Special badge[7] in lieu of bugle on 4-bar chevron worn point uppermost on both forearms of jackets and greatcoats	Special badge[7] worn in lieu of bugle worn on 4-bar chevron
Bugle-major, other regiments	Bugle over 4-bar chevron worn point uppermost on both forearms of jackets and greatcoats	Bugle worn over 4-bar chevron
Corporal-of-horse, Household Cavalry	Crown over 3-bar chevron worn on both upper arms on jackets and greatcoats	
Corporal-of-horse, other regiments		Small crown worn over 3-bar chevron; not worn on greatcoats
Squadron, battery or company quarter-master-serjeant	Small crown over 3-bar chevron worn on both upper arms of jackets and greatcoats	Small crown worn over 3-bar chevron
Colour-serjeant and company quarter-master-serjeant ranking as colour-serjeant, Foot Guards	Small crown over 3-bar chevron worn on both upper arms of jackets and on right forearm of greatcoats	
Colour-serjeant	Small crown over 3-bar chevron worn on both upper arms of jackets and greatcoats	Small crown worn over 3-bar chevron
Staff serjeant	Small crown over 3-bar chevron worn on both upper arms of jackets and greatcoats	Small crown worn over 3-bar chevron
Band corporal-of-horse, Household Cavalry	Crown over lyre on wreath over 3-bar chevron worn on upper arms of jackets and great coats	Crown over lyre on wreath over 3-bar chevron
Band serjeant, serjeant or lance-serjeant, Foot Guards	3-bar chevron worn on both upper arms of jackets and on right forearm of greatcoats	
Band serjeant or lance-serjeant, other regiments	Crown over lyre on wreath over 3-bar chevron worn on both upper arms of jackets and 3-bar chevron on both upper arms of greatcoats	Crown over lyre on wreath over 3-bar chevron; not worn by bands of Cavalry of the Line
Serjeant or lance-serjeant, other regiments	3-bar chevron worn on both upper arms of jackets and greatcoats	3-bar chevron
Kettle-drummer, 3rd Hussars[8]	3-bar chevron worn on both upper arms of jackets and greatcoats	3-bar chevron
Band corporal, corporal or lance-corporal, Foot Guards	2-bar chevron worn on both upper arms of jackets and on right forearm of greatcoats	

Above. Two badges of appointment not listed in official publications but often encountered. Top is a bagpipe badge worn by pipers of Scottish regiments (except Scots Guards); plain ribbons featured on the bagpipes of a similar badge worn by pipers of Irish regiments (except Irish Guards). Below that is a double bugle-horn badge worn by buglers of rifle regiments only.

Above: Special badges worn in conjunction with rank insignia by the Royal Artillery and Royal Engineers. The former are variations of the gun badge, RA; the latter is the RE grenade badge.

Table 4 (continued)

Rank or appointment	Description of chevrons and badges, 1936[1]	Description of chevrons and badges, 1941/1944[2]
Band corporal, Household Cavalry		Small crown over band badge over 2-bar chevron; not worn on greatcoats
Corporal, Household Cavalry	Crown over 2-bar chevron worn on both upper arms of jackets and greatcoats	Small crown worn over 2-bar chevrons; not worn on greatcoats
Band corporal, other regiments		Crown over lyre on wreath (band badge) over 2-bar chevron; not worn by bands of Cavalry of the Line
Band-corporal or bombardier, other regiments	Crown over lyre on wreath over 2-bar chevron worn on both upper arms of jackets; 2-bar chevron only worn on both upper arms of greatcoats	
Band bombardier, Royal Artillery		Crown over lyre on wreath (band badge) over 2-bar chevron
Bombardier, corporal	2-bar chevron worn on both upper arms of jackets and greatcoats	2-bar chevron
Lance-corporal, Household Cavalry	Crown over 1-bar chevron worn on both upper arms of jackets and greatcoats	Small crown over 2-bar chevron; not worn on greatcoats
Band lance-corporal, Household Cavalry		Crown over band badge over 2-bar chevron; not worn on the greatcoat
Band lance-corporal, Foot Guards		Crown over lyre on wreath (band badge) over 2-bar chevron
Lance-corporal, Foot Guards		2-bar chevron
Band lance-corporal or lance-bombardier	Crown over lyre on wreath over 1-bar chevron worn on both upper arms of jackets; 1-bar chevron only worn on both upper arms of greatcoats	Crown over lyre on wreath (band badge) over 1-bar chevron; not worn by bands of Cavalry of the Line
Lance-corporal, lance-bombardier	1-bar chevron worn on both upper arms of jackets and greatcoats	1-bar chevron
Bandsman, Household Cavalry	Crown over lyre on wreath on both upper arms of jackets only	
Bandsman and musician, Foot Guards	Crown over lyre on wreath worn on both upper arms of jackets only	
Bandsman and musician, other regiments		Crown over lyre on wreath (band badge); not worn by bands of Cavalry of the Line
Trumpeter, Household Cavalry	Crossed trumpets worn on both upper arms of jackets only	
Trumpeter, other regiments	Crossed trumpets worn on both upper arms of jackets only	Crossed trumpets
Kettle-drummer, Household Cavalry	—	
Drummer, Foot Guards	Drum worn on both upper arms of jackets only	
Drummer, other regiments	Drum worn on both upper arms of jackets only	Drum
Bugler	Bugle worn on both upper arms of jackets only	Bugle

[1]The information listed in this column has been extracted from tables published in *Regulations for the Clothing of the Army, 1936*, Appendix 5, pages 158 to 163, under the heading 'Badges, Chevrons, Armlets and Medals'.

[2]The information listed in this column has been extracted from tables published in *War Clothing Regulations, 1941*, Appendix IV, pages 63 to 65, under the heading 'Badges, Chevrons and Armlets', and in *War Clothing Regulations, 1943*, Appendix III, pages 126 to 128, under the heading 'Badges, Chevrons and Armlets'; both publications have identical information. It should be noted that there was far less information contained in these two wartime publications regarding badges and chevrons of rank as compared with the information published in the prewar clothing regulations.

[3]The initial letters for the Royal Army Ordnance Corps were not given in the 1936 edition of Clothing Regulations.

[4]The reversal of the position of the gun badge from the gun being worn *over* Royal Arms in wreath, *over* Royal Arms and *over* large crown in wreath to *below* Royal Arms in wreath, *below* Royal Arms and *below* crown in wreath was introduced in March 1937 and published as *Amendments No. 2 to Clothing Regulations, 1936*, page 4 (54/Artillery/1087).

[5]The large crown in wreath worn by quarter-master-serjeants ranking as Warrant Officers Class II was changed in March 1937 to a crown in wreath as part

of the amendments introduced in March 1937 (as shown above under footnote 4) and published in *Amendments No. 2 to Clothing Regulations, 1936,* page 4.

[6]ACI 398 dated 17 September 1938 (which dealt with the introduction of the rank of Warrant Officer Class III into the Regular Army) stated that until such time as the future dress of the Army was decided, warrant officers Class III when in Service Dress were to wear as their badge of rank a crown of the kind previously worn by company serjeant-majors etc. Warrant officers Class II, for whom the crown had hitherto been authorized as the badge of rank, were in future to wear the crown-in-wreath with Service Dress, which from that time (until 1947) became the badge of rank of all warrant officers Class II. For further details concerning the rank of Warrant Officer Class III, see page 14.

[7]The special badge for a bugle-major of the Royal Engineers worn superimposed upon a 4-bar chevron is not described in any Army orders or regulations. It was of elaborate design, consisting of a lyre surmounted by a grenade and supported by crossed trumpets; around these were arranged bugle-horns, more trumpets and a pair of tambourines, the whole being set against a stand of six flags, two Union flags, two Red Ensigns and two small blue banners. When worn on Service Dress the special badge was in drab worsted with the flags in colour. The badge was 4½in high by 3½in wide.

[8]The 3rd Hussars kettle-drummer is listed in the 1936 Clothing Regulations between band-serjeants and trumpet-majors (page 161) in the section dealing with ranks or appointments of non-commissioned officers. In the 1941/1943 War Clothing Regulations the 3rd Hussars kettle-drummer is listed under the sub-heading 'Other Ranks' – page 65 (1941) and page 128 (1943).

Note: In addition to the badges and chevrons detailed in this table, NCOs above lance-serjeant of

the Royal Artillery wore a 'gun' on their jackets and Battle-Dress blouse ¾in above any trade badge, if worn, or the point of the 'V' of their chevrons; serjeants only also wore the 'gun' above their 3-bar chevrons on the greatcoat. The barrel of the 'gun' faced to the wearer's front. The 'gun' badge was introduced by ACI 173 dated w/e 20 June 1934. The instruction stated that it had been decided that serjeants of the Royal Artillery were to wear the 'Gun, gilding metal' above the rank chevrons on the greatcoat as well as the Khaki Drill and Service Dress jackets, and that approval was given for a free initial issue of two 'Guns, gilding metal' to all such personnel and also to non-commissioned officers on promotion to the rank of Serjeant. A further ACI, No. 237 for w/e 29 August 1934, extended this dress distinction to serjeants of the Royal Artillery in the Territorial Army.

NCOs above lance-serjeant of the Royal Engineers wore a 'grenade' on their jackets, blouses and greatcoat ¾in above any trade badge, if worn, or the point of the 'V' of their chevrons.

All personnel of the Royal Tank Corps and later the Royal Tank Regiment wore on the right upper arm of their Service Dress jackets and Battle-Dress blouses a distinctive arm badge of a 'tank'; see page 76 for further details.

Boy NCOs at educational establishments before the war wore modified pattern (smaller) chevrons (1-bar or 2-bar) above the elbow on both arms of Service Dress jackets and greatcoats.

In the Grenadier Guards the practice since before the reform of Army dress in 1855 has been that non-commissioned officers wear a flaming grenade above their rank chevrons. This was worn both on the Service Dress jacket and Battle-Dress blouse. Warrant officers Class II and colour-serjeants of the Grenadier Guards wore, in addition to the grenade, crossed swords. These were worn on both forearms (see also page 26).

Opposite, far left: Warrant officers and NCOs of 1st SAS, 3 May 1944. Left to right: RSM Graham Rose, MM and bar, from Mansfield; Sjt. F. White, DCM, MM, of Manchester; and S. Sjt. Maj. David Kershaw, MM, of Birkenhead.

Opposite, left: CSM Reginald Bolland, MBE, DSM, of The Devonshire Regiment, 21 March 1944.

Far left: CQMS F. D. Gibbons, who received the Military Medal at the age of 49 after 32 years in the Queen's Royal Regiment (West Surrey); 5 March 1945.

Left: Sjt. David Grieve of Glasgow, a member of the Airborne Corps, was awarded the Military Medal for his part in a parachute raid on France; July 1942.

Far left: S. Sjt. H. Andrews, DFC, of the Glider Pilot Regiment; 3 May 1944.

Centre: L/Sjt. H. Lippitt, Grenadier Guards, a member of the 6th Guards Tank Brigade, receives from Field Marshal Montgomery the ribbon of the Military Medal for bravery during the fighting west of the River Rhine; 1945.

Left: L/Cpl. J. Hall of Blackpool, a PT instructor and member of the Border Regiment, photographed with his two-year-old daughter, Josephine, on the day he received his Distinguished Conduct Medal; 21 May 1942.

Table 5. Rank and Appointment Chevrons and Badges for Warrant Officers and Non-Commissioned Officers peculiar to Certain Regiments and known to have been worn with Service Dress, Battle-Dress and Greatcoats, 1935–45[1]

Rank or appointment	Description of chevrons and badges
Regimental serjeant-major, Foot Guards	Large size Royal Arms worn on both upper arms of Service Dress jacket and Battle-Dress blouse[2]
Company serjeant-major, Grenadier Guards	Crown above crossed swords over grenade worn on both forearms of Service Dress jacket; worn during period 1915–38
Platoon serjeant-major, Grenadier Guards	Crown above crossed swords over grenade worn on both forearms of Service Dress jacket and Battle-Dress blouse; worn during period 1938–47
Company serjeant-major, Grenadier Guards	Crown in wreath above crossed swords over grenade worn on both forearms of Service Dress jacket and Battle-Dress blouse; worn during period 1938–47
Squadron quarter-master-serjeant, Middlesex Yeomanry and 1st Queen's Dragoon Guards	Crown over 4-bar chevron worn point downwards on upper right arm of Service Dress jacket
Staff serjeant-farrier, Royal Horse Artillery	Crown over gun badge over 3-bar chevron on which was worn horse shoe trade badge for Farrier. Worn on upper right arm
Squadron quarter-master-serjeant, The Queen's Bays (2nd Dragoon Guards)	4-bar chevron worn point downwards
Colour-serjeant, Grenadier Guards	Grenade over crossed swords over 3-bar chevron; worn on both upper arms of Service Dress jacket and Battle-Dress blouse
Lance-corporal, The Queen's Bays (2nd Dragoon Guards)	2-bar chevron worn point downwards on upper arm
Corporal, Royal Gloucestershire Hussars	Crown over 2-bar chevron worn on upper arm
Lance-corporal, Royal Gloucestershire Hussars	Crown over 1-bar chevron worn on upper arm

Right: RSM A. Spratley of the Grenadier Guards (6th Guards Tank Brigade) displaying a fine example of the large-size Royal Arms worn by RSMs of the Foot Guards.

[1]The information compiled here has been gleaned from a number of sources, some of them unofficial, and should therefore be treated with caution. Some of the information is not complete to official Clothing Regulations standards.

[2]The large size Royal Arms badge, which is still in use today, was 5½in high by 5¼in at its widest point (the Royal Arms, worsted pattern, in use today is 6in high by 5½in at its widest point). This special badge has been worn by regimental serjeant-majors of the Foot Guards above the elbow on the Service Dress jacket since at least 1905, and during the 1939–45 war it was worn on the upper arms of the Battle-Dress blouse. It is not listed in any Clothing Regulations as the badge is unofficial and paid for out of regimental funds. It was (and still is) only permitted to be worn by regimental serjeant-majors of Guards battalions, the Guards' Depot, the Guards Training Battalion, the Honourable Artillery Company (the regimental serjeant-major of which was normally a Guardsman), the Royal Military College (later renamed the Royal Military Academy, Sandhurst; again, the regimental – later Academy – serjeant-major was a Guardsman), and superintending clerks of the regimental headquarters of the five Foot Guards regiments. It was not permitted to Guardsmen holding extra-regimental appointments carrying the rank of Warrant Officer Class I.

The worsted pattern of the Royal Arms badge in use before and during the 1939–45 war was worked in pale khaki tan and pale fawn coloured threads onto a khaki drab backing. The crown cap, the garter to the coat-of-arms, the five outer petals of the Tudor rose and the ribbon of the motto were all of dark chocolate brown, the garter being of velvet and the crown cap, rose petals and ribbon of cloth. The eyes of the lion and unicorn supporters and the lion of the Royal Crest were very small beads of jet. The coat-of-arms in the centre of the badge was worked in red, blue and yellow coloured silks, and the mouths and tongues of the three beasts were in red silk. Very fine detailing was carried out with single black threads. The whole design was cushioned to a depth of approximately 2/5in.

Right: Men of the Grenadier Guards prepare for the attack across the River Po, Italy, 24 April 1945. The man wearing the beret bears on his forearm the insignia of a Company serjeant-major. Next to him, wearing a cap comforter, is a Grenadier Guards Pioneer serjeant. (See also the photograph on page 143.)

Right: Distinctive badges and chevrons of rank and appointment. 1, Regimental Serjeant-Major, Foot Guards; 2, Company Serjeant-Major, Grenadier Guards, 1915–38, and Platoon Serjeant-Major, Grenadier Guards, 1938–47; 3, Company Serjeant-Major, Grenadier Guards, 1938–47; 4, SQMS, Middlesex Yeomanry and 1st Queen's Dragoon Guards; Staff Serjeant-Major, RHA; 6, SQMS, The Queen's Bays; 7, Colour Serjeant, Grenadier Guards; 8, Lance-Corporal, The Queen's Bays; 9, Corporal, Royal Gloucestershire Hussars; 10, Lance-Corporal, Royal Gloucestershire Hussars.

Regimental Arm Badges (Metal) worn by Warrant Officers and NCOs of Cavalry Regiments

Regulations for the Clothing of the Army, 1936 states in Appendix 8, page 179, that arm badges (metal) were to be worn by warrant officers and NCOs of Cavalry of the Line. The badges, which were required to be of authorized regimental design and could only be worn at the discretion of the commanding officers, were worn on the right arm of the Service Dress uniform (and later the Battle-Dress blouse) in various positions. NCOs had theirs either on or above their rank chevrons, and the badges were worn above the chevrons by full ranks only, full corporals, serjeants and warrant officers. In the case of squadron quarter-master-serjeants, the badge was worn above the chevrons but below the crown. Warrant officers wore their regimental badge below their badge of rank on the right forearm.

Table 6. *Descriptive Listing of Metal Arm Badges known to have been worn by Warrant Officers and NCOs of Cavalry of the Line Regiments on Service Dress and Battle-Dress,[1] 1936–45 and 1939–45.*

Regiment	Description of badge, colour of backing and application
1st King's Dragoon Guards	A monogram composed of the entwined letters K.D.G. surmounted by an imperial crown worn with a red cloth backing by corporals and above
The Queen's Bays (2nd Dragoon Guards)	A wreath surmounted by an imperial crown and containing the word BAYS in old English lettering; at the base of the wreath a scroll bearing the motto Pro Rege et Patria ('For King and Country'); worn without backing cloth by corporals and above[2]
3rd Carabiniers (Prince of Wales's Dragoon Guards)	Two carbines in saltire (crossed) surmounted by the Prince of Wales's crest, which consisted of three feather plumes encircled by a coronet with ribbon bearing the motto Ich Dien ('I serve'); the whole in white metal except for the coronet which was in gilding metal, all mounted on a white metal oval plaque; worn by lance-corporals and above[3]
4th/7th Royal Dragoon Guards	The eight-pointed star of the Order of St. Patrick upon the centre of which was a circlet bearing the motto Quis Separabit ('Who shall separate us?') and the date MCMXXII;[4] within the circlet was placed the Princess Royal coronet above the roman numerals IV and VII; the white metal badge mounted on to a circular backing of black cloth and worn by serjeants and above
5th Royal Inniskilling Dragoon Guards	The White Horse of Hannover (postured at full gallop or heraldically referred to as a 'horse courant') mounted on to a very dark green backing cloth which was cut to the general outline of the horse; worn on the chevrons of rank by serjeants and by other senior NCOs and WOs[5]
1st The Royal Dragoons	The Royal Crest with black cloth backing; worn by corporals and above
The Royal Scots Greys (2nd Dragoons)	A French eagle worn with a black backing cloth by serjeants and above[6]
3rd The King's Own Hussars	The White Horse of Hannover, taken from the arms of Westphalia (this badge was smaller than the one worn by NCOs and WOs of the 5th Royal Inniskilling Dragoon Guards, and although it too was postured at full gallop its hind legs were touching a grass mound); worn with a garter blue backing cloth by ranks from lance-corporal and above
4th Queen's Own Hussars	A monogram consisting of the letters Q.O.H. surmounted by an imperial crown above and the roman numeral IV below with a scroll bearing the motto Mente et Manu ('With heart and hand')
7th Queen's Own Hussars	A monogram designed to form, with the letter O, the letters Q.O., surmounted by an imperial crown; worn with a red cloth backing by corporals and above
8th King's Royal Irish Hussars	A crowned Irish harp, the spaces between the strings being filled in; worn with an emerald green cloth backing by corporals and above
9th Queen's Royal Lancers	Queen Adelaide's cypher, consisting of the letters A.R., entwined and reversed and surmounted by an imperial crown[7]; thought to have been worn with a red cloth backing and worn above rank chevrons from corporal and above
10th Royal Hussars (Prince of Wales's Own)	The Prince of Wales's crest worn in three sizes by lance-corporals, corporals and lance-serjeants and above; worn with a shaped red cloth backing
11th Hussars (Prince Albert's Own)	The Prince Consort's crest with the German motto Treu und Fest ('Faithful and steadfast'); worn by serjeants and above
12th Royal Lancers (Prince of Wales's)	Prince of Wales's crest worn with dark blue shaped backing cloth (referred to within the regiment as 'black'); worn by lance-corporals and above but excluding acting unpaid lance-corporals
13th/18th Hussars[8]	A monogram consisting of the letters Q.M.O. surmounted by an imperial crown; worn by corporals and above
14th/20th Hussars	A Prussian eagle worn on an oval plaque in brass for lance-corporals and in silver (white metal) for corporals and above[9]
15th/19th The King's Royal Hussars	The Royal Crest, worn with a shaped red backing cloth by corporals and above

Table 6 (continued)

Regiment	Description of badge, colour of backing and application
16th/5th Lancers	A crowned Irish harp with the spaces between the harp strings filled in; worn on the chevrons by corporals and above
17th/21st Lancers	The regimental 'motto'[10] consisting of a death's head with crossed bones below and a ribbon bearing the wording Or Glory; worn on chevrons by corporals and above
24th Lancers[11]	The roman numerals XXIV superimposed on and in front of crossed lances which extended to the outer rim of a circlet, at the base of which appeared the word Lancers, with the lance pennons flying outwards, the whole surmounted by an imperial crown
25th Dragoons[11]	The roman numerals XXV superimposed upon crossed swords with an imperial crown above and a scroll below inscribed 25th Dragoons, the whole mounted on a white metal oval plaque; worn directly on the rank chevrons by serjeants and by other senior NCOs and WOs
26th Hussars[11]	A Prussian eagle with imperial crown above, in its left talon a sceptre, in the right talon an orb, below which was a scroll inscribed XXVI Hussars, the whole mounted on a solid oval plate[12]
27th Lancers[11]	An elephant subscribed Hindoostan

[1]These arm badges were not so extensively worn in Battle-Dress: in all probability they were only worn on the individual's best Battle-Dress for parade functions and walking-out.

[2]The title 'Queen's Bays' is thought to have come into use in 1762 when the regiment was entirely horsed with bay horses and was then known as the '2nd or Queen's Regiment of Dragoon Guards'. The arm badge was authorized in May 1910.

[3]Arm badge introduced in 1922 at the time of the amalgamation of the 3rd Dragoon Guards and the 6th Dragoon Guards to form the 3rd Carabiniers (Prince of Wales's Dragoon Guards).

[4]The year the 4th (Royal Irish) Dragoon Guards and the 7th (Princess Royal's) Dragoon Guards were amalgamated to form the 4th/7th Dragoon Guards. As both regiments were 'Royal' regiments it was felt a serious omission that the distinction 'Royal' should have been dropped from the title of the new regiment; in 1936 Edward VIII restored the privilege and the 'Royal' designation was taken in that year.

[5]The White Horse was chosen to represent both the former 5th Dragoon Guards and the 6th Dragoons when these two regiments were amalgamated in 1922

to form the 5th/6th Dragoons. The title was altered in 1927 to the 5th Inniskilling Dragoon Guards. The distinction 'Royal' was awarded to commemorate the Silver Jubilee of King George V in 1935.

[6]Commemorated the capture of the Eagle of the French 45th Regiment at Waterloo.

[7]Queen Adelaide of Saxe-Mein was married to William IV.

[8]Regiment formed from the 1922 amalgamation of the 13th Hussars and the 18th Queen Mary's Own Royal Hussars. The 13th/18th Hussars was redesignated the 13th/18th Royal Hussars (Queen Mary's Own) in 1936.

[9]The colour of the Prussian eagle was later changed to black with a gilt crown, orb and sceptre.

[10]The 17th/21st Lancers have the peculiarity of calling a 'motto' what in other regiments is referred to as a 'regimental badge'.

[11]A war raised regiment.

[12]This style of arm badge was chosen to commemorate the close association the 26th Hussars had with the 14th/20th Hussars during their period of activation. The 14th/20th Hussars helped to raise the 26th Hussars in 1941.

Right: Men of the 11th Hussars (Prince Albert's Own), 16 May 1944. Left to right: Sjt. Leonard Bull, MM, SSM William McHardy, DCM, and Sjt. Hugh Lyon, MM and bar (see the photograph on page 151). The Prince Consort's crest can be seen worn above the rank chevrons by Serjeant Bull and below the WOII rank badge by SSM McHardy; see the photograph on page 141.

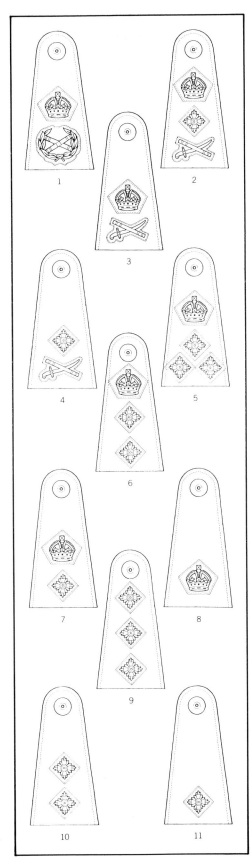

Right: Rank badges for officers. 1, Field Marshal; 2, General; 3, Lieutenant-General; 4, Major-General; 5, Brigadier; 6, Colonel; 7, Lieutenant-Colonel; 8, Major; 9, Captain; 10, Lieutenant; 11, Second Lieutenant. The versions shown are those that were worn on the Battle-Dress. Chaplains wore black badges of rank as follows: 4, Chaplain-General to the Forces; 6, Chaplain 1st Class (also known as Deputy Chaplain-General to the Forces); 7, Chaplain 2nd Class; 8, Chaplain 3rd Class; 9, Chaplain 4th Class.

Military Rank Distinctions for Officers

Officers' rank badges (metal for the Service Dress and greatcoat and in worsted for the Battle-Dress[1]; see also page 33) were carried on the shoulder straps. These straps were sewn into the scye or arm-hole seam at one end and fastened at the neck with a small, usually crested, button on the Service Dress and greatcoat or a vegetable composition or plastic button on the Battle-Dress. The width of the SD and BD strap at the shoulder end was 2in, tapering to 1¼in at the neck; straps worn on the greatcoat were slightly wider and slightly longer. The length of all straps was arranged so that the button was displayed slightly short of the collar 'fall' edge.

The first rank badge carried on the strap was normally situated about ½in from the arm-hole seam, although in the case of a captain it was often necessary to bring this insignia closer to the seam in order to find room for the three stars. The badges themselves were as follows.

Table 7. Rank Badges for Officers

Rank	Badge
Field-Marshal	Crossed batons on a wreath of laurel with crown above
General	Crossed sword and baton with crown and star above (crown nearest to shoulder strap button)
Lieutenant-General	Crossed sword and baton with crown above
Major-General	Crossed sword and baton with star above
Brigadier	Crown above three stars, the two lower stars side by side (the stars used in this instance were different from that used for other officers' ranks in that they were of a smaller dimension)
Colonel	Crown and two stars below
Lieutenant-Colonel	Crown and one star below
Major	Crown
Captain	Three stars
Lieutenant	Two stars
Second Lieutenant	One star

Variations in the design of officers' metal rank insignia.

The vast majority of metal stars worn by officers of the British Army were of one basic design and were often manufactured in gilding metal. Close examination of a newly struck star will show that the design consists of a cross patée surmounted by a green-enamelled laurel wreath which, in turn, encircles a medallion. The medallion incorporates three small crowns, two above one, surrounded with the motto Tria Juncta in Uno ('Three Joined in One') on red enamel. These three crowns

[1]It was announced by ACI 645 dated October 1939 that when personnel posted for duty as permanent staff on transports received acting rank which necessitated an alteration of their rank badges on their Service Dress jackets and greatcoats, the new badges of rank were to be of worsted and not of metal. The personnel concerned reverted to normal usage of rank badges on their reversion to normal duty.

represented the crowns of England, Scotland and Ireland united under His Majesty King George I. The motto is that of the Order of the Bath, which was founded in 1399 and revived as a military order by George I in 1725.

Other designs of 'stars' existed and these are illustrated on these pages. Some items were decorated with coloured enamelling, whilst other patterns were produced in both a black and a bronzed finish metal. The crown used with all officers' ranks was of the pattern known as the 'imperial crown', first adopted by King Edward VII in 1901 (and superseded in 1954 by the St. Edward's crown pattern).

Plastic insignia were produced during the war, usually coloured brown, dark brown or black and intended to replace the metal items as a form of wartime economy.

Right: Gen. Bernard Montgomery, complete with his famous black beret and wearing a grey wool Army pullover, displays on his Battle-Dress blouse the rank insignia of an Army General; June 1943.

Right: Variations of officer's rank stars. 1, Household Cavalry (SD, KD and BD); 2, Household Cavalry (greatcoat); 3, Grenadier, Coldstream and Welsh Guards (SD, KD and BD); 4, Grenadier, Coldstream and Welsh Guards (greatcoat); 5, Scots Guards (SD, KD and BD); 6, Scots Guards (greatcoat); 7, Irish Guards (SD, KD and BD); 8, Irish Guards (greatcoat); 9, Middlesex Regiment; 10, South Wales Borderers; 11, Somerset Light Infantry and Durham Light Infantry (SD); 12, 4th/7th Dragoon Guards (SD); 13, Lincolnshire Regiment (SD); 14, 15, Stars as worn by other regiments (15 being a size variation usually worn by brigadiers); 16, Rifle regiments and chaplains. Numbers 1-4 were Garter Stars; 9 and 10 were Eversley Stars. Number 12 was in silver; 1, 3, 5, 7, 9 and 13 were in gilt; 10, 14 and 15 were in gilt with coloured enamels; 2, 4, 6, 8 and 11 were bronzed; and 16 was in black metal.

Right: The rank insignia of a Brigadier, as worn on the Battle-Dress blouse. Brig. G. A. Pillean, MC, of the 197th Infantry Brigade, 59th (Staffordshire) Division, seen here on 12 January 1942.
Far right: A lieutenant of the Parachute Regiment, a former Grenadier Guards officer, with Lt.-Gen. Browning. Despite his transfer, the lieutenant has chosen to continue wearing the pattern of metal rank insignia worn by the Grenadier Guards; May 1944.

Right: Field Marshal Alexander pins the ribbon of the DCM on the tunic of a Polish soldier of the 3rd Carpathian Division (part of the 2nd Polish Corps) at Forli, Italy on 7 April 1945. Field Marshal Alexander is wearing the worsted version of the Royal Cypher 'G VI R' below his badge of rank as worn on the Battle-Dress blouse (see also the photograph on page 148). He has also been presented with the emblem of the 2nd Polish Corps, the 'Sirena' or Mermaid of Warsaw badge.

The Royal Cypher Shoulder Strap Emblem worn on Service Dress, Battle-Dress and Khaki Drill Uniform by Honorary Chaplains, Surgeons, Physicians, Equerries, Aides-de-Camp and Aides-de-Camp General to the King

Aides-de-camp general to the King. The Royal Cypher of the reigning monarch in gilt (15/16in high – excluding the imperial crown – and 1 5/16in wide) was worn on the shoulder straps of the Service Dress, Battle-Dress, Khaki Drill uniform and greatcoat immediately above the crossed sword and baton of the rank badges, except in the case of a field marshal, who wore the Royal Cypher below his badge of rank.

An aide-de-camp general who was a colonel or colonel commandant of a regiment or corps, and was wearing the regimental uniform of his regiment or corps, wore the Royal Cypher on the shoulder straps of garments, below the crown and stars of the rank badges of a colonel.

Ex-aides-de-camp general to the King. An aide-de-camp general to the King, after vacating the appointment, wore the gilt Royal Cypher or cyphers of the monarch or monarchs under whom he had held his appointment, in miniature, on the shoulder straps of all uniform garments. An ex-aide-de-camp general who was a colonel or colonel commandant of a regiment or corps, and was wearing the regimental uniform of his regiment or corps, wore the Royal Cypher on the shoulder straps of garments, below the crown and stars of the rank badges of a colonel.

Aides-de-camp to the King. Aides-de-camp to the King were required to wear regimental uniform; brigadiers, substantive colonels and officers holding the honorary rank of Brigadier-General or of Major-General wore the uniform of their rank. On the shoulder straps of the uniforms worn by brigadiers and substantive colonels, the gilt Royal Cypher of the reigning monarch was worn placed below the crown and above the stars of badges of rank, and in the case of aides-de-camp who held the honorary rank of Brigadier-General or Major-General the Royal Cypher was placed below the crossed sword and baton.

Ex-aides-de-camp to the King. Officers who vacated the appointment of aide-de-camp to the King on promotion to the substantive rank of Major-General ceased to wear the Royal Cypher and crown; ex-aides-de-camp to the King who were not promoted to the substantive rank of Major-General continued to wear the Royal Cypher and crown on all uniform garments, but the insignia was in miniature.

The Royal Cypher and crown was worn by ex-aides-de-camp to the King on retirement in the following manner. In the case of honorary major-generals and honorary brigadier-generals the Royal Cypher and crown (in miniature) was placed immediately below the crossed sword and baton. In the case of brigadiers and colonels, the Royal Cypher (in miniature) was placed immediately above the stars, the crown which formed part of the badges of rank serving also as the crown which was part of the Royal Cypher and crown.

Honorary physicians and honorary surgeons to the King. Officers who held these appointments wore the Royal Cypher, but they ceased to wear them when they ceased to hold the appointments.

General officers wore the Royal Cypher immediately below the crossed sword and baton. In the case of colonels, the Royal Cypher was placed immediately above the stars and below the crown.

Honorary chaplains to the King. The Royal Cypher of the reigning monarch was worn with Service Dress and was placed below the crown and above the stars of badges of rank worn on the shoulder straps. In the case of chaplains with the relative rank of Brigadier-General or Major-General, the Royal Cypher was placed below the crossed sword and baton. This distinction was not worn when the officers ceased to hold the appointment.

Change in size of shoulder strap Royal Cypher.

It was announced by ACI 992 dated 30 June 1943 that His Majesty the King (George VI) had been graciously pleased to approve the adoption for wear on Service Dress and Battle-Dress of a Royal Cypher of smaller size than had previously been worn (see *Dress Regulations for the Army, 1934*, para. 92 et seq and as shown on page 34) by officers holding the following appointments: Aide-de-Camp General to the King; Aide-de-Camp to the King; Equerry to the King; Honorary Physician to the King; Honorary Surgeon to the King; and Honorary Chaplain to the King. The Royal Cypher for wear by officers while actually holding any of the above appointments was now to be ¾in in height (excluding the crown) and ⅞in in width whilst the miniature for wear by officers after vacating an appointment was ½in and ¾in respectively.

In the interests of wartime economy officers were permitted to continue wearing cyphers then in their possession, and a change-over to the new size was made only gradually, as and when occasions arose. The question of the sizes of Royal Cyphers for use with orders of dress which were not being worn during the war (such as full dress) was held in abeyance for consideration at a later date.

Right: The Royal Cypher worn on officers' shoulder straps. 1, General aide-de-camp to the King; 2, Field Marshal aide-de-camp to the King; 3, General aide-de-camp to the King as a colonel or colonel commandant of a regiment or corps; 4, General ex-aide-de-camp to the King, having served also King George V and King Edward VIII; 5, General ex-aide-de-camp to the King as a colonel or colonel commandant of a regiment or corps, having served also King George V and King Edward VIII; 6, Brigadier aide-de-camp to the King; 7, Major-General (non-substantive rank) ex-aide-de-camp to the King; 8, Brigadier (retired) ex-aide-de-camp to the King; 9, Lieutenant-General as an honorary physician or honorary surgeon to the King; 10, Honorary physician, honorary surgeon and honorary chaplain to the King, ranking as a colonel (insignia and cypher for the honorary chaplain was in black); 11, Honorary chaplain to the King ranking as a major-general (insignia in black).

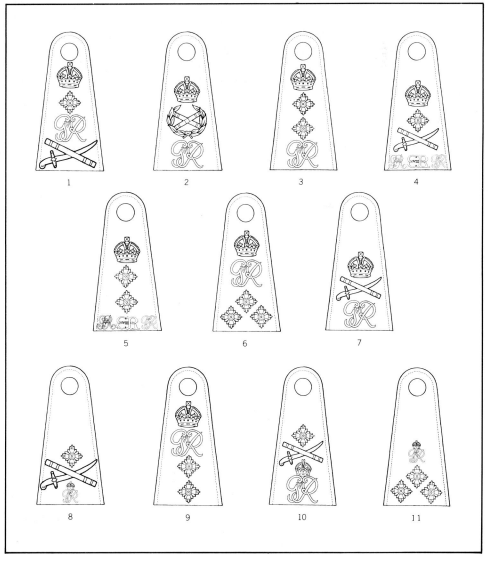

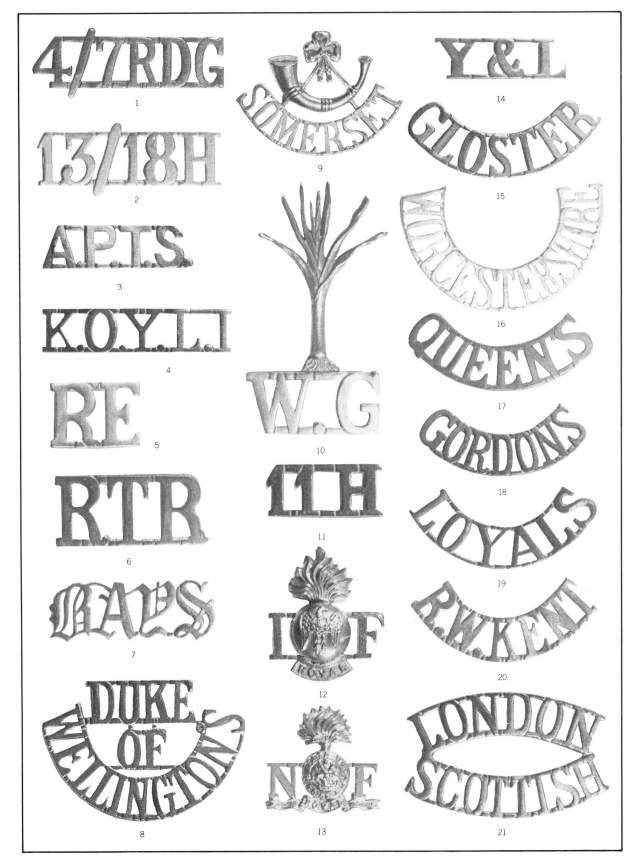

2. SHOULDER STRAP TITLES (METAL)

Metal Titles worn on the Shoulder Straps of Service Dress Tunics, Khaki Drill Jackets and Greatcoats

Metal shoulder titles were worn on both shoulder straps of those garments for which they were authorized. They were positioned with the lower edge of the title – or shoulder badge if one was authorized in lieu of a title – ½in above the seam that joined the shoulder strap to the sleeve. In those cases where a badge, such as a bugle or grenade, was authorized in addition to a title, the lower edge of the title was then worn ¼in above the shoulder seam. (For slip-on shoulder strap titles, see page 81.)

Table 8 is a listing of those metal shoulder titles that were in use from 1936 to 1939 and, in a number of cases (albeit with a much reduced usage), throughout the war years; the listing has been extracted from *Regulations for the Clothing of the Army, 1936*, Appendix 4, 'Titles etc. worn on the Shoulder Straps of Tunics, Jackets and Greatcoats'.

Left: Metal shoulder strap titles. 1, 4th/7th Royal Dragoon Guards; 2, 13th/18th Hussars; 3, Army Physical Training Staff; 4, King's Own Yorkshire Light Infantry; 5, Royal Engineers; 6, Royal Tank Regiment; 7, The Queen's Bays; 8, Duke of Wellington's Regiment; 9, Somerset Light Infantry; 10, Welsh Guards; 11, 11th Hussars; 12, Royal Inniskilling Fusiliers; 13, Royal Northumberland Fusiliers; 14, York and Lancaster Regiment; 15, Gloucestershire Regiment; 16, Worcestershire Regiment; 17, The Queen's Royal Regiment (West Surrey); 18, Gordon Highlanders; 19, Loyal Regiment (North Lancs); 20, Royal West Kents; 21, London Scottish.

Right: Sjt. Reginald Rimmer of the Royal Welch Fusiliers shows his daughter the George Cross he received from His Majesty King George VI at an investiture held at Buckingham Palace on 24 September 1941. Metal titles and emblems normally worn by other ranks on the shoulder straps of the SD jacket were not intended to be worn on the straps of the Battle Dress blouse. However, early in the Second World War several regiments adopted this unofficial practice.

Table 8. *Metal Shoulder Titles*

Regiment or corps	Title
Household Cavalry	
The Life Guards	L.G.[1]
Royal Horse Guards (The Blues)	R.H.G.[1]
Cavalry of the Line	
1st King's Dragoon Guards	K.D.G.
The Queen's Bays (2nd Dragoon Guards)	Bays[2]
3rd Carabiniers (Prince of Wales's Dragoon Guards)	3 D.G.
4th/7th Dragoon Guards[3]	4/7 D.G.[3]
5th Royal Inniskilling Dragoon Guards	Castle over 5 D.G.
1st The Royal Dragoons	Royals
The Royal Scots Greys (2nd Dragoons)	Greys
Royal Wiltshire Yeomanry[4]	Y/R. Wilts[5]
Warwickshire Yeomanry[4]	Y/Warwick
Yorkshire Hussars[4]	Y/Yorks Hussars
Nottinghamshire Yeomanry[4]	Y/Notts
Staffordshire Yeomanry[4]	Y/Stafford
Shropshire Yeomanry[4]	Y/Shropshire
Ayrshire Yeomanry[6]	Y/Ayrshire
Cheshire Yeomanry[4]	Y/Cheshire
Yorkshire Dragoons[7]	Y/Yorkshire D
Leicestershire Yeomanry[4]	Y/Leicestershire
North Somerset Yeomanry[8]	Y/N. Somerset
Duke of Lancaster's Own Yeomanry[9]	Y/D of L's Own
Lanarkshire Yeomanry[10]	Y/Lanarkshire
Northumberland Hussars[11]	N.H.
Lovat Scouts[4]	L.S.
Scottish Horse[12]	Scottish/Horse
Royal Armoured Corps[13]	R.A.C.
3rd The King's Own Hussars	3 H[1]
4th Queen's Own Hussars	4 H[1]
7th Queen's Own Hussars	7 H[1]
8th King's Royal Irish Hussars	8 H[1]
9th Queen's Royal Lancers	IX L[1]
10th Royal Hussars (Prince of Wales's Own)	10 H[1]
11th Hussars (Prince Albert's Own)	11 H[1]
12th Royal Lancers (Prince of Wales's)	12 L[1]
13th/18th Hussars[14]	13/18 H[1, 14]
14th/20th Hussars[15]	14/20 H[1, 16]
15th/19th The King's Royal Hussars	15/19 H[1]
16th/5th Lancers	16/5 L[1]
17th/21st Lancers	17/21 L[1]
North Irish Horse[4]	N.I.H.
Derbyshire Yeomanry[17]	Y/Derbyshire
Royal Gloucestershire Hussars[18]	Y/R.G.H.
Lothians and Border Horse[19]	Y/L & B. Horse
Fife and Forfar Yeomanry[20]	Y/Fife & Forfar
Westminster Dragoons[21]	W.D.
Sharpshooters[22]	Sharpshooters
Northamptonshire Yeomanry[23]	Y/Northampton
East Riding Yeomanry[24]	Y/E. Riding
Royal Artillery	
RHA batteries	R.H.A.[1]
Other batteries	R.A.[1]
Clerks' Section	R.A.[1]
Schools of Gunnery	R.A.[1]
Royal Malta Artillery	Maltese cross on jackets; R.M.A. on greatcoats
Hong Kong-Singapore RA	H.K.S.-R.A.[1]
Royal Engineers	R.E.[1]
Royal Engineers (Maltese Section)	R.E. over Malta
Royal Corps of Signals	R. Signals[1]
Foot Guards	
Grenadier Guards	G.G. and Royal Cypher, reversed and inter-twined within the garter surmounted by a crown[25]

Regiment or corps	Title
Coldstream Guards	C.G. and rose[25]
Scots Guards	Star on tunic, S.G. and thistle on jackets[25]
Irish Guards	I.G. and star[25]
Welsh Guards	W.G. and leek[25]
Infantry of the Line	
The Royal Scots (The Royal Regiment)	R.S.
The Queen's Royal Regiment (West Surrey)	Queen's
The Buffs (Royal East Kent Regiment)	Buffs
The King's Own Royal Regiment (Lancaster)[26]	King's Own
The Royal Northumberland Fusiliers	N.F. and grenade
The Royal Warwickshire Regiment	R. Warwickshire
The Royal Fusiliers (City of London Regiment)	R.F. and grenade
The King's Regiment (Liverpool)	King's[27]
The Royal Norfolk Regiment	Norfolk
The Lincolnshire Regiment	Lincoln
The Devonshire Regiment	Devon
The Suffolk Regiment	Suffolk
The Somerset Light Infantry (Prince Albert's)	Somerset and bugle
The West Yorkshire Regiment (The Prince of Wales's Own)	W. Yorkshire[28]
The East Yorkshire Regiment (The Duke of York's Own)	E. Yorkshire
The Bedfordshire and Hertfordshire Regiment	Bedfs. and Herts.
The Leicestershire Regiment	Leicestershire
The Green Howards (Alexandra, Princess of Wales's Own Yorkshire Regiment	Green Howards
The Lancashire Fusiliers	L.F. and grenade
The Royal Scots Fusiliers	R.S.F. and grenade
The Cheshire Regiment[29]	Cheshire
The Royal Welch Fusiliers	R.W.F. and grenade
The South Wales Borderers	S.W.B.
The King's Own Scottish Borderers	K.O.S.B.
The Cameronians (Scottish Rifles)	Cameronians[30]
The Royal Inniskilling Fusiliers	Inniskillings and grenade[31]
The Gloucestershire Regiment	Gloster
The Worcestershire Regiment	Worcestershire
The East Lancashire Regiment	E. Lancashire
The East Surrey Regiment	E. Surrey
The Duke of Cornwall's Light Infantry	D.C.L.I. and bugle
The Duke of Wellington's Regiment (West Riding)	D.W.
The Border Regiment	Border
The Royal Sussex Regiment	R. Sussex
The Hampshire Regiment	Hampshire[32]
The South Staffordshire Regiment	S. Stafford
The Dorsetshire Regiment	Dorset
The Prince of Wales's Volunteers (South Lancashire)[33]	P.W.V.
The Welch Regiment	Welch
The Black Watch (Royal Highland Regiment)	B.W.
The Oxfordshire and Buckinghamshire Light Infantry	Oxf. & Bucks. with bugle
The Essex Regiment	Essex
The Sherwood Foresters (Nottingham-shire and Derbyshire Regiment)	Foresters[34]
The Loyal Regiment (North Lancashire)	Loyals
The Northamptonshire Regiment	Northamptonshire
The Royal Berkshire Regiment (Princess Charlotte of Wales's)	Royal Berks.
The Queen's Own Royal West Kent Regiment	R.W. Kent

Regiment or corps	Title	Regiment or corps	Title
The King's Own Yorkshire Light Infantry	K.O.Y.L.I. and french horn with silver centre	Hallamshire Battalion of the York and Lancashire Regiment[4]	A white metal Tudor Rose above Y&L
The King's Shropshire Light Infantry	K.S.L.I. and bugle	Monmouthshire Regiment[4, 37]	T/Monmouthshire
The Middlesex Regiment (Duke of Cambridge's Own)	Middlesex	Cambridgeshire Regiment[4]	T/Cambridge
The King's Royal Rifle Corps	K.R.R.	London Rifle Brigade[4]	LRB
The Wiltshire Regiment (Duke of Edinburgh's)	Wilts	Queen Victoria Rifles[4]	QVR
The Manchester Regiment	Manchester	Rangers[4]	T/12/London
The North Staffordshire Regiment (Prince of Wales's)	N. Stafford	Kensington Regiment[4]	Princess/Kensington/Louise's
The York and Lancaster Regiment	Y. & L.	London Scottish[4]	London/Gordons/Scottish
The Durham Light Infantry	D.L.I. and bugle[35]	Queen's Westminsters[4]	T/16/London
The Highland Light Infantry (City of Glasgow Regiment)	H.L.I. and bugle	Tower Hamlets Rifles[4]	THR
The Seaforth Highlanders (Ross-shire Buffs, The Duke of Albany's)	Seaforth	London Irish Rifles[4]	LIR
The Gordon Highlanders	Gordons	Hertfordshire Regiment[4]	T/Herts
The Queen's Own Cameron Highlanders	Camerons	Herefordshire Regiment[4]	T/Herefordshire
The Royal Ulster Rifles	R.U.R.[30]	Royal Tank Corps[38]	R.T.C.[38]
The Royal Irish Fusiliers (Princess Victoria's)	R.I.F. and grenade[36]	Small Arms School Corps	S.A.S.C.
The Argyll and Sutherland Highlanders (Princess Louise's)	A. & S.H.	Royal Army Service Corps	R.A.S.C.[1]
The Rifle Brigade (Prince Consort's Own)	R.B.[30]	Royal Army Medical Corps	R.A.M.C.[1]
Liverpool Scottish[4]	Liverpool/T/Camerons/Scottish	Royal Army Ordnance Corps	R.A.O.C.
		Royal Army Pay Corps	R.A.P.C.
Buckinghamshire Battalion of the Oxfordshire and Buckinghamshire Light Infantry[4]	T/Bucks	Royal Army Veterinary Corps	R.A.V.C.
		Army Educational Corps	A.E.C.[1]
		The Army Dental Corps	A.D. Corps
		Corps of Military Police	C.M.P.[1]
		Army Physical Training Staff[39]	A.P.T.S.[39]
		Garrison Staff	Royal Cypher
		Military Provost Staff Corps	M.P.S.C.[1]
		School of Electric Lighting (boys under instruction only)	S.E.L.
		Royal Military Academy	R.M.A.
		Royal Military College	R.M.C.
		Army Technical School (boys)	A.T.S.[40]

[1]No titles were worn on tunics by these units.

[2]The style of lettering of the title Bays was in old English gothic.

[3]The 4th/7th Dragoon Guards became the 4th/7th Royal Dragoon Guards in 1936 with the shoulder title eventually being changed to 4/7 R.D.G.

[4]All the Yeomanry and Territorial units listed above and indicated with this footnote were first published in Army Council Instructions for 23 July 1941 for inclusion with the existing listing of regiments and corps of the Regular Army. Despite the delay of notification of these units in ACIs, many of them had been put on a war footing at the beginning of hostilities, if not earlier. Some units (as explained below) were converted from Yeomanry regiments to artillery regiments before the publication of the July 1941 listing, thereby making the listing partially obsolete. However, for the sake of uniformity and interest I have included them all in one 'master list' in their appropriate positions and have given further explanatory footnotes.

[5]The titles listed for the majority of the Yeomanry units were in two tiers, usually with the letter 'Y' placed above the title of the unit. This has been indicated above by the use of a vertical stroke placed between the letter 'Y' and the unit's name or between the words of the unit's name, each vertical stroke indicating each tier of letters or words. Strokes used in this manner should not be confused with the oblique strokes used to distinguish between numbered units, for example 4th/7th Dragoon Guards and 17th/21st Lancers.

[6]In 1940 the Ayrshire Yeomanry (Earl of Carrick's Own) was converted to the 151st Field Regiment, Royal Artillery. In 1947 it was transferred to the Royal Armoured Corps and reverted to its former title, The Ayrshire Yeomanry.

[7]The Queen's Own Yorkshire Dragoons was converted in 1942 to become the 9th Battalion The King's Own Yorkshire Light Infantry. In 1947 it was transferred to the RAC and reverted to its former title, the Yorkshire Dragoons.

[8]The North Somerset Yeomanry was converted in 1943 to become the 4th Air Formation Signals, reverting to its former title in 1947 when transferred to the RAC.

[9]The Duke of Lancaster's Own Yeomanry became the 77th Medium Regiment, RA, in 1940 but in 1947 transferred to the RAC and once again assumed its former title.

[10]In 1939 the Lanarkshire Yeomanry converted to become the

155th Field Regiment, RA. In 1947 it was transferred to the RAC and resumed the prewar title of The Lanarkshire Yeomanry.

[11]The Northumberland Hussars was converted in 1940 to become the 102nd Light Anti-Aircraft/Anti-Tank Regiment, Royal Artillery. In 1947 it was transferred to the RAC under the former title of The Northumberland Hussars.

[12]The Scottish Horse was converted in 1940 to the 79th Medium Regiment, RA. In 1947 it was transferred to the RAC, and was thereafter known by its previous title, The Scottish Horse.

[13]The Royal Armoured Corps was formed in April 1939 from Cavalry Regiments of the Line that had been mechanized and from the Royal Tank Regiment. The RAC was an administrative and training formation only, its badges and titles being worn only by RAC staff and recruits.

[14]In 1935 the 13th/18th Hussars was redesignated the 13th/18th Royal Hussars (Queen Mary's Own). Shoulder titles for officers were changed first to read 13/18 R.H. then later to read XIII/XVIII R.H.

[15]The 14th/20th Hussars was redesignated the 14th/20th King's Hussars in 1936.

[16]A title XIV/XX K.H. was worn by officers after 1936.

[17]From 1920 to 1939 this unit was known as the 24th (Derbyshire Yeomanry) Armoured Car Company, The Tank Corps. In 1939 it was transferred to the RAC under the title of The Derbyshire Yeomanry.

[18]In 1920 this unit became the 21st (Gloucestershire Yeomanry) Armoured Car Company, The Tank Corps. In 1939 it was transferred to the RAC with the title of The Royal Gloucestershire Hussars Yeomanry.

[19]In 1920 the Lothians and Border Horse became the 19th (Lothians and Border) Armoured Car Company of the Tank Corps. In 1939 it was transferred to the RAC and renamed the 1st Lothians and Border Yeomanry.

[20]In 1922 this unit was the 20th (Fife and Forfar) Armoured Car Company, The Tank Corps, and in 1939 was transferred to the RAC as the Fife and Forfar Yeomanry.

[21]The Westminster Dragoons (2nd County of London Regiment) was known as the 22nd Armoured Car Company, The Tank Corps, in 1922, and in 1939 became the 102nd Officer Cadet Training Unit. In 1940 the unit was transferred to the RAC as the Westminster Dragoons.

[22]The Sharpshooters were known in June 1922 as the 23rd London Armoured Car Company (Sharpshooters), The Tank Corps. In 1938 it became the 23rd Cavalry Armoured Car Regiment, and in 1939 part of the Royal Armoured Corps was split to form the 3rd and 4th County of London Yeomanry (Sharpshooters); in 1944 these were amalgamated to form the 3rd/4th County of London Yeomanry (Sharpshooters).

[23]In 1920 this unit was designated the 25th Armoured Car Company, The Tank Corps, and in 1939 was transferred to the RAC as the Northamptonshire Yeomanry.

[24]In 1920 this unit was converted to become the 26th Armoured Car Company, The Tank Corps, and in 1939 transferred to the RAC as the East Riding Yeomanry.

[25]Initials were not worn on Full Dress tunics and titles were not worn on the blue-grey (Atholl grey) greatcoats.

[26]This title was in use from 1881 until 1959, but prior to 1936 it was expressed as The King's Own (Royal Lancaster Regiment).

[27]The 5th and 6th Battalions of The King's Regiment wore bronzed finished shoulder titles and the remaining battalions had gilding metal.

[28]The 7th and 8th Battalions of the West Yorkshire Regiment wore bronzed finished shoulder titles, the remaining battalions having gilding metal.

[29]Despite its official title having been The Cheshire Regiment from 1881, the title used within the regiment is The 22nd (Cheshire) Regiment, a reference to its former title harking back to 1751.

[30]Shoulder title in bronzed finish.

[31]Pipe-majors and pipers of the Royal Inniskilling Fusiliers wore shoulder titles in white metal.

[32]The 8th Battalion of The Hampshire Regiment wore shoulder titles with a bronzed finish; the remaining battalions wore gilding metal titles.

[33]In 1938, by authority of Army Order 224, the title 'The Prince of Wales's Volunteers (South Lancashire)' was changed to 'The South Lancashire Regiment (Prince of Wales's Volunteers)'.

[34]The 7th Battalion of the Sherwood Foresters wore shoulder titles with a bronzed finish, other battalions having gilding metal.

[35]The 6th Battalion of the Durham Light Infantry wore a shoulder title with a bugle in a bronzed finish; the remaining battalions' titles were in gilding metal.

[36]Pipe-majors and pipers of the Royal Irish Fusiliers wore shoulder titles that were nickel silver.

[37]The 1st Battalion of the Monmouthshire Regiment wore bronzed finished titles, those of the 2nd Battalion being in gilding metal.

[38]In April 1939 the Royal Tank Corps was redesignated the Royal Tank Regiment; the shoulder title R.T.C. became R.T.R.

[39]The Army Physical Training Staff was redesignated the Army Physical Training Corps in 1940; shoulder titles were changed from A.P.T.S. to A.P.T.C.

[40]The title A.T.S. as used by boys of the Army Technical School should not be confused with that used by women of the Auxiliary Territorial Service. The former title had letters all of the same height whilst the later title had a large letter 'T' placed between the letters 'A' and 'S'.

3. COLLAR BADGES, GORGET PATCHES AND BUTTONS

Collar Badges

Metal collar badges, which were worn on SD tunics and KD jackets, but not on Battle-Dress blouses, were fixed midway between the top and bottom of the collar and 2in from the centre of the badge to the end of the collar. In the RA and RE the collar badges on the SD and KD jackets were worn in a diagonal position at an angle of 45°.

Officers below the rank of Substantive Colonel wore collar badges on the collars of their Service Dress jackets. These were normally in bronze finished metal, although other metals were used depending on the regiment, and were worn in either matching or mirror pairs.

As a form of wartime economy, officers of regiments raised during the 1939–45 war were not required to wear collar badges on their Service Dress jackets. Although the design of the badges was promulgated the badges themselves were not supposed to have been available until after the war was over; however, from a study of contemporary photographs it is evident that this ruling was not adhered to.

Gorget Patches

Cloth gorget patches were first introduced in 1887 for wear with Khaki Drill uniforms by general officers and certain officers of the staff and departments serving in India. In 1913 gorget patches were introduced to be worn on the collars of the open neck Service Dress jacket. These patches were also worn by all staff officers holding 'MS', 'G', 'A' and 'Q' appointments, as well as personal appointments, even down to subaltern level.[1]

In 1921 this proliferation of gorget patches was contained and from then on the wearing of gorget patches was restricted to officers of the rank of Substantive Colonel and above.

The 1934 edition of *Dress Regulations for the Army* lists the following coloured gorget patches.

Scarlet	Field-Marshal[2], General Officer[2], Brigadier and substantive Colonel, the latter not belonging to a corps or department[3]
Purple	The Chaplain-General, Chaplain with the relative rank of a General Officer[4, 5] and Chaplain with the relative rank of Colonel[6]
Dull cherry	General Officer late of the Royal Army Medical Corps[2] and Colonel of the RAMC[5]
Maroon red	Colonel late of the Royal Army Veterinary Corps[5]
Dark blue	Colonel of the Royal Army Ordnance Corps[7]
Cambridge blue	Colonel late of the Army Education Corps[5]
Emerald green	General Officer late of the Army Dental Corps[8] and Colonel late of the AD Corps[5]

Primrose yellow	General Officer late of the Royal Army Pay Corps[8] and Colonel late of the RAPC[5]

It is of interest to note that nowhere in the 1934 Dress Regulations for the Army or any of the Amendments to 1939 is there mention of the dark blue gorget patches worn by colonels of the Royal Engineers.

Gorget patches in beech brown were introduced for officers of the ATS from the rank of Controller and above on 7 February 1940. Major-generals, brigadiers and colonels of the REME were authorized to wear scarlet gorget patches under the authority of ACI 1605 dated 1 August 1942 which dealt with the formation of, and transfers to, the REME.

Gorget patches on the Battle-Dress blouse.

The subject of gorget patches worn on the Battle-Dress blouse was first raised in May 1940 (ACI 466 dated 15 May 1940). This instruction laid down that gorget patches were not to be worn on the Battle-Dress but that commanders of formations were to wear a scarlet cord boss set at the points of the collar of the Battle-Dress blouse. Sealed patterns of this special distinction for commanders were available for inspection at the War Office Pattern Room, at each command headquarters and at the General Headquarters British Expeditionary Force.

However, on 9 November 1940 ACI 1366 authorized that all officers for whom gorget patches were prescribed in Service Dress would in future wear gorget patches with Battle-Dress. The patches were similar to those authorized for Service Dress but were of miniature size, 2in long to the point and 1in wide, except that in the case of field-marshals and general officers plain gold braid 1/8in wide (corrected on 16 November 1940 to 1/5in wide) was worn down the centre of the patch instead of oakleaf embroidery as prescribed for patches worn with Service Dress.

The gorget patches were worn horizontally on each side of the opening of the collar of the Battle-

[1] MS = Officers of the Military Secretary's branches; G = Officers of the Chief of the Imperial General Staff's branches; A = Officers of the Adjutant-General's branches; Q = Officers of the Quarter-Master-General's branches.
[2] All gorget patches had a line of gold coloured oakleaves embroidered down the centre of the cloth patch, with a small gilt button positioned near to the pointed end of the patch.
[3] The line of silk gimp on these was in crimson.
[4] The small gorget button was black, not gilt metal.
[5] All gorget patches had a line of silk gimp of the same colour as the patch, positioned down the centre of the cloth patch, with a small gorget button in gilt metal positioned at the point of the patch.
[6] The small gorget button was black, not gilt metal, for chaplains.
[7] The dark blue gorget patches of the RAOC were changed in October 1941 to scarlet.
[8] These gorget patches were introduced by an Army Order dated June 1937.

Below: Men of the 1st Bn the South Staffordshire Regiment demonstrating the Boys' anti-tank rifle (.55in calibre with a magazine holding five rounds) during a series of exercises held at Mytchett near Aldershot, Hampshire, on 21 January 1938. The Staffordshire Knot collar badge, worn with its backing of brown holland cloth, together with the 'S STAFFORD' metal shoulder titles are clearly shown here; see also the photograph on page 225.

Right: Lt. B. H. Halsall, MC, a glider pilot of the Army Air Corps, after his investiture on 9 May 1944. Collar badges were for the duration of the war required to be worn only by officers of this war-raised Corps as an economy measure.

Far right: Gorget patches worn by a General Officer in shirt sleeve order. Maj.-Gen. C. G. C. Nicholson, CBE, DSO, MC and bar, photographed in November 1943 on the occasion of his receiving the US Legion of Merit.

Right: Lord Gort, VC, Inspector-General of Training on a tour of Northern Ireland in February 1941. The officer in the foreground is Brig. A.St.Q. Fullbrook-Leggatt, DSO, MC, of the 61st Infantry Division. He is wearing the special rank distinction of scarlet corded bosses on the points of the collar to his Battle-Dress blouse.

Right: Gorget patches worn by Brig. Geoffrey Harding, DSO, in Service Dress.

Far right: An example of gorget patches worn on the collar of the Service Dress jacket by a General Officer, Maj.-Gen. F. A. M. Browning.

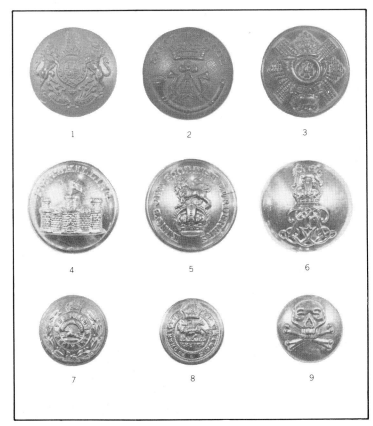

Below: Button types and sizes. 1, General List; 2, Rifle Brigade; 3, Highland Light Infantry; 4, Royal Inniskilling Fusiliers; 5, King's Own Scottish Borderers; 6, The Life Guards; 7, The King's Regiment; 8, The Royal Berkshire Regiment; 9, 17th/21st Lancers. Numbers 1–6 are tunic size; 7–9 are cuff buttons. Number 1 is a drab plastic wartime economy button; 2 is in black metal; 3 is in bronzed metal; and 4-9 are in gilding metal.

Dress blouse, with their points to the rear and the top of the patch ½in from the top of the collar; the scarlet cord boss previously authorized was abolished and no longer worn.

Uniform Buttons

The subject of regimental and corps patterned buttons is, like the subject of regimental and corps cap badges, far too extensive to be included in this work, and attention is drawn to the Bibliography on page 275 which includes a number of eminently useful books on the subject of military buttons for anyone who wishes to pursue this study further.

Before the war, according to *Dress Regulations for the Army, 1934*, where buttons were used on the fronts of tunics etc. they had to be spaced at equal distances from each other. All buttons, with the exception of those used by the Household troops and those worn on mess dress and on gorget patches, were die-struck; the buttons worn on articles of Service Dress were of gilding metal ungilt. Black buttons were worn on Service Dress by personnel of The Kings Royal Rifle Corps, the Royal Ulster Rifles, the Rifle Brigade, the Cameronians (Scottish Rifles) and members of the Royal Army Chaplains' Department.

It is of interest to note that not until 1937 were regimental buttons worn on the greatcoat. ACI 94 dated August 1937 announced that Regular Army personnel were in future to wear buttons of regimental pattern on the greatcoat as well as on the Service Dress jacket. Greatcoats from that date continued to be issued from RAOC stocks with buttons bearing the Royal Arms but were replaced by regimental buttons of the appropriate design on issue to the individual soldier.

The production of non-polishable buttons had been the subject of prolonged prewar research, but it proved at that time impossible to find a metal which was as serviceable as gilding metal whilst at the same time could not be polished – *could* not as opposed to *need* not. The buttons as used on the universal issue Battle-Dress were of vegetable composition and were initially fly-fitted; needless to say, they required no polishing, but for those used on the Service Dress, the greatcoat and the Field Service and Service Dress caps there was no alternative but to retain gilding metal buttons. Buttons worn on the drab Service Dress and Khaki Drill by officers of the five regiments of Foot Guards were arranged in a manner peculiar to each regiment: see page 160.

4.   ARMLETS

Far left: The Provost Marshal Maj.-Gen. Sir Percy Laurie, KCVO, CBE, DSO, former Chief of the Metropolitan Mounted Police, inspecting men of the Corps of Military Police attached to the 9th Armoured Division; Newmarket, Cambridgeshire, 29 July 1942. (See also the photograph on page 220.)
Left: A Brigadier of the Royal Artillery employed at a Command Headquarters (Home) wearing the red, black, red armlet with worsted gun emblem.

Prior to the Second World War the use of armlets, the majority of which were for wear by officers, was fairly extensive and rigidly controlled. Regulations for their use were set out in *Dress Regulations for the Army, 1934,* para. 164. General officers did not wear armlets, but brigadiers and substantive colonels holding appointments for which armlets were authorized, whether at the War Office or at command, divisional, brigade or area headquarters, wore the armlets with the appropriate lettering as shown in the accompanying tables; brigadiers and substantive colonels commanding formations wore the appropriate formation armlet without distinctive lettering.

Armlets were produced in cloth, and they were 3½in in width with the distinctive lettering in black cloth, except where otherwise stated. They were worn by all officers for whom they were authorized on the right arm, above the elbow with Service Dress, including the greatcoat when that article was worn. Armlets required by officers were provided by the officers themselves, sample armlets being kept at the headquarters of commands for their guidance.

ACI 115, published during week ending 14 February 1940 and entitled 'Armlets − Staff Officers', gave approval for the free issue of armlets to officers appointed to the Staff since 1 September 1939 who were eligible to wear an armlet under the provision of the 1934 Dress Regulation. One armlet with the appropriate letters for attachment was issued to each staff officer appointed since 1 September 1939 and who was not already in possession of an armlet. It was retained by the officer throughout his tenure of office, and when he relinquished his appointment or left the command etc. headquarters the armlet was withdrawn and held for re-issue under local arrangements.

These armlets were the distinguishing marks of officers holding staff appointments (GSOI, AAG etc.); they were not permitted to be worn by other officers serving at formation etc. headquarters who did not hold such appointments, neither were they worn by general officers.

Officers who took up appointments with formations in the British Expeditionary Force continued to be provided with armlets held as part of the war equipment of their formations. A free issue of armlets was not made to officers holding staff appointments to which they were appointed before 1 September 1939, these officers having already provided armlets for themselves under the provisions of *Dress Regulations for the Army, 1934,* para. 164.

ACI 1489 dated 7 December 1940 announced that for the duration of the war the instructions contained in the 1934 Dress Regulations were to be modified: for officers at home stations the armlet was not to be worn on all occasions, but only when staff officers were on duty with troops or when visiting the headquarters of formations, whilst at overseas stations they were worn as ordered by the general officer commanding in the light of local circumstances. Consequent on this announcement the free issue of an armlet to each staff officer as authorized by ACI 115 of 1940 (see above) was no longer necessary and was therefore discontinued. Armlets together with appropriate letters for attachment thereto were in future issued on demand by the COO, Central Ordnance Depot, Branston, through the normal channel and were held on charge as public clothing. In the case of officers who took up appointments with formations of a field force, armlets continued to be provided as part of the war equipment of the formation concerned. Armlets which had already been issued free to officers appointed since 1 September 1939 under the terms of ACI 115 of 1940 were withdrawn and similarly accounted for. Armlets continued to be considered as distinguishing marks and their use was restricted to holders of these appointments only.

The use of black crepe mourning bands.

When attending military funerals or memorial services connected therewith, officers and warrant officers had to wear a mourning band of black crepe material, 3¼in wide, around the left arm above the elbow. It was not worn at levées or at Court, except when the Court was in mourning, neither was it worn at ceremonies such as the unveiling of memorials and Armistice Day celebrations.

An officer or warrant officer in private mourning could, when in uniform, wear a mourning band as described above. An NCO or soldier in private mourning or at a military funeral was similarly permitted to wear a band of black material should he wish to do so.

On 5 April 1944 it was announced by ACI 493 of 1944 that the provisions of the *King's Regulations for the Army, 1940,* para. 1010 (a) as given above, were held in abeyance, and the wearing of mourning bands at Service funerals or memorial services connected therewith was discontinued for the duration of the war. However, this instruction did not prohibit the individual officer or other rank from wearing a mourning band, if he so desired, when in private mourning.

Armlets for Officers
War Office employed officers.
Armlet half red and half dark blue laid horizontally with the red uppermost; the Royal Crest in metal (usually gilding metal) with the following ¾in high red letters below:

M S	Officers of the Military Secretary's branches
G	Officers of the Chief of the Imperial General Staff's branches
A	Officers of the Adjutant-General's branches
Q	Officers of the Quarter-Master-General's branches
D G M P	Officers of the Director General of Munitions Production branches[1]
M G O	Officers of the Master-General of the Ordnance's branches

T A	Officers of the Territorial Army Directorate
P R	Officers of the Directorate of Public Relations[1]
P	Royal Army Pay Corps officers
A	Provost Marshal[2]
D J A	Officers of the Deputy Judge-Advocate's Department[3]

Officers with command headquarters (Home). Armlets divided horizontally in equal portions red, black and red, with the following distinctions and ¾in high scarlet letters, according to the appointment or employment of the officers concerned:

A M S	Assistant military secretary
A D C	Aides-de-camp
G	General Staff branch
A D Mn[4]	Brigadier or colonel in charge of administration
A & Q	Officers combining adjutant-general's and quarter-master-general's duties, e.g. assistant-adjutant and quarter-master-generals
A	Adjutant-General's branch of the Staff
Q	Quarter-Master-General's branch of the Staff
A gun[5]	Royal Artillery
E	Royal Engineers
S	Signal Service
S T	Supply and Transport Services
M	Medical Services (including the inspecting dental officer[6])
O	Ordnance Services
V	Veterinary Services
P M	Provost Marshal's officers[7]
P	Royal Army Pay Corps officers
A E C	Command Education officer
C	Assistant Chaplain-General
C Q M	The Camp Quarter-Master at Aldershot

Officers with appointments or employed with lesser formations within HQ Home Forces, in the BEF and in the Middle East.[8] Armlet half red and half dark blue laid horizontally with the red worn uppermost but without the Royal Crest; ¾in high yellow lettering on the lower dark blue portion of the armlet. The lettering used on these armlets was the same as that listed above under 'Officers with command headquarters (Home)'.

Staff officers at Headquarters, British Troops in Ireland. Command armlet of equal horizontal portions of red, black and red with ¾in high scarlet lettering positioned on the central black portion of the same configuration as listed in the previous section. Armlets were introduced for officers holding staff appointments at Headquarters, British Troops in Ireland, by authority of ACI 1101 dated 14 September 1940.

Officers at Headquarters, London District, Northern Ireland District[9] *and Divisional Headquarters.* A red armlet with the appropriate distinctive black lettering as laid down for officers at a command headquarters.

Officers at brigade headquarters. A blue armlet with the following distinctive black lettering:

| B M | Brigade-major |
| S C | Staff captain |

Other appointments had distinctive lettering as laid down for officers at the command headquarters (above).

Officers at area, district and garrison headquarters. A green armlet with the following distinctive black lettering:

| G A | Garrison adjutant |

Other officers had armlets as laid down for officers at a command headquarters; officers holding staff appointments at the Royal Tank Corps/the Royal Tank Regiment wore the armlet with lettering indicative of their appointment.[10]

Officers holding appointments at the Headquarters of the Anti-Aircraft Corps. A red, white and red armlet of horizontally equal portions with distinctive lettering that conformed to the instructions contained in *Dress Regulations of the Army, 1934*, para. 164, was introduced by authority of ACI 357 published during the week 24 August 1938 for wear by officers holding appointments for which armlets were authorized at the Headquarters of the AA Corps.

Officers with special duties. The following were worn by officers engaged on special duties:

Officers employed in connection with embarkation movements and transportation of troops. A white linen armlet.

Area fire superintendents. A khaki drab armlet with the word FIRE in blue letters.

Army Signal Service. A blue and white armlet (see below, page 49, for additional details).

War correspondents. An armlet of black and white alternate vertical stripes, 2in wide, with the word PRESS in ¾in high red letters (armlets were worn on both arms).

Air liaison officers. The armlet of their respective commands with the letters A L O[2].

Chief recruiting officers. A red armlet (division) with the letters C R O in black.[1]

Zone recruiting officers. A blue armlet (brigade) with the letters Z R O in black.[1]

Staff officers of the Auxiliary Military Pioneer Services. On 28 August 1940 approval was given under the authority of ACI 1006 of 1940 for staff officers of the AMPS to wear the armlet of the formation to which they belonged, bearing the letter L in appropriate colouring.

Motor contact officers. An armlet, horizontally divided in equal divisions of black, orange and black with a black letter C embroidered on the central orange portion was introduced by authority of ACI 1338 dated 6 November 1940 to be worn by officers employed as motor contact officers when on duty. These armlets were held on charge by the formation or unit to which the officer belonged and were issued out to officers as necessary.

Military attachés and officers holding staff appointments with military missions. These officers wore the armlet as laid down for officers holding War Office appointments (see above). The lettering in the case of military missions was as shown for War Office appointments; that for military attachés was with the letters M A.

Physical Training Officers. Officers graded as general staff officers wore the armlet of the formation to which they were attached with the letter G; supervising physical training officers wore the armlet of the formation to which they were attached, with the distinguishing letters P T.

Officers at stations abroad and in the Channel Islands.
Egypt, China and Malaya. Armlets as laid down for command headquarters (above).
Malta and Gibraltar. Armlets as laid down for divisional headquarters (above).
Guernsey and Jersey. Armlets as laid down for brigade headquarters (above).

Officers at other stations abroad. Armlets worn by officers at all stations abroad other than those mentioned in the previous section were all blue, with the appropriate distinctive lettering as laid down for officers at a command headquarters (above).

Intelligence Personnel Officers.[11] Intelligence officers of infantry battalions wore narrow green armlets; intelligence officers of infantry brigades wore a broad green armlet.

Officers of Royal Artillery and Royal Engineer survey companies.[12] These officers wore a blue and yellow armlet divided horizontally in equal parts with the blue portion uppermost.

Officers on board troop ships.[12] Officers acting as Adjutant, Baggage Master, Messing Officer and Quartermaster wore a white armlet with a blue centre line and black letters: ADJUTANT, BAGGAGE MASTER, MESSING OFFICER, QUARTERMASTER.

Officers of the Military Provost Staff Corps.[13] These officers wore black armlets with red letters M P S C.

Officers of the Field Security Police.[13] These officers wore green armlets with black letters F S P.

[1] The armlet for wear by these officers was introduced just prior to October 1938.
[2] The armlet for these officers was introduced just prior to June 1937.
[3] The armlet approved for wear by officers holding the appointment of Deputy Judge Advocate was authorized by ACI 261 published during w/e 20

March 1940. At home the War Office armlet with the letters D J A was worn and with the BEF the armlet of the appropriate formation (GHQ, Corps or Line of Communication) to which the wearer belonged was worn, also displaying the letters D J A. Officers taking up appointments with the BEF were provided with armlets held as part of the war equipment of their formations. Armlets were issued in accordance with the provision of ACI 115 of 1940 (see page 45).
[4] The letters A D Mn were in gold-yellow thread.
[5] In worsted.
[6] The inclusion of inspecting dental officers required to wear the medical services armlet was made some time prior to June 1937.
[7] On 1 June 1940 it was decided that all officers of the Provost Service would in future wear a distinguishing armlet. Officers holding provost appointments (e.g. A P M − Assistant Provost Marshal; D A P M − Deputy Assistant Provost Marshal) on the staff of, or attached to, headquarters of formations were to continue to wear the appropriate armlet as authorized in *Dress Regulations for the Army, 1934,* para. 164. Regimental officers who belonged to, or were appointed for duty with, units of the Corps of Military Police (including those referred to in *Dress Regulations for the Army, 1934,* para. 1789) were to wear an armlet of the same pattern as that issued to other ranks (see page 46, 'Officers with command headquarters (Home)').
[8] The armlets for wear by officers holding staff appointments under the Inspector General of the Home and Overseas forces were introduced by ACI 562 of August 1939.
[9] Northern Ireland District was added to London District and Divisional Headquarters just prior to June 1937.
[10] Staff officers of the RTR wore armlets with the addition of the distinctive 'tank' arm badge positioned above the lettering of the armlets (see items on display at the Bovington Museum).
[11] These armlets had been approved for wear by Intelligence personnel by authority of ACI 243 published during w/e 29 July 1931.
[12] Armlets listed in *Vocabulary of Clothing and Necessaries, 1936* (Part I).
[13] Armlets listed in *Vocabulary of Clothing and Necessaries, 1936* (Part I), amendments from 1 April 1938.

Below: Lt. Hugill of the 58th Rifle Brigade, 11th Armoured Division, shaking hands with King George VI. The Lieutenant is wearing the red armlet with black letter 'Q', indicating his appointment as an officer with the Quarter-Master-General's branch at the Division's Head-quarters.
Below right: A British war correspondent interviews Maj.-Gen. B. Miraslav of the Czechoslovak Independent Brigade; 30 May 1942.

Armlets for Other Ranks

Other ranks personnel employed as regimental police. Regimental Police personnel of all regiments wore black armlets (which before 1940 had been dark blue) with red cloth letters R P. Some regiments chose to wear a regimental cap badge set between the letters R and P, whilst other units went so far as to produce, at regimental expense, armlets with specially made brass letters R P. All regimental police armlets were worn on the upper left arm but in 1941 they were authorized to be worn on the upper right arm by regimental policemen of all units. However, under the authority of ACI 836 dated 29 May 1943, the RP armlet was ordered to be worn on the right cuff whether or not traffic control sleeves were worn – this was done in order to prevent confusion with the MP armlet worn by Military Police personnel on the right upper arm.

Military Police other ranks personnel. Personnel of the Corps of Military Police were required to wear, when on duty, a dark blue armlet (changed in 1940 to a black armlet) with the red cloth letters M P. This was worn on the upper right arm by each member of the CMP for both United Kingdom and foreign service.[1]

Garrison Military Police. Blue-black armlets with red cloth letters G M P, standing for Garrison Military Police, were worn on the upper right arm when on duty in the United Kingdom and on foreign service by each member of the Garrison Military Police.

Personnel of the Military Provost Staff Corps. These personnel wore black armlets with red cloth letters M P S C[2].

Personnel of the Field Security Police. These personnel wore green armlets with black cloth letters F S P[2].

Other ranks personnel of the RAMC and the Army Dental Corps. The Geneva Red Cross armlet was worn on the left upper arm by each man of the RAMC and the Army Dental Corps.

Opposite, top left: The white linen armlet worn as an emblem by officers responsible for the control of troop movements was also overprinted with the black letters 'RTO' (Railway Transport Officer). This Royal Engineer RTO is examining a German range-finder captured by a wounded French Commando, June 1944.

Opposite, top right: Three well known Cornish sportsmen, G. Robins, T. Mutton and W. Wills, all members of the DCLI Regimental Police, on duty at the Camp gates, Cookham, Surrey.

Opposite, below left: A Medical Services Brigadier on the Staff of the 2nd Corps, May 1941.

Above left: The Geneva Red Cross armlet as worn by Lt.-Col. Ferguson, RAMC, CO of the hospital ship *Duke of Argyle*; January 1945. The red cross on a circular white background worn on a khaki drab armlet was a variation on the all-white armlet.

Above centre and right: The standard issue Geneva Red Cross armlet. It is being worn (centre) by a private of the 50th (Northumbria) Tyne Tees Division and (right) by a captain in the RAMC.

Personnel employed on Sanitary Service. Sanitary Service personnel wore yellow armlets.[3]

Stretcher bearers. Other ranks personnel acting as stretcher bearers wore a worsted armlet with the red cloth letters S B (this item was seldom used during the 1939–45 war).[2]

Military hospital in-patients. Military personnel undergoing medical treatment as in-patients at military hospitals or convalescing wore, usually with the Army greatcoat, a blue armlet for walking-out.[3]

Intelligence personnel. Intelligence personnel of infantry battalions wore narrow green armlets and those of infantry brigades broad green armlets.[4]

Personnel of RA and RE survey companies. Personnel employed in Royal Artillery and Royal Engineer survey companies wore blue and yellow armlets divided horizontally in equal parts with the blue portion uppermost.[3]

Military fire service duty personnel. A khaki drab armlet bearing the word FIRE in blue cloth letters was worn on the right upper arm by each man of permanent military fire stations and each unit fire instructor when on duty in the United Kingdom only. In 1945 a new pattern of armlet was introduced which was closely associated with the special Army Fire Service printed tradesmen's badge (see page 55). In order that other ranks personnel of the Army Fire Service could be more easily distinguished when in shirt-sleeve order or when wearing the greatcoat on duty, a special armlet was introduced by ACI 1018 dated 29 August 1945; it comprised the Army Fire Service badge sewn on to a khaki cloth armlet and was worn on the upper right arm of shirt-sleeves or greatcoats. The scale of issue was one armlet per other rank of the Army Fire Service.

Remount personnel. Personnel of remount units wore a white drill armlet with black lettering REMOUNT.[3]

Checkers. Army personnel acting as checkers wore plain white drill armlets.[3]

Warders. Army personnel employed as warders wore khaki drab armlets with black lettering WARDER.[3]

Army Signals Service personnel. A free issue of two signals armlets was made to officers engaged on Army Signals Service (see page 46); to Royal Signals officers and regimental signalling officers; to Royal Signals NCOs in charge of regimental or battalion signal troops, sections or detachments, Royal Signals; to despatch riders, Royal Signals; to motor-cyclists of other arms while employed on despatch rider duties; and to Royal Signals personnel engaged in the construction and maintenance of signal lines. The horizontally divided white over blue armlets were worn on each upper arm and only during actual duty. They were worn when on active service or during unit or formation training but were not worn when there was a danger of the armlets attracting enemy fire to the wearer. These armlets were worn for two purposes: their use denoted persons engaged on urgent inter-communication duties and so ensured that they were not unduly delayed or hindered in carrying out those duties; and they enabled key inter-communication personnel to be immediately recognized.

War correspondents' servants. Armlets for use by other ranks acting as servants to war correspondents were similar to those worn by the officer correspondents themselves (see page 46). They were worn in pairs, one to each upper arm, and had black and white alternate vertical stripes 2in in width. They did *not* display PRESS.

[1]See footnote 7, page 47.
[2]Armlets listed in *Vocabulary of Clothing and Necessaries, 1936* (Part I), amendments from 1 April 1938.
[3]Armlets listed in *Vocabulary of Clothing and Necessaries, 1936* (Part I).
[4]These armlets had been approved for wear by Intelligence personnel by authority of ACI 243 published during w/e 29 July 1931.

Above: Military Police checking the papers of two German women in Bedburg, 19 February 1945.

Above right: Stretcher bearers of a Scottish regiment with the BEF in France, 1940. The white linen armlet with red cloth letters 'SB' was an improvement on the worsted item featured in the photograph right.

Right: A stretcher bearer wearing the worsted armlet, a remnant from the First World War seldom used during the 1939-45 conflict.

5. GOOD CONDUCT BADGES

A free initial issue of one set of good conduct badges, sometimes referred to as 'good conduct stripes' or 'good conduct chevrons', was issued to each soldier on his becoming entitled to wear such badges. The badges were worn point uppermost on the left forearm of Khaki Drill and Service Dress jackets, and Battle-Dress blouses, the centre of the lower edge being positioned 7in from the bottom of the sleeve.

Good conduct badges were not worn on Tropical shirts, on working clothing nor on great-coats, whilst worsted badges were worn on SD jackets and Battle-Dress blouses and cotton badges on Khaki Drill clothing. The qualification for these badges was contained in the Pay Warrant, and they could only be worn by soldiers below the rank of Corporal or its equivalent.

The issue of chevrons was subject to the following qualifying periods of military good conduct: one chevron for 2 years' good conduct service, two chevrons for 5 years, three for 12 years, four for 16 years and five for 21 years. Many instances exist where soldiers have completed anything up to and sometimes more than 50 years of good military service and have been progressively rewarded with as many as ten good conduct chevrons. However, when this has happened there seem to be discrepancies in the period of years that qualify for ten chevrons. At the Devonshire Regiment Museum, Exeter (now referred to as the Devonshire and Dorsetshire Regimental Museum), there is on view a No. 1 Dress tunic (period 1948−64) that once belonged to a Lance-Corporal T. Hooper. Hooper joined the Devonshire Regiment in 1917 and retired from the Devon and Dorset Regiment in 1964 with the claim that he was at that time the oldest serving soldier in the British Army. There are ten gold (dress quality) good conduct badges on the left sleeve of his tunic, which according to the information displayed with this garment represents over 47 years of good conduct.

The British Army magazine, *Soldier*, published an illustrated article on page 43 of their January 1951 issue, under the heading 'Long-Service Page', about two long-serving soldiers. Private A. 'Nick' Carter of the King's Shropshire Light Infantry retired from the Army in January 1951 after 50 years of unbroken service, having joined the KSLI just before the death of Queen Victoria in 1901. He is shown in the photograph that accompanied the article as wearing ten good conduct badges.

The second article was about 60-year-old Private Frederick 'Chuck' Sheffield of the Queen's Royal Regiment. He had served continuously since 1908 and at the time of the *Soldier* article was still in the Army. He was photographed wearing eight good conduct chevrons, which represented 43 years service.

All these examples are at variance with the periods of service required for six or more good conduct chevrons, which are six chevrons for 26 years, seven for 32 years, eight for 38, nine for 43 and ten for 48 years.

It is of interest to note that in *Vocabulary of Clothing and Necessaries, 1936* amended to 1939, Section CS, page 44, the maximum number of worsted good conduct chevrons shown as being available as a separate item is a five-bar set.

6. TRADESMEN'S, INSTRUCTORS' AND SKILL-AT-ARMS BADGES

Tradesmen's Badges 1936–43

Before the 1939–45 war, tradesmen's badges were, with only a few noted exceptions, produced in gilding metal and were fastened with a supporting plate and split pin or pins. After 1940 the needs of wartime economy brought about the introduction of all these badges in worsted.

They were worn on the right sleeve (except as otherwise provided) of the Service Dress jacket and, after 1939–40, the Battle-Dress blouse. They were not worn on Tropical shirts, PT smocks or working clothing, nor on greatcoats. NCOs wore them ¾in above the point of the inner angle of the top chevron; for other ranks, the lower edge of the badge was 9in from the top of the sleeve at the point of the shoulder. Warrant officers wore the badge below the rank badge.

The authority for the issue of these badges was the Part I order which appointed the individual to the duties for which the badges were intended.

Right: Tradesmen's badges, 1936–43. 1, Ammunition examiner; 2, Armament artificer, etc; 3, Army Fire Service; 4, Cook; 5, Farrier; 6, Pioneer, fusilier regiments; 7, Pioneer, light infantry and rifle regiments; 8, Pioneer, other units; 9, Radio mechanic; 10, Saddler; 11, Wheeler and carpenter; 12, Wireless mechanic; 13, Surveyor, RA, Class I; 14, Surveyor, RA, Class II and III; 15, Battery surveyor.

Table 9. Tradesmen's Badges

Class	Authorized badge	1936	Remarks[1] 1941	1943
Ammunition Examiner	A.E. in wreath	—	—	In worsted
Armament Artificer				
Armourer	Hammer and pincers	In gilding metal[2]	In worsted	In worsted
Fitter				
Smith				
Army fire fighting	Army Fire Service	—	—	Printed[3]
Cooks	C in wreath	—	—	In worsted
Farrier	Shoe	In gilding metal[2]	In worsted	In worsted
Pioneer, Fusilier Regiments	Grenade over crossed hatchets	In gilding metal[2]	In worsted	In worsted
Pioneer, Light Infantry and Rifle Regiments	Bugle over crossed hatchets	In gilding metal[2]	In worsted	In worsted
Pioneer, other units	Crossed hatchets[4]	In gilding metal[2]	In worsted	In worsted
Radio Mechanic[5]	Radio location	—	—	In worsted
Saddler and/or Saddle-Tree Maker	Bit	In gilding metal[2]	In worsted	In worsted
Tradesman, RAMC, Class II[6]	1 bar red braid[7]	In worsted	In worsted	In worsted
Tradesman, RAMC, Class I[6]	2 bars red braid[7]	In worsted	In worsted	In worsted
Wheeler and Carpenter	Wheel[8]	In gilding metal[2]	In worsted	In worsted
Wireless Mechanic	Wireless signals	—	—	In worsted
Surveyor, RA, Class I	S in wreath and crown	In worsted[9]	In worsted	In worsted
Surveyor, RA, Class II	S in wreath	In worsted[9]	In worsted	In worsted
Surveyor, RA, Class III				
Battery surveyor	S	In worsted	In worsted	In worsted

[1]The first bar was worn 6½in from the bottom of the right sleeve and the second bar positioned ½in above the first.

[2]Badge worn on both arms of jacket below rank badge by warrant officers, above chevrons by NCOs, and 9in from top of sleeve by other ranks.

[3]Army Fire Service badge introduced on 10 June 1942 by ACI 1237 for wear by all ranks of the Fire Fighting Wing of the Pioneer Corps; the badge was worn on both arms at the point of the shoulder.

[4]On tunics of Foot Guards, the following badges were worn above the crossed hatchets: a grenade (Grenadier Guards); a rose (Coldstream Guards); a star (Scots Guards and Irish Guards); and a leek (Welsh Guards).

[5]Worn lengthwise.

[6]Lance-corporals and privates only.

[7]The first bar was worn 6½in from the bottom of the right sleeve and the second bar ½in above the first.

[8]All wheelers who had qualified at the Military College of Science wore this badge.

[9]Worn on the right upper arm of jackets, above the chevrons by NCOs and 9in from the top of the sleeve by other ranks.

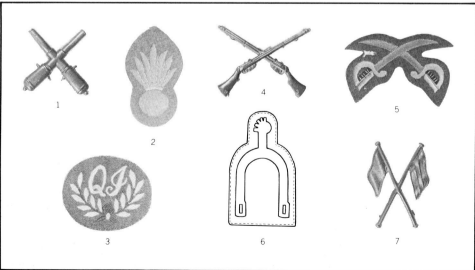

Above: The printed, Ordnance issue Army Fire Service arm badge, shown here worn with the formation badge for South-Eastern Command (UK) (above), the man's arm-of-service strip (green and red) and his crown rank chevrons (below); July 1942.
Left: Battery Sjt.-Maj. S. Hounsell, RA, from Gosport instructing on the Sparry No. 2 predictor at an anti-aircraft training school on the Orkneys; 1944.

Introduction of the Army Fire Service badge.

ACI 1237 dated 10 June 1942 introduced for wear by all ranks of the Fire Fighting Wing of the Pioneer Corps a circular cloth badge with the words 'Army Fire Service' surrounding an eight-pointed star in the centre, printed in yellow lettering on a background of scarlet material. This badge was worn on both arms of the blouse or jacket at the point of the shoulders.

Badges on the scale of four for each other rank were issued by the Commanding Officer, Army Fire Fighting Centre, Catterick Camp, Yorkshire. In the case of units serving abroad, indents to complete entitled personnel to the scale of four badges for each other rank were submitted through the usual channels. Badges required by officers were obtained on payment.

These Army Fire Service badges were not allowed to be worn by personnel who had not been transferred to the Fire Fighting Wing, Pioneer Corps. (See also page 49).

Instructors' Badges 1936–43

These badges were produced both in gilding metal – for use before and sometimes during the 1939–45 war – and in worsted during the war. Gilding metal badges were fastened to garments with a supporting plate and split pin or pins. They were worn on both sleeves of the Service Dress jacket, the greatcoat and, during the war, the Battle-Dress blouse. They were not worn on Tropical shirts or working clothing.

By those individuals who wore the crown in wreath badge and large crown, the badges were

Table 10. Instructors' Badges

Class	Authorized badge	1936	Remarks[1] 1941	1943
Gunnery				
Serjeant-Major, School of Artillery	Crossed guns[2]	On jacket and greatcoat in gilding metal[3]	Also on right arm of greatcoat in worsted[4]	Also on right arm of greatcoat in worsted[4]
Other instructors	Crossed guns[2]	On jacket in gilding metal[3]	In worsted[4]	In worsted[4]
RE				
Warrant Officer Instructor	Grenade	On jacket and greatcoat in gilding metal[3]	Also on right arm of greatcoat in worsted[4]	Also on right arm of greatcoat in worsted[4]
Instructors in field works below rank of Serjeant	QI in wreath[5]	On left forearm of jacket, only nearest cuff in worsted[3]	On left forearm below any other badges in worsted[4]	On left forearm below any other badges in worsted[4]
Musketry				
Serjeant-Major and warrant officer instructors at Small Arms School	Crossed rifles[2]	On jacket and greatcoat in gilding metal[3]	—	—
Other instructors, musketry	Crossed rifles[2]	On jacket in gilding metal[3]	On jacket in worsted[4]	On jacket in worsted[4]
Physical training[6]				
Warrant officers and NCOs of Physical Training staff	Crossed swords[2]	On jacket and greatcoat in gilding metal[3]	—	—
Other instructors[7]	Crossed swords[2]	On jacket in gilding metal[3]	—	—
Physical training instructors	Crossed swords	—	On jacket in worsted[4,8]	On jacket in worsted[4,9]
Riding instructors	Spur[2]	On jacket in gilding metal[3]	On jacket in worsted[4]	On jacket in worsted[4]
Signalling				
Assistant instructors of signalling	Crossed flags[2]	On jacket in gilding metal[3]	On jacket in worsted[4]	On jacket in worsted[4]
Other instructors	Crossed flags[2]	On jacket in gilding metal[3]	On jacket in worsted[4]	On jacket in worsted[4]

[1]As published in *Clothing Regulations* for 1936 and *War Clothing Regulations* for 1941 and 1943.
[2]The badges thus marked are listed in *Vocabulary of Clothing and Necessaries, 1936*, Part I, Section CB, amended to 1939 as being produced both in gilding metal (GM) and worsted. The quality of badge shown in the 1936 column is the quality as listed in *Regulations for the Clothing of the Army, 1936*, Appendix 5, 'Instructors Badges, All Services'.
[3]These badges were worn below rank badge by warrant officers and above chevrons by NCOs, unless stated otherwise.
[4]The badges thus marked were also worn on the Battle-Dress blouse. This information is not shown in the listing of instructors' badges as published in the 1941 and 1943 issues of *War Clothing Regulations*.

[5]Badge only produced in worsted.
[6]Including fencing and gymnastics in the Cavalry.
[7]Only warrant officers and NCOs in possession of Army Physical Training certificates granted at the expiration of the physical training course at Aldershot of at least three months' duration, endorsed by the superintendent of physical training in the command in which serving, and approved by the Inspector of Physical Training.
[8]Only warrant officers and NCOs in possession of Army Physical Training certificates, including fencing and gymnastics in the case of the Cavalry.
[9]Warrant officers and NCOs of the Army Physical Training Corps and Regimental NCOs awarded certificates by Section Officers of Physical Training Commands and Districts.

next highest competitor or withhold it at his discretion.

A skill-at-arms badge was worn until the individual forfeited it by competition, which included occasions on which the badge was reawarded during the absence of the holder. If a person reclassified for a badge he was awarded at the previous classification a fresh badge was not issued, but it could be renewed after two years.

In the event of no reclassification taking place within a unit for two years, a skill-at-arms badge was allowed to be worn by an entitled individual two years from the date of its last award or reclassification, but it ceased to be worn after that period until reclassification took place.

Skill-at-arms badges were embroidered (worsted silk lace on drab) and were worn by an entitled individual on the left forearm, except where otherwise stated in the listing below, of the Service Dress and Khaki Drill jacket and later the Battle-Dress blouse. They were not worn on the great-coat, Tropical shirts or working clothing. The position of the lowest badge on the sleeve, except where otherwise stated, was ½in above the centre point of the top chevron, the four-bar chevron or good conduct badge (or badges), the crown in its wreath, or large crown if worn; or 6½in from the bottom edge of the sleeve, if the sleeve had a plain cuff; or ½in above the point of the cuff, if the sleeve had a pointed cuff.

An exception to the above rule was made in the case of Cavalry regiments, who wor the cuff, if the sleeve had a pointed cuff.

An exception to the above rule was made in the case of Cavalry regiments, who wors who were employed as signallers but who were not in possession of an assistant instructor's certificate wore crossed flags (in gilding metal) on the left sleeve as a skill-at-arms badge.

No individual was permitted to wear two skill-at-arms badges of the same class awarded for individual merit; for example, a 'battalion shot' did not in addition wear the badge for 'company shot', although he was allowed to wear the badge for commanding a section in the best rifle shooting company. When two or more skill-at-arms badges were worn, they were worn in the order as laid down for the unit concerned, the first badge being nearest the cuff and each badge being ½in apart.

The qualifications for skill-at-arms badges were contained in the training manuals for weapons or equipment concerned. Competition badges as listed below were awarded before the 1939–45 war but not under wartime conditions.

Introduction of qualification badges for height-takers.

ACI 483 published during the week ending 16 November 1938 announced that a decision had been made to introduce a qualification badge for first class height-takers in anti-aircraft units of both the Regular and the Territorial Army. The badge was described as having the letter 'H' within a wreath in worsted for wear on Service Dress, and it was worn by qualified first class height-takers for one year only, subject to reclassification.

worn ½in below that badge. By NCOs they were worn ¾in above the point of the inner angle of the top chevron but below the small crown, except when badges of appointment, classification, qualification or tradesmen's badges were worn, in which case the instructor's badge was placed ½in above, with the small crown, if worn, surmount-ing the whole. By those persons who were not warrant or non-commissioned officers the instructor's badge was worn on the sleeve 9in below the point of the shoulder.

Instructors' badges were allowed to be worn by an entitled individual for five years (physical training instructors four years) after their last award or reclassification, but they could be withdrawn by order of the unit commander at any time during that period for inefficiency.

Skill-at-Arms Badges 1936–43

Skill-at-arms badges that were authorized for units (see below) were awarded annually by unit commanders, in accordance with the results of competitions which were held for these badges. The award to the individual was published in unit Part I orders, which showed those who reclassified for badges already awarded and those to whom an initial issue was to be made.

Skill-at-arms badges were not worn by warrant officers Class I, who therefore did not ordinarily compete for such badges. Where such an individual did compete and qualify for a skill-at-arms badge, such as 'battalion shot', the unit commander was allowed to award the badge to the

Right: Prewar competition badges. 1, 2, 3, 4, Skill in shooting, etc (rifle and light machine-guns); 5, Skill in shooting (machine-gun); 6, 7, 8, 9, Swordsmanship (cavalry); 10, 11, Two examples of lancer regiment competition badges; 12, 13, 14, Gunnery, Royal Artillery; 15, 16, 17, 18, Skill in driving.

Qualification badge for Gunner 1st Class, RTC/RTR.

Qualification badge worn on the sleeve by a Naval Gunlayer, Maritime RA. The badge signifies a 2nd Class Gunnery Rating, Anti-Aircraft, DEMS. It was in red worsted on a navy blue backing, and was worn on the khaki Battle-Dress blouse. RN badges for gunnery ratings came in three classes. 1st Class: crossed guns, star above and star with appropriate letter below (Q, Quarters; L, Layer; C, Control; A, Anti-Aircraft). 2nd Class: crossed guns, star above with appropriate letter Q, L, C or A below. 3rd Class: single gun (horizontal), star above with appropriate letter Q, L, C or A below.

Table 11. Competition Badges

Badge	Allocation
Skill in shooting, etc. (rifle and light machine gun)	
Star over crossed rifles	1 each squadron or company
Crown over crossed rifles in wreath	1 each Cavalry regiment or Infantry battalion
Star over crossed rifles in wreath	1 each Cavalry regiment or Infantry battalion
Crown over crossed rifles (worn on right forearm)	17 each Cavalry . regiment, 22 each Infantry battalion
Skill in shooting, etc. (machine gun)	
Star over MG in wreath	1 each MG squadron or support company
Swordsmanship (Cavalry)	
Crown over crossed swords in wreath (worn on right forearm)	1 each regiment
Crown over crossed swords	1 each squadron
Star over crossed swords	1 each troop
Crossed swords	1 for every 20 men competing in addition to the above

In lancer regiments crossed lances were substituted for crossed swords in each badge.

Badge	Allocation
Gunnery (Royal Artillery)	
Crown over G in wreath	1 each battery
	1 for detachment at Porton
	1 each HQ and DEs and DEs
Star over G in wreath, G in wreath	1 each battery
	1 for detachment at Porton except G in wreath
	1 each HQ and heavy brigades at Ceylon, Gibraltar, Malaya and Malta
Skill in driving	
Crown over whip and spur	1 each horse-drawn battery of field artillery
	1 each field unit, RE and R Signals
	1 for RE Mounted Depot
	1 for Signal Training Centre
	1 each animal transport company RASC
Whip and spur	3 each horse-drawn battery of field artillery
	3 each animal transport company RASC
	2 each field unit, RE and R Signals
	2 for RE Mounted Depot
	2 for Signal Training Centre
Crown over steering wheel	1 each mechanized battery, RA
	1 each mechanized unit, RE
	1 each mechanized unit, R Signals
Steering wheel	2 each mechanized battery, RA
	2 each mechanized unit, RE
	2 each mechanized unit, R Signals

Table 12. Qualification Badges

Badge	Qualification
1936 to 1945	
Crossed rifles	Rifle marksman
L.G. in wreath	Light MG marksman
M.G. in wreath	Heavy MG marksman and 1st class machine gunner, RTC and RTR
G in wreath (worn on right forearm)	1st class gunner, RTC and RTR
R in wreath	1st class range-taker of MG squadron or company; range-taker and position-finder and instrument number of RA unit
L in wreath (worn on left upper arm)	Layer, RA[1]
Star	1st class driver, RTC and RTR
Crossed guns	NCO who had been through gunnery staff course and had been recommended by the Commandant, School of Artillery
Crossed flags	Signaller
1941 to 1945 or later	
H in wreath	1st class height-taker, AA RA
P in wreath	RA personnel qualified in fortress plotting room (including fortress observation post) or battery plotting room duties
S.P. in wreath	Personnel granted special proficiency pay[2]
1943 to 1945 or later	
Army Flying Badge (worn on the left breast)	For each air observation post pilot and each glider pilot
Parachutist's badge (worn also on the gabardine – the Denison smock and parachute smock – jacket)	For regular parachute troops
Steering wheel	Drivers IC (internal combustion)

[1]Personnel of the Maritime RA who were qualified as naval gunlayers wore the naval pattern DEMS acting gunlayer's badge on the left forearm in the manner as detailed in the fifth paragraph of this section. The badge was issued on a scale of one badge for each qualified gunlayer; indents were submitted by Maritime RA regiments to HQ Maritime RA, and badges were supplied from naval sources under War Office arrangements. The badge was withdrawn when personnel in possession ceased to be employed as qualified acting gunlayers on Maritime RA establishment (ACI 1380 dated 18 September 1943). [2]This was the 1941 explanation for this badge, but in 1943 the explanation was expanded to read 'Privates on post 1925 rates of pay who were classified Class 1A and N.C.O's below the rank of serjeant who had been awarded the badge before 30th January 1943'.

Introduction of special qualification badges for radio and wireless specialists of the RAOC.

The following special badges were introduced by ACI 2155 dated 1 November 1941 for wear by personnel of the RAOC engaged on radio and wireless work, in order to indicate the specialist nature of their employment.

1. For armament artificers (radio) and radio mechanics (radio-location), a 'Badge, Radio Mechanics'. The design consisted of a red ring flanked on each side by three red zig-zag sparks embroidered on navy blue cloth.

2. For armament artificers (wireless) and wireless mechanics, a 'Badge, Wireless Mechanics'. This design consisted of a white ring flanked on each side by three white zig-zag sparks embroidered on navy blue cloth.

The above-mentioned badges were issued to the qualified personnel on their being mustered as armament artificers or as tradesmen Class III or above, and the wearing of the 'hammer and pincers' badge by such personnel was discontinued. The new badge was worn lengthwise on the right arm of the Battle-Dress blouse or Service Dress jacket, on the right forearm, below rank badge (warrant officers), on the right upper arms, above rank chevrons (NCOs), and on the right upper arm, below formation signs and distinguishing strip (other ranks).

Issues of the badges were made on the scale of one for each Battle-Dress blouse or Service Dress jacket, and for each KD jacket. The badges were not worn on Tropical shirts, greatcoats or working clothing.

Introduction of the skill-at-arms badge for internal combustion (engine) drivers.

A special badge for wear by qualified drivers IC was introduced by ACI 131 dated 21 January 1942. The badge took the form of a vehicle steering wheel. To qualify for the initial award of this badge, the undermentioned conditions had to be fulfilled.

1. Only internal combustion engine drivers were eligible.

2. The soldier must have had a minimum of one year's service as a qualified driver IC as laid down in the *Manual of Driving and Maintenance for Mechanical Vehicles (Wheeled), 1937*, Chapter XVIII, Section 135, para. 7.

3. The driver must have driven for one year without having been involved in any accident for which he was in any way responsible.

4. The driver must have had 50 hours' driving experience after having passed his tests as a driver IC to warrant the award of a badge.

In deciding on eligibility for the award of this badge, the commanding officer had to take into consideration such factors as reported cases of dangerous or negligent driving, even though these may not have caused accidents, and cases of neglected vehicle maintenance.

The badge was forfeited for six months after an accident for which the soldier was in any way responsible, or after a conviction by civil or military powers for dangerous driving. The award or forfeiture of a badge was entered in the soldier's

AB 64, Part I, page 4, under 'Particulars of Training'.

Neither the qualification nor the badge carried with it any extra pay or allowance. Issues were made on the scale of two badges for each other rank and one for each Battle-Dress blouse or Service Dress jacket, and the badge was worn on the left forearm. These conditions also applied to ATS internal combustion drivers.

Special Proficiency badge.

Consequent on the reclassification of the rates of pay of warrant officers, NCOs and other ranks of the Army introduced by the Royal Warrant dated 11 February 1943 (Army Order 14 of 1943), it was necessary to revise the qualification which entitled Army personnel to wear the Special Proficiency badge. It was decided that the following personnel only were entitled to the privilege.

1. Privates on post-1925 rates of pay who were classified Class 1A.

2. NCOs below the rank of Serjeant who were awarded the badge before 30 January 1943.

3. Personnel not affected by the above-mentioned Army Order, i.e. privates and NCOs below the rank of Serjeant and who belonged to corps whose depots were not situated in the United Kingdom or the Isle of Man, for so long as they were in receipt of special proficiency pay.

Those Special Proficiency badges that were in the possession of personnel other than those detailed above were withdrawn, returned to store and held for reissue to those entitled personnel as necessary.

Proposed qualification badges for wear by Irregular Commando Volunteers, and the origin of the Parachute badge.

On 9 June 1940 the War Office circulated a letter to the General Officers Commanding-in-Chief Northern and Southern Commands, with a copy to the Commander-in-Chief Home Forces, that was headed 'Volunteers for Special Service'. Signed by the Director of Recruiting and Organization, the letter set out the following six points.

'1. It is proposed to raise and train a special force of volunteers for independent mobile operations.

'2. You are requested to collect the names of up to 40 officers and 1,000 other ranks in your Command, who volunteer for this special service and whom you consider suitable for it.

'Volunteers will be employed on fighting duties only, and Commanding Officers should be assured that these duties will require only the best type of officers and men. All ranks will continue to wear their own uniforms but the question of awarding some special distinguishing badge is under consideration.

'Officers and men who have been approved for the Force will be taken off the strength of their units and trained in the United Kingdom. Individuals are not likely to remain in the Force for more than a few months.

'3. In compiling the list of volunteers, the following qualifications, shown in the order of their importance, must be borne in mind:—

'(a) *General*

All officers and men must be volunteers. They should be young and must be absolutely fit. They should be

Right: A serjeant of the Royal Artillery, a qualified 25pdr gun-layer and member of the 386th Field Battery, RA, from the 143rd Regiment, 49th (West Riding) Division, seen here at Alafoss, Iceland in May 1941.

Right: Armourer Staff Serjeant Mawdsley, a wireless armament artificer (foreground), and Craftsman Gillard, a wireless mechanic, both of the REME. Both men wear the 'Wireless Mechanics Badge' (white ring flanked by three white zig-zag sparks set on a dark navy blue backing) as well as the formation badge for British troops in Northern Ireland; December 1942.
Far right: Grenadier Guardsmen of the Guards Armoured Division – possibly of the 1st (Motor) Bn – all of whom are wearing the Special Proficiency Trade Badge.

able to swim and be immune from sea sickness. Those who have already seen active service and are able to drive a motor vehicle are particularly valuable.

'(b) *Officers*

Personality, tactical ability and imagination.

'(c) *Other Ranks*

A good standard of general intelligence and independence. Character must be such that a man can be relied upon to behave himself without supervision (i.e., there must be no risk of looting etc., by men operating independently).

'4. It is initially proposed to organize one 'Commando' from each of the Northern and Southern Commands. Each Commando will be led by a selected officer, and will consist of a number of 'Troops'. Each troop will be commanded by an officer (or a specially selected warrant officer or non-commissioned officer), and will have a strength approximating that of an infantry platoon.

'The officers selected as Commando leaders should be capable of planning and personally leading raiding operations carried out by parties chosen from their own Commandos. These officers should be selected entirely for their operational abilities; they will be relieved of all administrative detail by the appointment of an officer of sufficient administrative experience who will be attached to each Commando.

'Other ranks selected should, if possible, include a number of light tank drivers, and sappers who are well trained in demolition work. A high proportion of N.C.O's will be allowed on the establishment of the Commandos.

'5. All volunteers selected should be informed that they are liable to be returned to their units at the discretion of their leaders. The volunteers may also request to be returned to their units after the completion of any operation.

1

2

3

Above: Projected and prototype qualification badges. 1, A qualification badge for wear by irregular commando volunteers proposed in 1940; 2, First prototype parachutists' qualification badge, July 1940; 3, Early pattern parachutists' qualification badge. The specimen illustrated is sewn on the right lower sleeve of an American Army officer's tunic; the uniform, manufactured in New York, bears a tailor's label (no. 3346) dated '7/24/41' indicating that it was owned by a 1st Lieutenant Manning Jacob, although the rank insignia was that of a major in the US infantry. The conclusion I have drawn is that Lieutenant Manning Jacob was attached to the US forces, with the rank of major, in order to instruct parachutists (five months before the United States entered the war). The badge must have been one of the first British prototype parachute qualification badges to have been worn; compare the design with the badge illustrated on page 66.

'The same personnel will not be continuously employed over long periods on operations of this special nature.

'Before joining the Force each volunteer will be interviewed by an officer and told of the sort of duties he will be required to perform. He will then have the option of withdrawing his name should he wish to do so.

'6. Commando leaders will be officers below the rank of Lieutenant-Colonel. The selection of these officers is a matter of urgency, as candidates will have to be interviewed at the War Office before final selection is made. You are therefore requested to forward to the Under Secretary of State for War (M.O.8.) as soon as possible and under secret cover, the names of 6 or 8 officers selected from your Command who are recommended to lead Commandos.'

The proposed organization and employment of the Irregular Commandos which were to be formed from these (Special Service) volunteers were intended to contain certain volunteers who were to be employed as parachute troops.

Even at this early stage in the development of this force (16 June 1940) it was realized, and considered essential, that certain distinguishing marks would be needed in the walking-out dress of all ranks of the special force. The authorities at the War Office felt that some mark of distinction was required, but one which was not only easily removed when the need for secrecy demanded it but would also show at a glance that an officer or soldier was an active member of the Special Force, the purpose behind this being both to assist the 'esprit de corps' of the new force and also to prevent local authorities possibly interfering unnecessarily with the doings of the Irregulars, whose peculiar habits of living it was felt would have otherwise aroused suspicion.

Two forms of dress distinction were considered as fulfilling the requirements of this special force, a distinctive form of head-dress (which is dealt with on page 152), and two types of 'brevets', or badges of distinction.

In the case of these badges it was suggested that the two 'brevets' or badges of distinction should have been comparable to the 'wings' of the Royal Air Force and should be awarded to the following:
1. A member of the force who had taken part in a raid on the enemy.
2. A member of the force who had completed a course in parachute work, including a fixed number of jumps.
It was suggested that these badges be awarded in unit orders by a commanding officer and worn permanently, even after an officer or soldier had left the force.

Initially a small badge was proposed to be worn on the right breast. If it were produced in metal, it was felt that its value would be enhanced if the badge bore a serial number. The badge itself could be produced in silver for officers and brass for other ranks.

It was further felt that the design of the badge for force members who had taken part in a raid on the enemy − (1) above − should suggest a 'raider', possibly a fox, a tiger or a hawk, or even the plain letter R, whilst the badge for force members who had qualified as a parachutist (2) clearly had to feature a parachute.

The War Office authorities realized that the first badge might well prove unnecessary or undesirable, but the second was most definitely required for issue in July that year (1940).

Three days later, on 19 June, additional suggestions were made by the Assistant Director of Ordnance Supplies, Charles Montanaro, that a special badge for members of a raiding force may well lead to repercussions and that its necessity had to be well considered before it was introduced. He added that no distinction had until then been given to Infantry who had carried out raids on the enemy, and to do so then, he felt, would lead to their being inundated with similar requests from other quarters. He felt that if a badge had to be adopted for this purpose it should be as simple as possible in view of the necessity for reducing pressure on the manufacturing trade. The ADOS suggested that a black star worn on the sleeve would meet the requirements.

With regard to the Parachutist qualification badge, he strongly suggested that this be produced in worsted, with the design on the same lines as the badge worn by a machine gunner, range-taker or layer etc., to be worn on the arm. Supplies of a badge, provided approval were not delayed, were obtainable by July 1940.

Other suggestions put forward by Charles Montanaro were, first, on the lines of a distinctive form of head-dress (see page 152), and second, a special shoulder title which, he suggested, could take the form of the outsize letters S.F. in black. However, he immediately pointed out, since officers did not wear shoulder titles this idea was probably unacceptable, and instead he made a further suggestion that the letters could be worn on the breast, in black worsted (either in detachable form or sewn on the second suit of Battle-Dress or Service-Dress only), or in metal (in the form of a numbered brooch). The security aspect of this question, he concluded, needed to be borne in mind, particularly if detachable badges were introduced, although this, as he pointed out, was a matter for the General Staff.

On 28 June 1940 further comments were raised on this matter. When preparations for a raid were concentrated in an area, its members should not be readily identifiable as 'raiders', and it was felt that the emblem thus had to be one that was easily removed. This limited the choice of a dress distinction to either a forage cap (more correctly a Field Service cap) or a brooch badge. The necessity to remove dress distinctions for security reasons did not apply to a parachutist, who they felt could always wear a badge provided the volunteer had undertaken a jump. It was considered, however, that a little colour should be introduced into the design of the parachute badge in order to improve its appearance. It was even suggested that a brighter coloured badge might be considered to reward additional successful parachute jumps.

At this stage it was agreed to get Ordnance to make up samples of:
1. A parachute badge with some colour in it.
2. A black (Field Service) cap with tassels that were removable (see page 152).
3. A metal brooch.

Right: Designs submitted by J. R. Gaunt & Son Ltd. of Birmingham to the War Office for irregular commando volunteer badges. None of these designs was accepted.

Item (2), it was suggested, should be an issue item, but it was realized that the authority of the Army Council would be required as well as the approval and permission of the King.

In addition to all this, the suggestion was made that members of independent companies and of Commandos should wear coloured corded bosses, of the type then in use and being worn on the points of the Battle-Dress collar by substantive colonels and above (see page 41); there should be one colour for independent companies and another for Commandos, and if necessary the number of the individual unit in metal could be mounted on the bosses.

On 4 July 1940 samples of the Belgian style cap (see page 152) and coloured worsted parachute badges in alternative sizes and colours, together with six sketches provided by Messrs J. R. Gaunt & Son Ltd., with three further sketches provided later, all of which were suggested designs for a brooch badge (see illustrations above), were forwarded by the ADOS to Department MO9 for their consideration.

On 11 July a meeting was held, the proposals of which were to promote 'esprit de corps' and to encourage recruiting for Irregular Commandos by the introduction of a special head-dress, a metal brooch and special badges for parachutists. All of these items required the approval of the Army Council and, in the case of the special head-dress, that of His Majesty the King (see also page 152). It was pointed out that the War Committee had decided that no more metal shoulder titles were to be produced, and this would probably be the

reason which would rule out the metal brooch. No objection was made to the Parachute badge in principle, and it was suggested that qualifications should be laid down which did not render it too cheap.

On 13 July the ACIGS (Assistant Chief of the Imperial General Staff) went on record as saying that after discussion with the VCIGS the following decisions had been reached:

'(a) A special head-dress is not necessary.
'(b) No metal badges will be issued.
'(c) A parachute badge will be worn by those who have obtained a certain degree of proficiency in parachute landing.'

The degree of proficiency required to qualify for the parachute badge had still to be established.

On 25 July Department MO7 suggested, on the advice of G2 Special School, Ringway, that six practice parachute drops certified by troop leaders would be sufficient qualification for the badge. This was agreed by the Air Ministry, but on 31 July 1940 Department MO7 reassessed their first recommendation in the light of their visit to the Special School at Ringway. During this visit the Chief Instructor (RAF) felt that four parachute practice drops were all that was necessary to qualify and that it would have taken too long to have put all trainees through six drops; it was therefore suggested that the badge be awarded after completing only four drops, and the Air Ministry agreed to this proposal on the same day.

On 14 August 1940 the draft Army Council Instruction was drawn up and on 28 December 1940 it was published as ACI 1589.

8. SLIP-ON SHOULDER STRAP TITLES

Black on Khaki Worsted Shoulder Titles

Before the war metal shoulder titles worn on the other ranks' Service Dress and Khaki Drill uniforms (see page 37) were one of the most common methods used to display the wearer's corps, regiment or formation. When the Battle-Dress was introduced in March 1938 metal shoulder titles were not intended to be worn on its shoulder straps.

At the beginning of hostilities, and as an economy measure directed towards saving metal and also as a security device, slip-on titles of khaki cloth with lettering in black thread had been introduced to be worn, not just on the Battle-Dress blouse but also on the Khaki Drill jacket and the Khaki Drill shirt. Service Dress for other ranks was limited to personnel of certain horsed units (see page 178).

As well as the machine-stitched versions of the khaki cloth slip-on there also existed printed versions of the same thing. These are not as numerous as the former, original versions, and this seems to indicate that not only were they official ordnance issue but that they were introduced during the war.

I have not attempted to list all the known examples, together with their variations, but I have included a selection of some of the more common as well as some rare and unusual items as an illustrated plate.

Discontinuance of wear by certain units.

In September 1941, in an effort to economize on labour and materials, certain regiments and corps serving at home stations were ordered to discontinue wearing the slip-on shoulder strap titles. ACI 1681 of 1941, published on 6 September 1941, stated that due to the introduction of distinguishing strips the wearing of shoulder titles with Battle-Dress by personnel of certain units was to be discontinued. The regiments and corps thus affected were the Royal Artillery, Royal Engineers, Royal Corps of Signals, Royal Army Service Corps, Royal Army Medical Corps, Royal Army Ordnance Corps, Corps of Military Police, Royal Army Pay Corps, Army Education Corps, Army Dental Corps, Pioneer Corps, Intelligence Corps, Reconnaissance Corps, Army Catering Corps and Army Physical Training Corps.

ACI 1914 of 1942 added to this list the Army Air Corps, and by ACI 2304 dated 28 October 1942 the Royal Electrical and Mechanical Engineers were also added, but with the Army Physical Training Corps being struck from the list, presumably because their inclusion in the list in the first place had been in error as they did not wear a slip-on title, having the distinction shared with the five regiments of Foot Guards and the Household Cavalry of wearing a coloured and embroidered shoulder designation (see also page 89). Almost a year earlier, on 25 October 1941 (ACI 2091 of 1941) and only a matter of weeks after the initial order withdrawing these slip-on titles from the Corps of Military Police had been made, authority was given for the retention of shoulder titles worn with Battle-Dress by personnel of the Provost Wing of the CMP.

Shoulder titles had to be withdrawn with immediate effect from all personnel of the above

Right: An example of the Royal Artillery cloth slip-on shoulder title; see also the photograph on page 61.
Far right: An example of an unofficial slip-on shoulder strap title, worn by Commando Allender of Army Commando VI shortly after he had been awarded the Military Medal; 24 February 1942. Cmdo. Allender had won this conspicuous gallantry award before becoming a member of the Commandos.

Right: Slip-on shoulder strap titles (cloth). 1, Royal Artillery; 2, Royal Engineers; 3, Royal Corps of Signals; 4, The Queen's Royal Regiment (West Surreys); 5, The King's Own Royal Regiment (Lancaster); 6, The East Surrey Regiment; 7, Duke of Wellington's Regiment (West Riding); 8, The Border Regiment; 9, Hampshire Regiment; 10, The Dorsetshire Regiment; 11, Royal Berkshire Regiment; 12, The Rifle Brigade; 13, Royal Tank Regiment; 14, Army Catering Corps; 15, Corps of Military Police; 16, Auxiliary Military Pioneer Corps; 17, Non-Combatant Corps; 18, Parachute Regiment; 19, The Highland Regiment; 20, Royal Electrical and Mechanical Engineers.

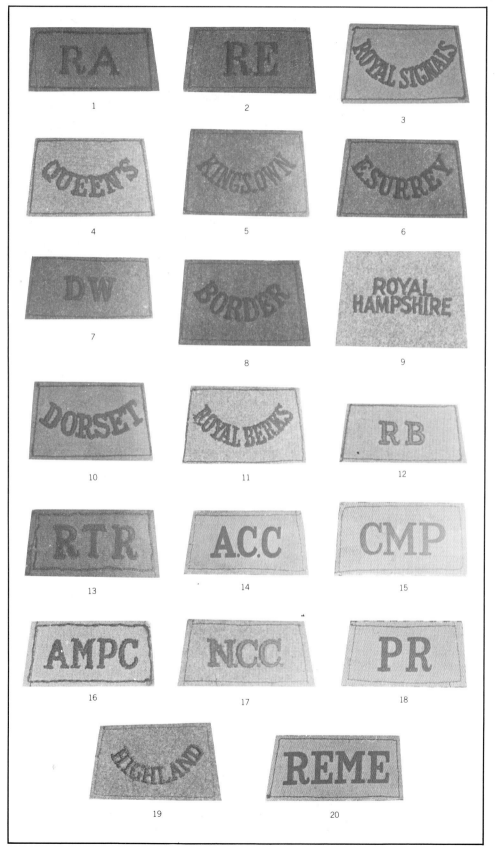

Right: A member of the Corps of Military Police wearing the CMP slip-on cloth shoulder title while on traffic control duty at Ballynure, County Antrim, Northern Ireland, in April 1941. (See also the photograph on page '221.)

mentioned regiments and corps, including any subsequent additions to this original list as shown, that were at home stations and were other than those troops wearing Service Dress and under orders for overseas service. These instructions did not apply to commands abroad where troops were clothed in Khaki Drill garments.

Battalion and Company Coloured Flashes
The use of coloured cloth 'flashes' worn on the shoulder straps of various types of drab clothing seems to date back to before the Great War of 1914–18. In all probability between the wars and during the Second World War the use of coloured shoulder flashes was widespread. I have made notes of many such flashes during the course of frequent visits to regimental museums and I have listed here two examples of these items in order to show the complex range of colours used.

Company colour tabs (flashes) worn by the 1st Battalion the Duke of Cornwall's Light Infantry, North-West Frontier, 1935.
    These were introduced to be worn on the shoulder straps of the shirt at the point of the shoulder when the troops were wearing shirt sleeve order; they were used by 1st Battalion DCLI troops on the North-West Frontier at Razmak in 1935. The slip-on tabs were worn in matching pairs and the tabs themselves seem to have been made from flag bunting material as follows.
Headquarters wing: all green.
'A' Company: all dark blue.
'B' Company: diagonally halved (but not from corner to corner), black and yellow.

'C' Company: diagonally halved (but not from corner to corner), red and white.
'D' Company: divided vertically, light blue, white and light blue.

Distinguishing colours of the Royal Tank Regiment.
    On display at the Royal Armoured Corps and Royal Tank Regiment Museum at Bovington Camp, Wareham, Dorset, is a finely painted display panel of all the known distinguishing colours worn as shoulder strap slip-ons by the RTR during the various stages of its history. Shown as neatly executed oblongs of colours, they represent the cloth shoulder 'flashes' worn by the Motor Machine Gun Service and the Machine Gun Corps of 1916, the Tank Corps of 1917 and the Royal Tank Regiment of 1939 onwards. Obviously not all the units shown on this panel existed at all times, the vast majority of them being battalion colours of the First World War Tank Corps.
    From this panel I have extracted those flashes that were worn by the Royal Tank Regiment during the 1939–45 war. It should be remembered that these colours were only worn between 1916 and 1919 and between 1939 and 1957; the coloured flashes were not worn from 1919 to 1939 nor were they worn on officers' Service Dress from 1939 onwards.
    There are only a very few actual examples of these coloured flashes on display in the museum, and where these can be seen it is very noticeable that they differ in size and shape as well as in the exact shade of colour from the neatly painted

oblongs of colours on the display panel. From notes I have made of these items in the late Major John Waring's collection housed at the Regimental Museum of the Royal Corps of Transport, Buller Barracks, Aldershot, it is apparent that there was quite a variance in the materials used in the production of these 'flashes'. Many were purpose-made in woven silk bands; others were made from coarse braiding, whilst still others were made from coarse braiding or from separate pieces of coloured materials sewn together to form a single 'flash'.

The size also varied in a number of instances. Not all were neat, 1½in deep flashes wide enough to slip over the shoulder strap of a Battle-Dress blouse; some were quite narrow and were actually sewn on to the shoulder strap at the base where it joined the shoulder.

Table 18. Royal Tank Regiment Shoulder Strap Flashes

Unit	Tab colour	Unit	Tab colour
1 RTR	Red lanyard worn around left shoulder; introduced after 1934 in place of the First World War all red slip-on		three portions, dark red in centre flanked on either side by dark blue[2]
2 RTR	All yellow slip-on flash worn from 1939 to 1940; after 1940 colour changed to yellow flash with central narrow band of red flanked on left side by similar width band of green and on right by band of brown (this flash still in use today)	41 RTR	Flash equally divided horizontally into buff over bottle green
		42 RTR	Flash equally divided horizontally into yellow over dark blue
		43 RTR	Flash equally divided horizontally into green over mauve[3]
		44 RTR	Flash equally divided horizontally into yellow over mauve
3 RTR	All green flash	45 RTR	Flash divided horizontally; narrow central band of yellow with green over and black under
4 RTR	Prior to 1922 all light blue flash; after 1922 colour changed to dark blue[1]		
5 RTR	Flash equally divided horizontally into red over light blue	46 RTR	Red Welsh dragon, rampant, set on small circular green background
6 RTR	Flash equally divided horizontally into red over yellow	47 RTR	Flash divided horizontally into three equal depth bands of buff over green over buff
7 RTR	Flash equally divided horizontally into red over green		
8 RTR	Flash equally divided horizontally into red over dark blue	48 RTR	Flash equally divided horizontally into yellow over black
9 RTR	Flash equally divided horizontally into red over brown	49 RTR	Flash equally divided horizontally into green over brown
10 RTR	Flash equally divided horizontally into red over white	50 RTR	Flash equally divided vertically into three portions, dark green centre flanked on either side by black[4]
11 RTR	Flash equally divided horizontally into white over black		
12 RTR	Flash equally divided horizontally into red over mauve	51 RTR	Flash equally divided horizontally into green over black
40 RTR	Flash equally divided vertically into	Band of RTR	Flash in Corps colours of green over red over brown, all equally divided horizontally[5]

[1]Item in the Waring Collection shows a royal blue flash with a narrow band of grey along upper edge.
[2]Item in Waring Collection shows a narrow elongated 'flash' with a dark cherry red centre flanked on either side by black; worn by 40th (King's) RTR (TA).
[3]Item in Waring Collection listed as being 1st pattern flash as worn by 43 RTR, 6 RNF, TA has equal horizontal bands of mustard yellow over cherry red.
[4]Item in Waring Collection shows flash listed as being for the 50 RTR but the colours are divided horizontally with a wide central band of green and narrow bands top and bottom in black.
[5]Item in Waring Collection lists this flash as being for the 1st Independent Squadron, RTR.

9. COLOUR SECTION

Right: Coloured rank badges. 1, Serjeant, The Middlesex Regiment (Duke of Cambridge's Own); 2, Corporal, 1st Battalion, The Royal Warwickshire Regiment; 3, Warrant Officer, Class II, The Royal Ulster Rifles.
Royal Arms badge with coloured edging. 4, Warrant Officer, Class I, Army Air Corps and Army Educational Corps; 5, Warrant Officer, Class I, Royal Artillery, Royal Army Ordnance Corps, Pioneer Corps and Corps of Military Police; 6, Warrant Officer, Class I, Army Physical Training Corps.
Gorget patches. 7, Scarlet corded boss worn on the collar of the Battle-Dress blouse by commanders of formations, May 1940 to November 1940; 8, Gorget patch (right side) worn in Service Dress by a Field Marshal (shown) and General Officers. Only the design of the button differs; 9, Gorget patch worn in Service Dress by Brigadiers and Substantive Colonels; 10, Gorget patch worn in Service Dress by a Colonel of the Army Dental Corps; 11, Gorget patch worn in Battle-Dress by a Colonel of the Royal Army Medical Corps; 12, Gorget patch worn in Service Dress by a Colonel of the Royal Army Pay Corps; 13, Gorget patch worn in Service Dress by a Colonel of the Army Educational Corps; 14, Gorget patch worn in Service Dress by a Colonel of the Royal Engineers and the Royal Army Ordnance Corps.
Armlets. 15, General Staff branch officer at Command Headquarters (Home); 16, Officers and Personnel of Royal Artillery and Royal Engineer Survey Companies; 17, Brigade-major at RTR Brigade Headquarters; 18, Motor Contact officer.
(Items not to scale.)

Right: Coloured backing and coloured Skill-at-Arms and Instructors' Badges. 1, Qualified Light Machine Gun marksman, Durham Light Infantry; 2, Signal Instructor, Royal Northumberland Fusiliers; 3, Drummer, East Surrey Regiment; 4, Qualified Heavy Machine Gun marksman, The Queen's Royal Regiment (West Surrey).

Shoulder strap slip-on coloured flashes. 5, 5th Royal Tank Regiment; 6, Band of the Royal Tank Regiment; 7, 'B' Company, 1st Battalion, the Duke of Cornwall's Light Infantry, NW Frontier, 1935.

Coloured backing to officers' badges of rank. 8, Crown worn by certain officers of the RAMC; 9, Star worn in the APTC; 10, Star worn in the Army Air Corps and Army Educational Corps; 11, Worn in the Royal Engineers and Royal Signals; 12, Worsted pattern star worn before the introduction of rank insignia with coloured backing; 13, Worn by Staff officers, officers of the Royal Artillery, RAOC, Pioneer Corps and Corps of Military Police; 14, Worn by officers of the Royal Army Chaplains Department; 15, Crown worn in the RAC, RASC and RAPC; 16, Star worn by officers of Rifle Regiments; 17, Star worn by officers of the Army Catering Corps.

Tartan and other flashes. 18, Tartan flash worn by the Black Watch; 19, Diced flash worn by the Argyll and Sutherland Highlanders.

Regimental and Corps designations, official and semi-official. 20, Welsh Guards (official); 21, Durham Light Infantry (semi-official); 22, The Buffs (official); 23, Royal Army Chaplains Department (official); 24, Army Air Corps (official); 25, The Royal Norfolk Regiment (official); 26, The Border Regiment (semi-official); 27, Army Dental Corps (official); 28, The Essex Regiment (semi-official).

Coldstream Guards Battalion numerals. 29, 3rd Battalion; 30, 4th Battalion.
(Items not to scale.)

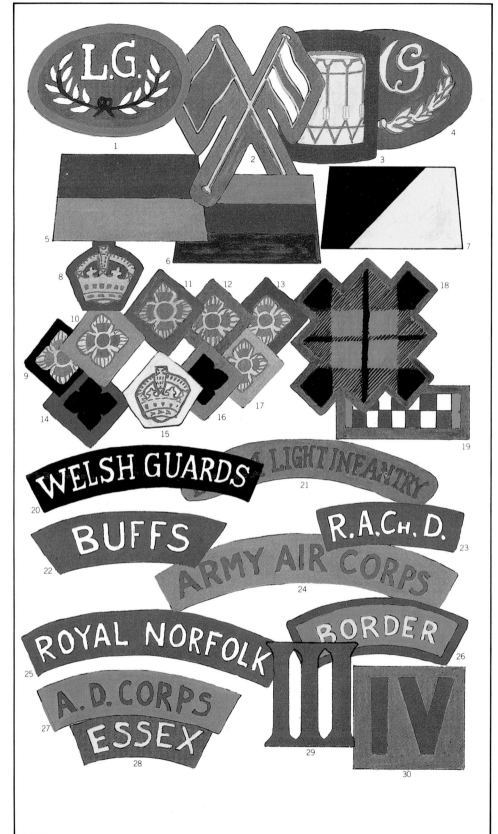

Right: Arm-of-service strips. 1, Staff, Corps of Military Police and Military Provost Staff Corps; 2, Royal Armoured Corps; 3, Royal Artillery; 4, Royal Engineers; 5, Royal Signals; 6, Infantry (except Rifles); 7, Infantry (Rifles); 8, Army Air Corps; 9, Royal Army Chaplains Department; 10, Royal Army Service Corps; 11, Recce Corps; 12, Pioneer Corps; 13, Royal Army Medical Corps; 14, Royal Army Ordnance Corps; 15, Royal Electrical and Mechanical Engineers; 16, Royal Army Pay Corps; 17, Army Educational Corps; 18, Army Dental Corps; 19, Intelligence Corps; 20, Army Catering Corps; 21, Army Physical Training Corps. Regiment and battalion arm flashes. 22, Royal Gloucester Hussars; 23, Fife and Forfar Yeomanry; 24, London Scottish; 25, The Suffolk Regiment; 26, The Somerset Light Infantry; 27, The Cheshire Regiment; 28, 2nd Battalion, The Devonshire Regiment; 29, 566th Heavy Anti-Aircraft Regiment, Royal Artillery; 30, The Northamptonshire Regiment; 31, 567th Light Anti-Aircraft Search Light Regiment, Royal Artillery. Formation signs. 32, 4th Corps and 64th Medium Artillery Regiment, Royal Artillery; 33, Northern Command (UK); 34, 8th Armoured Division; 35, 42nd Armoured Division; 36, Headquarters Line of Communication, 21st Army Group; 37, 21st Army Group (GHQ and L of C Troops); 38, 3rd Infantry Division; 39, Eighth Army; 40, 7th Armoured Division, first original pattern; 41, 4th Infantry Division (second pattern); 42, 18th Infantry Division; 43, 1st Anti-Aircraft Division (first pattern); 44, 56th (London) Infantry Division; 45, 46th (North Midland) Infantry Division; 46, 38th (Welsh) Infantry Division. Home Guard Insignia. 47, Universal pattern Home Guard shoulder title; 48, Proficiency badge; 49, Proficiency 'Bar'. (Items not to scale.)

Right: British Army camouflage patterns used on—1, Anti-Gas cape; 2, The Airborne Denison Smock; 3, The Windproof Smock; 4, The Special Operations Executive jump suit. (Items not to scale.)

1

2

3

4

10. SHOULDER DESIGNATIONS

The Origins and Use of the Embroidered and Coloured Shoulder Designation

Upon the introduction of Service Dress for other ranks in 1902 (Army Order 10 of 1920), the practice was introduced (Appendix A, para.[c]) whereby rank and file personnel wore curved strips of coloured cloth sewn to the upper part of the sleeves, about 1in below the shoulder seam of their Service Dress tunics and just clear of the shoulder flap of their greatcoats, on which was embroidered the title of their regiment, corps or department. The colour of the material used for the curved strips (which many years later were to be referred to officially as 'designations') and the colour of the embroidered lettering served to distinguish the wearer's arm of service.

Cavalry of the Line wore yellow titles with blue letters. The Royal Artillery had blue titles with red letters and the opposite applied to the Royal Engineers who had red titles and blue letters. Infantry of the Line wore red strips with white lettering and all intendant corps wore white strips, the Army Service Corps having blue letters, the Royal Army Medical Corps cherry red letters, the Army Ordnance Corps red and the Army Pay Corps yellow letters on their white titles.

Distinctive strips of green material were authorized for the rifle regiments in 1904, the lettering being in red for the King's Royal Rifles and in black for all others. These coloured distinguishing strips were abolished in about 1907 when they were replaced by metal shoulder titles.

During the Great War of 1914–18 the Brigade of Guards wore distinctive strips bearing the title of the regiment at the top of each sleeve of its Service Dress. The colours of the shoulder strips worn by the Foot Guards Regiments were the same as the regimental designations worn by the Foot Guards before and during the Second World War (see below).

After the Great War only the Grenadier Guards continued to wear their shoulder strips on their Service Dress, and the remaining four Foot Guard regiments ceased to use them. However, sometime in the early 1930s the former First World War shoulder designations were reintroduced for the five regiments of the Foot Guards and the practice was extended to the two Household Cavalry regiments.[1] The seven designations were The Life Guards, who had blue lettering on red cloth titles; the Royal Horse Guards, who had red lettering on dark blue cloth titles; the Grenadier Guards, who

[1] I have in my collection a sealed pattern of a Grenadier Guards' regimental designation, white lettering with serifs on red cloth strip. The designation was sealed on 19 March 1931.

Below: The Rev. J. Gwinnett of Cheltenham, a padre with the Airborne Forces. The Royal Army Chaplains' shoulder designation shown here is an example of an unofficial designation.

Below right: Another unofficial shoulder designation was the title 'Border' worn by troops of the Border Regiment. It was a multi-coloured designation with yellow letters on a dark green background edged with purple. The designation is displayed here by Pte. J. McCluskie, MM; April 1942. (See also the photograph on page 56.)

Right: A lieutenant-colonel of the 3rd Parachute Regiment wearing an unofficial shoulder designation; Netheravon aerodrome, October 1942. (See also the photograph on page 106.)
Far right: An early but unofficial shoulder designation for The Light Artillery displayed by a gunner at a demonstration staged by paratroops of the Airborne Division at Bulford on 9 July 1942.

had white lettering on red cloth; the Scots Guards, who had yellow lettering on royal blue cloth; the Welsh Guards, who had white lettering on black cloth titles; the Irish Guards, who had white lettering on emerald green cloth; and the Coldstream Guards, who had lettering in white on red titles. According to the former custodian of the Guards Museum in London, it was originally intended that the Coldstream Guards would have white lettering on blue cloth titles. However, this was not to be so and they received the same coloured designations as the Grenadier Guards. In order to further distinguish the two titles the corners of the Coldstream Guards' titles were rounded off whilst those worn by the Grenadier Guards remained as issued with square corners.

After September 1940, when the Army Physical Training Service became the Army Physical Training Corps, the latter were authorized to wear a shoulder designation with red lettering on a black cloth title.

Despite the introduction of the khaki slip-on worsted shoulder titles for wear on the Battle-Dress (see page 81). Many regiments and corps took to wearing unofficial designations embroidered in coloured threads on to coloured backings which in many cases were the colours used as their Full-Dress facings, although there was no authority for this and the War Office issued instructions on more than one occasion that they were not to be worn (ACI 2816).

It is impracticable to produce here a complete listing of all the known unofficial shoulder designations, even if it were possible to compile such a

listing; instead, I have had to content myself with an illustrated page of such insignia (opposite).

The Unauthorized Wearing of Unofficial Regimental Designations

Instructions regarding the wearing of dress by all ranks during the period of the war were those as given on page 125. Instructions regarding the wearing of distinguishing marks by Army personnel are given on page 94. These instructions were frequently not obeyed. The principal irregularities were the unauthorized wearing of berets and of unofficial regimental designations and the wearing of coloured lapels on Battle-Dress.

Army Council Instruction 2587 of 1941 (page 98) clearly laid down that the wearing of regimental designations was limited to the Household Cavalry and the Foot Guards. In October 1942, ACI 2816 dated 31 October 1942 stated that this provision had been extended to the wearing of the word Airborne by the Airborne Division (see page 80) and the letters A.P.T.C. by the Army Physical Training Corps. Proposals to extend this practice to other units on the ground of 'esprit de corps' were carefully examined but were not accepted. This decision was final and no further applications to wear such designations were allowed to be submitted. Officers commanding units were advised to take immediate steps to ensure that the above mentioned dress irregularities were dealt with and that all unauthorized articles and modifications of clothing, including regimental designations, ceased to be worn within one month of the date of publication of ACI 2816.

Right: Unofficial regimental and corps designations. 1, Yellow on purple; 2, Yellow on dark blue; 3, White on maroon; 4, Yellow on green with purple edging; 5, White on black; 6, Blue on red; 7, Yellow on black; 8, Yellow on black; 9, White on dark blue; 10, Red on green.

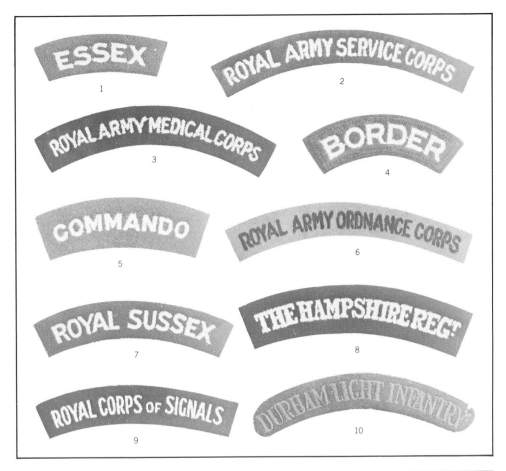

Right: Prewar and wartime official regimental and corps designations. 1, White on red; 2, Yellow on royal blue; 3, White on black; 4, Red on dark blue; 5, Red on black; 6, Blue on red; 7, White on red; 8, White on emerald green.

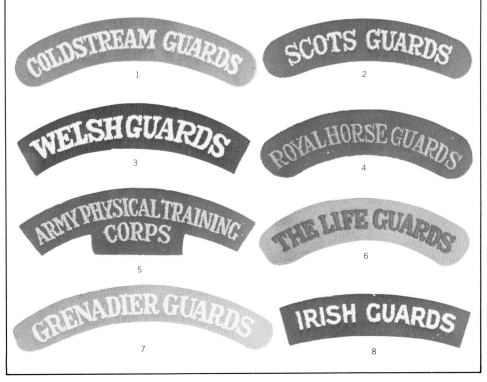

11. FORMATION AND UNIT COLOURED DISTINGUISHING MARKS, 1940–45

Army Council Instruction No. 419 issued by the War Office and promulgated during the week ending 1 May 1940 stated that 'Divisional Signs or badges will not be worn by British divisions during the war'. It went on to add: 'This policy will not apply to Dominion Divisions. Divisional Signs or badges may be worn by these formations at the discretion of the Dominion military authorities concerned'.

This attitude was clearly in line with the underlying purpose of the newly introduced Battle-Dress, the deliberate intention of which, due to its utilitarian qualities, was to deny to the enemy the means of distinguishing ranks and arms of service. However, even before the issue of ACI 419 of 1940, the policy was proving to be unsatisfactory, as can be seen from the extracts taken from the official correspondence (reproduced below) that took place between Lieutenant-General Viscount Gort, VC, the Commander-in-Chief of the British Expeditionary Force, and the War Office. The first letter General Gort wrote on the subject of rank badges, distinctive markings and the like was directed to the Under-Secretary of State at the War Office. It was dated 30 October 1939 and read as follows:

'1. I have the honour to make the following recommendations in regard to certain changes in order of dress which I desire to make applicable to the B.E.F.
'2. *"Officers Battle Dress Badges of Rank and Distinctive Markings"*.
It is very difficult to distinguish between officers and men when they are in Battle-Dress. I recommend that the ordinary badges of rank in metal or worsted should be worn on the shoulder straps but that if worsted they should be superimposed upon some coloured material to enable them to be more readily recognised close at hand but not too easily distinguishable at a distance.
'3. *"Badges and Regimental Titles"*.
I am of the opinion that Esprit de Corps should be interfered with as little as possible but I recognise that security has great importance. I recommend that the metal titles ordinarily in wear in service dress should be worn in Battle-Dress.

'These metal titles are easily removable in case it is desired to disguise the fact that any particular unit is in any particular place.
'As certain regiments have already gone to the expense of providing themselves with distinctive emblems and as others wear distinctive emblems in memory of the last war I recommend that the wearing of emblems should be allowed to continue in Battle-Dress.
'As every man carries an Army Book 64 in his pocket giving his full particulars, and as a man's regiment can be deduced from the blocks of numbers on his identity disc, I see no reason why the soldier should not continue to have his regimental title on his shoulder as he now does in Service Dress.
'If, by any chance, there is a shortage of metal, I recommend that coloured flashes, 2-inches square, should be worn on the sleeve 4-inches below the point of the shoulder. These flashes would be in regimental colours in the case of the Infantry and in different colours for the other Arms of Service. I only recommend the wearing of these flashes for Infantry if the metal titles cannot be obtained but flashes to denote the arm of the service would, in my opinion still be desirable even with the metal titles.

'I am definitely of the opinion, however, that Esprit de Corps particularly in the Infantry will suffer if soldiers in Battle-Dress are not permitted to carry on them an emblem showing the regiment to which they belong.
'If my recommendations are approved I consider the expense of coloured flashes should be borne by the Public.
'4. *"Covers for Steel Helmets"*
I wish to represent that in my view the covers now issued for steel helmets are not practicable in war. I understand that these covers are practically undecontaminable and will be a source of considerable danger in the case of an attack of mustard gas.
'Further in my view they are extremely unsightly and give a man a slovenly appearance. I recommend that dull (matt) paint should be used for steel helmets and that no regimental marking on steel helmets should be permitted.
'5. *"Officers' Caps in Battle-Dress"*.
Under War Office letter 54/Gen/8632 M.G.O., it is stated that officers must wear the drab cap in Battle-Dress.
'I recommend reconsideration of this in so far as it affects officers who are already in possession of caps in regimental colours.
'I do not wish to put newly joined officers to the expense of buying coloured caps and I recommend therefore that only those officers already in possession of coloured caps should be allowed to continue to wear them.
'6. I should be glad if early consideration can be given to these proposals to enable me to give effect to them with the least possible delay.'

The following is an extract from the report of a visit by the (late) DCIGS to the BEF on 20–21 October 1939:

'Para 7(f) "Officers Badges of Rank".
1. "It is impossible in the B.E.F. to tell a Colonel from a Private and the C-in-C would like the Battle-Dress to be provided with chevrons of rank similar to the French. I suggest a bar in red or yellow on one arm, one bar for a 2nd Lieutenant rising to five bars for a Lieutenant-Colonel would be sufficient."
2. The question came before the C.I.G.S. War Committee at its 29th meeting on 23rd October (1939). Paragraph 8 of the minutes reads as follows:
'Chevrons for the B.E.F.
D.C.I.G.S. said that chevrons as distinguishing marks between the different ranks were necessary for the B.E.F., A.C.I.G.S. said that D.S.D. in consultation with D.P.S. & D.O.S. was taking necessary action.
3. (a) Accordingly a Battle-Dress jacket was fitted with samples of proposed chevrons as badges of rank.
    (b) Meanwhile C-in-C had changed his mind and in his letter A/16/5 (P.S.) of October 1939 said: [see typed letter, above, from General Gort VC, C-in-C BEF, to the Under-Secretary of State at the War Office, dated 30 October 1939, para. 2].
4. The samples referred to in paragraph 2 above and the C-in-C's letter were brought simultaneously before the 35th meeting of the C.I.G.S. War Committee on the 3rd November 1939, and the following was agreed:
(i) Coloured chevrons on the sleeve of the jacket would not be suitable.
(ii) Metal rank badges would be out of the question due to the shortage of metal.
(iii) Samples of the ordinary worsted rank badges superimposed on a coloured material should be exhibited for consideration at an early meeting of the Committee'.

Parachute badge (parachute 'wings').

Regular parachute troops. Army Council Instruction 1589 dated 28 December 1940 announced that a decision had been made to introduce a special badge for wear by qualified parachutists. The badge was described as being of 'cloth worked with pale blue wings and a white parachute on a background of drab material'.

To qualify for the award of this badge, soldiers were required to make a specified number of parachute drops, although neither the qualification nor the badge carried with it any extra pay or allowances. The badges were to be worn permanently by qualified personnel even after they had ceased to be employed with parachute troops.

Issues of the 'wings' were made on the scale of two badges for each other rank, one for each Battle-Dress blouse or Service Dress jacket. On 12 February 1941 (ACI 204 of 1941) this issue was increased to three badges per other rank, the third issue of which was for wear on the gabardine jump jacket (see page 200); the badge was not permitted to be worn on the denim overalls nor on the greatcoat. The badge was worn on the right upper arm midway between the elbow and the point of the shoulder. Badges required by officers were issued on payment from unit stocks. Also on 12 February 1941, an amendment to the conditions of wear held that the badge would be withdrawn in the case of an active parachutist refusing to jump, but for no other disciplinary reason.

A further ACI, 1274 dated 17 June 1942, elaborated on the conditions for the award of this badge and who could wear it. As instructed by this ACI, the parachute 'wings' were to be worn on the right upper arm, 2in from the point of the shoulder and above any formation badge where this was worn. The badge was to be worn not only by qualified parachutists of the parachute brigades but also by all instructors regularly employed by Airborne Forces, the Experimental Establishment, or similar schools for parachutists.

The award of the badge was by now only to be made on the authority of the Commander Airborne Division. The requirements for the badge and the wearing of the same were as previously announced, and, as before, it carried no title to any extra pay or allowances.

In September 1942 (ACI 1890 dated 9 September 1942) a small amendment was made to the reasons for withdrawal of the badge: not only refusing to jump when ordered to do so, but also being absent without good cause from a parade for jumping were now sufficient reason for a parachutist to lose his 'wings'. ACI 2225 dated 21 October 1942 added the personnel of other units of the Airborne Division who were operational parachutists to the list of those persons who were permitted to wear the Parachute badge.

Members of the wartime SOE. The parachute qualification 'wings' were worn over the left breast pocket, above any medal ribbons where these were worn, on the Service Dress jacket and the Battle-Dress blouse by SOE agents who had made at least one operational drop into enemy-held territory and had successfully returned to the UK or other friendly territory.

Army Flying Badge (Air Observation Post pilots' and glider pilots' 'wings').

On 11 April 1942 Army Council Instruction No. 768 announced that an 'Army flying badge' had been approved to be worn on the left breast by qualified AOP pilots and glider pilots. The cloth badge was described as consisting of 'a pair of pale blue wings with the Royal Crest superimposed in the centre, the whole upon a black background'. The award of this badge did not carry with it any extra pay. Pilots were eligible for extra pay only during such time as they were being employed as air observation post or as glider pilots, but personnel who were awarded this badge were allowed to continue wearing it after they ceased to be employed as air observation post or glider pilots.

The qualifications for the award of this badge were as follows:
1. AOP pilots were eligible after successfully completing an Elementary Flying Training School course and the subsequent AOP pilot's course.
2. Glider pilots were eligible for the award of this badge after successfully completing Elementary Flying Training School, Glider Training School, and Glider Operational Training Unit courses. These last courses were substituted in September 1942 (ACI 1902 dated 9 September 1942) for Heavy Glider Conversion Unit courses; in November 1942 (ACI 2372 dated 7 November 1942) they were dropped altogether, leaving only the successful completion of an Elementary Flying Training School and Glider Training School course as qualification for the award of the badge.

The award of this badge was notified in Part II orders, which in the case of Air Observation Post pilots was by the School of Artillery at Larkhill, Wiltshire, and for glider pilots was by the Officer Commanding, the Glider Pilot Regiment. This was changed by ACI 1128 dated 19 August 1944 to read 'Glider pilots by the Commandant, the Glider Pilot Depot', and again by ACI 177 dated 17 February 1945 to read 'First Glider Pilots by the Officer Commanding glider pilot wing concerned under the authority of the Commander, Glider Pilots'.

An entry was made in AFB 199A in the case of officers and in AB 64 in the case of other ranks. Badges required by officers were issued to them on payment for the same.

Qualification badge for non-regular parachute trained personnel.

ACI 1274 dated 17 June 1942 also announced the introduction of a special cloth badge bearing a white parachute worked on a background of drab material which was to be worn by those personnel who had passed through a recognized parachute training school but who were not regular parachute troops or instructors.

Initially instructions were issued for the badge to be worn in the same position as the parachute 'wings', namely on the right upper arm 2in from the point of the shoulder and above any formation badge where this may have been present. It is possible that these instructions were in error in stating this, because five months later ACI 2225

Above: Maj.-Gen. Colin Gubbins of Ayrshire, Scotland, a General of Paratroops photographed on the day he was invested with the Companionship of the Most Distinguished Order of St. Michael and St. George, 8 March 1944. The qualification badge for non-regular parachute trained personnel can just be seen on General Gubbins' right forearm.

Above right: Sjt. Roscoe, a second glider pilot who was wounded at Arnhem and evacuated to England, 28 September 1944. The special badge for second glider pilots can be seen above the left breast pocket.

Right: Parachute and glider qualification badges. 1, Parachute badge (regular parachute troops); 2, Qualification badge for non-regular parachute-trained personnel; 3, Glider-trained infantry; 4, Army flying badge (Air Observation Post pilots' and glider pilots' wings); 5, Second glider pilots' badge; 6, Qualification wings, Special Air Service.

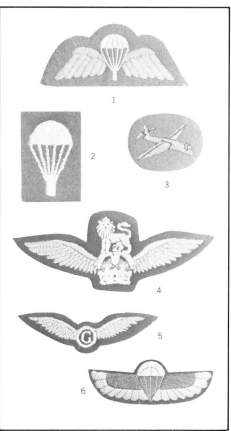

dated 21 October 1942 altered the position of wear for the 'light bulb' badge from the right upper arm to the lower right sleeve; it was in future to be worn on the forearm of the right sleeve of the Battle-Dress blouse or Service Dress jacket 6in from the lower edge of the cuff. Warrant officers wore their badge immediately above their badge of rank. However, a five-month period was long enough for some of these badges to be worn on the upper right arm, whether the original instructions were in error or not.

To qualify for the award, individuals were required to make a specified number of parachute jumps, and the badge was awarded by the commander of the school at which the individual qualified. Neither qualification nor the badge carried with it any entitlement to any extra pay or allowances.

Issues of the badge were made on the scale of two for each other rank, one per Battle-Dress blouse or Service Dress jacket; the badge was not worn on denim overalls nor on the greatcoat. Officers were required to purchase their badges.

Introduction of the second glider pilot's badge.

A special badge for second glider pilots, in addition to the Army Flying Badge, was introduced by ACI 1128 dated 19 August 1944. The second glider pilot's cloth badge took the form of a small pair of pale blue wings with the yellow letter G in a yellow circle set between the wings, the whole upon a black background. This badge was worn on the left breast by all qualified second glider pilots. To qualify for this award potential

Above: The badge for glider trained infantry, shown here on the right forearm of a member of the Airborne Forces undergoing training in protective tactics; 10 December 1942.
Above right: Staff Sjt. Bill Brough, MM, of Runcorn, a member of the 1st Special Air Service; 2 May 1944. The wartime SAS operational wings are shown worn over the left breast pocket. The modern SAS operational wings are fractionally smaller and slightly 'V'-shaped. (See the photograph on page 155.)

second glider pilots had successfully to complete the courses for second glider pilots at Elementary Flying Training Schools and Glider Training Schools.

The official entry on to officers' forms and other ranks' pay books and the conditions for officers obtaining this badge were as previously stated on page 65 for the Army Flying Badge. The award of the badge carried no entitlement or extra pay, and a second glider pilot who had been awarded the badge was allowed to continue wearing it even after he ceased to be employed as a glider pilot.

The notification of award of this badge was made by the Commandant Glider Pilot Depot, under the authority of the Commander Airborne Establishments (this last instruction was published under ACI 177 dated 17 February 1945).

Badge for glider trained infantry.

Infantry personnel who were trained as gliderborne infantry, and those who had made an operational glider landing, wore a small cloth oval badge on the right forearm of the Service Dress jacket or the Battle-Dress blouse. The badge, which was 1¾in across at its widest point, bore the design of a glider worked in mid-blue threads on to a khaki drab background. The glider faced from left to right, or forward when worn on the sleeve.

Examples exist, notably in the Museum of the Airborne Forces, Aldershot, of this pattern of badge with the addition of a coloured edging. This seems to have been purely a regimental or unit peculiarity, the colour of the edging matching the colour of the background to the regimental

designation worn by the glider-borne infantry. This badge must have been authorized by HQ Airborne Forces, but no official War Office authorization can be traced.

Qualification 'wings' as awarded to and worn by members of the wartime Special Air Service.

The design of this badge is attributed to Lieutenant J. S. 'Jock' Lewis, a former No. 8 Commando officer and one of Major David Stirling's first and most important SAS officers. Lewis was killed in action just before Christmas 1941.

The design chosen by Lieutenant Lewis is said to have been inspired by a frieze he saw whilst at a Cairo hotel (thought to have been either Sheppard's or the Heliopolis Palace Hotel). Based on a painting made of the ancient Egyptian symbol of Ra, the Sun God of Heliopolis, depicted as a spread-winged falcon, he devised a set of SAS wings. His design, which was initially made up under local Egyptian conditions, showed a white parachute fully developed with white rigging lines flanked by outspread dark blue and light 'pompadour' blue wings, with feather lines detailed in black and all worked on to a black backing.

The choice of two shades of blue was no doubt influenced by the turquoise (light blue) and lapis lazuli (rich blue) used on the original eighteenth dynasty falcon pectoral, but light and dark blue was also a fortuitous choice for the wings of the new badge as they were a visual reference to the Oxford and Cambridge rowing background of both

Lewis and Lieutenant Langton, two of the original SAS officers.

The badge, as far as I can ascertain, did not receive wartime War Office approval but instead was permitted to be worn in November 1941 by the authority of General Ritchie, who was then the commander-in-chief of the 8th Army. It continued to be used throughout the remaining war years until 8 October 1945 when the SAS brigade was disbanded.[1]

The wings were worn on the upper right arm below 'the point of the shoulder on the Service Dress and Khaki Drill jackets and the Battle-Dress blouse by those personnel who had made the required seven parachute jumps; the badge was also worn over the left breast pocket above any medal ribbons, if these were worn, by those SAS members who had been engaged in one or more conspicuous service operations or who had made one or more operational parachute drops during the Second World War only.

After the war those former members of the disbanded SAS serving in other units and who continued to wear their SAS 'sabre' wings in this manner were stopped from doing so by the Army Council. The War Office ruled that the only qualifying wings allowed to be worn by Army personnel in this position were qualified members of the Glider Pilot Regiment.

The 1944 Policy for the Wearing of Tradesmen's Badges, Instructors' Badges and Badges for Skill-at-Arms

The policy for the wearing of tradesmen's, instructors' and skill-at-arms badges underwent a complete review in 1944 in order to provide a basis for the wearing of these badges consistent with wartime requirements and at the same time to retain the desirable incentive which they

[1]The SAS 'wings' were authorized by ACI 995 of 1948. They were then described as being of 'cloth worked with a pair of dark blue and pale blue wings with a white parachute in the centre, on a background of dark blue material'.

provided. With effect from the date of publication, 16 September 1944, of ACI 1236, the following measures applied.

General.
1. Soldiers of the rank of Serjeant and above were not entitled to wear skill-at-arms or tradesmen's badges.
2. Any soldier below the rank of Serjeant was not permitted to wear more than two of these badges in the above three categories, i.e. one tradesman's badge and either one instructor's or one skill-at-arms badge, in addition to other badges authorized such as regimental designations, formation badges, etc.
3. Not more than one badge from each of the instructor's or tradesman's categories was permitted to be worn by any soldier.
4. The badges that were worn by a soldier had first to be approved by the soldier's commanding officer.

The instructions for the wearing of the badges in the three main categories were as stated in the list shown on page 55 entered in the column headed '1943'. This is based on the information to be found in *War Clothing Regulations, 1943*, Appendix III. The terms of ACI 1236 of 1944 also applied to auxiliaries of the ATS and VAD members enrolled for employment under the Army Council.

Tradesmen's badges, 1944.
1. Certain badges that had already been authorized in this category were retained. A list of these, showing the revised list of trades for which they were applicable, is given on page 70.
2. A new design of trade badge for Trade Groups A, B, C and D had been approved to cater for the trades for which the badges in sub-paragraph (1) above were not appropriate.
3. If a tradesman's badge was worn it had to be the badge of the trade in which a soldier was mustered.
4. Tradesmen's badges were only permitted to be worn by soldiers who qualified as Class I or Class II in their trade.

Right: Exhausted troops evacuated from Dunkirk asleep on the open deck of their rescue vessel, *Guinea*, June 1940. The soldier in the centre is wearing an unofficial trade badge which indicates that he is a driver of motor transport.

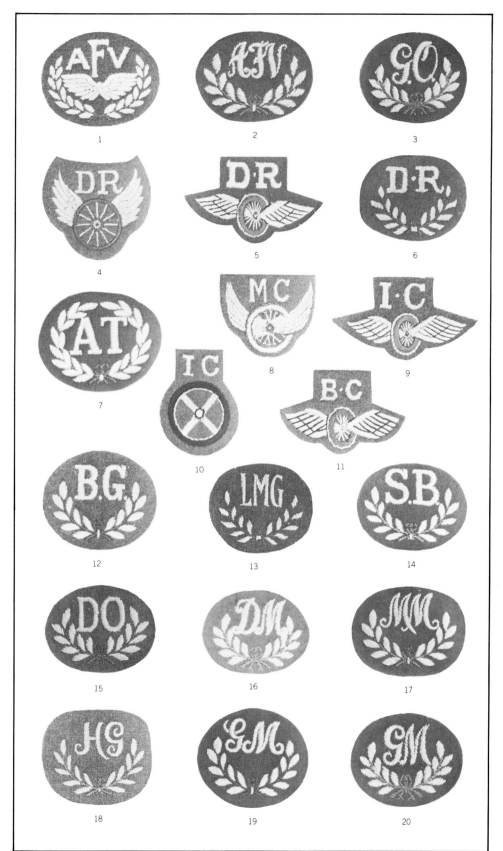

Right: Semi-official tradesmen's badges. This is but a small selection of the many examples known to have existed; the purpose of quite a number is now obscure. 1, 2, Armoured fighting vehicle crew; 3, Gunner/operator; 4, 5, 6, Despatch rider; 7, Anti-tank gunner; 8, Motorcyclist; 9, 10, Internal combustion (driver); 11, Bren gun carrier crew; 12, Bren gunner; 13, Light machine gun; 14, Stretcher bearer; 15, Driver/operator; 16, Driver/maintenance; 17, Mortar man; 18, Hotchkiss gunner; 19, 20, Gunner/mechanic.

Right: Tradesmen's badges, 1944. 1, Group A trades; 2, Group B trades; 3, Group C trades; 4, Group D trades; 5, Hammer and pincers badge; 6, Pioneer, fusilier regiments; 7, Pioneer, light infantry and rifle regiments; 8, Pioneer, other units.

Table 13. British Army Tradesmen's Badges, 1944

Group A trades	Group B trades	Group C trades	Group D trades
'A' badge	*'B' badge*	*'C' badge*	*'D' badge*
Chemical artificer	Barge engineer	Baker	Axeman
Chemical laboratory assistant	Boilermaker	Blockman	Checker (railway docks or
Draughtsman (architectural)	Bricklayer	Bookbinder	movement control)
Draughtsman (mechanical)	Clerk (shorthand writer)	Brakesman and shunter	Chiropodist
Draughtsman (topographical)	Coach painter	Butcher	Concreter
Draughtsman (railway or port	Cutter, cinematograph	Chemical laboratory attendant	Cycle repairer
construction)	Dental mechanic	Clerk (general duties)	Despatch rider (R Signals)[1]
Driver (transportation plant)	Dispenser	Clerk (field survey)	Driver (crane)
Electrician	Electrician (power station)	Clerk, orderly (AD Corps)	Engine hand (internal
Electrician (control equipment)	Electrician (wireman)	Clerk (RAMC)	combustion)
Electrician (vehicle and plant)	Electroplater	Clerk (RAOC)	Fireman (loco)
Electrician (maintenance)	Galvanizer	Clerk (RAPC)	Fireman (marine)
Electrician (diesel electric	Hospital Cook	Clerk, railway	Glass grinder
locomotive	Laboratory assistant	Clerk (special intelligence	Leather stitcher
Engine Artificer, RE	(pathological)	duties)[2]	Loftman (R Signals)
Experimental assistant	Lighterman (IWT)	Clerk, technical (MT) (RASC)	Operator fire control
(gunnery)	Mason	Clerk, technical (REME)	Operator switchboard (R Signals)
Helio worker	Masseur	Coach trimmer	Probationary armourer (REME)
Hospital cook	Miner	Dipper-checker (petroleum)	Probationary artificer (RA)
Lithographer (draughtsman)	Miner (mechanic or driller)	Draughtsman (R Signals)	Sawyer
Lithographer (machine minder)	Modeller (camouflage)	Driver road roller	Searchlight operator
Lithographer (prover)	Moulder	Engine attendant (RA)	Steel bender (ferro concrete)
Pharmacist	Operating room assistant	Lineman power	Stevedore
Photographer (cartographic)	Operator (excavator)	Lineman (R Signals)	Timberman (public works)
Photo writer	Operator (linotype)	Mental nursing orderly	Vulcanizer
Printer (machine minder)	Optician	Moulder (rubber stamp)	Waterman
Railway engine driver	Photographer (cinematograph	Nursing orderly	Stoker (stationary engine)
Saw doctor	or still)	Operator (dome teacher)	*Hammer and pincers badge*
Stereotyper	Photographic developer	Operator (tyre repair plant)	Motor assembler
Surgical instrument mechanic	Plasterer (camouflage)	Painter and decorator	*Grenade over crossed hatchets*
Surveyor (engineering)	Postal worker	Platelayer	*badge*
Surveyor (ordnance)	Projectionist (cinema)	Printer (compositor)	Pioneer of Fusilier Regiments
Surveyor (topographical)	Quarryman	Rigger	*Bugle over crossed hatchets*
Surveyor (trigonometrical)	Radiographer	Sanitary assistant	*badge*
Surveyor clerk	Railway engine driver (diesel)	Shoemaker	Pioneer of Light Infantry and
Traffic operator	Watchmaker	Special treatment orderly	Rifle Regiments
Trained nurse	Well borer	Stevedore (Class I)	*Crossed hatchets badge*
		Storeman (REME)	Pioneers of other units

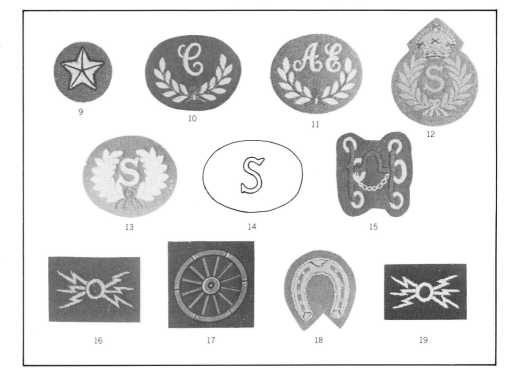

Right: Tradesmen's badges, 1944, continued. 9, Driver/mechanic; 10, Cook (other than hospital cook); 11, Ammunition examiner; 12, Surveyor, RA, Class I; 13, Surveyor, RA, Class II; 14, Battery surveyor; 15, Bit badge; 16, Wireless signals badge; 17, Wheel badge; 18, Farrier; 19, Radio location badge.

Group A trades	Group B trades	Group C trades	Group D trades
Hammer and pincers badge	*Hammer and pincers badge*	Storeman (supplies) (RASC)	*Star badge*
Armourer	Blacksmith	Storeman (survey)	Driver mechanic
Artificer, RA	Coppersmith	Storeman, technical and	
Electrical fitter, RA (AA SL,	Engine fitter (IC and pumps)	departmental (railway)	
or CA)	Engine fitter (mechanical	Storeman, technical (RAOC)	
Fitter	equipment	Storeman, technical (other than	
Fitter (engine room), RA	Engine fitter (steam	railway and RAOC)	
Fitter, gun (field, CD and AA)	reciprocating)	Surveyor (chemical warfare)	
Fitter (loco)	Fitter (petroleum)	Tailor	
Instrument mechanic	Fitter (railway signals)	Textile refitter	
Instrument mechanic (field	Grinder (precision)	Timberman (port construction)	
survey	Machinist (metal)	Transfusion orderly	
Millwright	Panel beater	Typewriter mechanic	
Shipwright	Plumber and pipe fitter	Warehouseman	
Steelwork erector	Sheet metal worker	*Hammer and pincers badge*	
Toolmaker	Welder	Riveter	
Turner	*'C' in wreath badge*	Tinsmith and whitesmith	
Vehicle mechanic	Cook (other than hospital cook)	*'S' badge*	
'AE' in wreath badge	*Wireless signals badge*	Battery surveyor	
Ammunition examiner[3]	Operator (keyboard and line)	*Bit badge*	
'S' in wreath badge	(R Signals)	Saddle tree maker	
Surveyor, RA Class II	Operator (special) (R Signals)	Saddler and harness maker	
'S' in wreath with crown	Operator (wireless and line)	*Shoe badge*	
Surveyor, RA Class I	(R Signals)	Farrier	
Wireless signals badge	*Wheel badge*	*Wireless signals badge*	
Electrician (R Signals)	Carpenter and joiner	Driver operator	
Instrument mechanic (R Signals)	Carriage and waggon repairer	Gunner operator	
Lineman mechanical (R Signals)	Wheeler	*Star badge*	
Operator (wireless and	Wood turner and machinist	Driver mechanical (AFV)	
keyboard) (R Signals)			
Wheel badge			
Pattern maker			
Radio location badge			
Telecommunication mechanic			

[1]The Royal Corps of Signals was the only corps or regiment to have despatch riders as an Army trade, although motor-cyclist messengers in other units were often loosely described as 'despatch riders'.
[2]No trade badge worn.

[3]The ammunition examiner's trade badge was first introduced in March 1942 by publication of ACI 659. Described as having the letters A.E. in a wreath, it was introduced for wear by classified ammunition examiners of the RAOC.

Instructors' badges, 1944.

As a wartime measure the existing instructors' badges were retained but no new badges were authorized in this category. The badges were as shown in table 14.

Table 14. **Instructors' Badges**

Class of instruction	Authorized badge
Gunnery serjeant-major, School of Artillery	Crossed guns
Other gunnery instructors[1]	Crossed guns
Warrant officer instructor, RE	Grenade
Instructor RE in field work below rank of Serjeant	Q.I. in wreath
Musketry instructors	Crossed rifles
Physical training instructors	Crossed swords
Riding instructors	Spur
Assistant instructors of signalling	Crossed flags
Other signalling instructors	Crossed flags

[1]Did not apply to the RAC.

On 28 March 1945 another ACI, No. 339, was published, which redesignated what had previously been known as instructors' badges as 'instructors qualification badges', and set out the qualifications required before a warrant officer or NCO was entitled to wear his or her badge.

The instructors' qualification badges listed in Table 15 were only worn by qualified warrant officers and NCOs who had obtained qualification 'AX' or higher according to the standard laid down at a recognized Army school or, in the case of the RA, who held the appointment of assistant instructor-in-gunnery. The qualification 'AX' applied equally to recognized Army schools outside the United Kingdom where an equivalent standard was maintained. Instructors' qualification badges were worn for a period not exceeding two years or in the case of the RA for the tenure of appointment as assistant instructor-in-gunnery, unless the holder had re-qualified under the terms given in column two of Table 15, or was granted a certificate by the commandant of the appropriate school if he or she was employed on the instructional staff at that time. This qualification certificate entitled the holder to wear the appropriate badge for a further period of two years.

With effect from 28 March 1945 only those who had reached 'AX' standard or who held the appointment of Assistant Instructor-in-Gunnery were permitted to continue to wear the appropriate badge; the two-year period of validity was dated from 28 March 1945.

The whole question of instructors' qualification badges was to be reconsidered at the end of hostilities in the light of postwar conditions.

Skill-at-arms badges, 1944.

As a wartime measure the existing skill-at-arms badges were also retained. Applications for the introduction of a new badge of this type were granted only in very exceptional cases (see the addition in November 1945 of the sniper's badge and the conditions of its award). A complete list of these authorized badges is as shown in Table 16.

Table 15. Instructors' Qualification Badges

Class of instruction	Qualification	Badge
Gunnery serjeant-major, School of Artillery	Gunnery Staff course or War Gunnery course	Crossed guns
Other gunnery instructors[1]		
Warrant officer instructor, RE	Qualified not lower than 'AX' at School of Military Engineering	Grenade
Instructor RE in field work below rank of Warrant Officer		Q.I. in wreath
Weapon training instructors	Qualified not lower than 'AX' at recognized Army school.	Crossed rifles
Physical training instructors	Holder of certificate awarded by supervising officer of physical training command or district	Crossed swords
Assistant instructors of signalling	Qualified not lower than 'AX' at recognized Army school	Crossed flags
Riding instructor	—	Spur

[1]Did not apply to the RAC.

Table 16. Skill-at-Arms Badges, 1944

Authorized badge[1]	Qualified personnel	Authorized badge[1]	Qualified personnel
Crossed flags	Signaller	P in wreath	Royal Artillery personnel qualified in fortress plotting room (including fortress observation post) or battery plotting room duties
Crossed guns	NCO who had been through Army Gunnery course at School of Artillery, School of Anti-Aircraft Artillery or Coast Artillery School, and was recommended by commandant of school concerned		
		Parachutist's badge	Regular parachute troops[3, 4]
		R in wreath	First-class range-taker of machine gun company, range-taker and position-finder and instrument number of Royal Artillery unit
Crossed rifles	Rifle marksman		
H in wreath	First-class height-taker, Anti-Aircraft Royal Artillery		
L in wreath	Layer, Royal Artillery, mortarman operating 3in or 4.2in mortar, anti-tank gun layer of an arm of the service other than Royal Artillery	Second Glider Pilot's badge	Second glider pilot[4]
		Steering wheel	Driver IC
		S.P. in wreath	Personnel granted special proficiency pay or equivalent
L.G. in wreath	Light machine gun marksman	Army Flying Badge	First glider pilot or Air Observation Post pilot[4]
M.G. in wreath	Medium machine gun marksman		
Naval Gunlayer's badge	Maritime Royal Artillery personnel for whom authorized[2]	Crossed rifles surmounted by S	Sniper[5]

[1]In general the conditions of award for badges were contained in the relevant training manuals.
[2]This badge was classed as a privilege accorded by the Royal Navy to NCOs of the Maritime Royal Artillery who had qualified as Acting Gunlayers (Defensively Equipped Merchant Ships) on a Royal Navy course; introduced by ACI 1380 dated 18 September 1943.
[3]In September 1944, at the time of the publication of ACI 1236 'Badges – Instructions for the Wearing of Tradesmen's, Instructors' and Skill-at-Arms Badges' (the last known set of instructions on this subject laid down and issued before the end of the war), it was intended that a modified badge would be issued to all personnel who had passed through a parachute training school but who were not regular parachute

troops or instructors. This modified badge presumably was to replace the already existing 'light bulb' badge introduced in June 1942 for just this category of non-regular parachute troops or instructors. However, no details have so far been discovered that explain the design of this proposed modified badge, and it may have been that no such badge was produced, especially as the War ceased eleven months later.
[4]The provisions set out under 'General' (above) did not apply. Any of the three skill-at-arms badges, the parachutist badge, the second glider pilot's badge or the Army Flying Badge, was permitted to be worn by all ranks who had duly qualified for the award.
[5]The sniper's badge was introduced on 10 November 1945 by ACI 1290 of 1945.

Wearing of the Regulation Flying Badge (RAF pilot's 'Wings')

According to *Dress Regulations for the Army, 1934*, para. 14, the Royal Air Force badge for pilots (pilot's qualification 'wings') was permitted to be worn by Army officers seconded to the RAF as soon as they had qualified as pilots. They were allowed to continue wearing their 'wings', but on the Service Dress only, on their return to the Army during any period of liability to serve with the RAF on mobilization.

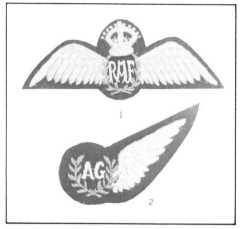

Far right: RAF pilots' qualification wings were permitted to be worn on Army uniforms by those persons entitled to this privilege. Here, HM King George VI is seen talking to Field Marshal Montgomery during his visit to a forward airfield in Belgium operated by the TAF; 15 October 1944
Right: 1, RAF pilot's wings; 2, Air Gunner's badge.

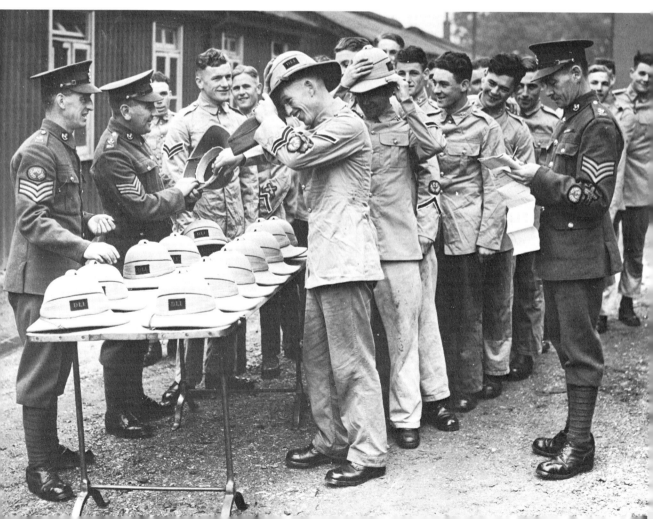

It was decided on 29 June 1940 by ACI 660 that the privilege of wearing the regulation flying badge would be permitted to both officers and other ranks of the British Army who had qualified for it under those regulations in force from time to time in the Royal Flying Corps, the Royal Naval Air Service and the Royal Air Force.

In all cases where a member of the Army desired to put his 'wings' up, confirmation regarding his qualification to wear the badge had first to be obtained by the commanding officer of that man's unit. The flying badge of the Royal Flying Corps was not allowed to be worn, and all officers and other ranks entitled to the privilege of wearing a flying badge were required to wear the pattern then current in the Royal Air Force. At the request of the RAF Council, the observer's badge was not permitted to be worn by officers or other ranks on the Army uniform.

Wearing of the Royal Air Force air gunner's badge by officers of the Army.

The only military personnel who were permitted to wear the air gunner's badge were Army officers loaned to the Royal Air Force for air gunner duties and who were fully qualified for the award of the badge as set out under the terms of Air Ministry Order A 89 of 1942 (reproduced below); they ceased to wear the badge on their return to Army duty. It is not clear whether the air gunner's badge was worn on the Army officers' Army uniform whilst the officer was attached to the RAF or whether he purchased an Air Force uniform to be worn during his time with the Royal Air Force and on which he wore the air gunner's badge.

Air Ministry Order A 89 'The Award of Air Crew Badges in Special Circumstances' dated 29 January 1942.

1. Air crew badges – i.e. observer's, air gunner's and radio operator's (air) – were normally awarded to officers and airmen who had been entered for air crew duties on satisfactory completion of the prescribed courses of instruction. The award of an air crew badge was an indication that the holder was qualified and available to perform operational duties as a regular member of an air crew.

2. As an exception to the normal rule, however, an air crew badge could be awarded to an officer or airman who, though not entered for or specially trained for air crew duties and not posted as a regular member of an air crew, had satisfied the following conditions:
(a) He had completed the full operational training unit course of training or, if it was impracticable for him to have undergone this training, had passed all the tests applied at the end of such a course;
(b) He had completed a minimum of thirty hours' operational flying that comprised not less than ten operational sorties (operational flying was defined for this purpose as flights undertaken against the enemy, and tests, development and instructional flights and flights of a similar nature were excluded);
(c) He had been certified by his commanding officer as having fulfilled conditions (a) and (b) and as being fully qualified; and
(d) He had signed a certificate to the effect that he undertook to keep himself efficient and fully qualified for the duties appropriate to the badge, and that he understood that he was available to be called upon to perform those duties in the air whenever required.

3. The appropriate badge could be awarded on the written authority of the air officer commanding the candidate's group or, in the case of an officer who did not serve in a group, of an officer of air rank at his command headquarters.

4. The awards of badges under this order were promulgated in unit personnel occurrence reports, this order and the authority of the officer making the award being quoted.

Coloured Backing and Coloured Skill-at-Arms and Instructors' Badges

Before the 1939–45 war certain regiments adopted the practice of wearing skill-at-arms and/or instructors' badges in gilding metal mounted on to a coloured cloth backing; some regiments also wore coloured skill-at-arms and instructors' badges in place of the worsted pattern badges normally worn. Listed in Table 17 are those regiments that were known to have adopted this practice.

Table 17. Regiments wearing Coloured Skill-at-Arms and Instructors' Badges

Regiment	Badge adopted in lieu of gilding metal badge	Badge adopted in lieu of worsted badge
4th/7th Dragoon Guards	Gold lace	Gold lace
4th Queen's Own Hussars	Gold on red background	Gold on red background
The Queen's Royal Regiment (West Surrey)	Mounted on blue cloth	—
The Royal Northumberland Fusiliers	Drummer's badge backed with red and gosling green cloth; bandsman's and signal instructor's badge backed with gosling green cloth; signaller's badge backed with gosling green cloth	
The Cheshire Regiment	—	Backed with cerise cloth
The East Surrey Regiment	Badges mounted on red cloth	—
The Duke of Cornwall's Light Infantry	Bandsman's, bugler's and pioneer's badges mounted on green cloth	—
The Royal Berkshire Regiment (Princess Charlotte of Wales's)	Mounted on red background	—
The Queen's Own Royal West Kent Regiment	Mounted on dark blue cloth	Mounted on dark blue cloth
The Durham Light Infantry	Mounted on dark green cloth	Mounted on dark green cloth

7. SPECIAL DRESS DISTINCTIONS

Special distinctive badges worn on the military uniform can be divided into two groups.
1. Those items awarded to units for recognition of past military valour or in recognition of an event that had taken place in the history of a regiment.
2. Those badges introduced during the 1939–45 war worn to indicate the special nature of the work undertaken by the personnel of a particular unit or formation.

Both these categories of special distinctive badges are separate from and should not be confused with, in the case of the former (1), regimental or units flashes and badges (see page 97) or regimental designations (see page 103), or in the case of the latter (2), formation badges (page 98) or qualification badges (see page 59).

The Gloucestershire Regiment Back Badge

The Gloucestershire Regiment has the unique distinction of wearing two cap badges, one at the front and the other, much smaller in size, at the back of their head-dress. This honour – the Back Badge – was awarded to the 28th of Foot (North Gloucestershire Regiment) to commemorate its gallant back-to-back stand at the Battle of Alexandria on 21 March 1801. The 28th of Foot were being attacked along their front by a strong column of French Grenadiers when they suddenly came under attack from their rear by French cavalry. Even though they 'appeared as enveloped in a complete blaze' the order was quickly given for the rear rank of the 28th to turn about, there being no time to form a square, and each rank fought its own battle, beating off simultaneous French attacks from both front and rear. In memory of this exploit the 28th were given the 'back number', the metal number 28 worn at the back of their head-dress, which was, however, later replaced by a small sphinx cap badge.

Personnel of the Gloucestershire Regiment wore this back badge both before and throughout the Second World War. It was produced in brass for the rank and file, in bronzed metal for officers and in plastic for general use. Home Guard units affiliated to the Gloucestershire Regiment were authorized to wear the back badge, and it was even worn as a small silver transfer on the back of the steel helmets (see page 224).

The Royal Welch Fusiliers Black Ribbon 'Flash'

All personnel of the Royal Welch Fusiliers wore the special dress distinction of a black ribbon flash on the back of the collar of the Service Dress jacket, the Khaki Drill jacket and the Battle-Dress blouse.

The back flash is probably one of the best known of all British Army dress distinctions. Its origin dates from the year 1834. When the wearing of wigs in the British Army had been abolished the fashion was introduced of tying up the long hair at the back of the head in a tail and enclosing it in what was known as a 'queue bag', the purpose of which was to protect the collar of the coatee from the powdered and greased pigtail.

The Gloucestershire Regiment back badge.

The Royal Welch Fusiliers black ribbon 'flash'.

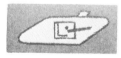

The Royal Tank Regiment arm badge.

The queue was secured by a bow of ribbons, and this custom continued in use until July 1808 when in its turn the queue was abolished and hair in the Army was cut short.

At this time the 23rd Regiment of Foot (Royal Welch Fusiliers) was stationed in Nova Scotia, where the queue continued to be worn for a number of years after it had been officially abolished. Even when the regiment ceased wearing hair in queues the officers continued to wear the queue ribbons, known by the slang term 'flash', attached to the back of their coat collars.

In November 1834, when the regiment arrived at Gosport from Gibraltar at the end of its overseas tour of duty, it was inspected by Major-General Sir Thomas McMahon. He noted this breach of Army regulations and ordered the queue ribbons to be done away with, their being a 'superfluous decoration'.

Colonel J. C. Harrison, Commanding Officer of the 23rd of Foot, lost no time in writing to the Colonel of the Regiment, Lieutenant-General Sir J. W. Gordon, who also happened to be the Quartermaster-General. He in turn represented the matter to Lord Hill, Commander-in-Chief, and within twenty-four hours the regiment had received a letter of reply from the Adjutant-General. It read as follows:

> Horse Guards,
> 28th November 1834
> Sir,
> By desire of the General Commanding-in-Chief, I have the honour to notify to you that, in consequence of your letter and Lord Hill's recommendation, the King has been graciously pleased to approve of the 'Flashes' now worn by the Officers of the Twenty-Third Foot, or Royal Welch Fusiliers, being henceforth worn and established as a peculiarity whereby to mark the dress of that distinguished regiment. I have Lord Hill's command to request that you will be pleased to cause this mark of His Majesty's gracious favour to be duly registered in the records of the Royal Welch Fusiliers.
>
> (Signed) John MacDonald,
> Adjutant-General

From November 1834 the flash was worn by officers, warrant officers and staff serjeants only, but on 2 June 1900, on the recommendation of Field-Marshal Lord Wolseley, the right to wear it was extended to all ranks of the regiment.

The flash consisted of five separate swallow-tailed black ribbons each 2¼in wide and approximately 9in in length, sewn together at one end (the end worn at the back of the neck) in such a fashion as to allow for the ribbons to splay out to a maximum width of approximately 6½in. The flash was attached to the collar by being either sewn into position or fastened with three small press-studs.

The Royal Tank Regiment Arm Badge

Personnel of the Royal Tank Corps and later the Royal Tank Regiment wore a special distinctive cloth badge on the right upper arm of the Service Dress and Khaki Drill jacket and, after 1939, the Battle-Dress blouse. The design of the badge was a representation of the First World War Mark I

Right: The RTR tank arm badge, shown here worn by a serjeant, probably from the 24th Army Tank Brigade.
Below: The Royal Welch Fusiliers' black ribbon 'back flash' displayed by members of the regiment as they parade for the Mayor of Belfast.

tank, known as 'Mother' and the first operational tank in use with the British Army. It was worked in white threads with black thread details on to a khaki drab background. A version worked in silver metallic threads was worn on the Full-Dress uniform.

The badge was originally worn on the right upper arm of the tunic at a depth from the shoulder seam of the thickness of four fingers. During the Second World War this was altered to a position on the right upper arm midway between the elbow and the point of the shoulder, below any formation sign where this may have been worn, except in the case of NCOs when the badge was worn positioned above the chevrons and below any formation sign. The tank faced towards the wearer's front.

The badge was originally bestowed on those officers and men who had successfully completed their training to take their place as a member of a tank crew. After the Great War the badge continued in use but was a general issue to all ranks of the Royal Tank Corps and, from April 1939, the Royal Tank Regiment.

The 1914–18 French Croix de Guerre Distinctions

Cap badge cockade worn by personnel of the 2nd Battalion The Devonshire Regiment.

To commemorate the exploits of the 2nd Battalion The Devonshire Regiment at Bois des Buttes, north of the River Aisne, on 27 May 1918, personnel of the battalion wore, prior to the outbreak of the Second World War, a cockade made from the ribbon of the 1914–18 Croix de Guerre positioned behind the cap badge on their Service Dress caps and worn each year on 27 May, the anniversary of the battalion's original gallant exploit.

During the 1939–45 war the 2nd Battalion The Devonshire Regiment, which saw service in Malta as part of the garrison under siege, Sicily, Italy, France (including D-Day) and Germany, wore a ½in deep shoulder flash of the 1914–18 Croix de Guerre ribbon on both shoulders, and for a short period they also wore a green and red lanyard.

Cockade and shoulder flash worn by personnel of the 4th Battalion The King's Shropshire Light Infantry.

In commemoration of the gallant exploits performed by the 1st/4th Battalion The King's Shropshire Light Infantry at La Montagne de Bligny on 6 June 1918, all personnel of the battalion were presented on 3 June 1922 by General Berthelot, the former commander of the 5th French Army, with cockades of 1914–18 Croix de Guerre ribbon to be worn on the left side of the Service Dress cap by all ranks.

On 1 August 1941, as an economy measure, the wearing of the cockade was restricted to the officers of the battalion and members of the band; all other battalion personnel wore, instead of the cockade, a ½in deep shoulder flash of 1914–18 Croix de Guerre ribbon (without the original bronzed palm emblem) at the shoulder point on both sleeves of the Battle-Dress blouse.

Special lanyard worn by personnel of the 6th Battalion The Black Watch.

In commemoration of their distinguished service in battles fought between 20 and 30 July 1918 about Chambrecy, the 6th Battalion The Black Watch received the 1914–18 Croix de Guerre avec Palme during the course of the victory celebrations held in Paris on 12 July 1919.

During the Second World War, personnel of the 6th Battalion The Black Watch wore a lanyard around the left shoulder in red and green, the colours of the Croix de Guerre ribbon, these lanyards being purchased under battalion arrangements.

Shoulder flash worn by personnel of the 7th (S) Battalion The South Wales Borderers.
The 7th (Service) Battalion of the South Wales Borderers received the Croix de Guerre avec Palme for its gallantry at Doiran, Salonika, on 18 September 1918.

When the battalion was re-formed in October 1940, permission was obtained from the War Office by the Commanding Officer, Lieutenant-Colonel E. M. G. Earle, for personnel of the battalion to wear the Croix de Guerre flash on the left arm of the uniform 2in below the shoulder seam. This privilege ceased in January 1942 when the battalion was converted to become the 90th Light Anti-Aircraft Regiment, Royal Artillery, and authority to wear the flash was withdrawn.

Cockade worn by personnel of the 8th Battalion The West Yorkshire Regiment (Leeds Rifles).

In commemoration of its exploits at Bois de Petit Champ and Bligny between 20 and 30 July 1918, the 8th Battalion The West Yorkshire Regiment (Leeds Rifles) was presented in 1918 by the President of the French Republic with the Croix de Guerre. A cockade made from the Croix de Guerre ribbon was worn on the left side of the Service Dress cap by all officers of the battalion on ceremonial occasions by gracious permission of His Majesty King George VI.

3rd French Division arm badge and special lanyard worn by personnel of the 9th Battalion The Royal Tank Regiment.

In commemoration of the Battle of Souvillers (otherwise known as the Battle of Moreuil) that took place on 23 July 1918, the 9th Battalion The Tank Corps was awarded the Croix de Guerre avec Palme, and as a token of the comradeship that had sprung up between the battalion and the French 3rd Infantry Division (La Grenadière) to whom they had been attached, the latter presented the battalion the honour of wearing on the left upper arm their own divisional emblem, a bursting grenade surrounded by a belt bearing the legend Qui s'y frotte s'y brule ('Whoever rubs me is burned'). This metal badge was worn by all ranks

Right: 1, 3rd French Division arm badge; 2, Polish 'Mermaid of Warsaw' arm badge. Personnel of certain British regiments that served alongside the Poles in Italy were awarded this distinction in recognition of comradeship in arms. 3, Arm badge for RASC waterborne personnel.

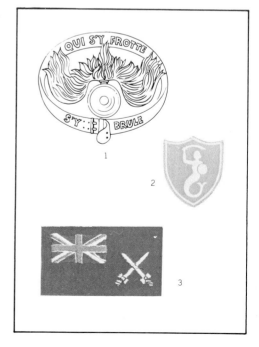

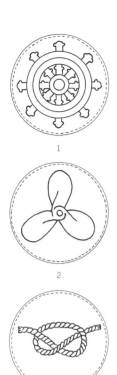

of the 9th Battalion The Tank Corps from July 1918 until its disbandment in 1919.

The traditions of the 9th Battalion were preserved by the 3rd Battalion the Royal Tank Corps, and on 27 November 1940 the 3rd Battalion provided the nucleus around which the new 9th Battalion The Royal Tank Regiment was reformed. Permission was once again granted for battalion personnel to wear the French 3rd Division metal arm badge, together with a lanyard in green and red, the colours of the French Croix de Guerre. The battalion was disbanded on 18 November 1945.

Shoulder flash and lanyard worn by the 128 (Wessex) Field Ambulance RAMC, TA.

This Territorial Army Field Ambulance unit was formed in 1920 as the direct successor of the First World War 24th Field Ambulance RAMC. During the Second World War this unit served with the Guards Armoured Division and its members were distinguished by wearing both the flash of the 1914–18 French Croix de Guerre ribbon on both upper arms of their Battle-Dress blouse and the red and green Croix de Guerre lanyard.

The Arm Badge for RASC Waterborne Personnel

A distinctive cloth arm badge in the design of the War Department Fleet ensign – a blue ensign with white crossed swords in the fly – was approved by ACI 230 dated 28 February 1945 for wear on the uniform of civilian personnel manning Royal Army Service Corps waterborne vessels.[1] The badge was worn at the top of each sleeve, immediately below the point of the shoulder, with the swords to the front. It was issued on the scale of one pair of badges for each Battle-Dress blouse or equivalent garment.

The Special Badge for Members of Bomb Disposal Units

At the end of 1940 it was decided to introduce a special badge for wear by personnel of bomb disposal units in order to indicate the dangerous nature of the work in which these men were employed. ACI 1562 dated 21 December 1940 introduced a cloth badge showing a representation of a bomb embroidered in gold-yellow threads with royal blue detailing on a bright red background, the whole being 3in deep by 2in wide.

These badges were worn only by men who were actually on the strength of bomb disposal units, but in November 1942 this stipulation was extended to drivers of No. 1 Land Incident Company RASC while actually employed with that company (ACI 2407 dated 11 November 1942). The badge was withdrawn from bomb disposal unit personnel on the expiration of their tour of duty.

Issue to other ranks was made on the scale of one badge for each Battle-Dress blouse or Service jacket, and for each Khaki Drill jacket. They were not worn on Tropical shirts, greatcoats or working clothing.

The badges were worn on the left forearm, 6½in from the bottom of the sleeve or immediately above any good conduct badges if these were present. Badges required by officers on the strength of bomb disposal units were obtained on payment as laid down under *Regulations for*

[1]It was announced in ACI 863 dated 21 July 1945 that the vessels known as the War Department Fleet and the vessels operated by the RASC had been incorporated under one administrative control; consequently, it had been decided that the title 'War Department Fleet' should be discontinued, and that in future all vessels operated by the RASC, including the War Department Fleet, should come under the general designation 'RASC Fleet'.

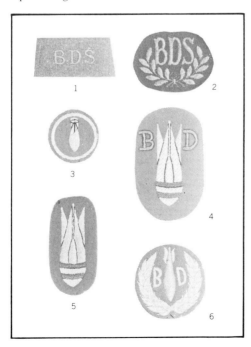

Right: The Airborne Strip, worn here by two members of the Rough Riders and one of the Anti-Tank Artillery; 1942.

The 'Airborne' strip.

Corps of Military Police distinctive arm badges. 1, Traffic control personnel; 2, Vulnerability points personnel.

the Clothing of the Army, 1936, para. 331 (see page 120).

Distinctive Arm Badges for the Corps of Military Police

Traffic Control personnel.

In addition to the white band painted around their steel helmets (see page 224) and the white traffic sleeves (see page 83), Traffic Control personnel of the CMP were further distinguished by wearing a 1½in square cloth badge just below the shoulder seam, and after June 1943 below the corps designation and above the arm-of-service strip. Positioned on its point, the blue cloth badge bore the red printed letters TC. It was worn on each sleeve of the Service Dress jacket, the Battle-Dress blouse, the Khaki Drill jacket and the greatcoat.

CMP(TC) personnel were organized into armed companies each responsible for a specific area. Although they belonged to the Corps of Military Police they carried out all instructions issued by Movement Control.

Vulnerability Points personnel.

Personnel of the CMP(VP) wore a special distinctive arm badge at the top of each sleeve of their Service Dress jacket, Battle-Dress blouse and greatcoat. The badge consisted of a 1½in square of blue linen on which were printed the red letters VP. It was worn just below the shoulder seam standing on its point.

The 'Blue Caps' (VPs), whose task it was to guard vulnerable points, worked in sections consisting of seven privates commanded by a lance-corporal working on a shift of an eight-hour tour of duty. They were armed with sub-machine guns and truncheons and used guard dogs for their night work. Their primary duty was anti-sabotage, and they were entrusted with the task of guarding installations and buildings regarded as vulnerable, such as ammunition and petrol dumps, docks, locks, bridges, power stations and even the BBC (see also page 224).

The 'Airborne' Strip

This was a narrow rectangular strip of maroon coloured cloth with the word 'Airborne' either embroidered or printed in pale blue. It was a wartime issue worn by operational airborne troops who were not parachutists in order to distinguish them from rear echelon personnel. The strips were worn on each upper arm of the Battle-Dress blouse, below the formation sign. Unlike the badge for glider trained infantry, there was official War Office authorization for the introduction of this strip; ACI 2816 dated 31 October 1942.

Right: Experimental backing colours for officers' rank insignia, BEF, 1939. 1, Plain worsted rank badges on Battle-Dress strap; 2, Worsted rank badge mounted on cloth backing the colour of the arm-of-service; 3, Worsted rank badges mounted on strips of arm-of-service coloured cloth; 4, 5, Variations on 3. These were worn in conjunction with a square patch of (prototype) arm-of-service coloured cloth (eg, scarlet for infantry, dark blue for RAOC) at the point of both shoulders.

At the 36th meeting of the CIGS War Committee on 6 November 1939 it was agreed 'that the D.S.D.(W) in consultation with D.P.S. and D.O.S. should make recommendations as to alterations to existing regulations for officers rank badges and other distinctive markings for all ranks in Battle-Dress to meet the request of the C-in-C, B.E.F.'

A letter dated 16 December 1939 from G. W. Lambert at the War Office to General Officer C-in-C, BEF, read thus:

'The Deputy Chief of the General Staff whilst at the War Office was able to inspect certain experimental flashes etc, for wear in Battle-Dress as follows:
a) Distinguishing marks to shew the arm-of-service to be worn at the top of the sleeve by both officers or O.R's eg:
Infantry = Scarlet
R.A. = Red and Blue
etc., according to the arm-of-service
b) A coloured backing to the badges of rank to be worn by officers only, in order to enable them to be more easily distinguished from other ranks than is at present the case with the regulation plain worsted rank badges.
'The patterns seen by the D.C.G.S. were considered to be too colourful and likely to make the officers too conspicuous and it was arranged that other samples should be produced and sent over to General Head-quarters for inspection.
'Six blouses, as detailed on page 4a, were dispatched to the B.E.F. Director of Ordnance Services on the 14th December 1939 with a request that a report be rendered to this office concerning the flashes and rank badges fitted to them, indicating whether any of the experimental patterns, and if so, which are considered to be suitable for the purpose in view and are recom-mended for adoption. In the case of the flashes it would be of assistance to know the colour suggested for each arm-of-service.
'Suggestions were required as to the best method of arranging for the conversion in France. If materials are sent out can arrangements be made to have the neces-sary cutting up and sewing done locally. It is thought that there might be considerable difficulty in providing the necessary number of badges complete with coloured material.'

A full reply from GOC-in-C, BEF, to all questions regarding coloured flashes and rank insignia backing was sent to the Under-Secretary of State at the War Office on 21 January 1940 under the code reference *A/16/5 (P.S.) Subject Dress*. It was signed by Lieutenant-General W. D. S. Brownrigg, A.G.
'1. With ref. to your letter 54/Gen/8778 (O.S.7.), dated 16 December 1939 I attach as an appendix to this letter the colours suggested for the various arms-of-service.
'2. I recommend that:
a) In Battle-Dress strips of the colours should be inserted at the top of the arm just below the shoulder strap and that greatcoats should be similarly marked (except in the case of the Brigade of Guards).
b) Similar colours be used as backing to the badges of rank to be worn by officers and the pattern selected is that in which coloured cloth is placed separately below each rank (Sample stamped with A.G. Branch G.H.Q. stamp).
c) Badges of rank should be worsted and not metal except in the case of the Brigade of Guards who specially ask permission to wear metal badges without any coloured material beneath.
d) In addition to the above strips which denote the various arms of service, corps or regimental flashes to be worn 4-inches below the point of the shoulder by such as desire to do so. These will be provided under unit arrangements and will not be a charge against govern-ment funds. Such flashes would usually be in corps or regimental colours and would be similar to those worn on the helmet in tropical countries.
'3. I recommend as an exception to para. 2 that the Brigade of Guards should wear no shoulder strip but would wear the regimental designation instead.
'4. I recommend that units who now have a right to wear distinctive emblems as a result of previous distin-guished service should be allowed to retain this right in Battle-Dress.
'5. The badges of rank for O.R's would be worn in Battle-Dress in the same manner as in Service Dress.
'6. If materials of the appropriate colours are sent to units in this country (France), it will be possible to arrange locally for cutting up and sewing.'

The list of colours sent by the GOC-in-C, BEF, to the War Office differed considerably from the

Right: The CO of 6th Armoured Division taking the salute at the drive past of the entire division on 12 September 1941. The white mailed fist set on a black square background was the formation badge of this division.

colours recommended by the War Committee to the Army Council, but the War Committee's recommendations in this respect were not sent to the C-in-C. An Army Council memorandum by CIGS (Secret OS 35) stated that the War Committee had considered these proposals and recommended that the Army Council agree with them. Charles Montanaro, ADOS, stated in a letter dated 21 August 1940, that:

'1. Non-Combatant Corps will not wear the coloured strips which mark the arm-of-service. No provision for them is necessary.

2. Rifle regiments will wear rifle-green instead or scarlet as for all other Infantry.

3. Infantry, including Rifles, when brigaded in divisions will wear their scarlet or rifle-green strips as follows:

Personnel of Senior Brigade = One on each arm
Personnel of Next Senior Brigade = Two on each arm
Personnel of Junior Brigade = Three on each arm

'(This will not apply to Foot Guards)'

Table 19. Original Colours suggested for First Arm-of-Service Strips

Corps etc.	Colour(s)	Remarks
RAC	Yellow and red	Halves divided horizontally, yellow on top
RA	Red and blue	Halves divided vertically, red in front
RE	Blue and red	Halves divided horizontally, red on top
RCS (R Signals)	Blue and white	Halves divided horizontally, white on top
Foot Guards	Nil	Regimental sign in scarlet[1]
Infantry	Scarlet	
RASC	Yellow and blue	Halves divided vertically, yellow in front
RAMC	Dark cherry	
RAOC	Dark blue	
RAPC	Yellow	
AEC	White[2]	
ADC	Green	
AMPC	Light blue[3]	
CMP[4]	Red[4]	

[1] 'Regimental sign' refers to regimental designation.
[2] 'White' crossed out in pencil on list, and 'Light blue' substituted.
[3] 'Light blue' crossed out in pencil, and 'Red and green' substituted.
[4] 'Corps of Military Police' and 'Red' added to original list in pencil.

Distinguishing Marks Worn on the Uniform, September 1940–December 1941

Thus it was that the whole progression of coloured signs, cloth badges, emblems and flashes first began, albeit in a limited way, to appear on the British Army Battle-Dress. By the time the war ended in September 1945 the complex system that evolved had undergone quite a number of changes, with regulations being enforced at periodic intervals in an effort to control and direct the whole colourful system. I have included here all the important instructions issued by the War Office governing the introduction and use of these signs in order to show the development of this subject.

Based on the recommendations produced from the correspondence and discussions held between General Gort and the War Office, ACI 1118, published on 18 September 1940 and entitled 'Dress – All Ranks', set out the first of a number of important instructions issued during the war that related to the subject of distinguishing marks etc. to be worn on the Army uniform (which in the main was the Battle-Dress). By its publication ACI 1118 of 1940 cancelled out ACI 419 of 1940, and over a period of time from December 1940 to September 1941 various minor changes and additions were made to ACI 1118 and eventually it was finalized as follows. Certain distinguishing marks had been approved for wear on the uniform during the period of the war, and these consisted of:

1. Command headquarters, corps, divisional, independent brigade group and independent brigade signs.

2. Arm-of-service distinguishing marks, including coloured backing to officers' rank badges.
3. Distinguishing marks for brigaded infantry in divisions, later to be referred to as 'brigade seniority strips'.
4. Regimental flashes.
5. Emblems that denoted previous distinguished service.
6. Badges on steel helmets.
These can now be discussed in more detail.

Command headquarters, corps, divisional, independent brigade group and independent brigade signs.

These signs were to be worn by officers and other ranks of all command headquarters, corps, divisional and independent brigade units at the top of both sleeves of the jacket or Battle-Dress blouse (for Household Cavalry and Foot Guards see below). The patterns of these signs were decided

Right: Formation signs. 1, Eastern Command (UK); 2, No. 2 Commando; 3, 10th Anti-Aircraft Division; 4, XXX Corps; 5, 6th Armoured Division; 6, Orkney and Shetland Defences; 7, IV Corps and 54th Medium Regiment, RA; 8, 59th (Staffordshire) Division; 9, VIII Corps (2nd pattern); 10, 78th Division; 11, 7th Armoured Division (1st pattern); 12, 46th (North Midlands and West Riding) Division; 13, 43rd (Wessex) Division; 14, South-Eastern Command (UK); 15, East Kent District (South-Eastern Command); 16, 4th Division; 17, Guards Armoured Division; 18, 6th Anti-Aircraft Division.

Left: A water-cooled Vickers machine gun being operated by its two-man crew from the 9th Bn the Royal Northumberland Fusiliers, part of the 18th Division; Trawsfuydd, 10 September 1941.
Below, far left: A clear example of a regimental flash, worn by Sjt. A. Parish, MM; November 1941.
Below left: A lieutenant-colonel of the 6th Bn the Northamptonshire Regiment, part of the 223rd Independant Infantry Brigade, 11th Corps wearing three red cloth strips below the formation badge, which identifies the 223rd as being the junior brigade within the division; 6 January 1942.

by the general officers commanding concerned and they in turn reported to the War Office their approved designs for the purpose of the records. Metal signs were not used in view of the necessity for conserving supplies.

Signs were provided under command headquarters, corps, divisional or independent brigade group arrangements, for which purpose a charge against the public, which did not exceed 1½d. for each individual concerned, was allowed. Any difficulties encountered in obtaining delivery of these signs were overcome by the Director General of Equipment and Stores at the Ministry of Supply putting formations in direct touch with manufacturers.

Arm-of-service distinguishing marks.

In order to enable officers when wearing Battle-Dress to be more readily distinguished from other ranks and in order to give a clearer indication of the various arms of the services, it was decided to adopt the following procedure for units other than the Household Cavalry and Foot Guards.
1. Officers were to wear a coloured backing to the worsted badges of rank worn on the shoulder straps of their Battle-Dress blouse. This coloured backing was not permitted to be worn with the metal rank badges worn on the greatcoat.
2. All ranks were to wear a strip of coloured material 2in by ¼in on each sleeve of the Battle-Dress blouse immediately below any corps or divisional etc. sign worn; similar strips were also to be worn on each sleeve of the greatcoat by personnel who wore Battle-Dress. The strip of material was to be worn horizontally on each sleeve of the garment concerned, and in the case of troops authorized to wear a corps or divisional

sign, the strip was worn immediately below the sign, troops not wearing corps or divisional signs having their strip at the top of the sleeve. In cases where a two-coloured strip was authorized to be worn (see listing on page 98), the complete strip was 2in long, half in each colour.
3. Warrant officers, NCOs and men were to wear on the shoulder straps of the Battle-Dress blouse the authorized worsted titles (see photograph of selected examples on page 82), except as otherwise ordered by the local military authority during active operations.
4. Officers of the Household Cavalry and Foot Guards wore metal rank badges of the authorized pattern on the Battle-Dress blouse without coloured backing; all ranks wore the authorized regimental designation in worsted at the top of each sleeve of the blouse, above their corps or divisional signs.

Distinguishing marks of brigaded infantry in divisions (except Brigade of Guards).

The number of strips to be worn on each arm by personnel of infantry battalions in divisions was determined by the brigade seniority, i.e. one strip on each arm by the senior brigade, two by the next senior and three strips to each arm by the junior brigade.

Regimental flashes.

Units which desired to do so were permitted to wear a flash in regimental colours on the sleeve. They were provided at regimental expense and no charge against the public was allowed to be incurred in connection with them. Regimental flashes when worn were situated immediately below the coloured arm-of-service strips.

Right: Examples of regimental and battalion arm flashes. 1, Fife and Forfar Yeomanry, red band over yellow band on dark blue; 2, 1st Battalion The Queen's Royal Regiment (West Surrey), dark blue (worn at the point of the shoulder before the introduction of regimental designations); 3, East Riding Yeomanry, maroon/blue-grey/maroon; 4, The Wiltshire Regiment, maroon; 5, 13th/18th Royal Hussars, White left, dark blue right (worn on the right arm below the shoulder designation); 6, The Sherwood Foresters, green (worn between the shoulder blades on the back of the Battle-Dress blouse; 7, The Devonshire Regiment, green over red; 8, 148th Regiment, RAC (formerly a battalion of The Loyal Regiment [North Lancs]), red/French grey/red edged in black; 9, The Royal Gloucestershire Hussars, red band separating upper yellow segment and lower dark blue; 10, The Somerset Light Infantry, yellow on dark green; 11, 4th Queen's Own Hussars, blue/buff/blue.

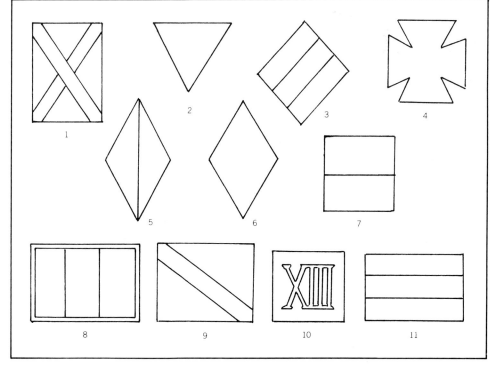

Emblems denoting previous distinguished service.

Units which had been authorized to wear distinctive emblems as a result of previous, pre-1939 distinguished service were permitted to exercise this right during the Second World War. Except where provision at the public expense had already been authorized under the then existing regulations, no charge against the public was permitted in connection with their provision. See also page 76.

Badges on steel helmets.

Regimental badges or flashes were permitted to be stencilled on to steel helmets at the expense of those units concerned.

Table 20. *Distinguishing Marks introduced by ACI 1118 dated 18 September 1940 for Wear on Battle-Dress (except by the Household Cavalry and the Brigade of Guards), with Dated Amendments*

Arm of Service	Colour of backing to officers' rank badges	Coloured strip to be worn below shoulder strap[1]
Staff[2]	Red	Red
RAC	Yellow	Yellow and red
RA	Red	Red and blue
RE	Blue	Blue and red
R Signals	Blue	Blue and white
Infantry (except rifles)	Scarlet	Scarlet
Infantry (rifles)	Rifle green	Rifle green
Reconnaissance Corps[3]	Green[3]	Green and yellow[3]
RAChD[4]	Black[4]	Black[4]
RASC	Yellow	Yellow and blue
RAMC	Dull cherry	Dull cherry
RAOC	Dark blue	Dark blue
CMP	Red	Red (with Military Police armlet)
RAPC	Yellow	Yellow
AEC	Cambridge blue	Cambridge blue
AD Corps	Green	Green and white
AMPC	Red	Red and green
Intelligence Corps	Green	Green
APTC[5]	Black[5]	Black, red, black[5]
General List	Scarlet	Scarlet

[1]Where two or more colours are shown, the first colour was worn to the fore.
[2]The 'Staff' referred only to colonels and above who did not normally wear the uniform of a particular regiment or corps, and also to those officers of the Extra-Regimentally Employed List.
[3]Introduced by ACI 420 of 1941.
[4]The Royal Army Chaplains' Department changed its coloured insignia from black to purple by authority of ACI 125 dated 25 January 1941; at the same time instructions were issued for a similar coloured backing to their rank badges to be worn by members of the RAChD on the Tropical shirt overseas. Chaplains had to make their own arrangements at their own expense for providing purple backing to their badges of rank and purple strips to wear on their Battle-Dress blouse and greatcoat. The shade of purple that was used was the same as that used on the RAChD mess dress.
[5]Introduced by ACI 660 of 1941. The coloured strips actually became available on 3 September 1941.

The provision of distinguishing marks.

The arrangements arrived at for the supply of the coloured arm-of-service strips was as follows. Officers who were already in possession of Battle-Dress at the date this ACI was published (18 September 1940) were allowed to have one Battle-Dress blouse and one greatcoat fitted with the necessary coloured backing to their rank badges, strips or worsted designations as authorized at public expense (which included both material and labour); officers who obtained their Battle-Dress after September 1940 had to provide any necessary distinguishing marks at their own expense. A different system applied for other ranks; the expense of supplying and fitting the necessary distinguishing marks to their Battle-Dress was met from public funds.

Distinguishing Marks worn on the Uniform, December 1941–June 1943

The next set of instructions, published as ACI No. 2587 of 1941, regarding the wearing of signs, distinguishing strips, flashes, etc. was dated 27 December 1941. This naturally cancelled out the previous ACI 1118 of 1940, together with all its additions and amendments introduced on 26 July 1941 (ACI 1329 of 1941). It set out the following approved formation badges[1], arm-of-service strips[2], rank badge backing and regimental flashes for wear on uniform during the period of the war. Similar distinguishing marks were also introduced to be worn by personnel of the Auxiliary Territorial Service.

Formation badges.

These badges were to be worn by all ranks of command headquarters, corps, divisions, independent brigade groups, independent brigades, and any other units for which War Office approval had been given. Regiments of the Royal Artillery which were unlikely to remain in a particular formation for any length of time did not, however, wear the formation badge.

The badge was worn at the top of both sleeves of the Service Dress jacket and Battle-Dress blouse; it was not worn on the greatcoat, Khaki Drill jacket or Tropical shirt. The design of these badges was decided upon by the formation commander concerned. This allowed for a whole variety of emblems, shapes and colours to be used, some of which were based on the signs previously used by units during the Great War, whilst others were a pun upon the commanding officer's name. The variety of these signs can best be seen by referring to pages 95 and 100.

Two specimens of each badge were forwarded to the War Office, Department AG 4(c), for record purposes. Once a design had been submitted to the War Office no alteration to the badge was permitted without the authority of the Adjutant-General's department. In April 1942 instructions were issued (ACI 852 of 1942) that only printed

[1]Described in ACI 1118 of 1940 as 'Divisional Signs'.
[2]Described in ACI 1118 of 1940 as 'Arms of the Service – Distinguishing Marks'.

(Ordnance issue) badges were to be purchased; metal and embroidered badges were not to be used, in an effort to conserve supplies.

Personnel who transferred from one formation to another had to hand in their formation badges before leaving the old formation, and fresh badges were issued out from the pool of badges held by the new formation.

When garments were replaced, serviceable formation badges had to be transferred from the old to the new garments.

Arm-of-service strips and regimental designations (regiments and corps other than the Household Cavalry and Foot Guards).

In order that a clear indication of a person's arm-of-service was possible, all ranks had to wear a strip of coloured material. The listing of these strips was, with just a few exceptions (which are reproduced on page 102), identical to the previous listing published under ACI 1118 of 1940 and shown on page 98. These strips were worn on each sleeve of the Battle-Dress blouse immediately below any formation badge worn. Those troops who at that time did not wear formation badges wore their arm-of-service strips 3½in from the top of the sleeve of the blouse in order to allow for the possible wearing of any future formation badges. No adjustment to strips already in wear were allowed to be made in those cases where an alternative position had been adopted. Arm-of-service strips continued to be worn at the top of each sleeve of the greatcoat by personnel who wore Battle-Dress; however, these strips were not to be worn on Service Dress or Khaki Drill jackets or Tropical shirts, nor on the greatcoats of personnel not supplied with Battle-Dress.

The size of these strips continued to be the same − 2in long by ¼in deep − and they were still worn horizontally. However, with the introduction of strips of three colours the different coloured sections were equally spaced over the 2in length in the order as set out in the listing, the first named colour being worn to the front.

Infantry brigaded in divisions continued to wear the system of one, two or three strips indicating brigade seniority.

Warrant officers, NCOs and men of the Royal Armoured Corps, the Infantry of the Line, and the Corps of Military Police (Provost Wing) wore the authorized shoulder titles on the shoulder straps of their Battle-Dress blouse, Service Dress or Khaki Drill jacket or Tropical shirt, except as otherwise ordered by the local military authority for security reasons during active operations. These slip-on titles were not worn on the greatcoat. Shoulder titles were not permitted to be worn on the shoulder straps by personnel of any other regiment or corps except on the Tropical uniform. The regimental designations that until this time

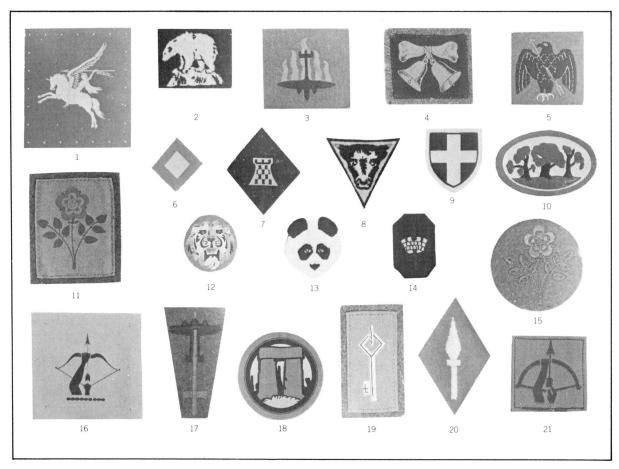

Right: The formation sign (large size), worn by personnel of the South-Eastern Command (UK); 5 July 1941.

Far right: Tp. Sjt. J. Hoppe, 64th Medium Regiment, RA, 2nd Army, of Ferryhill, County Durham. The Pegasus sign worn on the right forearm was a special distinction presented to the men of this artillery regiment by Maj.-Gen. R. L. Urquhart as a mark of gratitude from the commander and troops of the 1st Airborne Division for the gunners' vital cooperation and invaluable support at the time of the 1st Airborne's breakout from the Arnhem pocket.

Right: An example of an early divisional sign as worn by men of the 7th Bn the Argyll and Sutherland Highlanders from the 51st Highland Division at Milleboche, 7 June 1940. Signs such as these were not permitted to be worn in Battle-Dress prior to September 1940 although a number of units with the BEF in France and Flanders in 1939–40 adopted these signs, which had been used by their predecessors during the First World War.

Left: Formation signs. 1, Airborne divisions; 2, 49th (West Riding) Division (1st pattern); 3, 5th Anti-Aircraft Division; 4, 47th (London) Division; 5, 11th Anti-Aircraft Division; 6, 42nd (East Lancs) Division; 7, XI Corps; 8, 79th Armoured Division; 9, 38th (Welsh) Division; 10, XII Corps; 11, 55th (West Lancs) Division; 12, South-Eastern Command (UK); 13, 9th Armoured Division; 14, London District; 15, 55th (West Lancs) Division; 16, Anti-Aircraft Command (2nd pattern); 17, 1st Anti-Aircraft Division (1st pattern); 18, Salisbury Plain District (Southern Command); 19, Gibraltar Garrison; 20, I Corps; 21, Anti-Aircraft Command (1st pattern).

Above: An example of an incorrectly mounted badge, featuring the 5th (London) Division 'black cat' together with three Royal Engineers blue-and-red arm-of-service strips positioned as if for brigade seniority strips.

Above: An example of a divisional sign (5th Division) sewn onto a patch of khaki cloth together with three brigade seniority bars (scarlet) and arm-of-service strip (rifle green). This method of positioning insignia was adopted by regimental tailors to save time and effort.

Right: The shoulder designation 'Royal Corps of Signals' worn by members of the Air Landing Brigade (Signals Group); Bulford, 24 November 1942.

had been provided regimentally were not to be worn by personnel of any regiment or corps.

Arm-of-service strips and regimental designations for the Household Cavalry and Foot Guards.

The arm-of-service strip was not worn by personnel of the Household Cavalry or the Foot Guards, but all ranks did wear the authorized regimental designation in worsted at the top of each sleeve of the Service Dress jacket and Battle-Dress blouse above the formation badge. In February 1942 (ACI 263 of 1942) this authorization was altered so that these regimental designations were worn only on the Battle-Dress blouse by all ranks and in the case of other ranks only on the Service Dress jacket. These designations were not worn on the greatcoat.

Rank badge backings.

Officers, other than Household Cavalry and Foot Guards officers, continued to wear coloured backing to their worsted badges of rank on the shoulder straps of their Battle-Dress blouses. With one exception and one addition, these colours were the same as those shown in the previous listing on page 98. Coloured backing was still forbidden to be used on the rank badges worn on the greatcoat, but this prohibition was now extended to the officer's Service Dress jacket. Officers of the Household Cavalry and Foot Guards continued to wear metal rank badges on the Battle-Dress blouse without coloured backing.

Regimental flashes.

The wearing of a flash in regimental colours on the sleeve of the Service Dress jacket and Battle-Dress blouse immediately below the arm-of-service strip was extended to include individual regiments of the Royal Artillery. They still had to be provided at regimental expense.

Dress distinctions previously granted.

Units which had been authorized to wear distinctions in dress in recognition of distinguished services, or for some other reason, were permitted to exercise their right both in Service Dress and Battle-Dress.

Table 21. Coloured Rank Badge Backings and Arm-of-Service Strips as introduced by ACI 2587 dated 27 December 1941 which differed from ACI 1118 of 1940

Arm-of-service	Colour of backing to officers' rank badges	Coloured strip to be worn on each sleeve
Staff[1]	Red	Red
Recce Corps[2]	Green	Green and yellow
RAOC[3]	Red[3]	Red, blue, red[3]
Pioneer Corps[4]	Red	Red and green
ACC[5]	Grey[5]	Grey and yellow[5]

[1]The term 'Staff' was extended to include officers of the rank of Colonel and above of corps granted combatant status (ACI 2453 of 1942).
[2]The Reconnaissance Corps, now referred to as the 'Recce Corps', a convenient abbreviation and the official form.
[3]The previous RAOC rank badge backing colour of dark blue and arm-of-service strip colour of dark blue were changed to red and red, blue, red respectively on 3 February 1943 by ACI 193 of 1943. RAOC officers of the rank of Colonel and above continued to wear distinguishing marks in red (as originally authorized by ACI 2453 of 1942); they had previously worn dark blue (18 September 1940–26 December 1941), red (27 December 1941–19 May 1942 and dark blue (from 20 May 1942 (ACI 1074 of 1942) to 2 February 1943).
[4]Previously shown as AMPC (Auxiliary Military Pioneer Corps), the title of this unit was changed to Pioneer Corps.
[5]The Army Catering Corps (ACC) distinguishing marks were first introduced on 25 June 1941 by ACI 1054 of 1941.

Distinguishing Marks worn on the Uniform from June 1943

By far and away the most comprehensive and important set of instructions regarding distinguishing marks to be worn at home was published under ACI 905 dated 12 June 1943. These instructions drew together all the innovations that had previously been introduced and at the same time set the pattern of coloured insignia of all types that continued to be worn right up to the end of hostilities and in most instances beyond into the 1950s.

Under the heading of 'Dress – Distinguishing Marks to be worn at Home', the following regimental designations, formation badges, arm-of-service strips, regimental flashes, rank badge backings and slip-on shoulder titles were approved for wear on uniform at home during the (remaining) period of the war. No distinguishing marks other than those as given in this ACI and which are listed below or those authorized by Army Regulations were permitted to be worn.

The instructions regarding the removal of distinguishing marks in preparation for embarkation and the wearing of such marks overseas are set out on page 111.

Regimental designations.

In order to indicate the regiment or corps to which personnel belonged and at the same time to foster 'esprit de corps', all ranks below that of Colonel serving at home (except personnel of the

Right: Regimental designations. (See Tables 22, 23 and 24.)

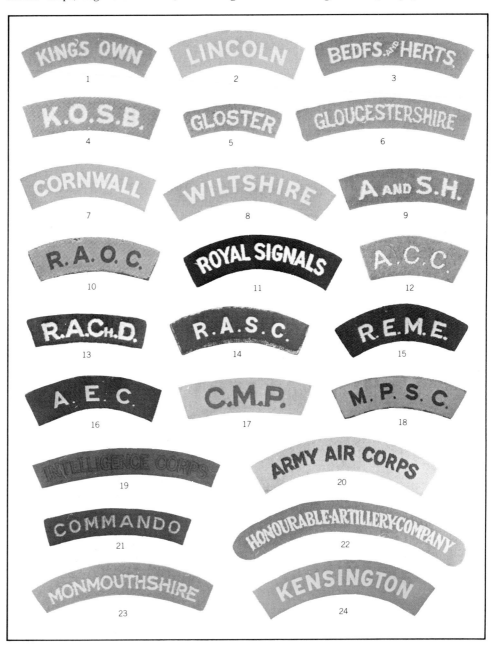

Regiment or corps[1]	Text of regimental designation	Regiment or corps[1]	Text of regimental designation
Royal Armoured Corps	Royal Armoured Corps	The Gloucestershire Regiment	Gloster[5]
Royal Artillery	Royal Artillery	The Worcestershire Regiment	Worcestershire
Royal Engineers	Royal Engineers	The East Lancashire Regiment	East Lancashire
Royal Corps of Signals	Royal Corps of Signals[2]	The East Surrey Regiment	East Surrey
The Royal Scots	Royal Scots[3]	The Duke of Cornwall's Light Infantry	Cornwall[6]
The Queen's Royal Regiment	Queen's	The Duke of Wellington's Regiment	Duke of Wellington's
The Buffs	Buffs	The Border Regiment	Border
The King's Own Royal Regiment	King's Own	The Royal Sussex Regiment	Royal Sussex
The Royal Northumberland Fusiliers	R. Northumberland Fus.	The Hampshire Regiment	Hampshire
The Royal Warwickshire Regiment	Royal Warwickshire	The South Staffordshire Regiment	South Stafford
The Royal Fusiliers	Royal Fusiliers	The Dorsetshire Regiment	Dorset
The King's Regiment	The King's Regiment	The South Lancashire Regiment	South Lancashire
The Royal Norfolk Regiment	Royal Norfolk	The Welch Regiment	Welch Regiment
The Lincolnshire Regiment	Lincoln	The Black Watch	Tartan patch
The Devonshire Regiment	Devon	The Oxfordshire and Buckinghamshire Light Infantry	Oxf. & Bucks.
The Suffolk Regiment	Suffolk		
The Somerset Light Infantry	Somerset L.I.	The Essex Regiment	Essex
The West Yorkshire Regiment	West Yorkshire	The Sherwood Foresters	Foresters
The East Yorkshire Regiment	East Yorkshire	The Loyal Regiment	Loyals
The Bedfordshire and Hertfordshire Regiment	Bedfs. and Herts.	The Northamptonshire Regiment	Northamptonshire
		The Royal Berkshire Regiment	Royal Berkshire
The Leicestershire Regiment	Leicestershire	The Queen's Own Royal West Kent Regiment	Royal West Kent
The Green Howards	Green Howards		
The Lancashire Fusiliers	Lancashire Fusiliers	The King's Own Yorkshire Light Infantry	K.O.Y.L.I.
The Royal Scots Fusiliers	Royal Scots Fusiliers[3]		
The Cheshire Regiment	Cheshire	The King's Shropshire Light Infantry	K.S.L.I.
The Royal Welch Fusiliers	Royal Welch Fusiliers	The Middlesex Regiment	Middlesex
The South Wales Borderers	S.W.B.[4]	The King's Royal Rifle Corps	K.R.R.C.
The King's Own Scottish Borderers	K.O.S.B.[3]	The Wiltshire Regiment	Wiltshire
The Cameronians	Cameronians[3]	The Manchester Regiment	Manchester
The Royal Inniskilling Fusiliers	Inniskillings	The North Staffordshire Regiment	North Stafford

[1]For details regarding the text of the regimental designations worn by personnel of the Household Cavalry (The Life Guards and Royal Horse Guards), the Foot Guards (Grenadier Guards, Coldstream Guards, Scots Guards, Irish Guards and Welsh Guards) and the Army Physical Training Corps, see notes to listing of 'Colour of Background and Lettering of Regimental Designations'.
[2]ACI 1207 dated 9 September 1944 changed the wording Royal Corps of Signals to read Royal Signals.
[3]These Scottish Infantry Regiments elected to wear tartan flashes in place of the regimental designation already produced for them. This was announced by ACI 1593 of 1943 dated 30 October 1943. For details and a description of individual tartan patterns see page 109.
[4]The text of the regimental designation S.W.B. was changed to South Wales Borderers by ACI 1593 dated 30 October 1943.
[5]The text of the regimental designation Gloster was changed to Gloucestershire by ACI 1593 dated 30 October 1943.
[6]The text of the regimental designation Cornwall was changed to D.C.L.I. by ACI 1207 dated 9 September 1944.

Right: Troops of the 1st Company, Oxf. and Bucks. Light Infantry, 53rd Division, at Heike, The Netherlands; 23 October 1944.
Far right: Reconnaissance Corps assault troops locating mines during manoeuvres; February 1944. On their RAC steel helmets the men carry basket-markers. These are placed over detected mines which are then defused by the following troops.
Top right: A private from the Royal Ulster Rifles, a member of an Air Landing Battalion in full battle order complete with .303in rifle.

Regiment or corps[1]	Text of regimental designation
The York and Lancaster Regiment	York and Lancaster
The Durham Light Infantry	Durham L.I.
The Highland Light Infantry	Tartan patch
The Seaforth Highlanders	Tartan patch
The Gordon Highlanders	Tartan patch
The Queen's Own Cameron Highlanders	Tartan patch
The Royal Ulster Rifles	Royal Ulster Rifles
The Royal Irish Fusiliers	Royal Irish Fusiliers
The Argyll and Sutherland Highlanders	A. and S.H.[7]
The Rifle Brigade	Rifle Brigade
Reconnaissance Corps	Reconnaissance
Army Air Corps[8]	Army Air Corps
Glider Pilot Regiment	Glider Pilot Regt.
Parachute Regiment	Parachute Regiment
Royal Army Chaplains' Department	R.A.Ch.D.
Royal Army Service Corps	R.A.S.C.
Royal Army Medical Corps	R.A.M.C.
Royal Army Ordnance Corps	R.A.O.C.
Royal Electrical and Mechanical Engineers	R.E.M.E.
Royal Army Pay Corps	R.A.P.C.[9]
Royal Army Veterinary Corps	R.A.V.C.
Army Education Corps	A.E.C.
The Army Dental Corps	A.D. Corps
The Corps of Military Police	C.M.P.
Military Provost Staff Corps	M.P.S.C.
Pioneer Corps	Pioneer Corps
Intelligence Corps	Intelligence Corps
Army Catering Corps	A.C.C.
Small Arms Schools Corps	S.A.S.C.
Commandos	Commando

[7]The regimental designation A.&S.H. was exchanged for a diced flash as announced by ACI 1898 dated 25 December 1943. Stocks of the existing regimental designations were first to be used up before the red and white diced flashes were taken into use. For a description of this flash see page 109.

[8]Except personnel of the Glider Pilot Regiment and the Parachute Regiment.

[9]The text (initial letters) of the regimental designation R.A.P.C. was changed to Royal Army Pay Corps by ACI 510 dated 5 May 1945.

Table 23. *Colour of Background and Lettering of Regimental Designations introduced by ACI 905 dated 12 June 1943*

Arm-of-service[1]	Colour of background	Colour of lettering
RAC	Yellow	Red
RA	Blue	Red
RE	Red	Blue
R Signals	Blue	White
Infantry (except rifles)[2]	Scarlet	White
Infantry (rifles, except KRRC)[2]	Rifle green	Black
Infantry KRRC	Rifle green	Red
Reconnaissance Corps	Green	Yellow
AAC	Cambridge blue	Dark blue
RAChD	Purple	White
RASC	Blue	Yellow
RAMC	Dull Cherry	White
RAOC	Scarlet	Dark blue
REME	Dark blue	Yellow
RAPC	Yellow[3]	Black[3]
RAVC	Grey	Red
AEC	Dark blue	Cambridge blue
AD Corps	Green	Red
Pioneer Corps	Red	Green
Intelligence Corps	Green	Black
ACC	Grey	Yellow
CMP	Red	Black
Military Provost Staff Corps	Red	Black
Small Arms Schools Corps	Black	Cambridge blue
Commandos	Dark blue	Red
Honourable Artillery Company		
HAC Artillery Unit	Blue	Red
HAC Infantry Unit	Scarlet	White
The Lovat Scouts	Scarlet	White

[1]With regard to the authorized regimental designations for wear by personnel of the Household Cavalry, the Foot Guards and the Army Physical Training Corps, which are not listed above, the following applied:

Household Cavalry		
The Life Guards	Red	Blue
Royal Horse Guards	Dark blue	Red
Foot Guards		
Grenadier Guards	Red	White
Coldstream Guards	Red	White
Scots Guards	Blue	Yellow
Irish Guards	Green	White
Welsh Guards	Black	White
APTC	Black	Red

[2]ACI 1593 of 1943 amended 'rifles' and 'Infantry rifles' to read 'rifle regiments' and 'Infantry rifle regiments' respectively.

[3]ACI 666 of 1945 dated 6 June 1945 amended the RAPC colours of yellow and black to dark blue and yellow respectively.

Table 24. Territorial Regiments and Battalions with Distinctive Titles as published in ACI 905 dated 12 June 1943, with Dated Amendments

Regiment/Battalion	Parent corps	Designation	Colour of ground	Colour of lettering
Lovat Scouts	Scouts	Lovat Scouts	Scarlet	White
Honourable Artillery Company	Honourable Artillery Company:			
	Artillery Unit	H.A.C.	Blue	Red
	Infantry Unit	H.A.C.	Scarlet	White
Cambridgeshire Regiment	Suffolk Regt	Cambridgeshire	Scarlet	White
Herefordshire Regiment	KSLI	Herefordshire	Scarlet	White
Hertfordshire Regiment	Bedfs & Herts	Hertfordshire	Scarlet	White
Monmouthshire Regiment	SWB	Monmouthshire	Scarlet	White
Artists Rifles	Rifle Bde	Artists Rifles	Rifle green	Black
Brecknockshire Bn	SWB	Brecknockshire[1]	Scarlet	White
Buckinghamshire Bns	Oxf & Bucks	Buckinghamshire	Scarlet	White
Glasgow Highlanders[2]	HLI	Tartan patch	—	—
Hallamshire Bn[3]	York and Lancaster	Hallamshire	Scarlet	White
Kensington Regt	Middlesex Regt	Kensington	Scarlet	White
Liverpool Scottish[2]	Camerons	Tartan patch	—	—
London Irish Rifles	RUR	London Irish Rifles	Rifle green	Black
London Scottish	Gordons	London Scottish	Scarlet	White
Tyneside Scottish[2]	Black Watch	Tartan patch	—	—

[1]The designation Brecknockshire was changed to South Wales Borderers by ACI 1593 of 30 October 1943.
[2]These Scottish Territorials elected to wear tartan flashes of the same pattern as worn by Regular Scottish rifle regiments to which they belonged. For details and descriptions of individual tartan patterns see section on 'Tartans' on page 109.
[3]Hallamshires were 'Terriers' of the York and Lancaster Regiment and came from a district of Sheffield. Hallamshire has never been a county. A gazetteer over 120 years ago stated 'Hallamshire – a Lordship round Sheffield, West Riding of Yorkshire, of uncertain extent'. The Hallamshire Rifles were raised as part of the Volunteer Rifle Corps during the Napoleonic invasion threat. In the South African War the Hallamshires provided companies for the 1st Battalion the York and Lancaster Regiment and in 1908 became the 4th (Hallamshire) Battalion the York and Lancaster Regiment; a second 4th Battalion was created in 1914.

Below: Their Majesties, King George VI and Queen Elizabeth are introduced to Airborne troops. The King is shown shaking hands with the Rev. Jenkins, a padre with the paratroops. (A couple of months before this photograph was taken the Rev. Jenkins had almost lost his life in a parachuting mishap when after making a practice jump he was caught up under the aircraft where he hung for almost 20 minutes before being hauled back inside. Immediately after his ordeal the padre had ordered the pilot to fly once more over the dropping zone, whereupon he again jumped, this time making a safe landing.) Compare this final form of Chaplains Dept. shoulder designation with that shown on page 90. The shoulder title 'YORKSHIRE' with dark blue lettering on a pale blue cloth slip-on was worn by members of the 12 (Yorkshire) Parachute Battalion.

General Service Corps, Extra-Regimentally Employed List, General List, Territorial Army Special List and Non-Combatant Corps) were to wear a regimental designation at the top of both sleeves of the Battle-Dress blouse or, for other ranks only, on Service Dress jackets when applicable to the scale of clothing. The designations were not worn on greatcoats.

The designations were printed on cloth, except in the case of the Household Cavalry, the Foot Guards and the Army Physical Training Corps, who wore worsted embroidered regimental designations of a pattern already approved. Highland Regiments, which by October 1943 were being referred to as 'Scottish Infantry Regiments', were permitted to wear their tartan flashes in lieu of the designations as listed on page 104, but not both. Where tartan flashes were worn they were positioned at the top of the sleeve.

Formation badges.

The wording of this section of the ACI was similar to that employed for ACI 2587 of 1941 and set out on page 98, and all the instructions previously published still applied. Formation badges were now being worn at the top of both sleeves of the Service Dress jacket and Battle-Dress blouse, immediately below the regimental designation. However, on 3 May 1944 new instructions were issued (ACI 650 of 1944) regarding the type of formations required to wear formation badges: army groups, armies, corps,

divisions, independent brigade groups and independent brigades. Army Commands and Districts in the United Kingdom were required to ensure that formation badges were worn by all troops in the order of battle of these formations. The command concerned had to arbitrate in cases where there was doubt whether a unit should wear the command or district badge. Except as shown in the following paragraph, units and establishments under War Office control did not wear a formation badge.

Pioneer groups and companies under War Office control wore a command or district badge depending upon their commitments. The command in which they were located decided which type of badge was worn.

Formation badges were also worn by the permanent staff only of reserve divisions, the 77th (Holding) Division and the 148th Training Brigade, together with any other units for which War Office approval had been given. A unit temporarily allotted to a particular formation, for example a regiment of the Royal Artillery, did not normally wear a formation badge. The final decision in cases of doubt rested with the commander of the formation concerned.

Arm-of-service strips.

The instruction regarding arm-of-service strips was similar to that previously published under ACI 2587 of 1941. Only one new addition and one alteration were made to the existing listing of coloured backing to officers' rank badges and arm-of-service strips, but for ease of reference the final and most complete listing of these items is given on page 109.

Regimental flashes.

The policy governing regimental flashes remained the same. They were permitted to be worn in addition to the newly introduced printed regimental designations, but they were not to bear a badge, an emblem, lettering or figures and were not to exceed an area 3in square. In the case of regiments or units which had been transferred to other corps, the flash could be in the colours of their present or former corps.

Rank badge backings.

The policy already in effect continued in use both with regard to regimental and corps officers and officers of the Household Cavalry and the Foot Guards.

Slip-on shoulder titles.

Slip-on shoulder titles were not to be worn when units were in possession of the regimental designations. They were demanded by units when mobilized for overseas service and taken overseas in bulk. This was in line with the policy regarding security and is fully explained on page 111, under the heading 'Removal of Distinguishing Marks for Embarkation and Wearing of Distinguishing Marks Overseas'. Slip-on titles rendered surplus by the introduction of the regimental designation were returned to the RAOC through the usual channels.

Below: The use of the early 'COMMANDO' designation, white letters on black backing, seen here worn by (left) Sjt. Ernest 'Knocker' White, DCM, and L/Sjt. Roy Herbert, DCM, MM; May 1942. These white-on-black items were replaced in 1943 by red on navy blue designations.

1

2

3

Above: Tartan shoulder flashes. 1, Royal Scots Fusiliers; 2, The Black Watch; 3, Argyll and Sutherland Highlanders.

Dress distinctions previously granted.

No alteration was made to the previous existing instructing regarding dress distinctions denoting previous distinguished military service.

Steel helmet markings.

Regimental badges or flashes continued to be stencilled onto steel helmets, the expense of which was met from unit funds.

Table 25. Coloured Rank Badge Backings and Arm-of-Service Strips which were to be worn on Battle-Dress, published by ACI 905 dated 12 June 1943

Arm-of-service	Colour of backing to officers' rank badges	Coloured strip to be worn on each sleeve
Staff[1]	Red	Red
RAC	Yellow	Yellow and red
RA	Red	Red and blue
RE	Blue	Blue and red
R Signals	Blue	Blue and white
Infantry (except rifles)[2]	Scarlet	Scarlet
Infantry (rifles)[2]	Rifle green	Rifle green
Recce Corps	Green	Green and yellow
AAC[3]	Cambridge blue	Cambridge blue and dark blue
RAChD	Purple[4]	Purple
RASC	Yellow	Yellow and blue
RAMC	Dull cherry	Dull cherry
RAOC	Red	Red, blue, red
REME[5]	Dark blue	Dark blue, yellow, red[6]
RAPC[7]	Yellow	Yellow
AEC	Cambridge blue	Cambridge blue
AD Corps	Green	Green and white
Pioneer Corps	Red	Red and green
Intelligence Corps	Green	Green
ACC	Grey	Grey and yellow
APTC	Black	Black, red, black
CMP	Red	Red
MPSC[8]	—	Red
General List	Scarlet	Scarlet

[1] 'Staff', in column 1 above, referred to officers of the rank of Colonel and upwards only, who did not normally wear the uniform of a particular regiment or corps, and to officers on the Extra-Regimentally Employed List.

[2] Infantry rifles were referred to as 'infantry rifle regiments' as instructed by ACI 1593 dated 30 October 1943.

[3] The formation of the Army Air Corps was authorized by Royal Warrant dated 24 February 1942. ACI 713 dated 4 April 1942 announced the colouring for the distinguishing marks to be worn, which were as shown in the table.

[4] Similar coloured backings to rank badges were also worn by members of the RAChD on the Tropical shirt overseas.

[5] The Royal Electrical and Mechanical Engineers had been formed in the summer of 1942 by authority of Army Order 70 of 1942.

[6] REME arm-of-service strips became available for distribution from 6 October 1942 (ACI 2147 of 1942).

[7] Subsequent to the publication of ACI 905 of 1943, the colour of the arm-of-service strip was changed from yellow to yellow, blue, yellow (authorized by ACI 1827 of 1943).

[8] The MPSC (Military Provost Staff Corps) was added to this listing by ACI 313 dated 1 March 1944.

An interesting innovation that was brought about a few weeks after the end of the Second World War but which I consider worthy of inclusion in this book was the introduction on 13 October 1945 of coloured edging to the badges of rank worn by warrant officers Class I, including those of the ATS. The colours employed were identical to the backing of officers' rank badges as shown in the listing on page 109. For full details of these badges see page 18.

Details of Tartan and other similar Shoulder Flashes elected to be worn in place of Regimental Designations by Certain Scottish Infantry Regiments

The Royal Scots: a square of Hunting Stuart tartan, 2½in × 2½in.

The Royal Scots Fusiliers: 42nd tartan, cut to the shape of a fusilier grenade.

The King's Own Scottish Borderers: a square of Leslie tartan, 2in × 2in.

The Cameronians (Scottish Rifles): a square of Douglas tartan, worn on its point.

The Black Watch: a flash of 42nd tartan cut to the shape of the Star of the Order of the Thistle.

The Highland Light Infantry: a square of MacKenzie tartan, 1¾in × 1¾in.

The Seaforth Highlanders (except 5th Bn): an oblong of MacKenzie tartan, 3in wide × 1¾in deep.

The Gordon Highlanders: a narrow curved strip of Gordon tartan 7in in length sewn directly below and in line with the shoulder seam.

The Queen's Own Cameron Highlanders: an oblong of Cameron of Erracht tartan, 3in wide × 1¼in deep.

The Argyll & Sutherland Highlanders: a diced flash of two horizontal rows of red and white checks edged left and right with dark green, usually worked on to a backing of khaki drab cloth.

5th Bn The Seaforth Highlanders: 2½in wide × 2¾in high patch of 42nd tartan.

9th (Glasgow Highland) Battalion, Highland Light Infantry: a 2½in square of 42nd tartan.

The Tyneside Scottish: a 2½in square of 42nd tartan.

The Liverpool Scottish: a 1in deep × 2in wide patch of Forbes tartan.

Royal Air Force Regiment Distinguishing Arm Badge

During 1942 a number of Army officers were required for regimental duty with the Royal Air Force Regiment to fill posts in the ranks of Squadron Leader and Flight Lieutenant; Army majors selected were to fill the post of Squadron Leader and captains or subalterns filled the Flight Lieutenants' posts.

Army officers who served on probation or were loaned to the RAF retained any acting or temporary rank (or were granted acting rank) appropriate to their new appointment. They were liable to be reposted for duty with the Army when required, subject to the agreement of the Air Ministry, they continued to receive from Army sources pay and allowances at the rates and under

Right: RAF Regiment distinguishing arm badge.

Right: A Colonel of the RAF Regiment serving in Belgium wearing the Regiment's distinguishing arm badge (shoulder designation) and, despite repeated instructions forbidding the practice, the RAF Observers' brevet.

Right: Men of the 2nd Bn Coldstream Guards training for Combined Operation Raids, 1942. The red cloth numerals are just visible on the upper left arm just below the regimental designation.

the conditions appropriate to Army officers, and lastly they retained their Army rank, wearing the Army uniform of their original corps or regiment but with the addition of the distinguishing arm badge consisting of the words 'RAF Regiment' in light blue lettering on a dark blue background.

Regimental and Battalion Arm Flashes

The practice of wearing cloth flashes on the military uniform is old, dating back to at least the South African Wars. It was widespread during the Great War, and the use of flashes was officially revived during the Second World War by the authority of Army Council Instruction 1118 dated 18 September 1940 (see page 97 et seq).

The flashes worn on the arm, and occasionally on the back of the Battle-Dress blouse high up between the shoulder blades, are closely related to tartan flashes (see page 109) and painted or stencilled flashes worn on the steel helmet (see page 224). Pagri and pith helmet flashes are really a separate subject (see page 146 for pagri flashes), although in a number of instances both former pagri and pith helmet flashes were pressed into service and used as arm flashes.

Regimental and battalion cloth flashes, despite their being widely used, can be very difficult to identify. Somewhat akin to the conditions governing the use of coloured field service caps and lanyards, these flashes were provided at regimental expense, and because of this there is no known official listing of these items; in all probability nobody will ever know their full range.

The colours employed on these flashes were either an arbitrary choice used for practical reasons (red for the 1st Battalion, blue for the 2nd, green for the 3rd, etc.) or they were facing colours used by a regiment and adapted into an arm flash. The shape of these flashes varied greatly and included square, oblong, diamond, oval, circular and triangular designs, although the size was regulated at no larger than 3in square.

I have illustrated a selection of these arm flashes on page 97.

Battalion Numerals worn by Personnel of the Coldstream Guards

Of the five regiments of the Foot Guards, the Coldstream Guards were alone in distinguishing the members of their various battalions by wearing 'battalion numerals'. This practice had originated during the latter years of the Great War and had continued in use ever since. The numerals, which were roman, were cut from scarlet cloth and were worn sewn on to the sleeve of both the Service Dress jacket and the Battle-Dress blouse, just below the shoulder title and above any formation badge when this was worn.

The figure used for the 1st Battalion the Coldstream Guards was a simple straight cut bar of scarlet cloth 1½in in length and ¼in wide; the scarlet cloth used came from unserviceable scarlet Full Dress tunics. The 2nd Battalion employed two of these bars of scarlet cloth sewn to the shoulder in parallel, whilst the 3rd Battalion had a specially made cutting instrument which cut out from the scarlet cloth in a single piece the roman numeral 'III' (see sketch). The 4th, 5th and 6th Battalions had numerals in the same style as those used for the 1st and 2nd Battalions but sewn on to a backing cloth of khaki material; this in turn was stitched to the shoulder of the Battle-Dress blouse (see sketch).

The Removal of Distinguishing Marks in Preparation for Embarkation and the Wearing of Distinguishing Marks Overseas

June 1943, just one year away from the Allied invasion of mainland Europe, saw the issuing of a series of instructions, the object of which was to ensure the maximum possible security coverage regarding the order of battle of British troops embarking for service overseas.

Having published detailed instructions governing the wearing of distinguishing marks on uniform at home, further instructions were issued by ACI 906 dated 12 June 1943 which concerned the removal of, and the wearing of, such distinguishing marks by all formations, units, drafts and individuals either when proceeding overseas or on arrival in all overseas commands. A notable exception was made to this ruling when the 21st Army Group embarked for the invasion of the Continent in June 1944. All formation badges, designations, flashes and steel helmet markings continued to be worn by all those troops who went from their concentration areas in England straight into battle in Normandy.

The instructions, as set out below, did not apply to sea voyages within the United Kingdom or between the Faroes and the United Kingdom.

Embarkation.

All ranks, including personnel accompanying motor transport or stores, were required to travel to their port of embarkation wearing Battle-Dress and steel helmets. No other form of dress – and this included such items as kilts – was permitted to be worn until the convoy in which the men were travelling was well out of sight of land. Normal forms of head-dress were permitted to be worn during any periods spent at transit camps but were forbidden during journeys between transit camps and docks.

Before moving to the port of embarkation the following distinguishing marks as defined by ACI 905 of 1943 were to be removed from clothing under arrangements made by officers commanding units, or in the case of drafts, by the OC the assembly area (the removal and replacement of distinguishing marks was normally undertaken by the individual soldier).

1. Regimental designations.
2. Formation badges.
3. Regimental flashes, including tartan flashes.
4. Any dress distinctions which indicated a particular regiment.
5. Regimental badges and flashes on steel helmets (to be painted out if they were not removable).

Only arm-of-service strips and officers' rank badge backing were retained in wear. Formation signs on vehicles had to be adequately obscured and even equipment, regimental and personal baggage had to have any visible markings that revealed the identity of a formation, unit or regiment removed or obscured, but the order did not apply to personal numbers, mobilization serial numbers, draft identification letters or distinguishing colour bars.

Regimental designations were required to be returned to ordnance in bulk before moving to the port of embarkation. In the case of drafts they were returned by the OC the assembly centre. In no case were regimental designations to be worn overseas, and the slip-on shoulder titles for wear overseas in place of the regimental designations that were withdrawn were indented for on the scale of one pair of titles per man on the mobilization establishment plus an extra ten per cent.

Men from detention barracks and their escorts.

All distinguishing marks, as specified above, were removed from the clothing of men from detention barracks before proceeding to the port of embarkation prior to their being sent overseas. When an escort was provided by a unit which had received embarkation orders all distinguishing marks as specified above were also removed from their clothing before proceeding to the port even if the men forming the escort were embarking or not. When an escort was provided by a unit not under embarkation orders, escorted prisoners if possible had to be handed over outside the dock area to the local assistant provost marshal or to the commandant of the transit camp; the latter was

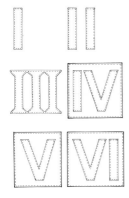

Above: Shoulder numerals worn by personnel of Coldstream Guard battalions.

then made responsible for escorting the prisoner to the ship. If all this was not possible, then the escort had to deliver the prisoner to the ship, in which case distinguishing marks on the clothing of the escort were not required to be removed. On 21 July 1943 ACI 1093 announced that personnel of the Corps of Military Police were exempted from the order requiring them to remove – or paint out – regimental flashes, dress distinctions and regimental badges or flashes on steel hemets. They still had to remove regimental designations and formation signs, but slip-on shoulder titles were taken into wear before moving to the port of embarkation.

Ports of call.

The form of dress laid down in the section 'Embarkation' (above) was also adopted when troops were allowed ashore on short pass at ports of call. The Tropical helmet without badge or flash was permitted to be worn in lieu of the steel helmet, and Khaki Drill uniform without regimental badges could be worn in place of the Battle-Dress if desired. If Khaki Drill clothing were worn, normal buttons were allowed (for example, rifle regiments were permitted to wear their black buttons). In the case of ports where transhipment took place, and where the stay of troops was likely to be protracted, a certain amount of relaxation regarding the above regulations was allowed at the discretion of the local commander. Service Dress or Khaki Drill with regimental badges and buttons was allowed to be worn, together with any authorized distinctive head-dress. Under no circumstances, however, were formation badges or slip-on shoulder titles permitted.

Arrival and disembarkation in overseas commands.

From the time when a troopship entered port and during disembarkation, the instructions as set out in the section 'Embarkation' (above) applied. If it were necessary, Khaki Drill clothing was allowed to be worn in place of Battle-Dress, in which case no regimental badges or dress distinctions other than regimental buttons were permitted. If Tropical helmets were worn they were not allowed to bear a regimental badge or flash.

Distinguishing marks on uniforms were only resumed in a command overseas when ordered by the C-in-C concerned. The following were permitted to be worn as and when authorized.
1. Formation badges.
2. Regimental flashes, including tartan flashes.
3. Slip-on shoulder titles.
4. Dress distinctions granted to particular regiments.
5. Regimental badges or flashes on steel helmets or Tropical helmets.
Arm-of-service strips and rank badge backings were allowed to be worn at any time. Formation signs were replaced on vehicles when authorized by the C-in-C of the overseas command concerned.

In July 1945, two months after the victory in Europe, further instructions were issued regarding the removal of formation and unit distinguishing marks before embarkation or emplaning for over-

seas destinations. These were in essence much as had been previously published except that they were now directed at troops proceeding as formations, units or detachments of units moving overseas to destinations other than the European continent. Signs, badges, designations, etc. which revealed the identity of a particular formation or unit, as opposed to a regiment or corps, were required to be removed before moving to the sea or air port of departure, but all other distinguishing marks or articles of dress, such as regimental designations, flashes, buttons and badges, which did not reveal the identity of a particular formation or unit as opposed to regiments or corps were allowed to be retained.

The ruling governing the distinguishing marks worn by prisoners from detention barracks and their escorts was much as had previously been published. The distinguishing marks that had to be removed or were permitted to be worn were as listed above. Slip-on shoulder titles were still in use for wear on Khaki Drill clothing being worn by troops en route to or after arrival at overseas destinations. The replacement of formation signs and unit distinguishing marks removed in accordance with the above instructions was only permitted on orders of the C-in-C of the overseas commands concerned, and particular attention had to be paid to this instruction by formations and units disembarking in the Far East.

12. WOUND STRIPES AND SERVICE CHEVRONS

Above: Wound stripe.
Below: Service chevrons for two, three and four years.

Left: Maj. D. F. Cartwright, MC, of the Norfolk Yeomanry wearing three wound stripes; 25 October 1944.

Wound Stripes

Issue of wound stripes.

The method for the issue of wound stripes as set out under ACI 233 dated 16 February 1944 was as follows.

Units stationed in a theatre of war.

1. All ranks who considered that they were entitled to wound stripes (for wounds or injuries received during the current war) had to initiate a claim to the officer commanding their unit for the number of gold wound stripes to which they considered they were entitled; stripes for wounds received after the date of this Army Council Instruction (February 1944) were claimed in the same way. When the commanding officer of the man's unit was satisfied that the claim was justified, he authorized the issue of the appropriate number of wound stripes (a list of wounds or injuries which qualified military personnel for entitlement to wound stripes is given below).

Entry of the casualty in the records of the War Office Casualty Branch was the final authority for entitlement, but reference to that branch was only made in doubtful cases which could not be decided from the records of units or 2nd Echelons in the field − see (4) below.

2. A gold wound stripe could also be claimed for each wound or injury sustained before enlistment in His Majesty's Forces whilst serving in the Home Guard or other qualifying service in which wound stripes were awarded (see listing below of qualifying services). Officers commanding units could authorize the issue of wound stripes for such injuries on production to them of proof that a wound stripe would have been issued in such cases in the Home Guard or other qualifying service concerned. Documentary evidence from a Home Guard unit or other qualifying service was normally required, but where the production of such evidence was difficult or possibly caused delay, officers commanding units in a theatre of war were permitted to authorize the issue of wound stripes pending receipt of proof.

3. Claims for the single red wound stripe in respect of wounds received in previous wars was dealt with in the same way. Entitlement was proved by the production of discharge papers or other documents in the individual's possession, or by any other available evidence.

4. In any case in which the officer commanding a unit was unable to satisfy himself that a claim was justified, he had to refer the claim to General Headquarters 2nd Echelon for a decision. If GHQ 2nd Echelon could not verify any claim from records in their possession, they had to refer the case for decision to the War Office in the case of officers and to the appropriate record office in the case of other ranks.

Units stationed other than in a theatre of war.

1. Officers commanding units were required to verify from AFB 199A, AFB 103, Part II/Part III Orders or other records in their possession the number of gold wound stripes (for wounds or injuries received during the current war) to which each individual was entitled and to authorize the issue of the appropriate number of stripes; in the same manner they authorized additional wound stripes to personnel who were recorded as having been wounded after the date of this ACI in Part II or Part III Orders and unit documents.

2. A gold wound stripe was also issued to personnel for each wound or injury sustained before enlistment in His Majesty's Forces whilst serving in the Home Guard or other qualifying service in which wound stripes were awarded. Officers commanding units were permitted to authorize the issue of wound stripes for such injuries on production to them of proof that a wound stripe would have been issued in such cases in the Home Guard or qualifying service concerned. Documentary evidence from a Home Guard unit or qualifying service was normally required, but where the production of such evidence proved difficult or liable to cause delay, officers commanding units overseas were allowed to authorize the issue of wound stripes pending receipt of proof.

3. Officers commanding units were required to verify entitlement to the single red wound stripe for wounds received in previous wars, from discharge papers or other documents in the individual's possession or by any other available evidence, and then authorized the issue of one red stripe in the appropriate cases.

4. Where there were cases of doubt, a War Office decision was sought (officers) or reference was made to the appropriate record office (other ranks), entry of the casualty in the records of the War Office Casualty Branch being the final authority.

Qualification for wound stripes.

The following wounds or injuries were considered sufficient for the qualification for wound stripes (military personnel were regarded as a rule as on duty unless actually on leave or pass).

In an operational command (other than an RAF operational command in the United Kingdom). Wounds or injuries due to enemy action whether received on duty or otherwise (there were exceptions − see below).

In an operational RAF command in the United Kingdom. Wounds or injuries due to enemy action, sustained when on duty in the air or on the ground.

In a non-operational command when on duty. Wounds or injuries due to enemy action received when on duty.

The wounds or injuries above included, for example, those inflicted by Allied projectiles (or parts of them) when these had been fired at the enemy; those caused by rescue work in bombed buildings or bombed defences; those suffered as a result of a collision of a vessel with a British mine; injuries sustained by members of an aircraft crew as a result of an aircraft crash, or aircraft damage, or fire in an aircraft, provided that these were due to enemy action (injuries sustained by those persons who rescued or attempted to rescue members of a crew in such circumstances were sufficient to qualify provided that the rescuers or the persons who attempted the rescue were in a class qualifying for the stripe, and crashes in operational sorties were included); injuries sustained in the performance of mine or bomb duties; injuries due to enemy gas, if at any time this was used, or injuries due to blast; and injuries not due to enemy action but sustained in forward operational areas by soldiers whilst engaged in battlefield conditions against the enemy.

Wounds or injuries due to the following causes were not a qualification for the stripe.

In a non-operational command when not on duty. Wounds or injuries due to enemy action sustained when not on duty. In certain circumstances it was necessary also to exclude wounds or injuries due to enemy action sustained by personnel on leave in an operational command.

In an operational or non-operational command. Injuries due to accidents on duty or that arose directly out of employment but were not directly attributable to enemy action, e.g. collisions between ships at sea (unless in battle), car accidents, flying accidents on duty that were not due to enemy action (but excluding operational sorties), the handling of lethal weapons and gun explosions, whether accompanied by a large 'active service risk' or otherwise. Injuries sustained by personnel in forward operational areas in contact with the enemy were, however, often classified as wounds, and personnel so injured were eligible.

In no circumstances were self-inflicted wounds a qualification.

The Issue of and Qualification for Service Chevrons (All Units)

Officers commanding units were required to verify from AB 439 in the case of officers and from unit documents and/or AB 64 Part I, in the case of other ranks, the number of service chevrons to which all ranks under their command were entitled, and they then authorized the issue of the appropriate number of chevrons. The issues were made as single chevrons or in sets of two, three or four. When an individual became entitled to an additional chevron the previous issue was withdrawn and a new, increased set issued.

Periods of imprisonment or detention that exceeded 28 days, absence without leave or desertion, and time that was spent in the Reserve (or, in the case of women, on the ATS Unemployed List) was deducted when estimating each period of 12 months' service.

In the case of personnel who, before enlistment in the armed forces, were members of the Home Guard or were enrolled for whole or part-time duty in a qualifying service (see listing below), the period of service therein was aggregated in estimating the number of chevrons to which such personnel were entitled.

Officers commanding units were permitted to authorize the issue of additional chevrons in respect of Home Guard or other qualifying service, provided that personnel who claimed such additional chevrons produced proof of their period of accountable service. Claims on behalf of ex-members of the Home Guard which required to be

verified were passed by the units with which the individuals were serving to the TA association of the county in which they had served with the Home Guard, in the case of theatres of war through GHQ 2nd Echelon.

Documentation for Wound Stripes and Service Chevrons

In the case of other ranks, an entry attested by the signature of an officer, and dated, was made on AB 64 Part I, page 4, which stated the number of wound stripes and service chevrons authorized up to their date of issue. Future issues of wound stripes were entered in the same way.

No entry regarding the entitlement or issue of wound stripes and service chevrons was made in Part II/III Orders, nor in the individual's documents except AB 64 Part I (other ranks only) as described above. Future issues of service chevrons were not recorded in AB 64 Part I after the initial entitlement had been settled and entered, but they were checked out in accordance with rules as shown above under the headings 'Issue of wound stripes', 'Qualification for wound stripes' and 'The Issue of and Qualification for Service Chevrons (All Units)'. The stripes and chevrons were not awards but were worn in recognition of service which was already then recorded in personal documents.

Application by entitled personnel who were not serving at the time stripes and chevrons were introduced had to be made, in the case of officers direct to the Under-Secretary of State for War at the War Office, Whitehall, London, and to the appropriate record office for other ranks for an initial free issue of one set of wound stripes and chevrons in respect of Army service. No additional free issue was made, however, if the applicant was supplied with wound stripes or service chevrons whilst serving with the Forces. In all cases replacement under this ruling was at the expense of the individual, and an announcement to this effect was published in the national press. Action regarding missing personnel was, at the time of this Army Council Instruction, deferred pending verification of their situation.

Instructions regarding the procedure that had to be followed for the Home Guard were quite separate (see Part VI of this book), and for colonial forces under War Office control the procedure was as set out above under the headings 'Issue of wound stripes', 'Qualification for wound stripes' and 'The Issue of and Qualification for Service Chevrons (All Units)'.

Units, other than units of the Home Guard and LAA units of the TA Reserve (for whom special instructions were issued), indented the RAOC for supplies of wound stripes and chevrons for free issue to all ranks on the basis of $1\frac{1}{2}$in of gold braid for each wound received in the 1939–45 war, $1\frac{1}{2}$in of red braid for a wound or wounds received in previous wars, and one set of chevrons for each garment in the approved scale on which they were authorized to be worn for each person entitled to them. Except as detailed above, wound stripes and service chevrons were replaced free of charge when they were no longer fit for further wear, but all ranks were required to make good any deficiencies, loss or damage that arose from neglect or carelessness.

The conditions of this ACI also applied to the ATS.

Qualifying Services for Wound Stripes and Service Chevrons

Civil Defence services. Ambulance (including Sitting Case Cars); Decontamination; First Aid (including the nursing service for public air raid shelters, first aid post and points, public cleansing centres and mobile cleansing units); Messenger; Report and Control; rescue (including former first aid party); Warden (including shelter wardens); and Civil Defence Reserve.

Other services. Merchant Navy and the fishing fleet serving at sea; Royal Observer Corps; Civil Air Transport; Coast Guard; lighthouse and lightvessel keepers who served under the three lighthouse authorities; Police, Royal Marine Police Special Reserve and Railway and Dock Police; National Fire Service (including service in a local authority fire brigade or the Auxiliary Fire Service before nationalization); fireguards performing duties under local authorities or at business or Government premises; Port of London Authority River Emergency Service; Civil Nursing Reserve; and nurses in hospitals for which Government departments or local authorities were responsible, or those in the recognized voluntary hospitals.

Below: Gunner Norman Dunn, RA, from Bradford (left) and Gunner John Swinburn, RA, from Liverpool, both of whom were awarded the George Medal for rescuing the rear gunner of a crashed aircraft. Gunner Dunn is wearing four service chevrons on his right cuff.
Below right: White distinguishing marks worn by Officer Cadets. Cadet Pooley of the RAC is wearing a white ivorine cap badge diamond and white shoulder strap tapes.

13. OFFICER CADET INSIGNIA

Officer cadets undergoing instruction at officer cadet training units wore as a form of identification a white band of cloth, approximately 1½in deep around the lower part of whatever form of head-dress they wore.

In June 1940 (ACI 661 dated 29 June 1940) it was decided that in addition to this white cap band all officer cadets were to wear a strip of white tape at the base of the shoulder straps on their Service Dress jackets and Battle-Dress blouses. The material to be used for this purpose was cotton tape, ½in wide and sufficient for two sets of strips per cadet, which had to be obtained under local arrangements.

A year later, on 27 June 1942, ACI 1358 instructed that officer cadets undergoing training at Royal Armoured Corps OCTUs who were in possession of the black RAC beret (caps RTR) were authorized to wear a white ivorine disc as a background to their cap badge in order to distinguish them as cadets. The ivorine disc, a form of white plastic, was 1¾in in diameter.

In an effort to economize in materials, a further Army Council Instruction was issued on 28 October 1942 (ACI 2301 of 1942) which introduced white cloth peaks to be worn on the Field Service caps in place of the then current white cloth band. All new intakes of officer cadets, with

the exception of RAC cadets, were required to wear these white peaks, lightly stitched to the body of the cap in order to prevent loss, under the folding peak of the Field Service cap. Stocks of white cap bands were to be used up before the issue of the white peaks for the Field Service caps began, and white cap bands and white peaks were allowed to be worn concurrently in any one unit. The usual warning in these cases of change-over was issued, stating that officer cadet training units were not to indent for these new peaks as a wholesale change-over merely to ensure uniformity.

With the introduction of the General Service cap in September 1943 (see page 155), the existing head-dress distinguishing marks worn by cadets at OCTUs were radically reviewed. The small white ivorine discs, the white ivorine diamonds and the white peaks worn on the Field Service caps were all made obsolete, and in their place an unpierced white ivorine disc, 3in in diameter, was gradually introduced for wear by all cadets except those mentioned below. These new discs were issued on a scale of one for each new cadet and were eventually taken into use by all OCTU cadets, and in exactly the same manner as before they formed a white distinguishing background to the cadets' cap badges. However, due to the fact that there was no standard position for the shanks of cap badges, these new discs were issued unpierced. It was the responsibility of the individual cadet to pierce the ivorine disc himself to enable the shank of his badge to be inserted neatly.

Current stocks of white peaks were required to be used up by personnel still in possession of Field Service caps, although in the event that the stocks of white peaks became exhausted while the Field Service caps were still available cadets were permitted to wear the white ivorine disc on the Field Service cap. The white ivorine diamond continued to be worn by OCTU cadets of the RAC until stocks of the items became exhausted.

Those cadets under instruction at OCTUs who were authorized to wear the Service Dress cap (including women cadets of the ATS wearing the ATS cap) were required to wear the former pattern of officer cadet's white cap band, which was reintroduced into service on a scale of two bands for each cadet.

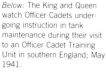

Below: The King and Queen watch Officer Cadets undergoing instruction in tank maintenance during their visit to an Officer Cadet Training Unit in southern England; May 1941.

14. CAP BADGES

The subject of cap badges is far too extensive to be covered in detail here, and anyone wishing to read about the vast range of badges that existed before and during the 1939–45 war is directed to the Bibliography to be found at the end of this book. Here are listed a number of titles which are recommended as first class reference material dealing with the subject. I have included in the present work only some of those orders and instructions that governed the introduction and use of cap badges before and during the Second World War.

Field Service Cap

On 28 September 1940 it was announced by ACI 1168 of 1940 that cap badges were to be worn on the left side of Field Service caps, with the centre of the badge 3½in from the front of the cap and normally 1½in from the top seam. Large cap badges were placed at such a distance below the top seam that the bottom of the badge was just clear of the visor.

Previously in March (ACI 262 for w/e 20 March 1940) it had been announced that the pattern of cap badge with a straight shank had been found to be insufficient to secure the badge when it was worn with the Field Service cap, and

in order to overcome this problem a clip had been introduced which when fitted to the badge secured it fast to the cloth of the cap. A free issue of one clip was made to all personnel wearing a cap badge with a vertical shank in the Field Service cap and thereafter free issues of clips were made to all recruits as part of their initial outfit on enlistment.

Change in pattern of badge for Royal Artillery personnel.

On 9 July 1941 it was announced in ACI 1179 of 1941 that in future the 'grenade' badge, normally used as a collar badge by RA personnel, was to be worn on the Field Service cap by Royal Artillery personnel in lieu of the existing 'gun' badge, although the 'gun' badge continued to be worn with the stiff Service Dress cap by personnel of Royal Artillery horsed units. As of the date of this ACI no further provision of badges of the latter pattern was made except to meet the requirements of personnel of RA horsed units. The change-over from the 'gun' badge to the 'grenade' badge was a gradual one, and for some time, until existing stocks were exhausted, both badges were evident.

Service Dress Cap (Soft and Stiff Versions)
The 1943 Clothing Regulations stated that cap badges were to be worn in the centre of the cap band at the front of the Service Dress cap.

Berets and Bonnets
The 1943 edition of Clothing Regulations stated that badges were to be worn on the left side about 1in from the front of the beret or bonnet and about 1½in above the band, and placed so that the badge rested above the forehead.

Cap Badges for Officers
When on duty officers were permitted to wear on the regulation head-dress, and at their discretion, either
1. The gilt, silver, etc. badge as authorized by *Dress Regulations for the Army, 1934* for wear with the forage cap; or
2. The bronze badge also as authorized by *Dress Regulations for the Army, 1934* for wear with the Service Dress cap.
If necessary, to obtain uniformity among officers when on duty, a commanding officer could order officers to wear on the regulation head-dress the badges of the type worn by other ranks, i.e. of gilding metal or plastic.

It was considered desirable that each corps or regiment should decide which type of badge to be worn off duty was to be regarded as the more appropriate. This decision did not modify the discretion of individual officers in their choice of badges as shown above, but the information did assist officers who transferred between arms, and others who sought guidance. The decision with regard to the appropriate badge, within the scope allowed by this ACI, rested with colonels of regiments and colonels commandant of corps.

Bronzed badges that were already in the possession of officers were retained in wear until needing replacements in the normal course. Colonels of regiments and colonels commandant of corps were requested to notify the War Office of their decisions as early as possible. In the case of those regiments and corps that had been formed during the war, for whom patterns of forage cap badges had not hitherto been approved, a sample of the badge which was desired to be adopted, or a sketch indicating the type of metal (gilt, silver, etc.) proposed for the badge or its component parts, had to be forwarded for consideration and, if approved, was sealed as the authorized pattern (ACI 692 dated 10 May 1944).

Cap Badges for Wear by Officer Cadets
Cadets of Infantry were required to wear the cap badge of the regiment to which they belonged, whilst cadets of the Cavalry and the Royal Armoured Corps wore the cap badge of the regiment to which they belonged, or, if they had never been posted to a regiment, they wore the Royal Arms in the case of Cavalry cadets and the RAC badge in the case of Royal Armoured Corps cadets.

Royal Armoured Corps Cap Badges

First pattern cap badges (and other insignia) for recruits.

In February 1940 (ACI 174 dated w/e 28 February 1940) it was decided that in view of the fact that recruits for the RAC were not appointed to regiments until the termination of their training, a design for a cap badge to be worn during this period had been approved as follows: within a laurel wreath surmounted by an imperial crown, the letters 'RAC' in monogram. This ACI also described other items of insignia, such as the collar badges (which were as for the cap badge but smaller) and the shoulder title (which consisted of the letters 'RAC'). However, it added that in keeping with wartime settled policy collar badges were not provided during the war and that the shoulder titles were of the worsted embroidery type. Special pattern buttons were not provided, general service (Royal Arms) buttons being worn instead.

Second pattern cap badge (and other insignia) for personnel and new entrants.

On 7 March 1942 it was announced in ACI 500 of 1942 that the new designs for the RAC badges and buttons that had been under consideration since 1941 had finally been approved. These were as follows.

Cap badge. In front of two concentric circles broken and barbed at the top, a gauntlet, clenched, and charged with a billet inscribed with the letters 'RAC', the whole ensigned with the imperial crown.

Collar badge. As for cap, but smaller.

Buttons. A gauntlet, clenched and charged with a billet inscribed with the letters 'RAC'.

Officers' cap badges were in silver or white metal and collar badges were bronzed; other ranks' cap and collar badges were in white metal. However, collar badges and regimental buttons were not issued to other ranks during the war.

Cap Badges for Wear on the Black Beret by Officers of Cavalry and Yeomanry Regiments

It was found that the bronzed cap badges which were prescribed for wear by Cavalry and Yeomanry officers with Service Dress and Battle-Dress were not sufficiently distinctive for wear on the black beret, and so regiments which so desired were permitted to wear on this form of head-dress badges of gilt or gilding metal of the type which were authorized for wear on the coloured forage cap with peak as described in *Dress Regulations for the Army, 1934*, para. 26. In those cases where the option was exercised, all officers of a regiment were required to wear the same type of badge with the beret when instructions had been issued for this head-dress to be taken into use.

Cap Badges (and other Insignia) for Recruits undergoing Training with Cavalry Training Regiments

Recruits with Cavalry training regiments, who were not appointed to regiments until the termination of their training, wore cap badges, buttons and shoulder titles as follows.

Cap badge. The Royal Arms.
Buttons. The Royal Arms.
Shoulder titles. The letters 'CAV.T.R'.

Collar badges were not worn during the period of the war and the shoulder titles were in worsted embroidery (ACI 817 dated 27 July 1940).

The Introduction of Plastic Badges

In December 1941 (ACI 2594 dated 27 December 1941) it was decided, in order to conserve metal, that cap badges be produced in plastic for the Royal Artillery, Royal Engineers, Royal Corps of Signals, Royal Army Service Corps, Royal Army Medical Corps, Royal Army Ordnance Corps, Corps of Military Police, Royal Army Pay Corps, Army Educational Corps, Army Dental Corps, Pioneer Corps, Intelligence Corps, Reconnaissance Corps, Army Catering Corps and the Army Physical Training Corps. Existing stocks of metal cap badges had to be used up before the issue of plastic badges began. Metal and plastic badges were allowed to be worn concurrently in any one unit, but units were not permitted to indent for plastic badges as a wholesale change-over merely to ensure uniformity.

Six months later ACI 1337 dated 24 June 1942 announced that, in order further to conserve metal, badges for all arms of the service would in future be produced in plastic. The only exceptions to this decision were made where it was found that the production of a badge in plastic material was impracticable.

The majority of plastic cap badges were produced in a dark brown coloured plastic, although other metallic colours existed and these were employed in an effort to mimic the colour of the original metal cap badge which they were intended to replace. Thus such badges were also produced in black, dull metallic yellow and dull grey silver, but to my knowledge no attempt was made to produce a plastic badge with two colours of plastic

in the same way as bi-metal cap badges were produced.

Coloured Backings and Tartan Backings to Regimental Cap Badges

The practice of wearing a piece of coloured cloth as a backing to the cap badge was adopted at various times by a number of regiments. In some cases the practice originated from some aspect of regimental history and was the means whereby a visual reference was made to a particular regimental tradition or to a past military engagement or the like. However, the use of some coloured cap badge backings by some regiments or units was purely arbitrary.

Two kinds of backing existed. There were those that appeared beyond the edges of the badge, either as a geometric shape or cut to the general outline of the badge itself. The other sort were patches of cloth placed directly behind a badge with the colour of the cloth patch only showing through the voided areas of the badge. Coloured backings were worn behind the cap badges on the Service Dress cap, the universal Field Service cap, the coloured Field Service cap, the beret and the General Service cap.

The coloured patches of cloth or regimental flashes worn on the pagri of the universal Foreign Service khaki helmet, the khaki solar pith hat or the felt bush hat are not considered as cap badge backings and are dealt with as a separate subject (see pages 143, 145 and 146); the white ivorine discs or ivorine diamonds worn by officer cadets are also not classed as coloured cap badge backings as defined above (see page 115).

Tartan backings were worn by personnel of Scottish line infantry regiments, usually on the khaki Balmoral bonnet (the Tam-o'-Shanter). A schedule of these backings is given opposite.

Designation	Method of Wear	Worn by
Royal Stuart tartan	Worn with broad and narrow lines of colours intersecting vertically and horizontally	Pipers of the Scots Guards,[2] The Royal Scots and The King's Own Scottish Borderers (except the 4th Bn); 9th Bn The Highland Light Infantry (except pipers); pipers of the Tyneside Scottish[3]
42nd or Government tartan	Edges of 3in square patch cut in line with overall squared, but large dark green, dark blue and black tartan patterning	The Argyll and Sutherland Highlanders; The Royal Scots Fusiliers (except pipers); 9th Bn The Highland Light Infantry (except pipers); Tyneside Scottish;[3] 5th Bn The Seaforth Highlanders
Mackenzie tartan	3in square patch cut diagonally so that black edged white stripe passed from top left to bottom right corner, crossing over the black edged scarlet stripe which passed from top right to bottom left corner	The Seaforth Highlanders (except 5th Bn)
Mackenzie tartan	3in square patch cut square so that black edged white and black edged scarlet stripes intersected vertically and horizontally	The Highland Light Infantry (except 9th Bn); 6th Bn the Highland Light Infantry
Gordon tartan	Patch cut square with narrow yellow stripes intersecting vertically and horizontally in centre of patch	Gordon Highlanders
79th or Cameron of Erracht tartan	Patch cut square intersected by vertical yellow stripe	The Queen's Own Cameron Highlanders
Douglas tartan	Patch cut square intersected by vertical white stripe	The Cameronians (Scottish Rifles)
Leslie tartan	Patch cut diagonally so that narrow white stripe passed from top left to bottom right corner intersecting with scarlet stripe which passed from top right to bottom left corner	The King's Own Scottish Borderers (except pipers)
Hunting Stuart tartan	Square patch cut diagonally so that scarlet stripe passed from top left to bottom right corner intersecting with yellow stripe passing from top right to bottom left corner	The Royal Scots (except pipers)
Forbes tartan	Square patch cut diagonally so that white stripes passed from top left to bottom right corner intersecting with another white stripe passing from top right to bottom left corner	Liverpool Scottish
Buccleuch tartan	Square patch of black and white checks cut at right angles to checking and intersected with light blue stripe	Pipers of 4th Bn The King's Own Scottish Borderers
Erskine (red) tartan	Square patch cut at right angles to large green and scarlet check patterning	Pipers of The Royal Scots Fusiliers
Hodden-Grey	Square of unpatterned Hodden-Grey material	London Scottish

Left: An unusual photograph of an officer of the Black Watch, Capt. C. A. Sutherland, MBE, wearing the badge normally worn with the glengarry. The red feathered hackle was the badge usually worn with the Balmoral bonnet. The badge has a backing of 42nd Government tartan. Capt. Sutherland is wearing Battle-Dress with a Sam Browne belt and cross strap which, again, is unusual; July 1941. He may have been a member of a Home Guard unit, which could explain his dress peculiarities.

[1]As this schedule deals with the tartan backings worn with cap badges on the khaki Balmoral bonnet (Tam-o'-Shanter) it should be noted that as a particular distinction personnel of The Black Watch (Royal Highland Regiment) did not wear a cap badge or a tartan backing with the TOS; it was considered sufficient for them to be distinguished by wearing the famous red hackle (see page 149).

[2]Officers of the Scots Guards wore a 2½in wide by 2in deep patch of specially woven Royal Stuart tartan on the left side of their khaki Service Dress caps.

[3]The Tyneside Scottish were reactivated in 1939 as the 12th (Tyneside Scottish) Battalion the Durham Light Infantry. Later that year they were transferred as the 1st Battalion the Tyneside Scottish, The Black Watch (Royal Highland Regiment). It is doubtful that they wore a tartan kilt, although they were authorized to wear tartan backing to their cap badges – Royal Stuart tartan for their pipers and 42nd or Government tartan for all other ranks.

PART III
Uniforms and Clothing

1. GENERAL INSTRUCTIONS

Officers' Uniforms and Clothing

Before the outbreak of the Second World War and the coming of the British Army Battle-Dress, instructions regarding the uniforms and clothing as worn by officers of the Army were clearly set out in *Dress Regulations for the Army, 1934* under Section I, 'General Instructions'.

Commanding officers were forbidden to introduce or to sanction any deviation from the sealed patterns of dress, clothing, equipment and badges, and they were held responsible for the cost of replacing or restoring to the approved pattern any articles worn in their units which were found not to be in conformity with the sealed pattern. When obtaining uniform and equipment, officers were advised to make sure that articles they were to obtain were according to the sealed patterns, even if this had to be done by personal comparison. Sealed patterns of garment, buttons, badges of rank, special badges and devices (including lace, embroidery, horse furniture and appointments) were deposited at the War Office for their reference and guidance; duplicates of the sealed patterns of badges were also kept by officers commanding regiments, battalions and infantry depots. No unauthorized ornament or emblem was permitted to be worn with uniform, but special emblems were allowed to be carried on the head-dress on anniversaries, provided that War Office authority had been obtained.

An officer on leave from abroad had to be in possession of uniform for use if he was detailed for duty at home or on his return voyage; in a foreign country, he was not allowed to wear uniform without first having obtained the permission of His Majesty's representative, which was granted only when the officer was employed on duty or attending Court or State ceremonies to which he had been invited. Permission to wear military uniform at foreign manoeuvres could only be obtained from the Under-Secretary of State at the War Office. Officers who were on leave from, or under orders for, stations abroad were allowed to wear the foreign pattern head-dress. Regulation uniform was not allowed to be worn at events such as fancy dress balls, but there was no objection to military uniforms of obsolete pattern being worn at such occasions.

Officers were required to wear uniform when on duty, and it was left to the discretion of the senior officer in a garrison whether to permit officers to wear plain clothes when not on duty. When attending manoeuvres, field training, camps of exercise and experiments at schools of instruction, all officers had to wear uniform.

When Service Dress was worn on parade or duty, officers wore breeches and boots as laid down for their respective services, Service Dress trousers and shoes not being worn on such occasions except at stables or during fatigue duties in barracks, or when officers were employed in offices. At stations abroad where Khaki Drill was worn, it was left to the discretion of general officers commanding to authorize such modifications as were considered necessary due to climatic conditions.

In order to achieve uniformity in the patterns and materials of Service Dress uniform within regiments and corps, it was essential that colonels commandant of corps and colonels of regiments took steps to prescribe the necessary details concerning the dress to be worn by officers serving in their respective corps or regiments. These involved the nature of the materials used in the manufacture of jackets, breeches, trousers, gloves, shirts and collars, the pattern of ties, and, in the case of breeches of the mounted pattern, whether buttons and button-holes or eyelet-holes and laces were to be worn. An alternative sealed pattern shade of light drab was approved for breeches of the mounted pattern. The sealed pattern shades of Service Dress materials were supposed to be strictly adhered to at all times.

Expenses.

The question of the expenses for which officers were liable in connection with the provision of their uniform during the war came under close and constant consideration by the War Office in view of the urgent need for economy in all things military. A number of Army Council Instructions were issued on this subject throughout the war.

ACI 1033, dated 31 August 1940, dealt with the expenses incurred by officers in the provision of their uniform. The 1940 rate of outfit allowance was lower than that in issue before the war, and this made it essential that all unnecessary expenditure on the provision of officers' outfits should be eliminated. The following instructions on this matter were issued.

1. The provisions as published in *Dress Regulations for the Army, 1934* which delegated to regimental authorities the selection of the type of material to be used by officers for their Service Dress garments were held in abeyance until further notice. Whilst it was realized that a good 'turn out' was essential at all times, the abandonment of ceremonial parades etc. during the war, and the introduction of the scheme under which officers were permitted to have uniforms made up in War Department material, rendered it both unnecessary and impracticable for uniformity of material to be adopted by officers in a regiment at that time. Each officer was permitted to wear material of whatever type he desired, provided that it was one of those normally used for Service Dress or Battle-Dress, such as barathea, whipcord or serge, and was of the correct drab shade.

2. Every officer was permitted to obtain his outfit from the tailor of his choice, and officers were not to be influenced to patronize any particular firm. The practice of nominating certain 'regimental tailors' in lists of items of uniform sent by regiments to young officers ceased.

3. Except in cases where a change of pattern was involved, e.g. transfer to or from Scottish regiments, officers who anticipated being transferred from one regiment to another were allowed to continue to wear the garments in their possession. Refunds of expenses, which might otherwise have been admissible, were not made to officers who obtained new garments contrary to these instructions.

4. A simplified pattern of greatcoat for officers (see page 171) was introduced, and this could be adopted by individual officers at their discretion. It was allowed to be worn side by side with the full regulation pattern in the same unit.

Instances had been brought to the notice of the War Office which indicated that some officers commissioned since the outbreak of hostilities had been induced by their regiments to incur heavy expenditure in the provision of extraneous items of kit which were quite unjustified during the national crisis and were not covered by their outfit allowance.

Officers transferred.

ACI 404, dated 22 March 1941, dealt with the question of the dress of officers transferred, posted or attached to regiments or corps other than their own. In the light of the conditions that prevailed in 1941 and with a view to reducing expense to the public and to individuals by the changes of uniform, the following instructions were published for the guidance of all concerned.

Service Dress

1. Except in the case of officers transferred from, or to, regiments or corps for which items of special pattern were authorized by *Dress Regulations for the Army, 1934* or other War Office authority (e.g. Foot Guards, Scottish regiments or the Royal Tank Regiment), officers were required to continue to wear the uniform in their possession at the date of their transfer, making changes only in the badges, buttons and any other authorized dress distinctions.

2. Officers transferred from, or to, regiments or corps for which items of distinctive pattern were authorized by *Dress Regulations for the Army, 1934* or other War Office authority, were required to change such garments to the pattern authorized for their new regiment or corps except for their footwear.

3. Officers transferred from a regiment etc. authorized to wear black boots to a unit in which brown boots were regulation footwear were required to wear out their black boots before changing over to the brown pattern; both types were permitted to be worn side by side in a unit, and, for the sake of economy, no pressure was allowed to be exerted on officers to make them change-over prematurely to the brown pattern. In cases where a change from brown to black boots was involved, the former were blacked.

4. Changes were not allowed to be made on account of variations in the types or shades of material used in different regiments or corps (see also ACI 1033 of 1940, page 121).

Battle-Dress. Changes were made in badges and other authorized distinctions, including those as detailed in ACI 1118 of 1940 (see page 95). A change of regulation head-dress was also made where appropriate. The matter of boots and the differences in uniform materials were applied to the Battle-Dress and were as set out above under (3) and (4).

Officers posted or attached.

Service Dress. As this order of dress was not normally worn on unit parades, officers posted or attached to a regiment or corps other than that to which they belonged were required to continue wearing the uniform of their own regiment of corps; they were not permitted to change to the uniform of the regiment or corps to which they were posted or attached.

Battle-Dress. In order to ensure that all officers of a unit were dressed alike when in Battle-Dress, those posted or attached to a regiment or corps other than their own had to adopt the procedure as set out above under 'Officers transferred'. This also applied when officers of the General List were posted or attached for duty with a regiment or corps, including those officers appointed as adjutant-masters of Home Guard battalions.

As late as the summer of 1943 this whole matter of the need to conserve both labour and materials was still being raised. Army Council Instruction 1250 dated 21 August 1943 considered it essential, both from the point of view of reducing individual expenses and on account of the urgent national need for economy in labour and materials, that officers be allowed to purchase their uniforms and outfit in the most economical manner. The following provisions were therefore made as a wartime measure, and all COs were required to ensure that they were properly understood:

1. Any tailor was allowed to be patronized. An officer was allowed to purchase his outfit from a tailor of his choice, and he was not allowed to be influenced to patronize any particular firm. The prewar practice of nominating 'regimental tailors', despite the instructions carried in ACI 1033 of August 1940 forbidding it, still had to be brought to the notice of regiments and units as late as August 1943.

2. Any material could be used provided that it was of the correct shade. An officer was allowed to wear material of whatever type he desired provided it was one of those normally used for Service Dress (barathea, whipcord or serge). It had to be of the regulation drab shade. This regulation drab shade was on view at the War Office Pattern Room, and sample pieces were supplied to regimental authorities and military tailors on request. In connection with the subject of uniform material, attention was called to the 1940 scheme enabling officers to purchase Service Dress garments made up in War Department material at reduced prices and the scheme introduced in 1943 whereby officers could obtain Service Dress garments made up in standard trade materials at controlled prices.

3. The modified pattern of Service Dress jacket had to be adopted. This measure was introduced by AC1 501 of 1942 (see page 159), and commanding officers had to ensure that all officers purchasing a Service Dress jacket, whether as an initial outfit or as a replacement, had it made up to the modified pattern.

4. A simplified pattern of greatcoat could be purchased. Although this measure had been introduced early in the war it was still being brought to the attention of officers as an alternative to the regulation style greatcoat for wear by individuals at their own discretion.

5. Officers were not to be influenced to buy extraneous articles of kit. All necessary articles required by an officer were as published in the pamphlet *Instructions Regarding Kit and Equipment for Officers, 1942*; any items not shown in this listing were considered to be extraneous, and no influence was brought to bear on officers to buy them.

6. Officers proceeding overseas were allowed to buy Tropical Clothing of other ranks' quality. Commanding officers were required to afford every facility to officers under orders for overseas to obtain their requirements from Army sources on payment and after the surrender of the appropriate number of clothing coupons.

Any provisions of *Dress Regulations for the Army, 1934* which were in conflict with any of the above instructions were held in abeyance until further notice.

Other Ranks' Personal Clothing, Necessaries and Unit and Station Public Clothing

All articles of authorized clothing and necessaries used by soldiers of the British Army were supplied by the Royal Army Ordnance Corps and were classified under three headings, as follows.

Personal clothing. This comprised such uniform articles as Service Dress, Battle-Dress, caps, jackets and trousers and ankle boots. The clothing was normally struck off charge upon issue to the soldier and was regarded as personal to the man, although he had no absolute right to the property issued.

Necessaries. These comprised such incidental articles as drawers, shirts and brushes. These articles were also normally struck off charge on issue and were regarded as personal to the soldier.

Public clothing. All other forms of authorized clothing and on issue were retained on ledger charge. Public clothing was sub-divided into unit public clothing, which was held on a unit's ledger charge and was issued either generally for retention during the term of a man's service (e.g. the greatcoat) or to certain personnel only for a specific purpose (e.g. motor-cyclist clothing); and station public clothing, which comprised articles held on charge by the officer in charge of the barracks and issued on inventory for the use of specific services, articles held on armament charge by officers in charge of armament sub-districts, and also articles held on 'articles-on-charge' in ordnance depots.

In 1943 the distinction between Public and Personal Clothing was abolished and all articles of clothing and necessaries were issued as permanent issues. Such articles remained public property and the individual soldier was held responsible for any loss or damage.

Regulation clothing.

Soldiers were clothed exclusively from Army sources. They were not allowed to wear or required to obtain articles which were not either sanctioned by the published Clothing Regulations or authorized by scales published from time to time by the War Office, and the wearing of articles of clothing and necessaries which departed in any way from the sealed patterns was strictly forbidden without the prior sanction of the War Office. Moreover, the alteration, either for payment or for any other purpose, of articles of clothing and necessaries that involved any departure from the sealed patterns was also strictly forbidden without the previous sanction of the War Office, the only alterations allowed in articles which were issued by the RAOC being those which were necessary to ensure a correct fit.

Any commanding officer who introduced or sanctioned for experimentation or any other purpose any unauthorized deviation from the sealed pattern of dress, clothing, equipment or badges was held responsible for the cost of replacing or restoring to the approved pattern any of these articles worn in his unit that may have been found not in conformity. No unauthorized ornament or emblem was permitted to be worn with uniform, and watch chains and trinkets were not permitted if they were visible.

A soldier was not permitted to leave his quarters unless he were properly dressed. Smoking in the streets in public when on duty was forbidden. It was the duty of all officers, warrant officers and NCOs to report irregularities of dress or misdemeanours of soldiers on pass or furlough to the commanding officer of the soldiers' unit, whether or not the men belonged to their own corps.

Soldiers were clothed in accordance with the scales of clothing and necessaries as laid down in War Office Clothing Regulations. These scales were applicable to other ranks only unless otherwise noted. Except where special War Office authority for free issue had been given, officers making use of War Department vehicles, motorcycles, etc. had to provide themselves with any

special protective clothing needed, and this was usually obtained from the RAOC on payment.

The recruit and his kit.

When a recruit had been supplied with a suit of Service Dress or Battle-Dress, a pair of ankle boots and underclothing, he was provided with packing materials obtained from the RAOC for the disposal of his plain clothing. The plain clothes within the limit for each man of one parcel as prescribed by the then current Post Office guide were despatched at the public's expense except where the individual soldier was able to make suitable arrangements for its disposal during a period of leave shortly after receipt of his uniform, or at any time depending on the proximity of his home. A record of the disposal arrangements made by each recruit was kept in the unit, and officers commanding ensured that all parcels were properly packed and addressed before despatch.

Part-worn articles were issued whenever available, except, for recruits, one suit and one pair of boots which were new. Articles of obsolescent pattern that were still authorized for wear were issued as long as stocks existed and before articles of a later pattern were issued. The correct fitting of boots was considered a matter of importance, and it was the commanding officers' responsibility to see that this was carefully carried out.

Regimental numbers.

Clothing and necessaries on issue from a unit's stores were marked with the soldier's Army number and the initials of his regiment or corps, but no markings which referred to his battalion, company, etc. were permitted. (For a listing of Army numbers allotted to corps etc., see Appendix I.) In the case of the identity discs, the soldier's Army number, his initials, surname and

Right: Men from the first draft of 34,000 Militiamen who started training with the regular forces during the weekend of 15 July 1939. These Militiamen are seen leaving the quartermaster's store at the Depot of the Queen's Royal Regiment (West Surrey), Guildford, having been issued with clothing and equipment.

Right: A new recruit at an
Infantry Training Centre
drawing his kit from the
quartermaster's stores, an
important part of his fitting-out.
Far right: Two photographs of a
British soldier's full kit; March
1942.
Below: These two photographs
demonstrate the sterling service
provided by the Tailor Corps.
An officer of the repair department, RAOC, first inspects men
wearing (left) badly fitting
Battle-Dress and then (right)
after the same suits have been
properly tailored to fit the
individual soldier; September
1941.

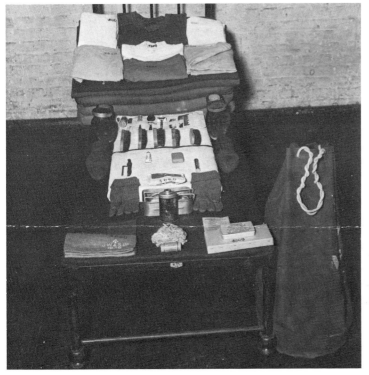

his religious denomination were shown. (For further details regarding the identity disc see page 254.)

Articles lost, stolen or damaged.

Clothing and necessaries other than cleaning and toilet articles were replaced free when no longer fit for further wear, but in the case of an article lost, made away with, or rendered prematurely unserviceable through carelessness or neglect, the soldier was placed under stoppages in order to make good its value. Loss by theft of, or malicious damage to, clothing and equipment issued to a soldier was made good at the soldier's expense, unless some other person were convicted of the offence. Where the commanding officer was satisfied that the loss or damage to clothing or equipment issued to individual soldiers was due to enemy action or active service operations, he was permitted to authorize replacements or repairs at public expense. In any other circumstances the matter was dealt with under King's Regulations.

The officer commanding a unit was responsible for ensuring that the clothing and necessaries of the soldiers under his command were serviceable and complete to scale and that all clothing and boots were carefully fitted in the presence of company commanders or an officer deputed by him for that purpose. It was considered of the utmost importance that each soldier was at all times in possession of one suit of clothing, one pair of boots and underclothing in sufficiently good condition to withstand three months' wear under active service conditions.

The high standard of cleanliness of uniforms and equipment normally expected in peacetime was not maintained during the war, especially under active service conditions. In the interests of economy, clothing was cleaned only when this was essential, webbing equipment was scrubbed and not blancoed, and brasses were allowed to tarnish or replaced altogether by gun-metal fittings.

Pre-War Service Dress for Officers of All Grades

The 1934 edition of *Dress Regulations for the Army* consisted of 192 pages (excluding the amendments), many of which were devoted to the listing of different types of uniform dress for wear by all grades of officers. Service Dress for the majority of these officers, as worn before the 1939–45 war, was included in the types of dress available to them, but this information is scattered throughout the book. I have therefore brought together all this information into one manageable chart (see Table 27 overleaf).

Wartime Dress Regulations, All Ranks, General Instructions, 1940–45

In May 1940, in the absence of a revised or new issue of Dress Regulations, the War Office published the first of a number of instructions dealing with the subject of dress for all ranks of the British Army. Army Council Instruction No. 466 for the week ending 15 May 1940 set out instructions regarding dress for the duration of the war which were published for general information and

Table 27. Items of Service Dress Uniform worn by Officers of the British Army, 1934–39

Each circle represents an individual item worn as part of the Service Dress (Home and Foreign Service) by the officer listed below.

	SD cap (p.133)	Forage cap/cover (p.129)	Beret (p.151)	Glengarry (p.138)	Tam-o'-Shanter (p.139)	Cap comforter (p.157)	SD jacket (p.158)	Breeches (p.161)	Tartan breeches (p.162)	Trousers (p.161)	Kilt/cover (p.189)	Spats	Leggings (p.168)	Puttees (p.166)	Hose tops (p.168)	Boots (p.163)	Spurs	Gloves (p.169)	Sam Browne (p.198)	Sword (p.199)	Broadsword (p.199)	British Warm (p.173)	Khaki greatcoat (p.170)	KD jacket (p.176)	KD trousers (p.174)	Khaki helmet (p.143)
Field-marshal	○						○	○								○	○	○	○			(16)				
General officer (general, lieutenant-general, major-general)	○						○	○								○	○	○	○					○	○	○
Brigadier and substantive colonel not belonging to a corps or department	○						○	○								○	○	○	○			○		○	○	○
Household Cavalry officer	○	①				○	○	○								○	○	○	○	○		(15)	(15)			
Dragoon officer	○					○	○	○								○	○	○	○	○			○	○	○	○
Hussar officer	○		○			○	○	○								○	○	○	○	○			○	○	○	○
Lancer officer	○					○	○	○								○	○	○	○	○			○	○	○	○
Royal Horse Artillery officer	○					○	○	○								○	○	○	○	○			○	○	○	○
Royal Artillery officer	○					○	○	○								○	○	○	○	○			○	○	○	○
Royal Engineers, officer of	○					○	○	○						○		○	○	○	○	○			○	○	○	○
Royal Corps of Signals, officer of	○					○	○	○						○		○	○	○	○	○			○	○	○	○
Infantry, Foot Guard Regiments, officer of	○	①				○	○	○		④						○	(12)	○	○	○			○			○
Infantry of the Line officer except fusilier, Scottish and rifle regiments	○					○	③	④		○						○		○	○	○			○			○
Fusilier, except Royal Scots Fusiliers	○					○	○	④		○						○		○	○	○			○			○
Scottish (Highland) Regiment officer (except HLI)		2		○	○	○	○		⑤		⑦	⑧	⑨		○	⑩	⑬	14	○		○			○	○	○
The Highland Light Infantry, officer of		2		○	○	○	④	⑤					⑨	○		⑪		14	○		○			○	○	○
Scottish (Lowland) Regiments, The Royal Scots, The Royal Scots Fusiliers and The King's Own Scottish Borderers, officer of		2		○	○	○	④											14	○		○			○	○	○
The Cameronians, officer of		2		○	○	○	④			○						○		○						○	○	○
Rifle Regiments, except Cameronians, officer of	○					○	○	○		○						○		○						○	○	○
Royal Tank Corps, officer of			○			○	○	○		⑥			⑨			○		○						○	○	○
Royal Army Chaplains Department, officer of	○	○					○	○								○		○	○				○			
RASC, officer of	○						○	○								○	○	○	○				○			○
RAMC general officer, late of		○					○	○								○		○	○				○			
RAMC, colonel, late of		○					○	○								○		○	○				○			
RAMC officer	○						○	○		○						○		○	○				○			
RAOC general officer, late of		○					○	○								○		○	○				○			
RAOC, colonel, late of		○					○	○								○		○	○				○			
RAOC, officer	○						○	○							○	○		○	○				○			
RAPC, general officer, late of		○					○	○								○		○	○				○			
RAPC, colonel, late of	○	○					○	○								○		○	○				○			
RAPC officer	○						○	○								○		○	○				○			
RAVC, general officer, late of		○					○	○								○		○	○				○			
RAVC, colonel, late of		○					○	○								○		○	○				○			
RAVC officer	○						○	○								○		○	○				○			
AEC, colonel, late of		○					○	○								○		○	○				○			
AEC officer	○						○	○							○	○		○	○							
The Army Dental Corps, general officer, late of		○					○	○								○		○	○				○			
The Army Dental Corps, colonel, late of		○					○	○								○	○	○	○				○		○	○
The Army Dental Corps, officer	○					○	○	○		○					○	○		○						○	○	○
Royal Engineers Services, staff for	○					○	○	○		○					○	○		○					○	○	○	○

[1] Worn without cover in Service Dress, in addition to the SD Cap.
[2] Glengarry often substituted for the Tam 'o Shanter.
[3] Oxf. & Bucks. wore 2½in. loop of drab Russia cording attached to a small bronze button on front edge of collar.
[4] Dismounted officers: knickerbocker pattern; others: mounted pattern.
[5] Worn by mounted officers.
[6] 1923–39 – below Major: 'Plus Two' trousers, puttees, black ankle boots in SD; Major and above: mounted breeches, field boots, spurs.
[7] Full dress Kilts worn with KD apron but without sporran.
[8] Khaki spats worn by dismounted officers.
[9] Mounted officers wore black leather leggings.
[10] Mounted officers: black boots; dismounted officers: black shoes.
[11] Dismounted officers: brown ankle boots with puttees; mounted officers: black boots and black leggings.
[12] Mounted officers wore brass spurs and brass chains.
[13] Mounted officers wore steel jack spurs.
[14] Undress brown leather gloves worn with SD.
[15] SD greatcoat changed in June 1937 to British Warm.
[16] Atholl Grey type.
CMP mounted officers: Cavalry dress; dismounted: Infantry dress.

compliance. Over the next five years these instructions were periodically added to and slightly altered, but in essence they remained the same until well after the war was over.

Order of dress.

1. Full Dress and Mess Dress was not to be worn on any occasion.

2. Undress was permitted to be worn by all ranks in the evening. This dress was optional and it was emphasized that individuals who then did not already possess it were not required to provide it against their will. It was not to be worn during the day on any occasion. However, in March 1942 Undress uniform was permitted to be worn by all ranks when on seven days' leave or longer at any time of the day, if they so wished. This dress, besides being an optional item, carried no allowance of clothing coupons under the clothing rationing scheme in order to enable either officers or other ranks to obtain it.

Officers proceeding out of barracks or camps in this dress were required to wear the Sam Browne belt (without brace or frog) or a cloth belt of the type (in the material and colour of the jacket) approved for wear with Service Dress (see below), whilst officers of rifle and Scottish regiments were permitted, alternatively, to wear the belts etc. authorized for them as shown in *Dress Regulations for the Army, 1934*, para. 90, sub-para. 7b. In keeping with the prewar policy, other ranks did not wear waist-belts with Undress.

3. Officers and other ranks from an expeditionary force on leave in the United Kingdom and Northern Ireland were allowed to regard the wearing of uniform whilst on leave as optional. In November 1940 these instructions were enlarged upon to allow all ranks on seven days' leave or longer taken in the United Kingdom to wear if they wished plain clothes while they were away from their stations; all ranks on leave in the United Kingdom from an expeditionary force had permission to wear plain clothes irrespective of their period of leave. These instructions were reiterated by ACI 851 dated 22 April 1942.

4. All ranks, whether they were on leave or at their stations, were permitted to wear plain clothes for the purpose of athletic exercises for which a special dress was necessary.

5. Except as otherwise provided above, Service Dress or Battle-Dress was worn by all serving personnel on all occasions.

Medals. The wearing of decorations and medals ceased during the war. Medal ribbons were worn on Undress, Service Dress and Battle-Dress.

Belts and swords.

1. Officers and warrant officers Class I, when wearing the Sam Browne belt without the sword, also wore it without a brace or frog, except that when the revolver was carried a brace over the right shoulder could be worn if desired in order properly to support the revolver holster; if a sword were carried, then the frog had obviously to be worn.

2. From May 1940 the sword was worn by officers and warrant officers Class I of horsed units only, and the following procedure was adopted. Newly appointed officers, except those of horsed

units, had to provide themselves with a sword, while the provision of a Sam Browne belt was optional. Instead of the Sam Browne belt a cloth belt in material which matched the Service Dress jacket was allowed to be worn. This belt, which happened to be similar in design to that then worn by officers of the Royal Air Force, was 2in in width and was fitted with a plain metal buckle. The cloth belt was allowed to be worn by any other officer as an alternative to the Sam Browne belt at his discretion. Warrant officers Class I did not wear the cloth belt.

Head-dress. See page 129.

Change of uniform on promotion. Officers who, on promotion to full Colonel (including Acting, Temporary or War Substantive rank) or appointment as Brigadier or Acting Major-General, were removed from the list of their regiment or corps were no longer required to adopt the uniform prescribed for these ranks in *Dress Regulations for the Army, 1934*, para. 261 et seq. They were permitted to continue wearing regimental uniform with scarlet gorget patches on Service Dress and the appropriate badges of rank. If they were promoted to the substantive rank of Major-General, the uniform that was prescribed for that rank was then adopted forthwith.

Gorget patches worn on Battle-Dress. For details of prewar and wartime gorget patches, including gorget patches worn on Battle-Dress, see page 41, listed under a separate heading.

Buttons of modified pattern and worsted rank badges. Officers who were unable to procure the then current regulation pattern articles were allowed to use buttons in composition of a colour that matched the garment for which they were required, or of brown leather, on all jackets etc. for which they were prescribed; they were also permitted to use rank badges in worsted embroidery in place of metal insignia. This did not authorize any change in articles that were then already in wear, and this expedient was intended to apply only when the regulation patterns were definitely unobtainable. ACI 1535 dated 22 July 1942 elaborated slightly on the previous instructions in stating that, in the event of officers being unable to procure the regulation pattern metal articles, alternative types were allowed to be used on all garments for which they were prescribed: cap badges in composition (later referred to as 'plastic'); collar badges in composition; rank badges in composition or worsted; and buttons in composition or leather. It should be remembered that plastic cap badges were first introduced in December 1941 (ACI 2594 dated 27 December 1941 – see page 118.)

The carrying of canes. The practice of carrying regimental or other types of canes or whips by other ranks ceased.

Wearing the letter 'T'. The letter 'T' referred to in *Territorial Army Regulations, 1936*, paras. 527 and 548, ceased to be worn by officers and other ranks for whom it had hitherto been prescribed. Battalion numerals were also omitted from the shoulder titles worn by other ranks of TA infantry battalions.

Footwear and anklets. See page 163.

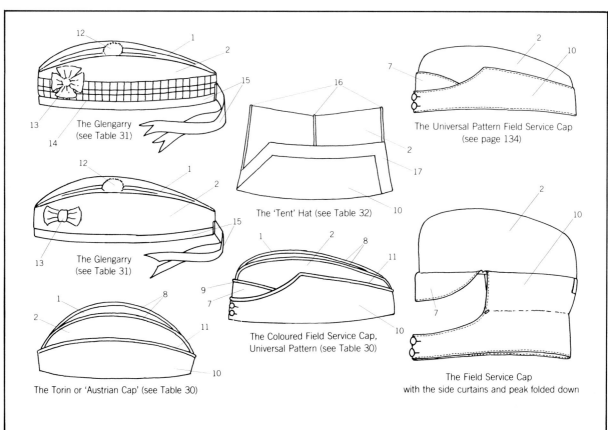

The Glengarry
(see Table 31)

The Glengarry
(see Table 31)

The Torin or 'Austrian Cap' (see Table 30)

The 'Tent' Hat (see Table 32)

The Coloured Field Service Cap,
Universal Pattern (see Table 30)

The Universal Pattern Field Service Cap
(see page 134)

The Field Service Cap
with the side curtains and peak folded down

2. HEAD-DRESS

The Universal Pattern Forage Cap

The universal pattern forage cap was very much a prewar item of head-dress worn by officers of all ranks but with varying amounts and patterns of embroidered decoration displayed on the peak which together with the cap badge differentiated between the grades of ranks. According to *Dress Regulations for the Army, 1934*, only general officers, brigadiers, substantive colonels and other entitled officers as listed below were permitted to wear the forage cap with Service Dress uniform. When this took place the forage cap had to be worn with a khaki drab, removable cloth cover which extended over the crown and body of the cap, leaving the cap band and the badge clear.

The crown of the cap, which was normally $10\frac{3}{8}$in in diameter but could be $\frac{1}{8}$in either larger or smaller for every $\frac{1}{4}$in variation in cap size, was joined to the body of the cap by a single welt. The body, made up in four pieces, was in turn joined to the cap band by a second welt, whilst a third ran around the base of the stiffened band covered by a cloth band $1\frac{1}{2}$in deep which nestled neatly between the two lower welts. The chin strap was of patent leather, $\frac{3}{8}$in wide, fastened on to the cap by two $\frac{1}{2}$in diameter gilt buttons placed immediately behind the corners of the peak. The peak itself sloped at an angle of $45°$ and was 2in deep at the middle when worn with embroidery and $1\frac{3}{4}$in deep when plain.

Above: A selection of headwear is displayed here by officers of the Staff at the Royal Military College Officer Cadet Training Unit, photographed with King George VI and Queen Elizabeth on 22 March 1945.

British Army head-dress types. 1, Crown; 2, Body; 3, Crown welt; 4, Band welt (upper); 5, Band welt (lower); 6, Cap band; 7, Peak; 8, Crown piping; 9, Peak piping; 10, Curtain; 11, Curtain piping; 12, Toori; 13, Badge ribbon; 14, Diced band; 15, Rim and silks; 16, Piped seams; 17, Curtain lace; 18, Head band; 19, Chin strap; 20, Chin strap buttons.

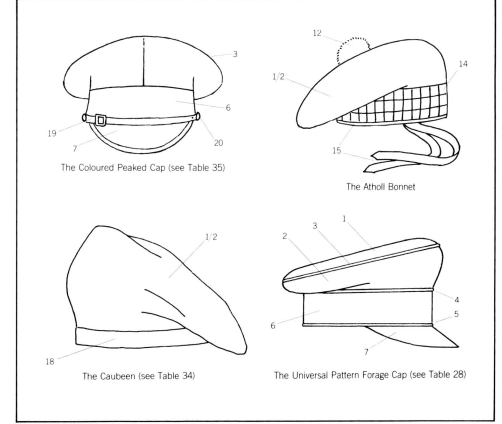

The Coloured Peaked Cap (see Table 35)

The Atholl Bonnet

The Caubeen (see Table 34)

The Universal Pattern Forage Cap (see Table 28)

Wearer	Crown body	Crown welt	Cap band	Band welt (upper)	Band welt (lower)	Peak	Badge
Field-marshal	Dark blue cloth	Dark blue	Scarlet cloth	Scarlet	Scarlet	Two rows of gold oakleaf embroidery[2]	In gold embroidery on blue cloth, the Royal Crest[3] above crossed batons within a laurel wreath
General officers[4]	Dark blue cloth	Dark blue	Scarlet cloth	Scarlet	Scarlet	Two rows of gold oakleaf embroidery[2]	In gold embroidery on blue cloth, the Royal Crest with crossed sword and baton within a laurel wreath, the blade of the sword in silver
Brigadiers and substantive colonels	Dark blue cloth	Dark blue	Scarlet cloth	Scarlet	Scarlet	One row of gold oakleaf embroidery on lower edge	The Royal Crest in gold embroidery on on blue cloth
Chaplain-General and chaplains with relative rank of General Officer	Black cloth	Purple	Purple cloth	Purple	Purple	Two rows of black oakleaf embroidery[2]	In gold embroidery on black cloth, the Royal Crest with crossed sword and baton within a laurel wreath, the blade of the sword in silver
Chaplains with relative rank of Colonel	Black cloth	Purple	Purple cloth	Purple	Purple	One row of black oakleaf embroidery on lower edge	Upon a wreath of laurel and oak, in gilt, a Maltese cross (eight points) in silver; in the centre of the cross a circle, in gilt, on a blue enamel ground with the motto 'In This Sign Conquer' pierced; within the circle a quatrefoil voided; the whole ensigned by the imperial crown in gilt
Deputy chaplain-general	Black cloth	Purple	Purple cloth	Purple	Purple	One row of black oakleaf embroidery on lower edge	The Royal Crest in gold embroidery on black cloth
General officer late RAMC	Dark blue cloth	Dull cherry	Dull cherry cloth	Dull cherry	Dull cherry	Two rows of gold oakleaf embroidery[2]	In gold embroidery on blue cloth, the Royal Crest with crossed sword and baton within a laurel wreath, the blade of the sword in silver
Colonel late RAMC[5]	Dark blue cloth	Dull cherry	Dull cherry cloth	Dull cherry	Dull cherry	One row of gold oakleaf embroidery on lower edge of peak	The Royal Crest in gold embroidery on blue cloth
General officer RAOC	Dark blue cloth	Scarlet	Blue cloth	Scarlet	Scarlet	Two rows of gold oakleaf embroidery[2]	In gold embroidery on blue cloth, the Royal Crest with crossed sword and baton within a laurel wreath, the blade of the sword in silver
Colonel RAOC	Dark blue cloth	Scarlet	Blue cloth	Scarlet	Scarlet	One row of gold oakleaf embroidery along lower edge of peak	As for collar of tunic, but larger
General officer late RAPC[5]	Dark blue cloth	Primrose yellow	Blue cloth	Primrose yellow	Primrose yellow	Two rows of gold oakleaf embroidery[2]	In gold embroidery on blue cloth, the Royal Crest with crossed sword and baton within a laurel wreath, the blade of the sword in silver
Colonel RAPC	Dark blue cloth	Primrose yellow	Blue cloth	Primrose yellow	Primrose yellow	One row of gold oakleaf embroidery along lower edge of peak	The Royal Crest in gold embroidery on blue cloth
General officer late RAVC	Dark blue cloth	Maroon	Maroon cloth	Maroon	Maroon	Two rows of gold oakleaf embroidery[2]	In gold embroidery on blue cloth, the Royal Crest with crossed sword and baton within a laurel wreath, the blade of the sword in silver
Colonel late RAVC	Dark blue cloth	Maroon	Maroon cloth	Maroon	Maroon	One row of gold oakleaf embroidery on lower edge of peak	The Royal Crest in gold embroidery on blue cloth
Colonel late AEC	Dark blue cloth	Cambridge blue	Cambridge blue cloth	Cambridge blue		One row of gold oakleaf embroidery on lower edge of peak	The Royal Crest in gold embroidery on blue cloth
General officer late The AD Corps[5]	Dark blue cloth	Emerald green	Emerald green cloth	Emerald green	Emerald green	Two rows of gold oakleaf embroidery[2]	In gold embroidery on blue cloth, the Royal Crest with crossed sword and baton within a laurel wreath, the blade of the sword in silver
Colonel late The AD Corps	Dark blue cloth	Emerald green	Emerald green cloth	Emerald green	Emerald green	One row of gold oakleaf embroidery on lower edge of peak	The Royal Crest in gold embroidery on blue cloth

Right: Senior officers' cap badges. 1, Field marshal; 2, General officer; 3, Brigadier and substantive colonel.

Wearer	Crown body	Crown welt	Cap band	Band welt (upper)	Band welt (lower)	Peak	Badge
Officers Household Cavalry[6]	Dark blue cloth	Scarlet	Scarlet cloth	Dark blue	Dark blue	Gold embroidered peak[7]	Within the Garter the Royal Cypher pierced on a ground of red enamel; the motto of the Garter pierced on blue enamel; the Garter surmounted by a crown; the whole of the badge in gilt
Officers Grenadier Guards[6]	Dark blue cloth	Dark blue	Plain black mohair braid	Dark blue	Dark blue	Embroidered peak	A grenade in gold embroidery
Officers Coldstream Guards[6]	Dark blue cloth	Dark blue	Plain black mohair braid	Dark blue	Dark blue	Embroidered peak	In silver, the Star of the Order of the Garter; the Garter and motto in gilt metal, over blue enamel, the cross in red enamel
Officers Scots Guards[6]	Dark blue cloth	Gold cord	Diced red, white, blue	Dark blue	Dark blue	Embroidered peak[8]	In silver, the Star of the Order of the Thistle; the circle with motto and the centre in gilt metal
Officers Irish Guards[6]	Dark blue cloth	Dark blue	Plain black mohair braid	Dark blue	Dark blue	Embroidered peak	The Star of the Order of St. Patrick in silver, the motto and circle in gilt metal on a blue enamel ground; within the circle the cross in red
Officers Welsh Guards[6]	Dark blue cloth	Dark blue	Plain black mohair braid	Dark blue	Dark blue	Embroidered peak	A leek in gold embroidery on black cloth

[1]This schedule is based on information extracted from *Dress Regulations for the Army, 1934.* The universal pattern forage cap was superseded by the introduction of the Field Service cap (details of which are contained on page 134 of this work) in June 1937. The forage cap was authorized to be worn by officers of those ranks as listed in this schedule on occasions other than on active service, annual training and manoeuvres when wearing Service Dress.

[2]The official description given for the configuration of the two rows of oakleaves (both in gold and black embroidery) set on the peaks of these forage caps, as published in *Dress Regulations for the Army, 1934* (various pages), is as follows: 'Two rows of gold (or black) oakleaf embroidery on the lower edge of the peak'.

As loath as I am to suggest that the War Office is in error, it is obvious that this statement is not correct. Any peak that carried two rows of oakleaves, either gold or black, had one row positioned along the upper edge just below the cap band and a second row running along the lower edge of the peak. Despite the fact that three separate sets of amendments were published between 1937 and 1940, no correction was made to the original statement. Note: All regimental officers of the Household Cavalry and of the Brigade of Guards wore a single bar of gold embroidery ¾in in width on the lower edge of the peak of their forage caps.

Although officers other than those listed in this schedule wore forage caps, they were not permitted to wear them with drab Service Dress. However, for the sake of interest the following information is given.

1. Field officers of rifle regiments wore a single row of black embroidered oakleaves on the lower edge of the peak of their forage caps.

2. Chaplains to the Forces, 2nd, 3rd and 4th classes, although they did not rank as field officers, wore a black embroidered bar ¾in in width on the lower edge of their forage cap peaks.

3. Field officers of all other regiments and corps, including colonels-in-chief, colonels commandant, colonels and brevet colonels, wore a single bar of gold embroidery ¾in in width on the lower edge of the peak of their forage caps.

The peaks of the forage caps for all other officers were worn plain, i.e. without embellishment.

[3]The Royal Crest consisted of a lion standing astride a royal crown. The attitude of the lion is referred to heraldically as 'lion passant guardant', that is with its hind legs standing on the right-hand portion of the crown as viewed from the front, with its forelegs astride the opposite, left-hand portion of the crown. The head of the lion is turned to its left to face towards the observer. This emblem is occasionally referred to in slang terms as 'a dog and basket'.

[4]General officers were generals, lieutenant-generals and major-generals.

[5]Added to the existing *Dress Regulations for the Army, 1934* by Amendment No. 1 dated June 1937.

[6]Officers of the Household Cavalry and five regiments of Foot Guards are listed in *Dress Regulations for the Army, 1934,* para. 26, page 6, as being permitted to wear the forage cap with Service Dress uniform, but in the same publication, for officers of the Household Cavalry (para. 349, page 46) and for officers of the Foot Guards (para. 709, page 78), no provision is made under the heading 'Service Dress, Home Service' for the forage cap to be worn.

[7]Chin-straps worn with the forage cap were of regimental pattern.

[8]Neither chin-strap nor buttons were worn on the forage cap in the Scots Guards.

The Service Dress Cap for Wear by Officers[1]

Stiff pattern. This was of the same shape as the forage cap (as described on page 129) but was manufactured of khaki drab material to match the officers' Service Dress. The peak was plain and stiff and the crown stiffened with a wire former. These caps had a brown leather chin-strap held in place by two small bronze buttons for all regiments other than officers of rifle regiments, who had chin-straps of black patent leather and black buttons. All officers wore cap badges in bronze finished metal, which later were sometimes replaced by plastic badges (see page 118).

Soft pattern. This item, a survivor from the time of the Great War, and having been introduced in 1925 by Army Order 234 of 1925, was still in use in 1934 according to the then current Dress Regulations but it is doubtful if it saw much use as an item of officers' head-dress by the time war broke out. No references are made to it in any wartime Army Council Instructions.

It was in fact of the same shape and colouring as the stiff pattern Service Dress cap except that the

[1]The caps as described here were for wear by officers below the rank of Substantive Colonel in the Cavalry, Infantry of the Line, Royal Artillery, Royal Engineers, Royal Corps of Signals and other corps and departments. For the pattern of Service Dress cap as worn by field-marshals, general officers, brigadiers and substantive colonels, as well as officers of the Foot Guards and Chaplains' Department, see below.

plain khaki peak was flexible and the crown of the cap was not wired. It was intended that this item be carried or worn on active service, during periods of training and during manoeuvres.

The Service Dress Cap for Wear by Other Ranks

This cap was produced from khaki serge material of a quality that was similar to, if not actually matching, that used for the khaki Service Dress or Battle-Dress as worn by the rank and file.

A brown leather chin-strap with brass buckles and a small brass stud (all of which required careful polishing) was worn on the front of the cap, fastened to the sides of the cap band about 1in back from the corners of the peak by two small brass buttons. The wearer's regimental or corps cap badge was worn on the front of the cap, usually positioned half way on the upper edge of the cap band and on the lower edge of the body of the cap.

The cap, once it had been issued, was usually 'moulded' into shape by the wearer in accordance with the prevailing regimental fashion. (In order to achieve uniformity within a regiment this work was often undertaken by the regimental tailor.)

All caps had the facility to be 'set up' in the front. This was achieved by the use of a short, flat, metal strip inserted into a specially provided pocket on the inside of the front of the cap under the oilcloth sweat band. The metal strip was attached to the internal wire grommet that formed

Table 29.   The Khaki Service Dress Cap worn by Officers as listed, 1934–45[1]

Wearer	Cap band	Badge details etc.
Field-marshal	Scarlet	As forage cap; chin-strap buttons in gilt
General officers[2]	Scarlet	As forage cap; chin-strap buttons in gilt
Brigadiers and substantive colonels	Scarlet	As forage cap; chin-strap buttons in gilt
General officer late RAMC	Dull cherry	As forage cap
Colonel RAMC	Dull cherry	As forage cap
General officer late RAOC	Scarlet	As forage cap
Colonel RAOC	Scarlet	As forage cap
General officer late RAPC	Primrose yellow	As forage cap
Colonel RAPC	Primrose yellow	As forage cap
General officer late RAVC	Maroon	As forage cap
Colonel RAVC	Maroon	As forage cap
General officer late AD Corps	Emerald green	As forage cap
Colonel AD Corps	Emerald green	As forage cap
Colonel AEC	Cambridge blue	As forage cap
Officer Grenadier Guards[3]		Grenade in gold embroidery
Officer Coldstream Guards[3]		The Star of the Order of the Garter in silver metal, as described for forage cap but smaller
Officer Scots Guards[3]		The Star of the Order of the Thistle in silver metal, as described for forage cap but smaller[4]
Officer Irish Guards[3]		The Star of the Order of St. Patrick in silver metal, as described for forage cap but smaller
Officer Welsh guards[3]		A leek in gold embroidery on black cloth, as described for forage cap but smaller
Chaplain		As described for forage cap worn by chaplains with the relative rank of Colonel but the whole in black metal; black chin-strap and buttons also worn

[1]Authorized for wear by officers as listed here on active service, annual training and manoeuvres.
[2]General officers consisted of generals, lieutenant-generals and major-generals.
[3]*Dress Regulations for the Army, 1934* refers to the head-dress worn by Foot Guards officers as a soft pattern Service Dress cap. Service Dress caps in use by Guards officers differed from those in use with the rest of the British Army in that they were manufactured from a darker, browner shade of khaki

drab than normally used. The slope of the peak was more pronounced even than with the forage cap, the crown of the cap was smaller and the front of the cap was 'set up'.
[4]Officers of the Scots Guards wore a small piece of Royal Stuart tartan cloth measuring 2½in wide × 2in deep on the left side of the Service Dress cap. The tartan material was produced in finely woven silks, and because of its small size the dark green and black stripes were ½in wide and the red stripes ²⁄₅in wide.

the shape to the crown of the cap, and once in position it forced the grommet up at the front of the cap which had the effect of raising the upper edge of the crown whilst at the same time stretching smooth the material in the front.

The peak to this style of cap was covered in khaki serge material. On prewar- and early wartime-produced caps the peak was stitched in parallel lines, the purpose of this being to stiffen the peak and to help it to retain its shape. However, this time-consuming practice was later done away with and plain peaks were produced with sufficient in-built stiffening to maintain their own shape, even after being drenched with rain.

The Universal Pattern Field Service Cap

The universal pattern of the khaki drab Field Service cap was reintroduced into the British Army at the time of the introduction of the Battle-Dress. It was authorized to be worn by officers and other ranks alike, the only difference being in the quality of the material used in its manufacture: officers had Field Service caps produced in fine quality barathea, whilst the caps mass produced for other ranks were of plain khaki drab serge.

The Field Service cap was required to be worn one size larger than other head-dresses in order that a proper fit was secured. When worn correctly the cap was placed on the right side of the wearer's head with the front of the cap positioned just over his right eye.

Regimental or corps cap badges were worn in bronzed metal for officers and gilding metal by other ranks towards the front on the left side of the cap. Two small buttons, in a metal that matched the cap badge, were used to fasten the ends of the curtain flaps that were secured in front of the cap; both the side curtains and the small peak were able to be folded down if required, but this was usually only done when the cap was worn during very cold

weather as the curtain flaps afforded some protection to the wearer's ears and the back of his neck.

This form of cap was occasionally referred to as a 'forage cap' or 'side-cap'.

The Introduction of the Coloured Field Service Cap, June 1937

Strictly speaking, June 1937 saw the re-introduction of this form of head-dress. The first recognizable pattern of coloured Field Service cap was introduced to be worn by British troops in India by a circular dated 15 February 1894. Two years later, under Army Order III of June 1896, officers were directed to wear the pattern of coloured Field Service cap in use with the other ranks. However, as all this is outside the time scale of this work it is not my intention to dwell on the origins of the cap, and for the purposes of this book the familiar coloured Field Service cap was introduced as published under Amendment No. 1 of June 1937 to the existing *Dress Regulations for the Army, 1934*. In para. 31A, under the heading 'Cap, Field Service' it stated:

'Similar in shape to the Glengarry, about 4½-inches high and 3¾-inches across the top; a folding peak at the front and flaps at the side let down which, when folded, fasten at the front with two small regimental buttons.

'The colour of the cap, crown and piping will be decided by the colonels commandant or colonels of regiments or corps. The badge will be of authorized regimental pattern.

'For field-marshals, general officers, brigadiers, and substantive colonels not belonging to a corps or department, the following pattern has been approved:—
Blue cloth with scarlet cloth top; gold French braid welts on cap and flaps and at front and back seams. Badges and buttons as for forage cap.

'This cap, the use of which is entirely optional, may be worn with mess dress and on other informal occasions; it will not be worn on any occasion when on parade or duty, and will be maintained in addition to, and not in substitution of, the forage cap.'

Right: Sjt. A. Cairns, DCM, MM, a Glaswegian member of the Durham Light Infantry, wearing the universal pattern khaki Field Service cap; 16 March 1944.
Far right: Lt.-Col. J. Durnford-Slater, DSO, who led the Commando raid on Vaagso, wearing the Royal Artillery Coloured Field Service cap with Service Dress; 7 July 1942.

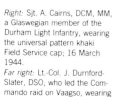

Table 30. Schedule of Coloured Field Service Caps (Universal Pattern)[1]

Item	Regiment or corps	Crown	Crown piping[2]	Body	Peak	Peak piping[3]	Curtain	Curtain piping[2]
1	1st The Royal Dragoons	Dark blue	Yellow Gld	Red	Dark blue	—	Dark blue	Yellow Gld
2	The Royal Scots Greys	Dark blue	Yellow Gld	Dark blue	Dark blue	—	—	—
3	Royal Wiltshire Yeomanry	Red	White Slv	Red	Red	—	Red	White Slv
4	Yorkshire Dragoons	White	White Slv	White	Dark blue	White Slv	Dark blue	White Slv
5	Yorkshire Hussars	Red	White Slv	Red	Red	—	Red	White Slv
6	The Queen's Bays	Dark blue	Yellow Gld	White	Dark blue	—	Dark blue	—
7	3rd Carabiniers	Yellow	Yellow Gld	Dark blue	Dark blue	—	Dark blue	Yellow Gld
8	5th Royal Inniskilling Dragoon Guards	Pale yellow	Yellow Gld	Pale yellow	Light green	Yellow Gld	Light green	Yellow Gld
9	3rd The King's Own Hussars	Red	Yellow Gld	Red	Red	—	Red	Yellow Gld
10	4th Queen's Own Hussars	Dark blue	Yellow Gld	Yellow	Dark blue	—	Dark blue	—
11	7th Queen's Own Hussars	Red	Yellow Gld	Red	Red	Yellow Gld	Red	Yellow Gld
12	9th Queen's Royal Lancers	Dark blue	Yellow Gld	Dark blue	Dark blue	—	Dark blue	Yellow Gld
13	10th Royal Hussars	Red	Yellow Gld	Red	Red	Yellow Gld	Red	Yellow Gld
14	11th Hussars	Cherry red	Yellow Gld	Cherry red	Cherry red	—	Cherry red	Yellow Gld
15	12th Royal Lancers	Red	Yellow Gld	Red	Red	—	Red	Yellow
16	13th/18th Royal Hussars	White	Yellow Gld	White	Dark blue	—	Dark blue	Yellow Gld
17	14th/20th King's Hussars	Red	Yellow Gld	Red	Red	Yellow Gld	Red	Yellow Gld
18	15th/19th The King's Royal Hussars	Red	Yellow Gld	Red	Red	Yellow Gld	Red	Yellow Gld
19	16th/5th Lancers	Red	Yellow Gld	Red	Dark blue	—	Dark blue	—
20	17th/21st Lancers	White	Yellow Gld	White	Dark blue	Yellow Gld	Dark blue	Yellow Gld
21	Derbyshire Yeomanry	Red	Yellow Gld	Dark blue	Dark blue	—	Cambridge blue	Yellow Gld
22	Fife & Forfar Yeomanry	Red	White Slv	Red	Dark blue	White Slv	Dark blue	White Slv
23	3rd & 4th County of London Yeomanry (Sharpshooters)	Pale yellow	Yellow Gld	Light green	Light green	—	Light green	Yellow Gld
24	Lothians and Border Horse	Light blue	Yellow Gld	Light blue	Light blue	—	Light blue	Yellow Gld
25	Northamptonshire Yeomanry	Light blue	White Slv	Light blue	Dark blue	—	Dark blue	Dark blue
26	East Riding Yeomanry	Light blue	—	Light blue	Light blue	—	Light blue	—
27	Lanarkshire Yeomanry	Red	Yellow Gld	Red	Dark blue	Yellow Gld	Dark blue	Yellow Gld
28	Duke of Lancaster's Own Yeomanry	Red	Yellow Gld	Cambridge blue	Cambridge blue	Yellow Gld	Cambridge blue	Yellow Gld
29	Leicestershire Yeomanry[4]	Red	White Slv	Red	Red	White Slv	Red	White Slv
30	Northumberland Hussars	Light blue	White	Light blue	Dark blue	White	Dark blue	White
31	Shropshire Yeomanry[4]	Red	Yellow Gld	Dark blue	Dark blue	—	Dark blue	Yellow Gld
32	Hampshire Carabiniers[4]	White	Yellow Gld	White	Dark blue	White	Dark blue	Yellow Gld
33	Royal Devonshire Yeomanry[4]	Red	White Slv	Red	Dark blue	White Slv	Dark blue	White Slv
34	Loyal Suffolk Hussars[4]	Red	Yellow Gld	Red	Dark green	Yellow Gld	Dark green	Yellow Gld
35	Queen's Own Worcestershire Yeomanry[4]	Red	—	Red	Dark blue	Yellow Gld	Dark blue	Yellow Gld
36	Oxfordshire Hussars[4]	Red	—	Red	Dark blue	Yellow	Dark blue	Yellow
37	Norfolk Yeomanry[4]	Yellow	—	Yellow	Yellow	—	Dark blue	—
38	Glamorgan Yeomanry[4]	Red	—	Red	Dark blue	Yellow Gld	Dark blue	Yellow Gld
39	Berkshire Yeomanry[5]	Scarlet	White	Dark blue	Yellow	—	Dark blue	White
40	Inns of Court Regiment[5]	Green	—	Dark blue	Green	—	Dark blue	Green
41	Essex Yeomanry[4, 5]	Scarlet	Yellow	Scarlet	Scarlet	—	Green	Yellow
42	North Irish Horse[5]	White	White	Dark green	Dark green	—	Dark green	White
43	Royal Artillery	Red	—	Red	Dark blue	Yellow Gld	Dark blue	Yellow Gld
44	Royal Engineers	Dark blue	Yellow Gld	Dark blue	Dark blue	—	Dark blue	—
45	Royal Corps of Signals	Light blue	Yellow Gld	Dark blue	Dark blue	Black	Dark blue	Yellow Gld
46	Queen's Royal Regiment	Light green	Red	Dark blue	Dark blue	—	Dark blue	—
47	The Buffs	Dark blue	Buff	Dark blue	Dark blue	—	Dark blue	—
48	The King's Own Royal Regiment	Red	—	Dark blue	Dark blue	—	Dark blue	—
49	The Royal Warwickshire Regiment	Dark blue	Red	Dark blue	Dark blue	—	Dark blue	—
50	The Royal Fusiliers	Cambridge blue	—	Cambridge blue	Cambridge blue	—	Cambridge blue	—
51	The King's Regiment	Dark blue	Red	Dark blue	Dark blue	—	Dark blue	—
52	The Royal Norfolk Regiment	Yellow	Black	Dark blue	Dark blue	Yellow	Dark blue	Yellow
53	The Lincolnshire Regiment[6]	Dark blue	—	Dark blue	Red	—	Dark blue	—
54	The Devonshire Regiment	Dark green	Red	Dark green	Black	—	Black	—
55	The Suffolk Regiment	Dark blue	Yellow Gld	Dark blue	Yellow	—	Dark blue	—
56	The Somerset Light Infantry	Rifle green	—	Rifle green	Rifle green	—	Rifle green	—
57	The West Yorkshire Regiment	Buff	—	Dark blue	Buff	—	Dark blue	—
58	The East Yorkshire Regiment	Dark red	White	Dark red	Black	—	Black	—
59	The Bedfordshire and Hertfordshire Regiment	Dark blue	—	Dark blue	Dark blue	-	Dark blue	—
60	The Leicestershire Regiment	Grey	—	Black	Grey	—	Black	—

Table 30 (continued)

Item	Regiment or corps	Crown	Crown piping[2]	Body	Peak	Peak piping[4]	Curtain	Curtain piping[2]
61	The Green Howards	Green	Yellow Gld	Green	Black	Yellow	Black	Yellow
62	The Lancashire Fusiliers	Primrose	—	Cherry red	Cherry red	—	Cherry red	Primrose
63	The Cheshire Regiment	Dark yellow	—	Dark blue	Dark blue	—	Dark blue	—
64	The Royal Welch Fusiliers	Dark blue	—	Dark blue	Dark blue	—	Dark blue	—
65	The South Wales Borderers	Light green	White	Light green	Light green	—	Light green	—
66	The Royal Inniskilling Fusiliers	Buff	—	Cambridge blue	Cambridge blue	Buff	Cambridge blue	—
67	The Gloucestershire Regiment	Pale yellow	Red	Dark blue	Dark blue	—	Dark blue	Red
68	The Worcestershire Regiment	Light green	Yellow	Light green	Dark blue	—	Dark blue	Yellow
69	The East Lancashire Regiment	White	—	Dark blue	Dark blue	—	Dark blue	—
70	The East Surrey Regiment	Black brown	Camel	Black	Camel brown	Cherry red	Black	White
71	The Duke of Cornwall's Light Infantry	Dark green	—	Dark green	Dark green	—	Dark green	—
72	The Duke of Wellington's Regiment	Dark blue	Yellow Gld	Dark blue	Dark blue	—	Dark blue	Yellow Gld
73	The Border Regiment	Light green	Pale yellow	Light green	Light green	Pale yellow	Light green	Pale yellow
74	The Hampshire Regiment	Yellow	—	Dark blue	Dark blue	—	Dark blue	Yellow Gld
75	The South Staffordshire Regiment	Dark blue	—	Dark blue	Dark blue	—	Dark blue	—
76	The Dorsetshire Regiment	Green	—	Green	Dark blue	—	Dark blue	Yellow Gld
77	South Lancashire Regiment	Cherry red	Yellow Gld	Dark blue	Cambridge blue	Yellow Gld	Dark blue	—
78	The Welch Regiment	Dark blue	Yellow Gld	Dark blue	Dark blue	—	Dark blue	
79	The Oxfordshire and Buckinghamshire Light Infantry	Rifle green	—	Rifle green	Rifle green	—	Rifle green	—
80	The Essex Regiment	Maroon	—	Maroon	Dark blue	—	Dark blue	—
81	The Sherwood Foresters	Rifle green	Yellow Gld	Dark blue	Rifle green	—	Dark blue	—
82	The Loyal Regiment	Dark blue	—	Dark blue	Dark blue	—	Dark blue	—
83	The Northamptonshire Regiment	Black	—	Black	Black	—	Black	—
84	The Royal Berkshire Regiment	Dark blue	Red	Dark blue	Dark blue	—	Dark blue	—
85	The Queen's Own Royal West Kent Regiment	Dark blue	Yellow Gld	Dark blue	Dark blue	Yellow Gld	Dark blue	Yellow Gld
86	The King's Shropshire Light Infantry	Rifle green	—	Rifle green	Rifle green	—	Rifle green	—
87	The Middlesex Regiment	Dark yellow	—	Dark blue	Dark yellow	—	Dark blue	—
88	The King's Royal Rifle Corps	Rifle green	Black	Rifle green	Rifle green	—	Rifle green	—
89	The Wiltshire Regiment	Buff	White	Dark blue	Dark blue	—	Dark blue	—
90	The Manchester Regiment	Dark blue	—	Dark blue	Dark blue	—	Dark blue	—
91	The North Staffordshire Regiment	Dark blue	—	Dark blue	Dark blue	—	Dark blue	—
92	The Durham Light Infantry	Light green	—	Light green	Light green	—	Light green	—
93	The Royal Ulster Rifles	Rifle green	Black	Rifle green	Rifle green	—	Rifle green	—
94	The Royal Irish Fusiliers	Dark blue	Red	Dark blue	Dark blue	—	Dark blue	—
95	The Rifle Brigade	Rifle green	Black	Rifle green	Rifle green	—	Rifle green	—
96	1st, 2nd and 3rd City of London Royal Fusiliers	Dark blue	—	Dark blue	Dark blue	—	Dark blue	—
97	4th City of London Regiment[4]	Red	—	Red	Dark blue	Yellow Gld	Dark blue	Yellow Gld
98	The London Rifle Brigade (Rifle Brigade), 5th City of London Regiment	Rifle green	Black	Rifle green	Rifle green	—	Rifle green	—
99	City of London Rifles, 6th City of London Regiment[4]	Red	—	Red	Dark blue	Yellow Gld	Dark blue	Yellow Gld
100	The Post Office Rifles, 7th City of London Regiment[7]	Dark blue	—	Dark blue	Dark blue	—	Dark blue	—
101	Queen Victoria's Rifles (King's Royal Rifle Corps), 9th London Regiment	Rifle green	Black	Rifle green	Rifle green	—	Rifle green	—
102	Hackney (Royal Berkshire Regiment), 10th London Regiment	Dark blue	Red	Dark blue	Dark blue	—	Dark blue	—
103	Finsbury Rifles, 11th London Regiment[4]	Red	—	Red	Dark blue	Yellow Gld	Dark blue	Yellow Gld
104	The Rangers (King's Royal Rifle Corps), 12th London Regiment	Rifle green	Black	Rifle green	Rifle green	—	Rifle green	—

Item	Regiment or corps	Crown	Crown piping[2]	Body	Peak	Peak piping[3]	Curtain	Curtain piping[2]
105	Princess Louise's Kensington Regiment (Middlesex Regiment), 13th London Regiment	Apple green	—	Dark blue	Apple green	—	Dark blue	—
106	Queen's Westminsters (King's Royal Rifle Corps), 16th London Regiment	Rifle green	Black	Rifle green	Rifle green	—	Rifle green	—
107	Tower Hamlets Rifles (Rifle Brigade), 17th London Regiment	Rifle green	Black	Rifle green	Rifle green	—	Rifle green	—
108	The Queen's (Queen's Royal Regiment), 22nd London Regiment and 24th London Regiment	Light green	Red	Dark blue	Dark blue	—	Dark blue	—
109	25th County of London Cyclist Battalion, London Regiment[8]	Light blue	Yellow Gld	Dark blue	Dark blue	Yellow Gld	Dark blue	Yellow Gld
110	The Artists Rifles (Rifle Brigade)	Rifle green	Black	Rifle green	Rifle green	—	Rifle green	—
111	The Monmouthshire Regiment (except 1st Battalion[4])	Dark blue	White	Dark blue	Dark blue	White	Dark blue	White
112	The Cambridgeshire Regiment	Light blue	—	Dark blue	Light blue	—	Dark blue	—
113	The Herefordshire Regiment	Mid-blue	Light green	Mid-blue	Mid-blue	—	Mid-blue	Light green
114	Royal Army Chaplains Dept., Christian and Jewish	Purple	Gold	Purple	Dark blue	—	Dark blue	Gold
115	Royal Army Service Corps	White	Black	Dark blue	Dark blue	—	Dark blue	Black
116	Royal Army Medical Corps	Maroon	Yellow Gld	Maroon	Dark blue	Yellow Gld	Dark blue	Yellow Gld
117	Royal Army Ordnance Corps	Dark blue	Red	Dark blue	Dark blue	—	Dark blue	Yellow Gld
118	Royal Army Pay Corps	Primrose yellow	Yellow Gld	Dark blue	Dark blue	—	Dark blue	Yellow Gld
119	Royal Army Veterinary Corps	Maroon	Yellow Gld	Maroon	Dark blue	—	Dark blue	—
120	Army Educational Corps	Cambridge blue	—	Cambridge blue	Dark blue	—	Dark blue	—
121	The Army Dental Corps	Grass green	Maroon	Grass green	Dark blue	—	Dark blue	Maroon
122	Pioneer Corps	Dark red	White Slv	Dark red	Light green	—	Light green	White Slv
123	The Intelligence Corps	Cypress green	Yellow Gld	Cypress green	Cypress green	Yellow Gld	Cypress green	Yellow Gld

Torin or 'Austrian cap' pattern

Item	Regiment or corps	Crown	Crown piping[2]	Body	Peak	Peak piping[3]	Curtain	Curtain piping[2]
124	4th/7th Dragoon Guards	Dark blue	Yellow Gld	Red			Dark blue	Yellow Gld
125	Royal Gloucestershire Hussars	Dark yellow	Yellow Gld	Dark blue			Dark blue	—
126	The King's Own Yorkshire Light Infantry	Pale green	—	Pale green			Pale green	—

[1]This and the following schedules are intended to apply to the period 1940–45, roughly from the time when coloured head-dress was permitted to be worn with Battle-Dress up to the time limit of this book. Many of these items of coloured head-dress existed long before 1940, such as the head-dress of the Foot Guards and the two patterns of Glengarries. The information compiled here has, in the main, been gleaned from *Regimental Badges and Service Caps*, published in 1941 by George Philip & Son, London, together with notes and observations made by myself. The Philip publication has, to my knowledge, been the only attempt at producing as complete a list of these coloured head-dress as is, or was, possible. However, it does suffer from a number of errors, notably in its interpretation of the exact shade of colours shown; moreover, it is not a complete listing of coloured head-dress, as the publishers themselves readily admit. It should be remembered that coloured Field Service caps as listed in the first schedule were, despite their being authorized by the Dress Committee of the Army Council, not an issue item, and possession of such items of head-dress was usually at the expense of the individual; because of this there was no official prewar or wartime listing of these caps.

Cap badges are not mentioned in these schedules (although they are shown in the original Philip publication, an important and notable feature of the booklet). Officers usually wore embroidered cap badges in silver or gold bullion and coloured silk threads. Other ranks wore badges in metal, some with coloured cloth backing, although even this 'ruling' was not hard and fast. The small buttons used at the front of the caps (first schedule) were almost

The colours of yellow and white shown as piping represent the cloth piping used on the coloured Field Service caps (first schedule) always of regimental or corps pattern in gilding metal, although silver/white metal and black were used where appropriate. Two silver buttons were used by the Royal Wiltshire Yeomanry (3); Yorkshire Dragoons (4); Yorkshire Hussars (5); Fife & Forfar Yeomanry (22); Northamptonshire Yeomanry (25); Northumberland Hussars (30); Royal Devonshire Yeomanry (33); East Yorkshire Regiment (58); Cheshire Regiment (63); South Wales Borderers (65) and the Pioneer Corps (122); two black buttons were used by Queen Victoria's Rifles (101) and three gilt buttons used by the Buffs (47). All the remaining caps used two gilt buttons.

Unless otherwise stated, the description of the colours given in these schedules, especially with regard to the piping used on the crown, peak and curtain, usually applied to caps as worn by other ranks (see footnotes 2 and 3 below). The exact shade of the colours I have listed is difficult to convey in words alone: dark blue almost always was a form of blue-black, and red could also be interpreted as scarlet. There were a number of shades of blue, green and yellow, and other reds are given as maroon, cherry red, dark red and even purple.

[2]Piping to the crown and curtain are given as being either in a colour or shown as a dash (—); the dash represents the fact that there was no separate piping that differed in colour from the crown or curtain respectively. Usually the crown or curtain was edged with a self-coloured raised seam, and although this gave the superficial appearance of piping, it should not be confused with added piping.

as worn by other ranks. Officers' caps, and in some cases caps worn by warrant officers, were usually piped in gold or silver tubular 'French' braid. Where the piping is shown as being either yellow or white and is followed by the letters 'Gld' or 'Slv' respectively, this is meant to show that the colours indicated in the original Philip booklet were assumed to represent gold and silver as worn by officers.

[3]Piping to the peak is shown as being either in a colour or in white/silver or yellow/gold. The use of a dash (—) in this column represents the same conditions as stated above in footnote 2.

[4]Regiment converted to an artillery role, becoming part of the Royal Artillery.

[5]The information for the coloured Field Service caps for this regiment was extracted from a series of three articles written by Captain D. G. Glover, AMA, and published in the *Bulletin of the Military Historical Society* (No. 71, February 1968, page 57; No. 116, May 1979 page 93; and No. 117, August 1979, page 6). Douglas Glover covers a much wider period of British Army history than I have attempted here, bringing his information up into the 1970s, and he also deals in greater depth than I have been able to. His articles are highly recommended for anyone wishing to pursue this field of military interest.

[6]The coloured Field Service cap described here was worn by officers of the 2nd Battalion the Lincolnshire Regiment.

[7]Regiment converted to an engineer role, becoming part of the Royal Engineers.

[8]Regiment converted to a signals role, becoming part of the Royal Signals.

Table 31.   Schedule of Coloured Field Service Caps (Glengarry Pattern)[1]

Item	Regiment	Crown	Toori	Body	Badge ribbon	Diced band	Rim and silks
127	The Royal Scots	Dark blue	Red	Dark blue	Black cross	Red and white, white and green, red and white	Black with swallow-tail cuts
128	The Royal Scots Fusiliers	Dark blue	Red	Dark blue	Black cross	Red and white, white and green, red and white	Black with straight cut ends
129	The King's Own Scottish Borderers	Dark blue	Red	Dark blue	Black cross	Red and white, white and green, red and white	Black with straight cut ends
130	The Seaforth Highlanders	Dark blue	Red	Dark blue	Black cross	Red and white white and green red and white	Black with swallow-tail cuts
131	The Gordon Highlanders	Dark blue	Red	Dark blue	Black cross	Red and white, green and white red and white	Black with straight cut ends
132	The Argyll and Sutherland Highlanders	Dark blue	Red	Dark blue	Black bow	Red and white, white and red, red and white	Black with straight cut ends
133	The Cameronians (Scottish Rifles)	Rifle green	Black	Rifle green	Black bow		Black with straight cut ends
134	The Black Watch	Dark blue	Red	Dark blue	None		Black with straight cut ends
135	The Highland Light Infantry	Rifle green	Dark green	Rifle green	Black bow		Black with straight cut ends
136	The Queen's Own Cameron Highlanders	Dark blue	Red	Dark blue	Black bow		Black with straight cuts
137	The London Scottish, Gordon Highlanders, 14th London Regiment	Dark blue	Royal blue	Dark blue	Black cross		Black with straight cuts

[1]See footnote 1, page 131.

The Glengarry

When the first of the coloured Field Service caps were introduced in June 1937, their shape was compared with that of the Glengarry (page 134).

The Glengarry was an item of head-dress worn by personnel of Scottish regiments. It was boat shaped, without curtains or a peak, and could be folded flat. All Glengarries sported a toori (a round tuft of closely packed coloured wool), all were edged around the rim in black silk and all had black silk ribbons hanging from the rear rim. Here the similarity among Glengarries worn by different Scottish regiments ceased. Some wore a diced band; red, black, dark green and royal blue toories were worn by different regiments; the badge ribbon worn behind the silver or white metal cap badge was either in the form of a black silk bow or a black silk cross; and some black silk ribbons that hung down from the hat were cut diagonally straight whilst others had a swallow tail cut. Details regarding the Glengarry worn by individual Scottish regiments are shown in Table 31.

Left: Men of the Royal Scots Fusiliers taking part in a pre-war army manoeuvre near Horsham, Sussex; 13 August 1936. All are wearing the Glengarry with coloured manoeuvre band.

Above: Sjt. M. MacKenzie, DCM, and CSM D. MacLeod, DCM, of the Seaforth Highlanders; 27 April 1941. Both men are wearing the Glengarry with diced band, SD and kilts.

Above right: Pipe Major David Duncinson, MM, of Grange-mouth, Stirlingshire, (left) and Sjt. John Smith, MM, of Denny, Stirlingshire, both of the Argyll and Sutherland Highlanders; 2 May 1944. The Pipe Major is wearing the plain version of the Glengarry and Sjt. Smith the other ranks' version of the khaki Balmoral bonnet.

Right: The Balmoral bonnet for Scottish officers worn by Maj. G. W. Dunn, DSO and bar, of the Black Watch; March 1944.

Far right: The Balmoral bonnet for Scottish other ranks worn by Cpl. Charles Jones, DCM, MM, of the Black Watch; 16 May 1944.

The Balmoral Bonnet

The Balmoral bonnet, also known as the Tam-o'-Shanter, was a khaki drab item, flat on top and with a khaki drab toori. It was usually worn with the soft crown pulled forward and the cap badge worn on the left side of the bonnet, normally with a backing patch of appropriate tartan cloth (see page 119). This item should not be confused with the khaki drab General Service cap (page 155). For ceremonial duties the Balmoral bonnet was produced as a dress item.

Other Distinctive Regimental Coloured Head-Dress

Table 32. Coloured Field Service Caps ('Tent' Pattern)[1]

Item	Regiment	Body	Curtain	Curtain lace	Seams
138	8th King's Royal Irish Hussars[2]	Emerald green	Emerald green	Gold[3]	Gold

[1]See footnote 1, page 131.
[2]The 'tent hat' was only worn by officers of the 8th King's Royal Irish Hussars; other ranks wore the universal pattern coloured Field Service cap in dark green piped around the crown and curtain in gold Russian braid.
[3]The 'tent hat' was trimmed with wide, flat gold lace that had a shamrock design woven into it. No buttons or cap badge were worn on this item of head-dress.

Table 33. Coloured Field Service Caps (Atholl Bonnet Pattern)[1]

Item	Regiment	Crown/body	Toori	Badge ribbon	Diced band	Rim and silks
139	Lovat Scouts	Dark blue	Dark blue	Black cross	Black and white, white and black, black and white	Black with straight cut ends
140	Scottish Horse	Dark blue	Red	Black cross	Red and white, white and green, red and white	Black with pointed cut ends

[1]See footnote 1, page 131.

Table 34. Coloured Field Service Caps (Caubeen Pattern)[1]

Item	Regiment	Body/Crown	Band
141	The London Irish Rifles|(Royal Ulster Rifles), 18th London Regiment	Rifle green[2]	Rifle green

[1]See footnote 1, page 131.
[2]Prewar photographs indicate that there were two versions of this Caubeen, the dark rifle green version worn by officers and senior warrant officers and a khaki drab version worn by other ranks (see photo on page 141). This distinctive head-dress was worn with an emerald green feathered hackle behind the cap badge.

Table 35. Schedule of Coloured Service Caps (Peaked Cap Pattern)[1]

Item	Regiment	Crown	Crown welt	Body	Cap band	Peak[2]	Chin-strap	Chin-strap buttons
142	The Life Guards[3]	Khaki	—	Khaki	Khaki	Khaki cloth	Brown leather	2 brass
143	Royal Horse Guards[3]	Khaki	—	Khaki	Khaki	Khaki cloth	Brown leather	2 brass
144	Grenadier Guards	Dark blue	Red	Dark blue	Red	Black patent with brass rim	Black leather	2 brass
145	Coldstream Guards	Dark blue	White	Dark blue	White	Black patent with brass rim	Black leather	2 brass
146	Scots Guards	Dark blue	White	Dark blue	Diced: red and white, white and blue, red and white	Black patent with brass band	None	None
147	Irish Guards	Dark blue	—	Dark blue	Emerald green	Black patent with brass rim	Black leather	2 brass
148	Welsh Guards	Dark blue	—	Dark blue	Black	Black patent with brass rim	Black leather	2 brass
149	The Honourable Artillery Company[4]	Dark blue	Red	Dark blue	Red and dark blue	Black patent with white metal rim	Black leather	2 white metal

[1]See footnote 1, page 131. The coloured peaked caps listed here have been included as they were worn with Service Dress and initially with Battle-Dress before the war.

[2]The black patent peaks of the coloured peaked caps of the five regiments of Foot Guards were used as a means of showing the wearer's rank. A single narrow brass rim was used by all other ranks, but in addition to this colour-serjeants and serjeants had two parallel brass strips; lance-serjeants and corporals, including those in the Corps of Drums, wore one brass strip in addition to the brass rim; and all remaining guardsmen and drummers including in both cases lance-corporals wore only the brass rim.

Warrant officers and non-commissioned officers senior to the above were distinguished by wearing rows of gold Russia braiding: warrant officers Class I had five parallel rows of gold Russia braid; warrant officers Class II and serjeants on the Staff with the rank of Quartermaster-Serjeant had four rows; serjeants on the Staff below the rank of Quartermaster-Serjeant and band-serjeants had three rows; band corporals had two rows; and lance-corporals in the band

and bandsmen had one row of Russia braid.

[3]Although other ranks of the Household Cavalry wore plain khaki Service Dress caps for much of their time, on occasions they wore their coloured peaked caps with Service Dress. As with the Foot Guards, the rank of the wearer was shown on the black peak of his forage cap. However, only gold Russia braiding was used in the Household Cavalry. The system adopted was as follows: warrant officers Class I had five parallel rows; warrant officers Class II, trumpet-majors and band corporals-of-horse had four rows; staff-corporals and squadron quartermaster-corporals had three rows; corporals-of-horse had two parallel rows; and corporals, and bandsmen and trumpeters (including, in both cases, lance-corporals), had a single row. Other lance-corporals and troopers had plain peaks.

[4]For warrant officers, NCOs and men of the HAC the system of showing rank on the peak of the forage cap was the same as that used by the Grenadier Guards, with the exception that the trimming used was of white metal and not brass.

Above left: The use of the coloured Forage Cap by members of the Household Cavalry when in Service Dress. Mounted personnel of The Life Guards (foreground) on their way to Windsor pass a mounted unit ot the Royal Horse Guards, bound for Knightsbridge barracks, along the Great West Road; 11 October 1933. The Horse Guards are wearing their State Duty helmets with khaki SD.
Above: Welsh Guardsmen wearing their coloured Forage Caps with SD; 20 March 1937.
Above right: Members of the TA mount guard at Buckingham Palace for the first time; 6 July 1938. A sentry from the Honourable Artillery Company is seen here taking over guard duty from the 2nd Bn, Scots Guards. The HAC sentry is wearing the Company's coloured Forage Cap with its distinctive red cap band divided by a dark blue band.
Right: Grenadier Guards of the 2nd Bn receiving the universal 'Wolseley' pattern Foreign Service helmet (issued without a pagri) at Chelsea barracks in preparation for the regiment's departure to Egypt; 25 February 1936.

Tropical Head-Dress

The Universal Foreign Service Khaki Helmet.

This item was of the cork 'Wolseley' pattern, made with six panels of Khaki Drill and seams, with the edging of the brim bound in buff leather. The width of the brim that projected all round was 3in in the front, 4in at the back and 2in on either side, and the helmet was ventilated at the top with a zinc button covered with khaki cloth which fitted into a collet riveted on to a collar ⅜in wide. The brown leather chin-strap was ⅜in in width.

No badges, plumes, hackles or ornaments of any description, except regimental patches, were allowed to be worn with the khaki helmet, except that the Brigade of Guards wore regimental plumes and pagri badges; the Royal Fusiliers wore a white plume; the Black Watch wore a red hackle;

Top, far left: Men of the 1st Bn,
S. Staffs Regiment parade with
the recently approved web
equipment and their Foreign
Service helmets in preparation
for their departure to Palestine;
Dover, Kent, 8 September
1938.
Top left: The 1st Bn, Irish
Guards at their Pirbright camp,
Surrey being inspected by an
officer prior to their departure
for a tour of duty in Egypt; 14
November 1936. Each man is
carrying his Foreign Service
helmet in its own carrying bag.
Centre, far left: British troops
on air defence exercises in
north-west India. These men
are wearing the khaki Solar
Pith Hat with cloth cover;
1941.
Centre left: Men of the
Lancashire Fusiliers in Burma,
1943. The soldier in the right
foreground is wearing the regimental pagri flash, an upright
oblong of red cloth bearing a
white flaming grenade flanked
on either side with the letters
'L' and 'F'.
Below, far left: Gen. Sir Claude
Auchinleck, C-in-C India, talking
to an officer of the Sherwood
Foresters in December 1943.
The first fold in the pagri – a
strip of green cloth – is very
prominent on the khaki Solar
Pith Hat.
Below left: A gunner of the
Royal Artillery operating a
predictor in Burma. The red
and blue RA flash can be seen
worn on the pagri of the khaki
Solar Pith Hat.

the Duke of Cornwall's Light Infantry wore red feathers; the Lancashire Fusiliers wore a primrose hackle; and the Royal Berkshire Regiment wore a strip of red cloth 1¼in wide on the right side of the helmet. Regimental patches were worn on the left side of the khaki helmet. The white version of the universal Foreign Service helmet was used for ceremonial occasions and has not been included here.

Pagris worn on the universal khaki helmet were required to be affixed to it on arrival at stations abroad and not before embarkation (ACI 460, dated October 1938). The Buffs (Royal East Kent Regiment) wore a buff-coloured pagri.

Wearing of universal khaki helmets at Aden and in the Sudan.

It was announced in ACI 173 published during the week ending 18 May 1938 that the universal khaki helmet would in future be worn at Aden and in the Sudan instead of the Indian pattern helmet. No further Indian pattern helmets were provided after this date, but local stocks were required to be used up first.

Restricted wartime use of the universal khaki helmet (including the pith hat and slouch hat).

In view of the representation made to the Army Council and the War Office as a result of experiences gained in the Middle East and North Africa, it was decided in December 1942 that the universal khaki helmet and other Tropical head-gear for wear by British other ranks would be maintained and worn only at certain stations abroad as follows:

The universal khaki helmet.
1. Personnel serving in the Sudan, Transjordan and the desert areas of Lebanon on the scale of one for each other rank.
2. For personnel serving in Egypt (including the Western Desert), Palestine (excluding Trans-jordan), Lebanon (other than the desert areas), Syria and Cyprus, a stock of universal khaki helmets was held under command arrangements on the scale of four per cent strength of units serving in those areas, for use on special duties. Helmets were not permitted to be worn by the remainder.
Pith hat. Personnel serving in Persia/Iraq command only.
Slouch hat with special lining. Personnel serving in East and West Africa only.

Personnel who proceeded from the United Kingdom to tropical or semi-tropical areas for which the universal khaki helmet was previously authorized as regulation head-wear continued to be issued initially with universal khaki helmets before embarkation for use on the voyage. On arrival at their new station where the universal khaki helmet was no longer worn as according to the details above, they had to retain the helmet until they became acclimatized or it was replaced by the form of Tropical headgear in use at that station.

Those universal khaki helmets at stations abroad that were rendered surplus by these instructions were withdrawn and returned to the

RAOC who reconditioned and brought on charge those fit for reissue or disposed of those considered unserviceable under command arrangements (ACI 2661 dated 19 December 1942).

The Khaki Solar Pith Hat

Introduction for wear by officers of the Army in India.

Consequent on the deletion of the universal khaki helmet from peacetime and wartime scales of issue for British troops serving in India, the Commander-in-Chief India instructed, by the publication of ACI 284 dated w/e 13 July 1938, that the universal Foreign Service khaki helmet 'Wolseley' pattern was to be replaced by the khaki solar pith hat for wear by all officers of the Army in India (other than those wearing pagris) in all orders of dress.

Universal Foreign Service khaki helmets and Cawnpore tent club pith hats that were already in possession were allowed to be worn up to 31 December 1938 for all occasions that had hitherto been authorized, except for ceremonial parades or Field Service. The khaki solar pith hat for officers was identical to that worn by other ranks.

The universal khaki helmet continued to be the regulation head-dress for officers in stations abroad other than India.

Introduction for wear by all ranks serving in Burma.

ACI 415 dated week ending 28 September 1938 announced that, on instructions from the General Officer Commanding-in-Chief Burma, the universal Foreign Service khaki helmet 'Wolseley' pattern was replaced by the khaki solar pith hat. The provisions of ACI 284 of week ending 13 July 1938 (see above) regarding the introduc-tion of this item of head-dress to officers and other ranks in India also applied to all ranks serving in Burma.

ACI 451 dated week ending 26 October 1938 announced that a free issue of a universal Foreign Service khaki helmet 'Wolseley' pattern, complete with chin-strap, pagri and bag, would be issued to soldiers proceeding from India or Burma to an imperial station abroad.

The pagri (as worn on the khaki solar pith hat).

The cloth pagri was folded into four throughout its length, with the edges inside, before it was placed around the crown of the hat or head-dress. The folds when fitted showed ³/16in between each fold with an overall depth at each side of the head-dress of approximately 2¾in.

The pagri was crossed at either end and drawn tight, to even out the folds. The folds were spaced at equal distance, below the first fold, so that the last fold rested on the brim ½in below the welt where the crown of the head-dress joined the brim. The number of folds was normally restricted to six. Some British units serving overseas before the 1939–45 war were permitted to deviate from the method of wearing the pagri, as described above, and vary the number of folds used; these are shown in Table 36 overleaf.

Right: Pagri flashes. 1, The Queen's Royal Regiment (West Surrey); 2, The Manchester Regiment; 3, The Wiltshire Regiment; 4, The Essex Regiment; 5, The Rifle Brigade; 6, The King's Own Royal Regiment (Lancaster); 7, The Suffolk Regiment; 8, The East Surrey Regiment; 9, Royal Tank Corps; 10, Waziristan Medium Survey section, Royal Artillery; 11, Lancashire Fusiliers; 12, The Royal Berkshire Regiment.

Table 36. *Pagris and Pagri Flashes and Patches worn on the Khaki Solar Pith Hat by British Troops in India, circa 1939*[1]

Unit, regiment or corps	Pagri, flash or patch
4th Queen's Own Hussars	Top fold of pagri in blue cloth; second fold from the top in primrose cloth
9th Queen's Royal Lancers	Two top folds of pagri in red
The Royal Scots (The Royal Regiment)	Cloth patch comprising piece of regimental tartan 3in × 2in[2]
The Queen's Royal Regiment (West Surrey)	Dark blue cloth patch 3in × 2in with oblong piece of red cloth on top with Queen's embroidered thereon in white worsted; blue and grey strip of ribbon above first fold of pagri, grey on top
The King's Own Royal Regiment (Lancaster)	Blue cloth patch 3in × 2in embroidered in white King's Own
The Royal Northumberland Fusiliers	Red cloth pagri worn uppermost 1in high at sides and ½in high at back and front; khaki cloth pagri was 1½in high at sides
The Royal Warwickshire Regiment	Blue cloth patch 3in × 2in with orange coloured stripe through centre; khaki pagri had only six folds
The King's Regiment (Liverpool)	Red cloth patch 3in × 2in with 'King's' embroidered in white worsted
The Royal Norfolk Regiment	Patch of yellow cloth 3in × 2in with narrow black stripe down centre
The Lincolnshire Regiment	Blue cloth patch 3in × 2in with red sphinx embroidered thereon; blue and red stripe above first fold of pagri
The Suffolk Regiment	Yellow cloth castle
The Somerset Light Infantry (Prince Albert's)	Top fold of the pagri in rifle green cloth
The West Yorkshire Regiment (The Prince of Wales's Own)	Red cloth patch 2¾in × 2in with White Horse of Hannover embroidered thereon
The Leicestershire Regiment	Flash of silk regimental ribbon 3in long
The Lancashire Fusiliers	Letters L and F in white on either side of white embroidered Fusilier grenade, all on upright oblong of scarlet cloth
The Cheshire Regiment	Diamond patch 2in × 2in, left half cerise, right half buff; pagris adjusted in four folds
The South Wales Borderers	Fourth fold from top of pagri was green cloth, fifth fold white cloth
The Cameronians (Scottish Rifles)	Diamond cloth patch of Douglas tartan 3in × 2in, white vertical stripe through centre
The Gloucestershire Regiment	Back badge of authorized pattern (see page 76) was worn at back of helmet; not polished
The Worcestershire Regiment	Green cloth patch 1½in square worn diamond shape (on its point); helmet 'top' painted green
The East Surrey Regiment	Red cloth patch 3in × 2in with black background and East Surrey embroidered thereon in white worsted
The Duke of Cornwall's Light Infantry	Cloth flash 2¾in deep by 2½in wide, horizontally divided green, red, green, white, green, red, green in equal-width bands[3]; single 5½in long swan's feather (officers) or single 4½in long feather (other ranks), dyed red, worn on front of helmet (see also page 149)

Unit, regiment or corps	Pagri, flash or patch
The Duke of Wellington's Regiment (West Riding)	First fold of pagri was strip of scarlet cloth
The Royal Sussex Regiment	Patch of red cloth 3in × 2in with Royal Sussex embroidered in white worsted
The Hampshire Regiment	Cloth patch 2in × 3in consisting of 1in of yellow and black
The South Staffordshire Regiment	Green cloth flash 3in × 2in with vertical stripes of gold and red with black border
The Dorsetshire Regiment	Fourth fold from top of pagri was grass green strip of cloth
The South Lancashire Regiment (The Prince of Wales's Volunteers)	Khaki cloth patch 3in × 2in with white sphinx embroidered thereon
The Welch Regiment	Ribbed silk patch 2in × 2¼in with equal vertical white, red and green stripes
The Black Watch (Royal Highlanders)	Red feathered hackle on left side of helmet (see also page 000)
The Essex Regiment	Red cloth patch 3in × 2in with Essex embroidered thereon in white worsted
The Sherwood Foresters (Nottinghamshire and Derbyshire Regiment)	First fold of pagri was strip of green cloth
The Loyal Regiment (North Lancashire)	Cloth ribbon 3in × 2in with vertical cerise and French grey stripes with black dividing lines
The Northamptonshire Regiment	Cloth flash 3in × 2in, cerise and French grey in equal parts, divided by a black vertical line
The Royal Berkshire Regiment (Princess Charlotte of Wales's)	Blue diamond cloth patch 2in × 2in embroidered Royal Berkshire in red
The King's Shropshire Light Infantry	First fold of pagri was stripe of green cloth
The Middlesex Regiment (Duke of Cambridge's Own)	Cloth patch diamond shape, maroon and lemon yellow halves, yellow worn to front; top fold of pagri was yellow
The King's Royal Rifle Corps	Chin-strap worn on head-dress was black leather
The Wiltshire Regiment (Duke of Edinburgh's)	Maroon cloth Maltese cross 1½in square on white ground
The Manchester Regiment	First fold of pagri was (old gold) yellow; green diamond patch 2in square worn on its point mounted with gilding metal fleur de lys in centre
The North Staffordshire Regiment (The Prince of Wales's)	Patch of black cloth 3in × 2in; white Staffordshire knot with Prince of Wales plume and with North Stafford worked in red below knot
The York and Lancaster Regiment	Middle fold of pagri was black cloth
The Durham Light Infantry	Dark green cloth patch 3in × 2in
The Highland Light Infantry (City of Glasgow Regiment)	Triangular piece of tartan cloth[4]
The Queen's Own Cameron Highlanders	Cloth patch of Cameron tartan, 3in × 1½in[5]
The Rifle Brigade (Prince Consort's Own)	Green cloth patch 2in square with R.B. embroidered thereon in ¾in black letters
Royal Artillery	Cloth patch 2in square worn on its point, diamond shape, half red half blue; embroidered thereon in yellow numerals and letters as follows:
	Regimental headquarters. Roman numerals or letters in brass, denoting regiment with letter(s) for arm-of-service as for batteries.
	Batteries (except anti-aircraft). Arabic numbers or letters in brass denoting battery above service letters F (Field), P (Light and Mountain), M (Medium), H (Heavy), D.A.C., R.A.T.C., M.A.T.C.[6] or S. of A. (School of Artillery)[6]
	Anti-aircraft batteries and RA Survey Section. Roman numerals in brass denoting unit above service letter(s) A.A. (Anti-Aircraft Battery), S (RA Survey Section) or WAZ (Waziristan Medium Section, RA)[6]
Royal Engineers	Flash 2in square, red stripes ¼in wide at each edge, with 5/16in blue stripes at each side of 7/8in red stripe on centre; all stripes vertically arranged
Royal Corps of Signals	Cloth patch 3in × 2in, light blue, dark blue and green in 1in horizontal bars; ends of patch were tucked under lower edge and into fourth fold from top of pagri
Royal Tank Corps[7]	Cloth patch 3in × 2in, of green, red and brown in 1in horizontal stripes; unit number or letters R.T.C. embroidered in black on red portion of patch
Royal Army Medical Corps	Silk ribbon 3in × 2in, in corps colours, arranged vertically on stiff background, colours each ⅔in wide; dull cherry worn to front
The Army Dental Corps	Silk ribbon 3in × 2in in corps colours, arranged vertically on stiff background, emerald green and dark blue stripes each 7/8in wide with a ¼in dull cherry stripe between emerald green worn to front
The Royal Army Veterinary Corps	Cloth ribbon 3in × 2in, maroon, blue and gold in 1in vertical stripes
Army Educational Corps	Maroon and blue cloth patch, 1¾in square, worn on its point diamond fashion, blue on top with 5/32in black and green horizontal stripes through centre
Army School of Physical Training	Cloth patch 3in × 2in, red and black in 1in vertical stripes

[1]This schedule has been compiled from information extracted from *Clothing Regulations (India), 1939 (Appendices)*, Appendix XX, Table 2, pages 155–182. It excludes Indian and Gurkha troops. It is to be presumed that those British Army regiments not given in this schedule wore plain khaki pagris without any flash, patch or silk ribbon insignia.

[2]Although the pattern is not given in the original information, the patch used was of Hunting Stuart tartan.

[3]The cloth flash as described in the schedule was, according to the Regimental Museum of the DCLI at Bodmin, Cornwall, introduced in 1932 at the same time as the red feather head-dress embellishment, and was worn until 1936, when a new pattern of pagri flash was introduced. It was laid down in Regimental Standing Orders that the regimental colours were to be displayed as equidistant white and red stripes each one-fifth the width of the green backing. The new flash was divided horizontally into seven portions which were, from the top, green, red, green, white, green, red and green.

[4]Although the pattern is not given in the original information, the patch used was of MacKenzie tartan.

[5]The tartan used was Cameron of Erracht.

[6]No numerals used.

[7]The Khaki solar pith helmet was worn in addition to the black RTC beret.

The Bush (Slouch) Hat

Authorized use of the bush or slouch hat by personnel on leave in the United Kingdom.

All ranks whose authorized head-dress overseas was the bush (or slouch) hat were allowed to wear it in the United Kingdom, if they so desired, as follows.

1. During disembarkation leave upon posting to home establishments under PYTHON or on compassionate posting.

2. Whilst on leave in the United Kingdom under LILOP or LIAP schemes.

Officers were required to provide their own head-dress in the normal way. For other ranks personnel, the normal authorized head-dress, if not in their possession, was also issued to them before they proceeded on leave. Replacement of bush hats was not possible in the UK. Where other ranks personnel were not returning to the area in which the bush hat was worn, it was with-drawn from them at the expiration of their leave (ACI 45 dated 17 January 1945).

Head-Dress Embellishments

Feathers, feathered hackles and feathered plumes worn as head-dress embellishments.

As a distinctive form of head-dress embellishments, feathers and feathered hackles were worn both before and during the 1939–45 war. The hackles were made from short cut feathers and were bound into a small 'bush' and fitted with a short wire stalk or narrow loop. The feathers themselves were either of the natural white variety or were white feathers artificially dyed to various shades as required. Some hackles were of all one colour, whilst others were a combination of two bound together in such a manner that each colour was separate.

The hackles were normally worn fitted into the head-dress behind the cap badge (where this was

Table 37. Feathers, Feathered Hackles and Feathered Plumes known to have been worn with Service Dress Head-Dress of Various Patterns before and during the 1939–45 War

Item	Article and colours	By whom worn	Head-dress on which worn
Feathers			
1	Single red feather[1]	The Duke of Cornwall's Light Infantry	Foreign Service universal helmet (khaki) and khaki solar pith hat[2]
2	Black tipped feathers	The Highland Light Infantry	Dark green Glengarry
3	Blackcock feathers	The Royal Scots	Kilmarnock bonnet
4	Blackcock tail feathers	The London Scottish	Dark blue Glengarry
Hackles			
5	Red[3]	The Black Watch	Foreign Service universal helmet (khaki) and khaki solar pith hat, Tam-o'-Shanter bonnet
6	Green	The King's Own Yorkshire Light Infantry	Slouch hat
7	Emerald green	The London Irish Rifles	Caubeen
8	Primrose[4]	The Lancashire Fusiliers	Foreign Service universal helmet (khaki)
9	Saffron yellow	No. 5 Commando (Army)	Beret, green
10	Black	The Royal Ulster Rifles	Caubeen
11	Black	No. 9 Commando (Army)	Beret, green
12	Black	The Cameronians (Scottish Rifles)	Glengarry and slouch hat
Plumes			
13	White	Grenadier Guards	Foreign Service universal helmet (khaki)[5]
14	Red	Coldstream Guards	Foreign Service universal helmet (khaki)[6]
15	St. Patrick blue[7]	Irish Guards	Foreign Service universal helmet (khaki)[8]
16	White, green, white[9]	Welsh Guards	Foreign Service universal helmet (khaki)[10]
17	White	The Royal Fusiliers	Foreign Service universal helmet (khaki)

Far left: Gen. Auchinleck shaking hands with Sjt. H. Banning from Peckham, London, who was serving with a West African Regiment. All these troops are wearing the Bush or Slouch Hat; March 1944.

Left: A dark green feathered hackle worn in the dark green Caubeen by Lt.-Col. H. E. N. Bredin, DSO, MC, CO 2nd Bn, London Irish Rifles; 20 March 1945. (See also the photographs on page 141.)

Below, far left: Head-Dress embellishments: eagle feathers worn in the Glengarry by pipers of the 2nd Bn, Cameron Highlanders at Chelsea Barracks, 23 August 1934.

Below left: A Guard of Honour from No. 9 Commando, part of No. 2 Commando Brigade Headquarters, Mediterranean Theatre. Each man is wearing a black feathered hackle in his green beret; 6 April 1945.

[1]The 'single' red dyed feather was specially produced from two separate red feathers for wear by other ranks of the DCLI. The feathers, 4½in in length, were laid together, fitted at the quill end into a small, narrow, metal sleeve and trimmed at the top to form a rounded point. The feather used for officers' head-dress was a swan's feather dyed red and trimmed to a length of 5½in.

[2]This very attractive head-dress embellishment originated from the Battle of Paoli fought during the American War of Independence. 'On the night of 20th September 1777 a British force which included the Light Company of the 46th of Foot [which in 1782 was entitled the 46th (South Devonshire) Regiment and later still in 1881 merged with the 32nd of Foot – the 32nd (Cornwall) Regiment – to form the Duke of Cornwall's Light Infantry] surprised an American detachment under General Wayne killing and capturing 400 with a loss to themselves of only 8 killed and wounded. The Americans vowed they would give no quarter to the British troops they engaged, so the British units employed in the original attack dyed their hat feathers red in order that they might be more easily distinguished in the future'.

The red feather embellishment was authorized in 1932 to be worn on the front of the Foreign Service universal helmet (khaki) at foreign stations other than India and on the front of the solar pith hat when in India. It was tucked in under the pagri and worn directly behind and above the helmet badge; the feather lay flat against the curved front of the helmet. When both the Foreign Service universal helmet (khaki) and the solar pith hat were superseded by other forms of service head-dress, the red feather was no longer worn; instead, the Duke of Cornwall's Light Infantry took to wearing a red cloth backing to their cap badges (this was worn by all ranks of the regiment).

[3]The red hackle of the Royal Highlanders (The Black Watch) is arguably one of the most famous of all regimental hackles, instantly recognizable as on some forms of head-dress, such as Field Service head-dress, it was worn without a cap badge. The 42nd of Foot received the red hackle for their gallant action at Geldermalsen in Flanders in 1795 when, with another Highland regiment, it covered the retreat of the piquet of 80 men of the 11th Light Dragoons in the face of greatly superior French forces. In 1821 the Black Watch was granted the distinction of being the one regiment in the British Army with the sole right to wear the red hackle. In 1918 the Black Watch were given the authority by the War Office – War Office telegram 1901 (Q.M.G.7.) – to wear the red hackle with the Foreign Service universal helmet and with the Tam-o'-Shanter bonnet provided the hackles were purchased regimentally.

[4]The highly prized primrose hackle was granted to the Lancashire Fusiliers in 1901 as a tribute to the regiment's war record over more than 200 years, culminating in a display of great gallantry at Spion Kop in the South African War. Primrose should never be referred to as 'yellow' or even 'primrose yellow'.

[5]The white plume of the Grenadier Guards was worn on the left side of the head-dress, in the same manner as worn on the ceremonial bearskin caps.

[6]The red plume of the Coldstream Guards was worn on the right side of the head-dress.

[7]The St. Patrick blue plume was 6in in length and of feathers or bristle according to rank.

[8]The St. Patrick blue plume, feathered or bristle, was worn on the right side of the head-dress.

[9]The white/green/white plume was of cut feathers 9in in length.

[10]The white/green/white plume of the Welsh Guards was worn on the left side of the head-dress.

worn) in such a fashion that the wire stalk was out of view and only the feathered bush was visible. Feather embellishments were usually a single or at most two separate feathers.

The type, colouring and method of wear are described in the listing on page 149. This listing consists of information about feathers and hackles that are known to have been worn with Service Dress, including Battle-Dress and Khaki Drill clothing, both before and during the Second World War. I have deliberately not included feathered plumes as worn on Full Dress head-dress, but I have included head-dresses and their feathered embellishments where occasionally worn by pipers with Service Dress, Battle-Dress and Khaki Drill.

National flowers, the poppy and the 'Minden Rose' worn on uniform head-dress.

All ranks, when not on duty, were permitted to wear their national flower on their uniform head-dress as follows:

A rose by all English units on St. George's Day (23 April).

A thistle by all Scottish units on St. Andrew's Day (30 November).

A leek by all Welsh units on St. David's Day (1 March).

A sprig of shamrock by all Irish units on St. Patrick's Day (17 March).

These emblems were also permitted to be worn by English, Scots, Welsh and Irish soldiers serving in other units.

The red poppy was permitted to be worn by all units of the British Army on Armistice Day.

Red roses, known as 'Minden Roses' were worn in the head-dress of the following regiments on 1 August each year to commemorate the Battle of Minden fought on that day in 1759: the Suffolk Regiment; the Lancashire Fusiliers; the Royal Welch Fusiliers; the King's Own Scottish Borderers; the Hampshire Regiment; and the King's Own Yorkshire Light Infantry. Oakleaves were worn in the head-dress of members of the Cheshire Regiment on special regimental anniversaries.

Right: Two members of the Royal Northumberland Fusiliers wearing red and white roses in their head-dress. An English regiment, the Fusiliers commemorated St. George's Day (23 April) by wearing the English national flower in their head-dress. (See also the photograph on page 170.)

Authorized Head-Dress in the British Army as published in ACI 466 dated w/e 15 May 1940, with Notes and Amendments

Field-marshals, general officers and substantive colonels.

These officers were required to wear the following head-dresses on those occasions when the steel helmet was not worn.

With Service Dress. The 'Cap, khaki, Service Dress', with badge, coloured band and plain peak[1] as detailed in *Dress Regulations for the Army, 1934,* para. 30, or the 'Coloured cap, Field Service', with badge, also as detailed in *Dress Regulations for the Army, 1934,* para. 31A, whichever they so desired.

With Battle-Dress. The 'Coloured cap, Field Service', as detailed above.[1]

Officers below the rank of Substantive Colonel.

Consequent on the replacement of the 'Cap, Service Dress' by the 'Drab cap, Field Service', in the clothing scales of certain other ranks, the head-dress as set out below was to be worn on those occasions when the steel helmet was not worn.

1. The 'Cap, Service Dress' was to continue to be the regulation head-dress for wear with Service Dress by officers of units for which it was authorized for other ranks, e.g. horsed units and other horsed personnel.

2. In all other units in which officers were then wearing the Service Dress cap, or except those for which by 1942 a distinctive pattern was authorized (for example a beret, Tam-o'-Shanter, etc.), the regulation head-dress for wear with the Service Dress was the Drab cap, Field Service; the drab cap FS was to be worn with Battle-Dress. 'Caps, Service Dress' that were in possession were to be worn with Service Dress until replacements became necessary, when the drab cap FS was to be worn with Battle-Dress.

3. Officers of the Household Cavalry and the Brigade of Guards continued to wear the coloured forage cap when on duty in Service Dress. When wearing Battle-Dress, officers of the Brigade of Guards wore the drab cap FS or from November 1941 the beret, whichever was appropriate.

All officers and other ranks.

1. When not on duty, all ranks of all arms for which it was appropriate (see para. 3 below) were permitted to wear the coloured cap FS, with Undress, Service Dress and Battle-Dress instead of the regulation head-dress prescribed. The latter was invariably worn on duty.

2. The use of this alternative head-dress was entirely optional and no compulsion was placed on any individual to provide it. If adopted, it had to be maintained in addition to, and not in substitution of, the regulation article.

3. In those regiments for which a special type of head-dress was already approved, examples being Scottish regiments and the Royal Tank Regiment, the special head-dress continued to be worn.

[1]By July 1942, by instruction of ACI 1535, this paragraph was dropped from the original instructions.

Above: The black RTR beret, worn by Churchill tank crewmen of the 33rd Army Tank Brigade, part of the 3rd Infantry Division. These men were probably from the 43rd RTR and were taking part in a demonstration held at Brockenhurst, Longslade Bolton, Southern Command, on 13 August 1942.

Right: The 11th Hussars' beret, worn by Sjt. Hugh Lyon, MM and bar, who had the distinction of being the first Allied soldier to enter both Tripoli and Tunis; 16 May 1944. (See also the photograph on page 139.)

Berets

Origin of the black beret worn by personnel of the Royal Tank Regiment.

The black beret was officially adopted as the head-dress of the Royal Tank Corps as a replacement for the then standard issue Service Dress cap. This peaked cap, and even the unstiffened 'every day' tank park cap, had proved very unsuitable for use in tanks, not fitting close enough to the head. The peak of the cap prevented the wearer from keeping his eyes close to the vision slits or gun sights unless he turned his cap back to front or took it off altogether. Lastly, the khaki colour all too obviously showed up oil and grease stains.

All these drawbacks had come under discussion during the Great War, and particularly at a time when the 70th Chasseurs Alpins of the French Army were training with the Tank Corps in May 1918. General Sir Hugh J. Elles, Colonel Commandant RTC, was favourably impressed by the beret type head-dress worn by these French mountaineering troops, and still more so after trying on one of their berets. That impression led him to recommend in 1922 that a broadly similar type of head-dress should be introduced for wear by troops of the Tank Corps. However, the large beret worn by the Chasseurs Alpins was considered too 'sloppy', whilst the Basque beret as worn by the Chars d'Assault − the French tank troops − was thought to be too 'skimpy', and the final pattern chosen was a compromise and more akin to the Scottish Tam-o'-Shanter, which was in

fact the description used in submitting the proposal to King George V in November 1923. The black beret received His Majesty's approval in March 1924.

The dark brown and cherry red beret worn by all ranks of the 11th Hussars (Prince Albert's Own).

When the 11th Hussars were first mechanized in 1928 they adopted a brown beret with a cherry red band. This very distinctive beret was therefore the second oldest such form of headwear in use in the British Army, the first being the black beret

worn by personnel of the Royal Tank Corps (later the Royal Tank Regiment) approved for wear in March 1924.

The 11th Hussars beret was worn without a badge, a privilege granted to the regiment by King George VI who considered that its distinctive coloured head-dress alone was sufficient identification.

Head-dress for units of the Royal Armoured Corps.

The question of the most suitable type of head-dress for wear by RAC units had been under consideration since the beginning of the war, and on 19 November 1941, with the publication of ACI 2276, the following policy was agreed upon.

1. In tanks, all personnel of the RAC were to wear the crash helmet.

2. In armoured fighting vehicles (other than tanks), and on all occasions when on duty, all Cavalry units (except the 11th Hussars) and Yeomanry regiments were to wear the black beret as then authorized for the Royal Tank Regiment; the 11th Hussars were to wear the brown beret as then authorized; and the Royal Tank Regiment and Royal Armoured Corps regiments were to wear the black beret as then authorized for the Royal Tank regiment.

3. When not on duty, personnel of Cavalry and Yeomanry regiments were allowed to continue to wear a coloured Field Service cap as first provided for by ACI 466 of 1940, the relevant section of which regarding head-dress authorized in 1940 is set out on page 135.

Introduction of the black beret for wear by personnel of the Guards Armoured Division.

In November 1941 authority was given (ACI 2338 dated 26 November 1941) for personnel of the regiments of Foot Guards serving in the Guards Armoured Division to wear a cap (the official term used at this time to refer to the beret) of the pattern prescribed for the Royal Tank Regiment when on duty in tanks when the crash helmet was not being worn. It was also to be worn for performing maintenance duties connected with tanks. The regimental badge was worn in the front of the cap.

Guards officers were required to make their own arrangements for obtaining the new pattern beret, but it was not to be worn until a complete issue of the black beret had been made to other ranks of their unit; the existing head-dresses were retained for wear on those occasions for which the new beret was not prescribed. Other ranks of the Guards Armoured Division received an initial free issue of one 'Cap, RTR' per man and their Field Service cap or soft SD cap in their possession was withdrawn. The stiff Service Dress cap was retained for wear on those occasions for which the black beret was not prescribed.

In January 1942 authority to wear the black beret was extended to personnel of divisional headquarters, brigade headquarters, the Household Cavalry Armoured Car Regiment and armoured battalions serving in the Guards Armoured Division. (ACI 124, dated 17 January 1942).

Proposed head-dress for Irregular Commando Volunteers.

The subject of some form of distinctive head-dress for wear by the newly formed Irregular Commando Volunteers is closely associated with the subject of the proposed qualification badges for wear by these same volunteers as well as the first parachutist formations. The origins and purpose of the Irregular Commando Volunteers is explained fully on page 60, but I have separated the bulk of the material appertaining to the proposed head-dress and included it here in this section which deals with British Army head-dress for the sake of continuity.

As early as 16 June 1940 the authorities at the War Office considered it essential that some form of distinguishing mark would be needed in the walking-out dress of all ranks of the Special Force of Irregular Commandos. This dress distinction had to be easily removed when the need for secrecy demanded it, but it would at the same time indicate that the wearer – officer or soldier – was an active member of the Special Force.

The purpose behind the proposed introduction of some form of dress distinction was two-fold. First, it was felt that it would help to assist the 'esprit de corps' of the new force as well as encouraging recruitment; second, it would act as a recognizable distinction that would help to prevent local authorities possibly interfering unnecessarily with the Irregular Commandos, who, because of the unusual nature of their training and instruction, were bound to arouse suspicion amongst the British population. It has to be remembered that in 1940 everyone in the United Kingdom was waiting for the German invasion which many people felt would be preceded by massed parachute attacks.

In addition to two types of 'brevets' or badges of distinction being proposed (see page 62), a distinctive form of head-dress was considered. It was felt that a distinctive cap would have been suitable as not only could its use be forbidden when the need for secrecy arose but it also would be withdrawn when a volunteer left the special force. A sinister note in the colour or shape of the cap was initially suggested, with probably an all-black side-cap being worn without a badge or decoration.

On 28 June 1940 the idea of some form of black Field Service cap had developed to the point where it was suggested that the black cap should take the shape similar to that then being worn by Belgian troops and be worn with a detachable tassel (see page 129). It was suggested that this cap should be an issue item and it was realized that the authority of the Army Council would be required as well as the approval and permission of the King sought before any such item could be authorized for wear.

Slightly earlier, on 19 June 1940, Charles Montanaro, the Assistant Director of Ordnance Supplies, had committed his suggestions to paper under the heading of 'Force Distinctions'. In addition to the suggestions given on page 62 of this book he felt that a black cap of the type worn by Belgian troops was possible, with small tassels fastened front and back ('fore and aft'); a plain

Above: Sjt. Lawrie of Glasgow wearing the Airborne Forces maroon beret; 22 June 1945.

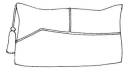

1

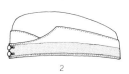

2

Above: Proposed head-dress for irregular commando volunteers. 1, Belgian-style cap with detachable tassel; 2, Khaki field service cap with black band.

black Field Service cap, he added, would have been too like many dark blue-black regimental Field Service caps already being worn. A second suggestion put forward by the ADOS was that a band of black cloth could be fitted to the existing khaki Field Service cap, on the same lines as the white cap band worn by officer cadets (see page 115).

On 4 July 1940 a sample of the Belgian style cap, along with two worsted parachute badges and sketches for six metal badges, was produced by the ADOS for appraisal by the War Office. In his covering note to these items, Charles Montanaro, referring to the Belgian style sample cap, wrote that as the cap was required to be distinctive this could only be achieved by adopting a pattern which differed from the Field Service cap. Black, he noted, was already worn by at least one regiment (the Northamptonshire Regiment, see page 136, item 83), and as regiments decided their own colours for their caps no colour was safe. The cap that was submitted was intended to show the general outline; details as to its finish were intended to be settled by arrangement. He concluded by stating that a cap, unlike a badge, ceased to distinguish the wearer when he was indoors (presumably on removal of his head-dress).

The Board meeting held on 11 July 1940 to review the items submitted and to decide whether they promoted 'esprit de corps' and encourage recruiting for the Irregular Commandos ruled against the adoption of the head-dress. It was considered 'particularly hideous', and its use was felt to have the opposite effect from that intended. The question of secrecy was mainly one for DMO&P (Department of Military Operations and Planning), and it was considered that the sudden departure from their station of a body of men who had hitherto been wearing the very singular head-dress would give away to all and sundry that some irregular operation was shortly going to take place: the use of this form of head-dress was therefore ruled out altogether. 'Esprit de corps' could be

sufficiently promoted by the introduction of a regimental badge, probably in worsted but not in metal.

Two days later, on 13 July 1940, the Assistant Chief of the Imperial General Staff, after discussion with the VCIGS, ruled that 'a special head-dress was not necessary'. This put an end to the idea of a 'sinister, black Belgian style head-dress, complete with tassels', and not until after the Commando raid on Dieppe did the question of some form of distinctive head-dress come up again, and when it did it took the form of the famous green beret.

Introduction of the maroon beret for wear by personnel of the Airborne Forces.

A maroon coloured beret was introduced for wear by personnel of the Airborne Forces on 29 July 1942 (ACI 1596). An initial free issue of the beret was made on the scale of one for each other rank. The Field Service cap already in their possession was retained, intended for wear when the beret was not worn. Officers who had to make their own arrangements to obtain this new head-dress were permitted to purchase berets of other ranks' pattern.

As a point of interest, light blue and claret were the prewar point-to-point racing 'silks' used by Major-General F. A. M. 'Boy' Browning. Frederick Browning had been appointed General Officer Commanding Airborne Forces in November 1941 and he was responsible for the adoption of the maroon coloured beret. A parade held at Wellington Barracks in which Guardsmen were paraded wearing a number of different coloured berets provided the senior personnel of the 1st Airborne Division with the opportunity to choose their future head-dress. Browning insisted on uniformity in head-dress and insignia for all volunteer troops that went to make up the Airborne Forces.

The choice of coloured head-dress was whittled down to blue or maroon, and maroon eventually prevailed. It is said that the colour maroon used for the airborne beret had been chosen by Daphne du Maurier, novelist wife of Major-General Browning.

Introduction of the green beret for personnel of the Special Service Brigade.

A green beret, of a similar design to that worn by the RAC, was introduced for wear by personnel of the Special Service Brigade (later called the Special Service Group) under the authority of ACI 2264 dated 24 October 1942. The use of the green beret was discontinued in 1946.

Introduction of the khaki beret.

A khaki coloured beret of a similar design to that worn by the Royal Armoured Corps began to be introduced for wear by personnel of the Reconnaissance Corps and motor battalions of Infantry on 17 October 1942 (ACI 2216 of 1942). On 20 February 1943 (ACI 282 of 1943), the use of the khaki beret was extended to include personnel of light scout car companies and field parks and the Light Scout Car Training Centre.

In a memorandum dated 8 June 1943 prepared by Major A. D. Melville, GS, MA, to VCIGS and addressed to the Military Members of the Army Council, the question of the wearing of the knitted khaki beret by colonels and upwards when in battle was raised. The memorandum stated:

'1. In North Africa many Commanders, including General Alexander and General Anderson, wear, with battle-dress, the knitted khaki beret authorised for Reconnaissance and Motor Battalions. This is believed to have arisen from the mistaken idea that this beret was for universal adoption in the Army.
'2. A.C.I. 1535 of 1942, paragraph 4(a), lays down that:

"Field Marshals, General Officers and Colonels will wear the following head-dress on occasions when the steel helmet is not worn;

"Cap, khaki, service dress with badge, as detailed in Dress Regulations for the Army, 1934 paragraph 30, or the Coloured Cap, Field Service with badge as detailed in Dress Regulations for the Army, 1934 paragraph 31A."

'3. A.C.I. 124 of 1942 grants permission, in the case of the Guards Armoured Division for personnel of Divisional and Brigade headquarters to wear black berets when on duty in or performing maintenance duties connected with armoured fighting vehicles.
'4. The new khaki serge cap, G.S., is being introduced this year as the official Army head-dress for wear by all officers below the rank of colonel excepting those for whom a specific head-dress has already been approved.
'5. The military members of the Army Council are invited to approve: That the knitted khaki beret be made the official head-dress for wear with battle-dress by all officers of the rank of Colonel and upwards.'

This question was raised at the conclusion of the meeting of No. 1 Selection Board on Tuesday 15 June 1943:

Extracts taken from the Minutes of the 59th Meeting of Military Members of the Army Council held on Friday 25 June 1943. 'Wearing of knitted khaki beret by colonels and upwards when in Battle-Dress'.
The Adjutant-General, introducing his paper, explained that senior officers in North Africa had found a beret very useful when going up to forward areas, particularly in AFVs. It was agreed that there was a general need for some form of head-dress other than the khaki SD cap, and after a short discussion the meeting agreed that the knitted beret should be the official head-dress to wear with Battle-Dress by all officers of the rank of Colonel and upwards.

The King's objections, if any, were sought on 24 July, and two days later a reply was received from the Palace. There were no objections from His Majesty except that the King thought that it would have been an excellent idea if the khaki beret was also worn with Service Dress.

The Chief of the Imperial General Staff held strong views regarding keeping the SD cap for wear with Service Dress, and other Military Members (of the Army Council) agreed with him. A change-over was considered inevitable and would probably be forced on them eventually, but in the meantime they recommended that matters should rest as they were.

By 9 August the King was happy as things then stood, and on 16 August 1943 the position was

assessed as being that the khaki beret was permissible with Battle-Dress and the cap SD with either Battle-Dress or Service Dress.

During the late summer of 1943 the subject of head-dress in the British Army with its numerous innovations and introductions was encapsulated in an ACI (No. 1408 dated 25 September 1943), which set out precise details of who wore what and when. Unauthorized forms of head-dress (a separate subject dealt with on page 90 of this book), which until the publication of this ACI were being worn contrary to regulations and were a source of constant irritation to the clothing authorities, were once again ordered to cease being worn.

The authorized head-dresses for all arms of the service at this time are as set out in Table 28 on page 156.

Semi-official use of grey berets by all ranks of the Royal Dragoons.

When war was declared in September 1939 the 1st Royal Dragoons were stationed in the Middle East and were still a Cavalry regiment. They moved from Palestine to Egypt during 1940, and just before Christmas that year they had their last inspection as horsed cavalry at their camp just outside Cairo.

In place of their horses they were equipped with armoured cars and were instructed in the art of mechanized armoured desert warfare by instructors from the 11th Hussars. The brown and maroon berets worn by their instructors may well have influenced the Royal Dragoons in their decision to adopt a cloth beret as the most suitable form of head-dress for wear inside their armoured cars. Colonel R. F. Heyworth, the colonel of the regiment, was anxious that the latter should have its own distinctive coloured head-dress, and grey was finally chosen. Grey was a neutral colour, very suitable for desert warfare as it toned in well with the desert surroundings. An order was placed with a tailor in Cairo who both provided the grey material and produced the finished berets. These were paid for out of regimental funds and were worn by all ranks of the regiment, being both smart in appearance and extremely popular with officers and men alike.

King George VI, the Commander-in-Chief of the Royal Dragoons, inspected the regiment when it was encamped at Tunis at the end of the North African campaign. He actually gave permission for the grey beret to be retained as the official head-dress, but shortly afterwards was reminded by the War Office that this was not possible as the King himself had previously decreed that the only exception to the regulation black beret worn by the Royal Armoured Corps was the brown and cherry red beret of the 11th Hussars.

After North Africa and the fighting in Italy, where the regiment continued to wear its cherished grey beret, the members returned to the UK to prepare for the invasion of Europe. The rank and file lost the semi-official use of the grey beret, only the officers retaining it in wear for some time, but eventually even they were forced to relinquish it. The cost of providing the grey

Right: The SAS beige beret
worn by Cpl. Moore, MM; 3
May 1944. (See also the photo-
graph on page 67.)
Far right: The General Service
Cap.

beret both as an initial issue as well as a replacement was a drain on regimental funds, and
although Field-Marshal Montgomery, who greatly
admired the beret, tried to win official approval for
its retention, even he lost the fight with the War
Office.

Unofficial white beret worn by some members of
'L' Detachment, Special Air Service Brigade.
  This white coloured beret was a short-lived item
of SAS head-dress. There is some doubt as to
whether it was made from white coloured material
as a deliberately produced beret or whether the
colour was the result of frequent washing of the
beige coloured berets in petrol to remove oil and
grease stains and the subsequent effect of
bleaching produced by the strong North African
sunlight which turned the beige berets white.
  Photographic evidence proves that the white
beret was worn during the early days of the North
African campaign at the time of 'L' Detachment.
Problems arose with the use of the white beret
when it was worn by members of the Special Air
Service when on leave in Cairo: not only did this
odd coloured head-dress attract attention but it
was often the cause of derision, albeit misplaced,
from other military personnel, resulting in the
inevitable fist fight and street brawl.
  The white beret was subsequently replaced by
the beige coloured beret.

Beige coloured beret worn by personnel of the
wartime Special Air Service.
  Although I can find no mention in any official
publication regarding the berets worn by members
of the wartime SAS (this colour of head-dress is
not given in any of the ACI listings of official head-
dress), the beige coloured beret was worn during
the last war. This is borne out by contemporary

photographs, some of which are reproduced in this
book. Although it was a common item worn by
many members of the wartime SAS and even for
important events such as investitures held at
Buckingham Palace, in all probability the beige
beret was a semi-official item of Army head-dress,
not actually receiving wartime approval from the
War Office.

The General Service Cap

As a wartime measure it was decided to introduce
a khaki cloth cap made on the beret pattern for
wear in lieu of the drab Field Service cap by all
personnel for whom the latter item of head-dress
was then prescribed. The new head-dress was
known as the 'Cap, General Service' – Cap GS –
and was immediately dubbed 'Cap, Ridiculous'. It
was not a popular item of head-dress, but because
it was for universal wear the troops eventually got
used to it.
  Although it was introduced initially in
September 1943, the new item had to be taken
into use gradually by other ranks, with order of
priority given to all troops abroad, followed by
field force units at home, then officer cadet training units, anti-aircraft formations and finally other
static troops. The drab Field Service cap then still
in use, or stocks of the same, had first to be used
up, and in order to dispose of existing stocks of
gabardine the first issues of the new General
Service cap were made of that material.
  The General Service cap was correctly worn
with the band positioned level around the head and
1in above the eyebrows, the crown of the cap
being pulled to the right. The badge was worn
over the left eye, placed centrally between the
headband and the crown of the cap. Each cap had
to be suitably marked to indicate where the badge
was to be placed. The badge required to be worn

Serial	Corps etc	Officers		Other ranks	Remarks
		Battle-Dress	Service Dress		
1	Officers of the rank of Colonel and above	Khaki beret or cap SD, or coloured cap FS	Cap SD or coloured cap FS	—	Officers covered by serials 2, 5, 7, 8 and 15 were to wear beret appropriate to those serials when serving with units therein referred to
2	Royal Armoured Corps (except 11th Hussars)	Black beret	Black beret	Beret RAC (black)	
3	11th Hussars	Cap, 11th Hussars (brown)[1]	Cap, 11th Hussars (brown)[1]	Cap, 11th Hussars (brown)[1]	
4	Household Cavalry and Brigade of Guards (except Guards Armoured Division)	Cap SD or cap FS	Cap SD or coloured forage cap	Cap SD stiff and cap SD soft, or cap FS	Cap GS was at this time being introduced to replace cap SD soft or cap FS (see below)
5	Personnel of the Household Brigade in divisional and brigade headquarters of Guards Armoured Division and the Household Cavalry (Armoured Car) Regiment and armoured and tank battalions in the Guards Armoured Division	Black beret	Black beret	Cap SD stiff and beret RAC (black)	Beret to be worn when on duty in tanks (when crash helmet not being worn) and when performing maintenance duties in connection with tanks; at other times normal regimental head-dress was worn by officers and the stiff SD cap by other ranks
6	Reconnaissance Corps; motor battalions of Infantry; light scout car companies; light scout car field parks; Light Scout Car Training Centre	Khaki beret	Khaki beret	Beret, khaki	
7	Airborne Forces	Maroon beret or cap FS	Maroon beret or cap FS	Beret, Airborne (maroon) and cap FS	
8	Special Service Brigade[2]	Green beret	Green beret	Beret, green	
9	Scottish Horse	Bonnet, Atholl	Bonnet, Atholl	Bonnet, Atholl	
10	Lovat Scouts	Bonnet, blue	Bonnet, blue	Bonnet, blue	
11	Scottish Infantry regiments; London Irish Rifles, 8th (Irish) Bn, the King's Regiment[3]; Scots Guards (pipers only)	Bonnet, Tam-o'-Shanter	Bonnet, Tam-o'-Shanter or (Scottish infantry regiments only) cap, Glengarry	Bonnet, Tam-o'-Shanter	
12	Irish Guards (pipers only); Royal Irish Fusiliers (pipers only); Royal Inniskilling Fusiliers	—	—	Bonnet, drab	
13	Instructors of Gunnery; Small Arms School Corps[4]	Cap SD	Cap SD	Cap SD stiff	
14	Horsed units; CMP; MPSC; NCOs and musicians under a director of music; enlisted boys	Cap SD	Cap SD	Cap SD stiff	CMP with field formations wore FS cap when not wearing steel helmets[5] (see below)
15	Officers attached to the RAF Regiment	Blue beret (RAF pattern)	Blue beret (RAF pattern)	—	
16	All other units and personnel	Cap FS	Cap FS	Cap FS	Cap GS was about to replace cap FS in due course (see below)

Caps, Service Dress. Where not included above, caps SD in the possession of officers were permitted to be worn with Service Dress but not Battle-Dress, except when specially authorized.

Coloured caps, Field Service. When not on duty, the coloured cap FS or, in the case of Scottish regiments, the Glengarry, could be worn by all ranks of all arms for which it was appropriate with Undress, Service Dress and Battle-Dress, instead of the head-dress prescribed.

Black beret. The black beret was the regulation head-dress of the units and individuals detailed in serials 2 and 5 only.

Khaki beret. Admissible for wear by the personnel detailed in serials 1 and 6 only; it was not to be worn in lieu of the cap GS.

Cap, General Service. See ACI 1407 of 1943 as shown on page 155. The cap GS, which was issued to officers through the RAOC on repayment, was not taken into use until it had been issued to the officers' unit as a whole. It was then the only regulation head-dress permitted to be worn on duty by the officers as detailed in serial 16 above (but see first paragraph above). The cap GS was not to be confused with the khaki beret.

Changes introduced. Attention was called to the following changes which were being effected at this time:
1. The introduction of the khaki beret for officers of the rank of Colonel and above, for wear on duty with Battle-Dress.
2. The abolition of the stiff SD cap for motor boat companies of the RASC, staffs of RTOs in London District and Personnel Selection Staff when the cap GS was issued.
3. The introduction of the stiff SD cap for CMP (Traffic Control Wing).

[1]For details regarding the 11th Hussars beret see page 151.
[2]ACI 42 of 1944 changed the title of the Special Service Brigade to 'Special Service Group'.
[3]ACI 649 dated 3 May 1944 added the 8th (Irish) Bn the King's Regiment to this listing.
[4]This Corps was added to this listing by authority of ACI 1879 dated 22 December 1943.
[5]These remarks were deleted from this listing by authority of ACI 1641 of 1943.

was the regulation pattern as authorized for the Field Service cap, in bronzed metal for officers and in metal or plastic for other ranks. Units which had been previously authorized to wear distinctions on head-dress in recognition of past services or for some other reason were permitted to wear such distinctions on the cap GS.

The cap GS of other ranks' pattern was worn by officers on those occasions as laid down for the cap FS, which it replaced. Serving officers had to adopt the cap GS for wear when other ranks of their unit were issued with it, but caps FS that were already in the possession of serving officers were allowed to continue to be worn with Service Dress until worn out. Newly commissioned officers were not entitled to wear the cap GS until they were serving with a unit to which the new form of head-dress had been issued, and to avoid unnecessary expense in the interim these officers were advised to equip themselves with the other ranks' pattern of the cap FS.

Instructions regarding the issue of the General Service cap to the Home Guard, senior and junior training corps and the Army Cadet Force were to be issued at a later date. However, a year later, in August 1944, these formations still had not received the cap GS, and pending even further instructions they had to continue making do with the khaki drab Field Service cap.

Covers worn on Cloth Head-Dress by All Ranks

Cloth covers worn on head-dress, forage or Service Dress, were intended either to conceal or to display. All were removable.

Khaki covers. Worn on the universal pattern forage cap by certain grades of officers when the forage cap was worn with Service Dress (see also page 129).

Red covers. Worn as an identifying emblem by all personnel of the Corps of Military Police (Provost Wing) when on duty.

Oxford blue covers. Worn as an identifying emblem by all personnel of the Corps of Military Police (Vulnerable Points Wing) when on duty.

White covers. Worn as an identifying emblem by assistant instructors in gunnery at Royal Artillery practice camps and schools of gunnery. The covers were only worn by assistant instructors while actually doing range work. The schools' instructors in gunnery wore, irrespective of their officers' rank, a red cap band on their SD caps as an identifying emblem for easy recognition when on the firing point. This practice was also carried out by those officers of the ATS selected to act as instructors of gunnery at schools of gunnery.

The Cap Comforter (Officers' and Other Ranks' Patterns)

Cap comforters of brown silk similar to the pattern as worn by the rank and file were worn, when necessary, by officers as part of their Service uniform. The pattern of cap comforter worn by other ranks was knitted in khaki coloured wool. This item is not listed in any of the scales of clothing published in the 1936 *Regulations for the Clothing of the Army* but is mentioned in the 1941 *War Clothing Regulations* as an item of necessaries issued to members of horsed units and other horsed personnel, pipe bands of the Foot Guards and of Scottish and Irish infantry regiments, and to all other personnel, which in other words meant all other ranks of the British Army. It was issued for home service on the scale of one comforter per man.

However, by 1942 the cap comforter was no longer considered an essential item for all personnel serving in the UK, and with effect from 4 November 1942 (ACI 2350 of 1942) the scale of issue was reduced to one cap comforter for each other rank of field force units, units of AA Command, troops in the Orkneys and Shetlands defences, and those engaged in coast defence duties, together with all drivers and crews of 'A' and 'B' vehicles. All other cap comforters in possession of personnel in the UK other than those detailed above, as well as stocks of comforters held by units for maintenance purposes, had to be returned to the RAOC forthwith.

The Balaclava Helmet

Despite its name, the Balaclava was not a form of steel helmet or even a tropical sun helmet: it was in fact a knitted, close-fitting hood that was worn over the head and neck with an opening for the wearer's face. Manufactured from drab khaki coloured wool, it was usually worn during cold weather, although it was used for stalking, sniping and night operations that required concealment.

It probably derived its name from the famous Crimean War battle when in all probability a similar type of knitted hood first made its appearance. It was a popular item worn during the Great War and continued in use throughout the Second World War. Its advantage was that it could be worn under the steel helmet, and if the neck and lower face of the helmet were rolled up around the head it formed a kind of cap comforter.

Below: The Balaclava helmet. Bdr. Howe (left) wearing the Balaclava under his steel helmet and Sjt. Goslin, with his Balaclava worn rolled up, both formerly of Bolton Wanderers Football Club are seen ramming home a 25pdr charge during an artillery exercise shoot; Southern Command, 11 March 1940.

3. OFFICERS' SERVICE DRESS

Pre-1942 Pattern Service Dress Jacket

Officers of all units except Foot Guards.

Manufactured from khaki drab material of sealed pattern, cut and shade, this garment was single-breasted, cut as a lounge coat to the waist with a back seam, loose at the chest and shoulders but fitted at the waist. It had a military skirt to the bottom edge, with an opening at the back from the bottom of the garment to the waist line. The depth of the skirt was 13in for an officer 5ft 9in in height, or of a proportionate variation for any difference in height. The step collar had a depth of opening about 3in.

The jacket had two cross-patch breast pockets above, 6½in wide and 7½in deep to the top of the pocket flap. The box pleats in the centre of the pockets were 2¼in wide, and the pocket flaps had

three points and were 6½in wide and 2¼in deep. There were two large, expanding pockets below the waist line at the sides of the jacket, 9¼in wide across the top of the pocket increasing slightly to 10½in at the bottom. The pockets were 8in deep to the top and were fastened here with a small button flap with button-hole to cover the pockets, 3½in deep and 10¾in wide. The tops of the pockets were sewn down at the corners in such a manner that when worn on service the pocket could be expanded at the top also. There was an inside watch pocket with a leather tab positioned above to take the chain or strap of the watch.

There were four large regimental buttons positioned down the front of the jacket. The jacket itself was lined or not as required by the individual, but if it were lined then the lining was of a colour similar to that of the jacket. The cuffs

had a pointed design 2½in deep, rising to 6in at the point. Badges of rank worn on the shoulder straps were in metal (see page 31 for details of rank insignia and page 33 for designs of rank stars). The shoulder straps were of the same material as that of the jacket and were fastened next to the collar with a small regimental button. No special material was specified for this jacket, but all officers of a unit were required to be dressed alike.

In Scottish regiments the fronts of the skirts were rounded off to Highland pattern and the sleeves were of gauntlet shape. Officers of the Foot Guards wore a special pattern of Service Dress jacket. (For details of both these patterns of jacket, see below).

Officers of Scottish regiments.

As has already been described above, the Service Dress jacket as worn by officers of Scottish regiments prior to 1942 was similar in cut to that worn by officers of all other British regiments with the exception of the Foot Guards. There were slight differences in certain features of the Service jacket worn by Scottish officers and these were as follows.

The garment was single-breasted, cut as a lounge coat to the waist with a back seam. It was loose at the chest and shoulders but fitted at the waist. It had a military skirt to the bottom edge with an opening at the back from the bottom of the garment to the waist line, except for that of dismounted officers of the Argyll and Sutherland Highlanders, which had slits at the sides, and also of the Cameronians (Scottish Rifles), which had no slit at all at the back. There were varying lengths of the skirt for officers 5ft 9in in height for the following regiments.

Royal Scots Fusiliers: 13in.
The Cameronians (Scottish Rifles): 11¾in.
King's Own Scottish Borderers, and Argyll and Sutherland Highlanders: 9¾in.
Queen's Own Cameron Highlanders and The Royal Scots: 7in.
Seaforth Highlanders: 8in.
Gordon Highlanders: 10in.
Highland Light Infantry: 9¾in.
The Black Watch: 10in.

The two pockets below the waist had three-pointed flaps 9in wide and 3in deep to the points. The depth of the pockets varied with the length of the skirt, and the front edge of each waist pocket was rounded off in sympathy with the rounded off shape of the skirt fronts of the jacket. The gauntlet cuffs were 2¾in deep, rising to a point at the back of the sleeve 6in high.

Wartime modified pattern of Service Dress jacket for officers of all units except Foot Guards.

Introduced during March 1942 as an economy measure (ACI 501 dated 7 March 1942), the modified pattern of Service Dress jacket, sometimes referred to as the 'austerity pattern SD jacket', differed from the previous, pre-1942 jacket in the following points.
1. There were no box pleats to the breast pockets.
2. The bottom pockets of the modified pattern

were of the slit type without pocket flaps, and were without buttons (the former bellows pockets being done away with).
3. The sleeves were plain without the built-on cuffs, except for those jackets worn by officers of Scottish regiments, which retained the gauntlet pattern cuff.

A considerable saving was made in both materials and buttons with this modified pattern of Service Dress jacket. All officers from that date when obtaining jackets, whether as an initial outfit or as a replacement, were required to have them made up to the new pattern. Both types were allowed to be worn side by side in a unit, and officers were not required to have their existing pattern of jackets altered for the sake of uniformity. These alterations also applied to the Khaki Drill jacket (see page 176) and to the jackets worn by officers of the ATS.

By ACI 340 dated 28 March 1945 it was announced that with effect from 15 January 1945 the Board of Trade had agreed and had notified military tailors that, to the extent that the materials and labour situation permitted, orders would be accepted for officers' Service Dress jackets of the pre-1942 pattern. As every effort to conserve materials and labour was still very necessary, any abnormal purchasing of the new jackets by officers was discouraged until the situation improved. Where officers, newly-commissioned or otherwise, were able to obtain the pre-1942 pattern jackets, they were allowed to purchase and wear, without restriction, the austerity pattern introduced by ACI 501 of 1942 (above). Both patterns were allowed to be worn side by side and no pressure of any sort was to be brought to bear on officers to convert or change garments in their possession before they were due for replacement in the normal course of events. Where jackets had, at the time of this Army Council Instruction, already been ordered in the austerity style, no pressure was allowed to be placed by officers on tailors to alter them.

The above instructions also applied to the Khaki Drill jacket (see page 176).

Service Dress jacket for officers of the Foot Guards.

Made of drab barathea cloth, with the under-collar of drab melton, the body lined with drab Italian cloth and the sleeves with cream coloured satin, this jacket was cut as a lounge coat to the waist, without seam at the centre of the back, fairly loose at the chest and shoulders, but fitting snugly at the waist, with a waist seam across the foreparts only. The skirt was 13in deep for an officer 5ft 9in high, but this varied slightly in proportion to the individual officer's height. There were two small seams in each forepart that ran from the waist to well under the breast pockets, and also two seams in each skirt running from the waist to underneath the pockets, with two vertical seams about 7½in long at the waist of the back. All these seams were for the purpose of defining the waist. Edges and flaps, except the top of the latter, were stitched ¹/₁₆in from the edge. Pockets and the top edges of flaps were ³/₁₆in wide.

The jacket had four plain patch pockets with three-pointed pocket flaps, one on each breast, the top edge of the breast pocket flaps in line ½in above the top button-hole. These pockets, which were well rounded at the bottom, were 6¼in wide at the top, graduating to 6¾in at the centre; they were 7½in deep from the top edge of the flap. The button-hole at the centre of the pocket flap fastened to a small size regimental button on the pocket. The point of the flap near the arm-hole was secured to the pocket with a snap fastener. Two similar pockets on each skirt, also rounded at the bottom, were 7½in wide at the top, graduating to 9¾in towards the bottom. The top edge of the pocket flap was 1in below the waist seam, and both the pockets and plain flap were without button-holes or buttons.

Shoulder straps were plain, of the same material as that of the jacket. They were 2¼in wide at the base, graduating to 1¾in up to where they became triangular in shape, nearest the collar. There was a button-hole in each strap, the top edge of which was 1¼in from the top of the shoulder strap. The sleeve ends were plain but had small size regimental buttons arranged in regimental groupings (see below). Large buttons of regimental pattern were worn down the front of the jacket, also arranged in regimental groupings (again, see below), but with the top button-hole 6½in down from the top of the forepart and the lowest button-hole 2¾in up from the waist seam. These measurements varied slightly according to the length of the jacket.

As already mentioned, there were small regimental pattern buttons on each cuff, one on each breast pocket and one on each shoulder in order to fasten down the shoulder straps. A plain gilt button was positioned at the left side of the front of the jacket on the waist seam, which fastened through a button-hole set in the right side of the waist seam. The front of this hole was 1¾in from the front edge of the jacket. The plain gilt waist button was flat in order not to interfere with the wearing of the waist-belt. All buttons had fixed shanks.

Above the waist seam on the left side, 2in from the front edge of the garment, were two gilt collar hooks placed 1¼in apart, the top one 1½in from the waist, let into the facing for the purpose of fastening to two eyes in the front edge of the right forepart. The jacket had two waist hooks, one on each forepart, placed about 2¼in from the side seams. There was a piece of drab braid ⅛in in diameter and 2¼in long for the waist-belt to pass through at each side of the back, near the waist, the bottom being ½in below the waist seam.

Arrangement of regimental buttons for Guards' regiments as worn on the Service Dress jacket and Khaki Drill jacket by officers of the Foot Guards.

Grenadier Guards. The three large regimental pattern buttons were spaced evenly down the front of the jacket, with a single small button on each cuff.

Coldstream Guards. The large buttons were spaced in three sets of two buttons. The cuffs had

two sets of two small buttons, the first one being positioned 1in from the bottom edge of the cuff.

Scots Guards. The fastenings comprised two sets of three large buttons down the front of the jacket with a line of three small buttons on each cuff.

Irish Guards. Two sets of four large regimental pattern buttons formed the fastening in the case of the Irish Guards, with a closely set line of four small cuff buttons at the hindarm.

Welsh Guards. A single row of five evenly spaced large buttons down the front of the jackets, with the same number of small, closely set buttons on each cuff.

It is of interest to note that no modification was made to the pattern of Service Dress jacket or Khaki Drill jacket as worn by officers of the Foot Guards. These garments were then considered already to be so similar in design to the simplified pattern brought into use in March 1942 that it was not necessary to alter them; undoubtedly this is yet another example of the Guards doing things correctly.

The Officer's Khaki Undress Reefer Jacket
The khaki Undress reefer jacket was a comparatively rare prewar item of dress for officers, introduced into service by authority of ACI 119 published during the week ending 1 May 1935. It was considered as an optional item of dress and its provision by individual officers was entirely voluntary.

The reefer jacket was approved for wear with Service Dress trousers and with breeches, but the Sam Browne belt was not worn with it. It was authorized for wear by officers when on duty in military hospitals, offices, schools, workshops and the like, and also when proceeding to and from such places of duty. It was not worn on parade with troops nor by combatant officers when on duty with their units; neither was it worn with trews.

The jacket was made from drab material of sealed pattern cut and shade. It was cut in the same style as a naval officer's Undress coat. It had a 4½in deep slit from the bottom of the skirt at each side of the jacket. The sleeves were plain, with two small regimental buttons and button-holes at the back of the wrist. There were two rows of large regimental buttons positioned down the front of the jacket, with three buttons in each row placed about 4in apart, the two rows being 7in apart. There were two bottom letter pockets with box flaps and two inside breast pockets. The shoulder straps were of the same material as the jacket itself and were sewn on to the shoulder at the base of the strap and fastened at the rounded top end, nearest the collar, with a small regimental button.

No gorget patches were worn on this garment, nor were collar badges. The lapels were without holes. All buttons and officers' badges of rank were in gilt metal except in rifle regiments and the RAChD where they were in black horn or metal.

No particular material was specified for the manufacture of this item, but all officers of a unit wearing it were required to be dressed alike.

Below: Officers' khaki undress reefer jacket.

4. TROUSERS, BREECHES, PANTALOONS AND TREWS

Officers' Service Dress Trousers

These nether garments were originally made from a drab mixture material very similar to trousers worn by civilians but without turn-ups and worn with braces. In 1933 trousers of barathea cloth with 1½in deep turn-ups were introduced, but turn-ups ceased to be worn about 1938.

Breeches

Mounted pattern.

'Breeches, Mounted Pattern' were worn by general officers, brigadiers, substantive colonels, officers of mounted units and mounted officers of dismounted units. They were of a drab coloured Bedford cord or Cavalry twill, of sealed pattern cut and shade and with drab coloured buckskin strappings. There was a small horn button positioned about 2½in from the bottom of each leg at the back, used for attachment to the legging

or field boot. The breeches were cut to reach to about 6in below the wearer's knee, fairly loose over the hip and thigh and with a good fullness in the top half over the knee.

The breeches were fly fronted, fastened with fly buttons, they had two cross pockets and at the back of the waist they were drawn together with a buckle and strap. There were side openings at the bottom of the legs about 5in long with either eyelet-holes for laces on either side or buttons and button-holes. The top eyelet-holes or buttons and button-holes were positioned about ½in from the top of the opening, with the other eyelet-holes or buttons and button-holes about ½in apart. It was optional for button-holes and buttons or eyelet-holes and laces to be worn, but all officers of a single unit for whom these breeches were authorized were required to wear the same pattern and material.

Knickerbocker breeches for officers.

Made from drab material to match the Service Dress jacket worn by officers, and of sealed pattern cut and shade, the knickerbocker breeches were cut fairly loose around the hips and had continuations of the same material about 3in deep, which could be fastened, if desired, with buttons and button-holes or with a strap and buckle. Any superfluous material at the bottom was fulled on all round when the continuations were seamed on. The fall over the knee was not allowed to exceed 4in. The breeches had fly fronts, the top button being on the inside of a fly while its button-hole was just behind the button catch seam. There were two side pockets, with a strap and buckle fastening at the back. The waist lining was of drab flannel.

Pantaloons

Withdrawal of a cotton cord pantaloons from personnel of mounted services at stations abroad.

Under the authority of ACI 403 dated w/e 21 September 1938, cotton cord pantaloons were no longer included in the scales of clothing for wear by personnel of mounted services in Cyprus, Egypt, Malta and Palestine, except in the case of grooms and men employed on animal transport duties, who continued to wear the cotton cord pantaloons when on duty. All other cotton cord pantaloons in the possession of other soldiers were permitted to continue in use until worn out; thereafter, such soldiers were required to wear trousers or Khaki Drill shorts.

Introduction of pantaloons for motor-cyclists.

Pantaloons for wear by motor-cyclists began to be issued from 26 July 1941 to other ranks personnel who were required to ride motor-cycles for a considerable portion of their period of duty. They were only to be worn when on riding duty and were worn in conjunction with the newly introduced special motor-cyclist boots (see page 166). On all other occasions these personnel were required to wear Battle-Dress trousers, ankle boots and web gaiters (ACI 1331 of 1941).

Below: The King with Generals Paget and Montgomery (right background) leaving a military headquarters at Tunbridge Wells on 16 June 1941. All are wearing officers mounted pattern breeches. This must be a comparatively rare photograph because it shows HM King George VI carrying a personal weapon. Most photographs of the King in military uniform during wartime show him unarmed.

Pre-War Clothing for Personnel of the Corps of Military Police

It was announced by ACI 124 dated w/e 7 April 1937 that a decision had been arrived at whereby all personnel of the Corps of Military Police were in future to be clothed on the 'mounted' scale, as set out in 'Scale 4 – Clothing for Mounted Men' published in *Regulations for the Clothing of the Army, 1936*. Spurs, however, were only issued to men who actually performed mounted duties.

A free initial issue of one pair of pantaloons was made to all personnel of the dismounted section serving at home and in Egypt and China; the second pair that were required to complete to scale were provided on repayment. At stations abroad other than Egypt and China pantaloons were not provided as they were not worn on those stations except by men who were engaged on mounted duties.

Tartan Trews and Tartan Breeches

Trews – the anglicized word is derived from the Gaelic 'triubhas' – were close (not tight) fitting trousers manufactured from tartan cloth. They required skilled tailoring in order to match the tartan pattern at the seams to preserve the continuity of the checks. Trews were worn by personnel of Scottish lowland regiments.

Tartan breeches were just that: breeches produced in tartan cloth and worn by military personnel of lowland regiments that were required to ride a horse.

Personnel required to wear tartan trews are given in Table 39.

Table 39. *Personnel of Scottish Regiments and Units authorized to wear Tartan Trews, 1935–45*[1]

Regiment or unit	Tartan
The Royal Scots (except 9th Bn)[2]	Hunting Stuart tartan
Pipers of the Royal Scots	Royal Stuart tartan
The King's Own Scottish Borderers (except 4th Bn and all pipers except those of the 4th Bn)	Leslie tartan
4th Bn King's Own Scottish Borderers (inc. pipers)	Buccleuch tartan
Pipers of the King's Own Scottish Borderers	Royal Stuart tartan
Royal Scots Fusiliers	42nd or Government tartan
Pipers of the Royal Scots Fusiliers	Erskin red (Dress Erskin) tartan
The Cameronians (Scottish Rifles)	Douglas tartan
The Highland Light Infantry (City of Glasgow Regiment) (except the 9th (Glasgow Highland) Bn HLI and pipers of 9th Bn)	Mackenzie tartan
Pipers of the 9th (Glasgow Highland) Bn HLI	Royal Stuart tartan
9th (Glasgow Highland) Bn HLI	42nd or Government tartan

[1]For a description of tartan patterns see page 192
[2]The 9th Battalion The Royal Scots wore kilts of Hunting Stuart tartan and not trews. Although they formed part of a Lowland Regiment, the 9th Battalion had originally been formed from Highlanders living in Edinburgh.

Below left: Buglers of The Highland Light Infantry wearing tartan trews sound the last post during a memorial service for the fallen heroes of the Zeebrugge raid buried in St. James's Cemetery, Dover; 23 April 1934.
Below right: Officers' tartan breeches.

5. FOOTWEAR AND HANDWEAR

Boots

Boots for Service Dress worn by mounted officers.

Field-marshals, general officers, brigadiers, substantive colonels and officers of the Cavalry, Foot Guards and Royal Army Veterinary Corps wore brown field boots of sealed pattern. These boots had soft legs stiffened to a depth of 4–6in from the top, laced at the instep with between seven and nine pairs of eyelet-holes, at the option of the officer. The boots had plain toe-caps with two rows of stitching $1/16$in apart, horizontal counter in line with the third lace-hole from the bottom and about $3\frac{1}{4}$in above the top of the heel. There was a leather garter at the top of the leg. The provision of spur rests was optional, as was a gusset with strap and buckle at the top of the boot. Other mounted officers wore brown ankle boots with leggings, except where otherwise specified.

For training and manoeuvres, officers for whom field boots were prescribed could, as an option, wear brown ankle boots and leggings instead of field boots.

Boots for dismounted officers.

Dismounted officers generally wore brown ankle boots with plain toe-caps.

Special pattern field boots worn by officers of the Royal Artillery.

RA officers wore brown leather field boots. The boots were laced at the instep with seven pairs of

Above: The special pattern field boot for officers of the Royal Artillery, 1933.
Below: Examples of boots worn by officers with Service Dress and breeches and with Battle-Dress trousers and anklets. The task of cleaning and polishing officers' boots was undertaken by the officers' batmen.

eyelet-holes, and they had plain toe-caps with two rows of stitching $1/16$in apart. There was a bellows tongue coming to within about 2in of the top of each boot and curved downwards towards the centre so as to obviate any pressure of the tongue on the shin bone. The tops of the boots were lined to a depth of about $4\frac{3}{4}$in.

The boots were fastened with three buckles and straps spaced equidistantly up the leg, proportionate to the length of the boot. The brass buckles were $\frac{1}{2}$in wide. The horizontal counter was positioned about $3\frac{1}{4}$in above the top of the heel, the front flap was stiffened with whalebone, and there was a backstrip about $\frac{3}{8}$in wide. Spur rests and a detachable garter, $\frac{1}{2}$in wide, at the top of the boot were optional.

These boots were introduced by authority of ACI 7 published during the week ending 11 January 1933.

Ankle boots.

British Army ankle boots, often referred to as 'ammunition boots',[1] were manufactured in leather, dyed black and came in sizes (the length of the boot) and fittings (the width of the boot). There were three fittings to each size: small ('S'), medium ('M') and large ('L'). A soldier's mobility depended on the proper fitting of his boots, and this therefore was considered a matter of the first importance. Properly fitted boots were neither too tight for comfort nor loose enough to bruise the foot in motion.

The removal of grease from ankle boots by the use of petrol, by the application of 'hot irons' or spoons, or by any other method, with a view to obtaining a high polish, not only shortened the life of the boots but it also reduced their waterproof qualities. Officers commanding units were instructed to forbid such practices within their units and were required to ensure that boots were treated with dubbin and that blacking was not used (see also page 165). However, by 1943 only one pair of boots per soldier was required to be treated with dubbin. The other pair, presumably his 'best pair', were allowed to be treated with black boot polish applied with a boot brush.

Specially adapted ankle boots for wear by personnel of the Corps of Military Police (Provost Wing). When ankle boots belonging to CMP (Provost Wing) personnel only were due for repair after October 1941, rubber or composition heels were, at the discretion of the OC the detachment, allowed to be fitted in lieu of metal heel tips and

[1]According to W. A. Thorburn, the former Curator of the Scottish United Services Museum, Edinburgh, Queen's Regulations of 1844, 1857 and 1862 refer to 'Ammunition Boots and Shoes', although this terminology was dropped by 1868 and thereafter. Mr. Thorburn maintains that the term 'ammunition boots' is a perfectly legitimate expression, based on the fundamental meaning of the word as a description of an item of military equipment and which simply meant 'Army issue' or 'issued from stores'. Ankle boots would seem to have been the last item of issue clothing to retain the original use of the word.

Right and below: The biggest British Army wargame for over ten years was held in August 1935 (see also the photograph on page 28). Both photographs show troops making their way to Salisbury Plain; although the progress of the horse-drawn gun team from the 17th Brigade, RA (right) seems more leisurely than most, as they have even found time for a rest on Old Dean Common, Surrey.

fillings where the personnel in question were required to do a considerable amount of patrol work on pavements. No alteration was permitted to new boots, and for medical reasons, which were not explained, the fixing of rubber soles could not be permitted (ACI 1983 dated 11 October 1941).

Hobbing or studding of Army ankle boots. Before the 1939–45 war, and for at least the first three or so years of the conflict, the soles of the ankle ('ammunition') boots were protected with 25 hobs or studs hammered into the leather soles in five rows each of five studs or hobnails, as shown in the photograph opposite. The toes of the soles were protected by toe-plates and the heel with heel cleats.

The need for economy during the war reduced the number of protective studs used from 25 to 15. These 15 studs were inserted in the soles in three rows of five studs, one row down the length of the centre of the sole and the other two rows on either side (ACI 823 dated 18 April 1942).

The need further to economize in the use of grindery was announced in August 1942 (ACI 1827 dated 29 August 1942) whereby the number of protector studs would be reduced even further to 13 per boot sole; they were positioned as shown in the accompanying sketch. Those units operating in hilly or downland country, where an anti-slip device was considered essential, were permitted, under the authority of the officer commanding the unit, to have hobnails fitted in lieu of protector studs. The shortage at this time in the supply of screws required that the fixing of toe-

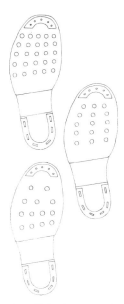

Below: Early pattern crepe sole leather ankle boots initially worn by British Paratroopers.

plates to ankle boots had to be modified by the omission of one screw per toe-plate. This modification in no way impaired the normal wear of the toe-plates (ACI 1857 dated 2 September 1942). The original order for the prohibition of the wearing of hobbed boots by drivers of mechanical vehicles had first been promulgated under the authority of ACI 246 for the week ending 14 July 1937; it had been brought to the notice of the Army authorities that an accident had been caused through the driver of a mechanical vehicle wearing hobbed boots, and in order to prevent any similar accidents happening the wearing of hobbed boots by personnel when driving mechanical vehicles was prohibited from that time.

However, on 21 March 1942 (ACI 611), it was announced that in future the prohibition against the wearing of hobbed or studded boots would only apply to personnel whilst undergoing instruction in driving, i.e. until the soldier had passed out as a qualified internal combustion engine driver (driver IC) or carrier driver. This instruction also covered ATS auxiliaries where it was applicable.

On 16 September 1942 (ACI 1969), the prohibition against hobbed or studded boots was extended to include personnel comprising crews of armoured fighting vehicles, and by 1943 crew members of Royal Army Service Corps waterborne transport were also included.

Anti-Gas Protection of Service Boots by the Use of 'Dubbin, Protective No. 1'

All service boots in wear in the British Army, including those in use by officers wearing Battle-Dress and by other ranks, and which also included ATS leather boots but not ATS shoes, were required to be treated with ordinary service dubbin or 'Dubbin, protective No. 1' as supplies of the latter commodity became available – which was after September 1942. It was forbidden to use blacking on these boots.

'Dubbin, protective No. 1' was being introduced into the Service in September 1942 for issue to all units other than the Home Guard, and it gradually replaced the ordinary service dubbin that had been in use since 1940. One tin, containing 2oz of dubbin, was issued to each soldier, and also to each ATS auxiliary in possession of ATS leather boots. When empty these tins were refilled from the bulk supply carried by the unit. Issue to officers was made on repayment.

The purpose of the dubbin was to resist the possible penetration of blister gas through the uppers of the boots. One pair of boots required ½oz of dubbin for each application, and the dubbin had to be applied at least once a week. Instructions for the application of the dubbin by the individual were as follows.
1. All mud and dirt had first to be removed with a damp cloth and the boot then wiped dry.
2. The dubbin was applied evenly over the whole of the uppers, including the tongue.
3. The dubbin was worked well into the boot by hand, with particular attention paid to the seams and to the join of the upper and the welt.

Dubbin was not allowed to be carried in the anti-gas service respirator.

Introduction of Special Boots for Motor-Cyclists

Special boots (and pantaloons – see page 161) for wear by motor-cyclists became available for issue on 26 July 1941 (ACI 1331 of 1941). These boots were for wear by any other rank who was called upon to ride a motor-cycle for a considerable portion of his period of duty. They were only intended to be worn by motor-cyclists when on riding duty; on all other occasions these personnel were required to wear ankle boots and web anklets with their issue Battle-Dress trousers.

On 17 May 1944 it was announced that as metal foot rests and kick starters were no longer being encased in rubber on newly manufactured motor-cycles (part of the Army's drive to conserve rubber) it was considered unsafe to continue to reinforce the right boot of each pair with a metal plate fitted to the waist of the boot. These metal plates were therefore removed from existing stocks of boots held by commands and wooden plugs were inserted in the old screw holes. This was carried out under command arrangement by either the unit shoemaker or by local contract. Serviceable stocks of these metal plates were retained in the commands for issue to the Pioneer Corps or other troops who were normally called upon to do digging (ACI 733 of 1944).

Below: Kit inspection for NCOs of the Royal Scots Greys as they prepare to leave their Hounslow Barracks for Palestine on 26 September 1938.

Puttees

Puttees (the word is Hindustani for 'bandages') were lengths of woollen cloth with tapes attached which were wound around the lower part of the legs to cover the tops of boots; their purpose was to prevent dust, mud and grit from entering the footwear. There were both long and short puttees, and in the main they were either khaki drab or sand in colour to match either the Service Dress or the Khaki Drill clothing.

Certain regiments of British troops stationed in India before the 1939–45 war adopted coloured puttees and hose tops; these regiments and their coloured puttees are listed in the schedule of puttees and hose tops given below.

The puttees, as authorized, were worn with Service Dress trousers, pantaloons, knickerbockers or kilts. Those worn by a dismounted individual commenced at the ankle and finished at the knee (except in the case of those wearing kilts when they finished below the calf), whilst those worn by mounted soldiers commenced at the knee and finished at the ankle. The puttees were wound around the leg beginning from the inside and working outwards (over the trousers which were required to be folded neatly inside) in a spiral manner, the 'folds' gradually increasing from the beginning until the desired length was reached, the puttee finishing on the 'outside' of the leg. One 'turn' was allowed to be made so that the puttee conformed to the shape of the wearer's leg.

Before the war puttees were worn with Service Dress on duty except on 'stables' or 'fatigue duties' in barracks, or when artificers were working at their trades, or by personnel employed in offices; they were not required to be worn when off duty in barracks, or on such occasions as were sanctioned by superior commanders. Puttees were not worn with Khaki Drill trousers by British soldiers on ceremonial duties in India.

When puttees were not worn by troops, trousers were invariably worn with Service Dress. The wearing of leggings or gaiters in lieu of puttees except by such individuals for whom they were authorized was forbidden.

Prewar use of puttees by all ranks.
On 18 May 1938 *The Times* reported that the War Office had stated that pending the issue of Battle-Dress and a decision on a new pattern of dress for ceremonial and walking-out, the following interim measures had been approved for Regular Army personnel at home stations and for the TA.

Field boots, leggings or puttees were to continue to be worn by officers on ceremonial occasions so long as puttees were worn by other ranks. Pending a decision on the dress of the future, trousers without puttees were allowed to be worn by all ranks on training and when employed on office work.

No young officers, except those of horsed units, needed to provide themselves with field boots or gaiters and breeches on joining: they would, if required to ride, retain and utilize such articles of dress as they wore as cadets when on mounted parades.

*Table 40. **Puttees and Hose Tops (Coloured) adopted by Certain British Regiments stationed in India, 1939**[1]*

Regiment or Corps	Puttees	Hose tops
The Royal Scots (The Royal Regiment)		Hunting Stuart tartan
The Queen's Royal Regiment (West Surrey)	Khaki	
The King's Own Royal Regiment (Lancaster)		Khaki
The Northumberland Fusiliers		Khaki
The Leicestershire Regiment		Khaki
The Lancashire Fusiliers		Khaki
The Royal Scots Fusiliers		Mar tartan[2]
The Cheshire Regiment		Khaki
The South Wales Borderers		Khaki
The Cameronians (Scottish Rifles)		Douglas tartan tops with green legs
The Gloucestershire Regiment		Khaki
The Worcestershire Regiment		Khaki
The East Surrey Regiment		Khaki
The Duke of Cornwall's Light Infantry	Green	Green
The Duke of Wellington's Regiment (West Riding)		Scarlet
The Dorsetshire Regiment		Green
The Oxfordshire and Buckinghamshire Light Infantry		Khaki
The Essex Regiment		Pompadour blue
The Loyal Regiment (North Lancashire)		French grey
The Royal Berkshire Regiment (Princess Charlotte of Wales's)		Khaki
The Queen's Own Royal West Kent Regiment	Dark drab	Universal[3]
The King's Shropshire Light Infantry		Dark green
The Middlesex Regiment (Duke of Cambridge's Own)		Maroon
The Manchester Regiment		Khaki
The Durham Light Infantry		Bottle green
Royal Tank Corps		Black

[1]This schedule has been compiled from information extracted from *Clothing Regulations (India), 1939 (Appendices)*, Appendix XX, Table 2, pages 155–182; it excludes Indian and Gurkha troops. No information was available in these Clothing Regulations for regiments and corps of the British Army other than those shown here.

[2]The colouring of the hose tops adopted by the Royal Scots Fusiliers is given as 'Mar tartan'. Mar tartan is in fact Hunting Erskine tartan, the original Earl of

Mar having been an Erskine. As an additional point of interest, with regard to tartan patterned hose tops it was decided by ACI 498 dated w/e 23 November 1938 to increase the initial issue of tartan hose tops to new recruits enlisted into Highland kilted regiments from one to two pairs, with effect from 1 November 1938.

[3]No explanation is given in the Clothing Regulations (India), 1939 as to what is meant by the term 'universal'.

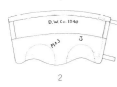

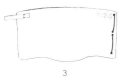

Above: Anklets. 1, The Webbing anklet; 2, inside surface of the Webbing anklet; 3, the leather gaiter.

Puttees continued to be worn on ceremonial parades and for walking-out purposes by other ranks pending the introduction of the new pattern of Battle-Dress trousers.

Anklets (Gaiters)

The British Army used two types of anklets, also referred to as gaiters, the most common type being of webbing and the other produced from leather, both black and brown. Brown leather anklets were produced for male personnel and special brown leather anklets for ATS personnel.

When being worn, anklets were required to fit easily but not loosely around the top of the wearer's boot. Anklets worn with early pattern Battle-Dress trousers that were provided with a short cloth tab and button on the bottom outer edge of each trouser leg were correctly worn as follows.

The bottom of the trouser leg was folded around the top of the boot and secured in position by fastening the strap and button on the trouser. The anklet was then folded around the leg, over the bottom of the trouser leg and around the top of the boot, with the highest points of the curve on the anklet in front and behind, the 'ears' being positioned over the ankle and the ankle straps facing towards the rear. The straps were then drawn through the buckles, starting with the

lower, to the full extent of their overlap. There had to be no sign of tightness or strain; if this occurred it indicated that the anklets being worn were too small. After the anklets had been put on, the trousers were drawn down 1in over the top of each anklet.

Anklets worn with Battle-Dress trousers that had plain trouser bottoms were worn as follows.

The trouser leg was folded over the top of the boot by holding the trouser bottom by the front and back seam and folding the crease to the outside of the leg. The anklet was then strapped around the ankle and the trouser leg was 'bagged' down over the top of the anklets.[1] Folding the trousers in this way prevented the insides of the trouser legs from rubbing together, which in turn

[1]Many former soldiers will remember the ritual of stamping the feet in order to make the freshly 'bagged' trouser bottom hang smartly over the top of the anklets. Those who were bold enough to risk the wrath of the RSM etc. took to wearing weights inside the bagged ends of the trousers. Bicycle chains, short lengths and properly degreased and cleaned, were used for this purpose, as were small lumps of lead threaded on to a length of twine to form a 'necklace' and worn inside the trouser legs, hanging down inside the bagging and thus keeping the latter over the top of the anklets. Needless to say, this practice was not permitted – officially – in the British Army.

avoided undue wear with all its consequent premature repair and replacement.

Modifications to Footwear and Anklets Regulations

ACI 1327 dated 26 July 1941 amended the original 1940 ACI 466 with regard to the type and colour of shoes permitted to be worn with military uniform. Officers were allowed to wear brown leather, but not buckskin, laced shoes, with or without toe-caps, whilst officers of Scottish regiments and officers of Royal Tank regiments wore black leather shoes on the following occasions.
1. With Service Dress when walking out, for work in offices or when not on duty with troops.
2. With Battle-Dress worn indoors when attending a dance.

Other ranks were permitted to wear black leather lace-up shoes, with or without toe-caps, on the following occasions.
1. With Service Dress when walking out.
2. With Battle-Dress when indoors attending a dance.
3. With Undress when walking out.

Somewhat later these instructions were simplified to read as follows.
1. All ranks were permitted to wear either brown or black civilian pattern boots or shoes with Service Dress or Battle-Dress on all those occasions previously referred to above.
2. All ranks were also permitted to wear black civilian pattern boots or shoes with Undress uniform when not on duty with troops or when walking out.
3. Boots or shoes of the suede type were not permitted to be worn on any occasion.

ACI 1239 dated 12 October 1940 stipulated that in future anklets were to be worn with Battle-Dress by all ranks when off duty out of barracks; this implied that up until that date anklets were not being worn with Battle-Dress outside barracks when off duty. However, a further ACI (No. 1328 dated 26 July 1941) stated that as part of the footwear concessions to all ranks, anklets were no longer to be worn when attending a dance indoors in shoes. At an even later date instructions were issued where all ranks were permitted to wear Battle-Dress without anklets—
1. When working in offices.
2. When not on duty with troops.
3. When walking out.

Leggings

Before the 1939–45 war brown leather leggings of sealed pattern that fastened up the front with laces and six studs were worn with both Service Dress and Khaki Drill clothing by mounted officers other than those who wore field boots.

Clogs

Clogs, known as 'Clogs, ordinary', which had been authorized by *Clothing Regulations 1926* and which were used for stable work, were discontinued as from the week ending 27 March 1935 by authority of ACI 85. All stocks of these clogs were withdrawn and returned to the RAOC.

Rope Soled Overshoes for Gun Crews of Coast Artillery Fixed Defence Units

In order to meet complaints of slipping on wet gun platforms, a pattern of rope soled overshoes was introduced in July 1940 (ACI 818 dated 27 July 1940) for wear over gun-floor shoes by gun crews of coast artillery fixed defence units. The overshoes were designated 'Overshoes, rope sole' and were made in sizes 6 to 12 for wear over gun-floor shoes of a similar size number.

The overshoes were issued on the following scales: 10 pairs for each 15in equipment manned; 8 pairs for each 9.2in; 7 pairs for each 6in; 5 pairs for each 4.7in; 4 pairs for each 12pdr 12cwt; and 8 pairs for each 6pdr twin Mark I equipment manned. This list was added to later in the year (ACI 1257 of 1940) to include 7 pairs for each naval 6in gun manned and 5 pairs for each naval 5.5in, 4.7in and 4in gun manned.

The Issue of Naval Pattern Boots for Personnel of Maritime Anti-Aircraft Regiments, Royal Artillery

Authority was given on 17 June 1942 (ACI 1288) for the issue of naval pattern boots, on the scale of two pairs for each other rank, to personnel of the Maritime AA Regiments, Royal Artillery. These boots were issued in replacement of the ankle boots.

Canvas Shoes

Canvas shoes were an issue item to all ranks who were required to perform physical training. They were also worn for certain sporting events, on troopships and in transport aircraft (to avoid damaging the interior of the ship or plane), in hospital and sometimes in barracks during times of relaxation.

The shoes were manufactured with uppers of darkish brown canvas and with the one piece heel and sole, plus a small toe-cap produced in black rubber, and they laced up at the front. They were supplied in one fitting only, and the size required by the individual corresponded to the size of his ankle boots.

Care had to be taken to ensure that these canvas shoes were not rendered prematurely unserviceable; the backs of the heels were often split open, invariably because the wearer forced his foot into the shoe or removed the shoe without first untying the laces. Disciplinary action was liable to be taken against the soldier whose shoes became unserviceable through this cause.

Hose Tops and Garter Flashes

Hose tops were footless hose. They were normally made from drab coloured knitted wool and were worn on the legs below the knee, with the lower end of the hose fitted over the upper end of the wearer's socks. They were only worn with Khaki Drill clothing when shorts were worn and, as khaki drab hose tops, were also worn by kilted regiments for field service use. Hose tops were usually held in position on the leg by having short length puttees wound around the ankle of the boots and the lower part of the hose tops or by the wearing of web gaiters.

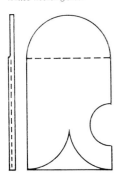

Above: Standard Army issue knitted woollen gloves.

Protective hand palm.

required to purchase at least six pairs. Long, khaki coloured woollen socks, officially referred to as 'stockings', were worn by officers when dressed in Khaki Drill clothing and wearing Khaki Drill shorts, the officers being required to have at least four pairs. For use by officers serving in cold climates two pairs of footless stockings and four pairs of natural grease, heavy woollen socks were required for service in Iceland and six pairs of heavy duty woollen socks for arctic climate use.

On 17 December 1930 (ACI 479) brown hospital socks were reintroduced for use by patients in military hospitals. These replaced the grey woollen socks marked with the hospital stamp that were then being used.

Personnel of the ATS were issued with three pairs of khaki ankle socks.

Gloves, Mittens and Gauntlets

Gloves worn by officers and other ranks.

Officers other than officers of rifle regiments were required to wear brown dogskin or buckskin gloves when on duty with troops when the latter were required to wear them. Rifle regiment officers wore black leather gloves. In Service Dress, gloves were also worn by officers when ordered to do so by their commanding officer. On all other occasions the wearing of gloves by officers was optional (ACI 2208 dated 17 October 1942).

Other ranks were permitted to wear brown leather civilian pattern gloves with either Service Dress or Battle-Dress when walking out (ACI 1603 dated 3 November 1943).

Wearing of black gloves with Service Dress by all ranks in rifle regiments.

The wearing of black gloves with Service Dress by all ranks in rifle regiments was approved by ACI 155 published during the week ending 13 May 1931. No free issue of black gloves was made to warrant officers, NCOs or men serving within rifle regiments at that time, but in the case of recruits of the Regular Army knitted black woollen gloves were supplied as an initial issue in place of the drab knit gloves previously issued.

Gloves, MT.

Gloves (or more correctly gauntlets) issued for drivers of motor vehicles were of natural leather and unlined.

Protective 'hand palms' issued for personnel handling ammunition packages.

As part of the Army's drive to conserve rubber, the War Office announced by ACI 1051 dated 16 May 1942 that the handles of ammunition boxes would, in future, be of bare wire without their covering of a protective rubber casing. In order to lessen the risk of damage to the hands of personnel whose task it was to lift and carry boxes of ammunition, approval had been given for the issue of what were called 'Palms, hand' as a form of protection. These were of simple construction and were made up locally, cut from short lengths of unserviceable fire hose (see sketch left).

Some regiments, in particular Scottish regiments, wore garter flashes with their hose tops; these were very similar to the garter flashes worn by Boy Scouts of thirty or more years ago. They were short lengths of coloured braid, usually finished in a swallow-tail cut, and were attached to the elasticated garter strap that was worn around the hose top underneath the hose where it was folded over. The flashes hung down from below these folded over sections of the hose tops and they were visible on the outer side of each calf.

I have yet to see anything that remotely resembles a listing of these garter flashes, but as far as I can ascertain the colours used for the flashes were related to companies and battalions.

Socks

Army issue socks for normal wear were manufactured in grey wool. Other ranks were issued with four pairs per man[1], and officers were

[1]The original issue of pairs of worsted socks per man prior to November 1941 had been three, but from 1 November 1941, by authority of ACI 2154, in order to extend the life of socks and with the consequential saving in wool the number of pairs of socks issued to men at home stations was increased to four. This increase permitted the wearing of two pairs weekly and helped to facilitate the mending of holes as soon as they appeared. The scale of socks issued to men at stations overseas remained at three pairs each until further notice. I have been unable to find any subsequent alteration to this number before 1945.

6. GREATCOATS, TRENCH COATS AND CAPES

Greatcoats

Officers' Old Style military greatcoat.

This garment was not worn by general officers, brigadiers and substantive colonels, nor by officers of the Household Cavalry and Foot Guards; they wore as Service Dress the ordinary British Warm.

The material was of regulation khaki drab mixture, milled and waterproofed. The coat was double-breasted, lancer style, to reach within a foot of the ground. The stand and fall collar was 3in wide at the fall and 1¾in wide at the stand, fastened with two hooks and eyes. Two rows of four buttons were positioned down the front of coat, vertically spaced 6in apart.

The back centre seam had a box pleat extending from the back of the neck to the waist, and a long vent was placed in the centre seam with two button-holes and buttons. The skirts were cut moderately full, and the back waist was slightly gathered by means of a 2in deep half-belt which was finished with square ends and carried three buttons. When fastened the belt became about 1–1½in narrower than the actual back of the coat.

The pocket flaps were made 7¾in long by 3½in deep and were placed on the slant. A sword slit 5in long was positioned in the underarm dart,

1½in above the left pocket. Inside the slit a closing flap was placed.

The sleeves were finished with gauntlet cuffs 6in deep and were unlined. Shoulder straps were sewn in scye and held in position at the neck with a small button. The width of the straps at the shoulder seam was 2½in, tapering to 2¼in at the neck. The coat was only lined in the shoulders, and it had a vertical inside breast pocket.

The alternative greatcoat for officers.

This new pattern greatcoat was intended as an alternative only to the previously described items, and those officers who already possessed the old pattern greatcoat were not required to go to the expense of including the new garment in their kit. Its wear was entirely optional.

The shape of the coat was similar to that used by officers of the Royal Air Force and was cut double-breasted with a two-way collar. Two rows of four regimental buttons spaced vertically 6½in apart were positioned with the top two buttons 9½in horizontally apart, the second two 7¾in apart, the third 5¾in and the lower pair 4in apart. The collar, made with a 3½in fall and a 1½in stand, was constructed so that it could be worn up or down and had a tab underneath.

The pockets were placed on the slant, with 7¼in wide and 3in deep flaps. The belt was cut in two sections, each of which reached the full width of the back waist, had three buttons and was sewn into the side seams. The sword slit was positioned 1½in above the left pocket and was let into the underarm dart. The slit was 5in long and had a cloth flap or facing inside.

The shoulder straps were made 2¾in wide at the shoulder and 1¾in at the neck. The straps were not inserted into the scye seam but extended over the latter by about ⅜in and were attached to the scye seam by a prick stitch. The straps reached to within 1in of the neck seam, were lined with melton cloth, and were fastened at the collar fall position by small regimental buttons.

The sleeves were plain except for a single line of stitching ⅝in from the bottom edge. The stitching throughout the edges of the garment, the flaps, belt and collar was ½in or ⅝in wide. The centre, back, side and other seams were plain. The shoulder straps were not stitched. The inside finish to the greatcoat was of Italian or any strong lining, with glissade used in the sleeves. The back was lined to the waist only, the lining in the foreparts being carried down to the side seams to below the level of the pockets. The coat had a 9in deep inside pocket inserted vertically at the junction of the facing and the lining and between the second and third buttons. There was also a ticket pocket inside the right side pocket.

The back, with its three seams and a long centre fly vent starting 7in below the waist and having two small buttons, was drawn into the waist by means of two 2in pleats situated about 2in away from the side seams. These pleats were held in position by a tacking stitch concealed under the two halves of the 2in deep cross belts; the latter extended across the back of the waist and had three button holes and buttons. The side and front waist

were shaped by means of darts and the skirt was moderately full.

The length of the greatcoat varied with the height of the wearer but it was suggested that a man 5ft 9in in height should wear a coat that reached to within 14in of the ground. The greatcoat was made from regulation khaki mixture material, milled and waterproofed.

The *Kings Regulations for the Army and the Royal Army Reserve, 1940*, Section X 'Dress, Clothing, Equipment, Medals and Decorations', page 354, para. 1008, stated that equipment was to be worn over the greatcoat. Greatcoats were required to be worn by officers on duty when the men were paraded with them. When carried rolled – by dismounted officers of foot units – the greatcoat was attached to the web sling. A commanding officer could allow greatcoats to be worn when he considered it necessary.

The prewar single-breasted greatcoat for wear by other ranks.

Prior to April 1939, greatcoats worn by other ranks were single-breasted. They were worn buttoned up to the neck by five large buttons, and the collar was worn closed at the neck. All other external features of the greatcoat were the same as those to be found on the double-breasted greatcoat.

Until August 1937 greatcoats were worn with Royal Arms buttons. After this date, by authorization of ACI 94 of 1937, buttons with a regimental or corps design were used.

The new pattern greatcoat for other ranks.

The Times announced on 21 April 1939 that a new pattern of greatcoat was being provided for other ranks of the British Army. It resembled the existing pattern of greatcoat as worn by officers in that it was longer in the skirt than was the then present OR pattern. It was double-breasted and was intended to be worn with the collar open.

The new pattern greatcoat was not to be issued until stocks of the superseded pattern were used up. No change was made in the patterns of the officer's greatcoat or in the blue-grey greatcoat of the Foot Guards.

The 1941 modification to the 1939 pattern dismounted greatcoat.

Following upon the recommendations submitted by Army commands, the following modifications in the design of the 1939 pattern dismounted greatcoat were introduced.
1. The length of the garment was decreased by 2in and the fall of the collar by ¾in in all sizes.
2. An inverted pleat was added to the back.
3. A large button, known as a 'jigger' button, was added to the inside of the left front, with a corresponding button-hole in the front of the right side, to prevent the right front from sagging.
4. A different type of material, calculated to afford additional warmth, was used for the lining.
5. The cut of the waist was modified to allow for increased freedom of movement.

Greatcoats to the improved design were introduced as supplies became available, stocks of the

Left: Col. L. M. Gregson, OBE, distributing shamrock to officers of the 1st Bn, Irish Guards at Pirbright Camp, Surrey, on St. Patrick's Day, 17 March 1934. (See also the photograph on page 150.) All are wearing the pattern of greatcoat worn by Guards officers.
Below: Maj.-Gen. J. E. S. Brind, the British Commander of the International Force in the Saar, inspecting British armoured cars at their barracks in the Petersburger-Hof, Saarbrucken, 10 January 1935. The accompanying officers are wearing the officers' old style military greatcoat.

obsolescent pattern being first used up (ACI 36 dated 8 January 1941).

Greatcoats condemned as unserviceable.

Before the war greatcoats were not condemned as unserviceable unless:

1. The collar, pocket flaps or front edges were worn threadbare, and expenditure on providing replacement new collars or pocket flaps was not considered an economical proposition.
2. The cuffs were worn through.
3. The button-holes were past repair.
4. The coat was so badly stained that, in the written opinion of a firm of cleaners, cleaning was of no use. Unserviceability of garments, including greatcoats, owing to staining was not normally considered as having been caused by fair wear, and soldiers were held liable for the damage unless they could show that the staining was due to wear under service conditions or by circumstances outside their control.

Between the wars condemned greatcoats were supplied for wear by soldiers of unsound mind at Netley whenever the Officer Commanding the Royal Victoria Hospital considered it necessary. During the war condemned greatcoats were retained by units for wear by their troops when on fatigues and as second coats for drivers of mechanical vehicles, tank and dragon crews etc., other than by those already issued with the tank crews oversuit.

Garments so retained were marked with the condemned stamp by the units concerned, and were recorded on the formal certificate which condemned them and also entered separately in the unit's administrative records.

The British Warm

This coat was the approved pattern for wear with Service Dress by general officers, brigadiers and substantive colonels; for officers below the rank of Substantive Colonel it was an optional garment for wear when not parading with troops.

For general officers, brigadiers and substantive colonels the material was of angola cloth of a light drab colour approximating to that of the alternative shade of 'Breeches, mounted pattern'. In all other cases the material and colour was left to the discretion of regiments and corps, provided that the shade was either that approved for Service Dress garments or was the alternative shade of the mounted breeches. All officers of any one unit had to be dressed alike.

The regulations for the British warm were as follows. The coat was double-breasted. It was cut to a little below knee length. It had two rows of three large leather covered buttons on each side, with a bone button under the lapel and two small leather buttons at the cuffs, the latter having slits 3¼in in length.

The back of the coat had three seams and a centre vent, commencing about 2½in below the seat line. The turn-down collar was 2in deep with lapel and step. It had two side pockets with 3in deep flaps and one inside breast pocket; an outside welted breast pocket was optional. There was also a ticket pocket in the left facing or in the right

outside pocket. There was a sword slit in the left underarm dart seam, inserted in the same way as in the greatcoat. Shoulder straps of the same material as the coat were sewn into the sleevehead seam and were held at the collar fall edge position by two small leather or bone buttons. Badges of rank in metal were worn mounted on to the shoulder straps.

The Military Trench Coat

The trench coat, which was lighter in weight than the greatcoat, was a popular garment worn by military officers during wet and rainy weather. It was made from khaki gabardine material. The coat was loose-fitting and had a two-row, three-button double-breasted front. An extra button at the top enabled the coat collar to be fastened close to the neck. There was also an extra piece of material put on the front of the shoulders as protection against the weather. The two rows of three buttons were spaced about 6in apart vertically and about 11in apart horizontally at the top and 8in apart at the waist.

The collar was made with a 3½in fall and a 1½in stand and constructed so that it could be worn up or down. There was a throat tab under the collar. Side pockets were placed on the slant with 3in deep flaps. The back had a pleat in the centre which was held at the waist by the full belt. The belt was 2½in deep, matching the coat, and had a single-prong, squared off slip buckle at the front. The sleeves had straps with buckles and were about 1¼in wide. Shoulder straps were made 2¾in wide at the shoulders and 1¾in at the neck, coming to a pointed end. The length of the garment varied with the height of the wearer but generally it reached to within 12in of the ground.

The Waterproof Cape

This was produced in drab twill, corresponding in colour to the khaki drab of the Service Dress. It was waterproofed with indiarubber and was fitted with a turn-down collar which could be turned up around the wearer's neck and fastened by the use of a fitted tab across the throat when necessary.

The cape fastened with a hook and eye at the throat and with five buttons and button-holes down the front. Two straps of the same material as the cape were attached to the junction of the collar and the cape on the inside; these straps passed over the shoulders, crossed on the wearer's breast, and were fastened with buttons and button-holes at the back that allowed the cape to be worn thrown back.

The cape was of sufficient length to come well below the knees of the wearer and had a perpendicular slit on each side of the front to allow for the free movement of the arms outside the cape when required.

This cape was used before the Second World War by troops walking out. It was not worn on parades or on duties under arms, but it was allowed to be worn by postmen, orderlies, clerks and other soldiers who were required to move around a camp or barracks during wet weather. It should not be confused with the waterproof ground sheet worn as a cape.

7. KHAKI DRILL AND JUNGLE GREEN CLOTHING

Khaki Drill Clothing No. 2 (Green) and No. 4 (Brown)

It was announced by ACI 230 published during the week ending 27 July 1932 that in order that No. 2 (green) Khaki Drill garments could be brought into general wear as soon as possible for all troops serving at imperial stations abroad and to ensure that during the transition period all men of a unit were dressed alike on ceremonial parades, either in No. 2 (green) or No. 4 (brown) Khaki Drill, the following procedure would be adopted.

In the case of units and drafts that were proceeding to stations abroad from the United Kingdom after 1 August 1932, one of the suits of KD supplied under *Clothing Regulations, Part I, 1926*, para. 217, to complete to the overseas scale was to be of No. 2 (green) drill; the balance was of No. 4 (brown) drill, until the stocks of the latter were exhausted.

Issues of No. 4 (brown) drill garments to troops serving at stations abroad ceased with effect from 1 April 1932 and all replacements were of No. 2 (green) drill in future.

At the time of this ACI, universal khaki helmets of No. 2 (green) shade were being issued in certain sizes, but there were also stocks of the No. 4 (brown) shade in other sizes which still had to be

exhausted. In order that the head-dress harmonize with the shade of Khaki Drill garments worn on ceremonial parades, arrangements were made for stocks of blanco of the two shades (corresponding with the shades of the d. ill clothing) to be placed on sale in regimental institutes at all overseas stations.

Khaki Drill Shorts and Trousers

It was decided in May 1935 (ACI 147 published during the week ending 29 May 1935) that Khaki Drill shorts for troops serving at stations abroad, other than in India, which were then authorized to be provided as optional garments under regimental arrangements were in future to be obtained on repayment from the RAOC. To this end a new pattern of drill shorts that embodied certain recommendations was sealed accordingly. The shorts continued to be an optional garment provided in lieu of the third pair of Khaki Drill trousers, and they were worn only at the discretion of officers commanding units and on such occasions, other than ceremonial parades, as determined by the general officer commanding.

Troops that proceeded abroad were no longer supplied before embarkation with the third pair of Khaki Drill trousers as referred to in *Clothing*

Above left: Lord Wavell, newly appointed Viceroy of India, inspecting men of a British guard of honour wearing Khaki Drill uniforms; Delhi, 1943.
Above right: Khaki Drill worn by British officers and NCOs during training manoeuvres in India, 1943.

Regulations, Part I, 1926, para. 217, but on arrival at the new station either one pair of Khaki Drill trousers or alternatively two pairs of the 'new pattern' Khaki Drill shorts were issued on repayment.

The current pattern of Khaki Drill shorts continued to be issued to personnel of the Hong Kong and the Singapore Royal Artillery, whilst stocks existed. Stocks of regimental pattern shorts were not taken over, but they were used up and issue of the new approved pattern delayed until such stocks were exhausted.

On 3 July 1935 (ACI 179 of 1935) it was further decided that the issue of Khaki Drill shorts − of No. 2 (green) drill − to men proceeding to imperial stations abroad was to be made before embarkation and not on arrival at the new station as laid down in ACI 147 of 1935; on 24 July 1935 ACI 196 announced that it had been decided that, subject to the approval of the GOC, Khaki Drill shorts were allowed to be worn on ceremonial parades at stations abroad.

ACI 299, published during the week ending 20 July 1938, dealt with the issue of Tropical shirts and Khaki Drill shorts to permanent staffs on transports. Approval had been given for the issue of two Tropical shirts and two pairs of KD shorts as public clothing to each man posted for duty in transports, in addition to the two KD suits authorized at that time under *Clothing Regulations, 1936*, para. 190.

Khaki Drill trousers began to cease being issued to troops serving overseas from February 1941. ACI 205 dated 12 February 1941 announced that from that date no further provision of the Khaki Drill trousers was to be made, but these garments continued to be issued until stocks were exhausted. When there were no further trousers available for issue, either as initial outfits or as replacements for unserviceable garments, an additional pair of Khaki Drill shorts with turn-ups ('Bombay Bloomers') were supplied in place of the trousers.

'Bombay Bloomers'

'Bombay Bloomers' was the derogatory name given by British troops to a particular style of Khaki Drill 'shorts' that were issued early on in the Second World War to troops serving in the Middle East. These sartorial monstrosities, which were both very unpopular and mercifully short-lived, were KD shorts which had very deep turn-ups. These reached up to the wearer's crutch and when worn in this manner were held in position with buttons. The purpose of these deep turn-ups was that they could be turned down, and by means of the white tapes threaded through the ends of the turn-ups could be bound to the wearer's ankles,

thus eliminating the need for changing into KD trousers.

The Khaki Drill Jacket

Officers other than Foot Guards.

The pattern of the Khaki Drill jacket worn by officers was as detailed on page 158 under the heading 'The pre-1942 pattern Service Dress jacket: officers of all units except Foot Guards'.

The wartime modified pattern of Khaki Drill jacket for officers of all units except Foot Guards.

This pattern of the Khaki Drill jacket was as previously described for the pre-1942 khaki drab Service jacket (page 158), together with the 1942 modifications listed on page 159. As with the khaki drab Service jacket, austerity pattern, the restrictions imposed in the manufacture of the modified pattern Khaki Drill jacket were lifted as from 15 January 1945 (see page 159).

Khaki Drill jacket for officers of the Foot Guards.

This item was of similar pattern to that of the Service Dress jacket described on page 159.

Tropical Clothing for Officers

Army Council Instruction 1868 dated 18 December 1943 advised that officers ordered for service in theatres in which Tropical clothing was worn were, with one exception, required to provide themselves with the 'normal scale' of Khaki Drill etc. as set out below. The Tropical clothing that was considered necessary for service in the Middle East had been adopted as the standard scale for this purpose. In the case of the one exception referred to above officers required a

'special scale' and the details of this are also set out in Table 41.

The mobilization instructions or draft warning orders indicated which scale 'normal' or 'special' officers were required to provide and also the

Table 41. Scales of Tropical Clothing for Officers

Item	Normal scale	Special scale
Helmet, UK[1]	1	—
Slouch hat, with lining	—	1
Bush shirts and/or Tropical shirts (both with long sleeves)[2, 3]	6	—
Tropical blouses (with long sleeves)[2]	—	3
Tropical shirts (with long sleeves)	—	3
Khaki Drill shorts, pairs[4]	3	3
Khaki Drill trousers, pairs[4]	3	2
Stockings, pairs	6	2
Hose tops, pairs	2	2
Puttees, long, pairs	—	2
Vests, thin	6	4
Drawers, thin, pairs	6	4
Boots, mosquito, pairs[5]	—	1
Pyjamas, suits	—	3
Socks, thin, pairs	—	3

[1]Required only for certain stations (mobilization instructions or draft warning orders gave details).
[2]Bush shirts and Tropical blouses – with gorget patches for officers of the rank of Colonel and above – had medal ribbons for all ranks where applicable.
[3]Bush shirts only, with worsted rank badges on plain backing.
[4]When providing themselves with Tropical clothing, officers were reminded that as an anti-malaria precaution Khaki Drill trousers were the standard legwear in all tropical areas, shorts being worn only at the discretion of the C-in-C.
[5]Issued free from store.

Above left: The Khaki Drill jacket for officers of Scottish regiments. Lt.-Col. J. D. Frost, DSO, MC, formerly of the Cameronians (Scottish Rifles) and a senior officer of the British Airborne Forces, meets General Eisenhower.
Above: Cpl. G. Snelgrove of Gloucester, serving with a West African unit, shakes hands with the C-in-C India. Cpl. Snelgrove is wearing the tropical combination suit: March 1944.

particular type of Tropical headgear, if any, required. The Tropical clothing was additional to the home outfit scale and it will be noted that, except as provided in the scale of Tropical clothing for officers proceeding to the USA or Canada, below, the Khaki Drill jacket was omitted. This garment was not an essential item under war conditions, and officers were not required to provide themselves with it.

The quantities shown in the two columns above were those suggested by the GOC-in-C concerned, but in view of the shortage of cotton material in the UK and its cost, and also the possibility that a unit or draft could be diverted to an alternative destination after sailing, officers were advised to limit their purchases before embarkation to their essential needs for the voyage; on arrival at their destination additional requirements could be obtained on payment from stocks held in officers' shops. Garments of other ranks' pattern could also be obtained from store, whilst local tailors frequently made up garments at a far cheaper rate than was the case with military tailors and outfitters at home.

In the case of officers who proceeded to the USA or Canada, the following scale applied (Tropical clothing was worn only between 1 May and 30 September in the USA and between 1 June and 1 September in Canada).
Khaki Drill jackets: 2
Khaki Drill trousers, pairs: 2
Tropical shirts with long sleeves: 3
Drawers, thin, pairs: 6
Vests, thin: 6

Officers were reminded that they were permitted to purchase from the RAOC before embarkation articles of other ranks' pattern

Tropical clothing, if available. If officers decided to purchase their clothing from the trade, it was essential for security reasons that they did not give their tailors etc. any idea of their destination or date of sailing, even if the destination and date were only based upon speculation.

In the case of officers who proceeded on the 'special scale' it was not necessary for them to take the full scale of articles peculiar to home outfit; one suit of Service Dress or Battle-Dress (later amended just to Battle-Dress), one greatcoat, one jersey pullover, one pair of shoes and sufficient warm shirts and underclothing were required for the voyage. Working overalls and waterproof coats were obtainable at their destination.

The Tropical Combination Suit

Produced from Khaki Drill material, this garment was a one-piece combination of a short sleeved, collarless shirt with shorts. It was buttoned down its entire front from the collar to the crutch. Three brass exposed buttons fastened the upper part of the garment; five brass buttons fastened the fly of the shorts, with the top button of the five at waist level left exposed.

There was a single breast pocket on the left without flap and two slit opening side pockets built into the shorts. The back of the shirt had a wide pleat and at the waist was a short strap with a two-pronged brass buckle that engaged with an opposite length of strap, both of which were adjustable to gather in the waist.

This was a working garment, worn usually for maintenance purposes.

Jungle Green Clothing

At the beginning of the 1939–45 war the clothing worn by British troops stationed in the Far East had been of the same type and colour as that worn in the Middle East. Khaki Drill clothing was found to be unsuitable for jungle warfare because it was insufficiently robust and, equally importantly, it was of an unsuitable colour – in the leafy half-light of dense jungle and against green jungle vegetation the colour of the khaki drill clothing was too light.

By 1942 new 'jungle green' clothing began to be introduced for the forces in Far East theatres. All outer clothing, such as long trousers, jackets, shorts and cellular shirts, were vat-dyed a dull dark green registered as Standard Camouflage Colour 19 (SCC 19); web equipment was similarly sulphur-dyed. Experience had shown this colour to have been the most suitable. Other clothing, such as underwear, socks, handkerchiefs and towels, was dyed to this or a slightly lighter shade of green in order to be as inconspicuous as possible when hung up to dry.

As early as April 1932 the military authorities in India had begun to change over their Khaki Drill clothing from No. 4 (brown) to No. 2 (green) (see page 174) as their standard shade of colour. However, their olive green faded to too light a shade with exposure and laundering to be suitable for jungle warfare. When faded, SCC 19 was comparable to the Indian No. 2 (green) when new.

8. SERVICE DRESS FOR OTHER RANKS

The Service Dress Jacket for Other Ranks, 1907–24

This pattern was produced from drab serge mixture. It was worn loose over the chest with a minimum of 5in spare over the chest measurements, and it had a turned down rolled collar. There were 'rifle patches' on both shoulders, two box pleated breast pockets with flaps and two side pockets with letter-box flaps. The jacket was pleated slightly at the waist, there was a wide, false pleat down the centre of the back, and it had sewn-in shoulder straps. The jacket was intended to be loose fitting and was not allowed to be tailored to a snug fit. Collar badges were not worn but badges of rank, and skill-at-arms and appointment badges, were worn and were of worsted. Brass shoulder titles were worn on the shoulder straps. The jacket was slightly modified during the Great War.

The Service Dress Jacket for Other Ranks, 1924–39

By authority of ACI 129 of 1924, the existing Service Dress jacket as described above became a 'second' jacket and its place was taken by an improved pattern jacket to be worn on ceremonial parades and for walking-out. The original pattern jacket – the second jacket – was retained for drill, training, field exercises and the like.

The new, improved Service Dress jacket was produced by altering the old pattern. The width around the breast and waist was reduced by about 3 or 4in and across the back by about ¼in, whilst the width of the upper portion of the sleeves was reduced and the collar was made higher. Collar badges, brass shoulder titles and all worsted badges were worn.

Warrant officers Class I were permitted to wear a superior type of Service Dress jacket with a stand-and-fall collar, but ACI 130 of 1924 forbade both the wearing of the officers' type of Service Dress jacket (see page 158) by warrant officers Class I and of the warrant officers' Class I SD jacket by warrant officers Class II. The 1933 edition of *Priced Vocabulary of Clothing and*

Right: Sjt. Smith, a Royal Fusiliers' drill instructor, demonstrating the standing load drill movement to recruits at the Hounslow Barracks, Middlesex, on 25 March 1938. The men are wearing the Service Dress jacket for other ranks.
Top, far right: The Service Dress Jacket for other ranks of Scottish Regiments, worn here by an advance party of Gordon Highlanders when they moved to Bridge of Don, Aberdeen from their old barracks at Castlehill on 14 August 1935.
Below, far right: Three versions of Army dress; from left to right, Service Dress, Battle-Dress and Shirt Sleeve order.

Necessaries lists the Service Dress jacket for warrant officers Class I as being of whipcord.

The Service Dress Trousers for Other Ranks, 1907–39

Before 1924, Service Dress trousers for other ranks were of drab mixture tartan. They were cut narrow on the lower half of the leg near to the ankle and were made short to reach the top of the ankle boot. They were not permitted to be worn in public without leggings or puttees being worn. After 1926 they assumed more normal proportions. SD trousers worn by warrant officers Class I in 1933 were produced in whipcord to match the quality of their Service Dress jackets, and all other trousers were manufactured in drab serge mixture.

The Use of Other Ranks' Pattern Service Dress, 1939–45

With the introduction of the Battle-Dress in March 1939 it was decided that Service Dress would only be worn by mounted troops of the Royal Artillery, a few horsed Royal Army Service Corps units and personnel of the Royal Army Veterinary Corps (ACI 466 of 1940).

The existing Service Dress was, in 1939, to be used for ceremonial and walking-out purposes only, except where Full Dress had already been authorized and where this was retained. However, even this provision seems to have lapsed, owing no doubt to the strains placed on the national economy by the war. Other ranks' Service Dress was, however, reintroduced in 1945 for wear by regimental bands (see below).

The Wartime Reintroduction of Service Dress for Other Ranks of Regimental Bands

To enable personnel of authorized bands to maintain a neat appearance (which was not always possible with loose-fitting Battle-Dress), it was announced in ACI 122 dated 3 February 1945 that Service Dress had been authorized to be worn as occasions demanded. In the case of bands of Scottish regiments, the kilt or trews, as appropriate, were allowed to be worn in lieu of Service Dress trousers, issues of the above items being made to the scales as shown below. In the case of bands that were under a director of music, the issue of two suits of Service Dress for each other rank on the establishment continued.

Authorized bands, other than Scottish regiments. The scale of issue for other ranks on the establishment of authorized bands, other than those of Scottish regiments and those under a director of music, was one Service Dress jacket, one pair of Service Dress trousers, one Battle-Dress blouse and one pair of Battle-Dress trousers. The issue of one stiff Service Dress cap was also authorized for such of the above personnel who were then in possession of the General Service cap or the Field Service cap. Where a beret or bonnet was authorized, the stiff Service Dress cap was not issued. The General Service cap or the Field Service cap was retained by band members for wear when training etc.

Authorized bands of Scottish regiments. The scale of issue on the establishment for each other rank of authorized bands of Scottish Regiments was as shown in Table 42.

The issue of one Glengarry cap was also authorized for the above personnel and for pipers of pipe bands of such regiments, in addition to the head-dress they were wearing at the time of this ACI. Approval had also been given for the issue, if desired, of a buff waist-belt to each other rank of all authorized bands.

On 29 August 1945 a further ACI, No. 1019 of 1945, was issued, adding the following items approved for use by personnel of all authorized bands: regimental buttons, black waist-belts for bands of rifle regiments, and the Mark II Sam Browne waist-belt with sword and shoulder belt for use by warrant officer bandmasters.

The regimental buttons were issued on a scale of one set for each Service Dress jacket. The black waist-belt for rifle regiments was for band personnel other than bandmasters, whilst the buff

waist-belt that had earlier been approved for each other rank of all authorized bands was, by the authority of this ACI, restricted to all bands other than bands of rifle regiments and to warrant officer bandmasters.

Table 42. The Wartime Reintroduction of Service Dress for Other Ranks of Authorized Bands of Scottish Regiments

Article	Kilted regiments	Trewed regiments
Other ranks' Service Dress jacket Scottish pattern	1	1
Kilt	1	—
Garters	1 pr	—
Hose tops, drab	2 prs	—
Purse and belt, complete	1	—
Trews	—	1 pr
Battle-Dress blouse	1	1
Battle-Dress trousers	1 pr	1 pr

Below: Pipers of the London Scottish and Royal Irish Fusiliers piping at a ceremony in 1942.

9. BATTLE-DRESS, SERGE AND DENIM

The 1932–34 Experimental Pattern Serge Uniform

In November 1932 it was officially announced that a new experimental Field Service uniform had been designed for troops of the British Army. Its use was intended to increase the soldier's comfort both when marching and when in action and to improve personal hygiene.

Manufactured from khaki coloured serge material, the uniform consisted of a four-pocket single-breasted jacket and matching trousers. Bronzed and/or gun-metal finished buttons, badges and shoulder titles that required no cleaning replaced the existing brass items.

The new jacket and a new, collar-attached khaki flannel shirt were both worn open at the neck, with the shirt collar turned down over the collar of the jacket. A khaki wool pullover, which replaced the former cardigan, was worn under the jacket in cold weather and was just visible above the opening at the front of the jacket. The jacket had a double vent at the back and the ends of the cuffs were fastened with buttons.

Web canvas leggings could be worn with the trousers or, if required, were replaced by short puttees. As an alternative to the trousers, long 'shorts' worn with short puttees and hose tops could also be worn. The boots were of a lighter pattern than previously worn.

The new gabardine head-dress, which was to be worn for service in the field and was referred to as a 'deer stalker' cap, was intended to replace the existing Service Dress peaked cap. It had no chin strap and carried no metal cap badge, and when not in use it could be folded and carried in one of the pockets of the jacket.

Right: Front and rear views of the 1932–34 Experimental Pattern British Army serge uniform, photographed at the Central Recruiting Office, Whitehall, on 28 November 1932.

New items of canvas webbing equipment were introduced at this time, together with alterations to existing items.

Two experimental platoons from two infantry battalions, the 2nd Battalion The Queen's Royal Regiment (West Surrey) stationed at Aldershot and the 2nd Battalion The Durham Light Infantry at Catterick, were chosen by the War Office and fitted out with the new uniform and equipment, instructed with the task of carrying out evaluation tests and controlled experiments on these items. These evaluation tests were conducted throughout the military training programme for the year 1933.

In November 1934 it was reported in the national press that the new experimental Field Service dress which had been under trials during the past eighteen months or so had reached the report stage and was then being considered by the Army's clothing and medical authorities. In general it was found that the new form of dress was both comfortable and hygienic and at that time it was considered likely that the whole design would be approved but that some modifications would be looked for. The wider trousers which were a feature of the new uniform were found to collect rain, and some of the men of the two experimental platoons favoured the old pattern of trousers with the tightly wound puttees. The angola wool shirt with its fixed collar worn open at the neck proved popular with the fifty-strong experimental platoons; it could also be worn closed at the neck with a tie. The 'deer stalker' cap, which gave protection against both sun and rain, had been improved with more stiffening, and this too was a popular item. Other items of clothing

that had been under trial were ankle boots of lighter weight, a pullover, web leggings, a waterproof greatcoat and an oilskin cape.

The 1938 'Overalls' Experimental Pattern Uniform

The prewar adoption by the British Army of new weapons such as the 'Bren' light machine gun and the 'Boys' anti-tank rifle, the reorganization of the Infantry into rifle and machine gun battalions and the evolution of new patterns of equipment all had their effect on the British soldier's fighting attire. In March 1938 further tests were carried out in order to devise an improved form of active service clothing and personal equipment. These tests involved all arms except horsed units.

A new version of the 1932–34 experimental pattern serge uniform, previously described, was produced in khaki coloured denim material, together with a new style of denim uniform, initially referred to as 'overalls' but which subsequently evolved into the ubiquitous British Army Battle-Dress.

These uniforms were designed primarily to lighten the weight then carried by the infantry soldier and to meet certain factors due to mechanization. They were also intended to make the wearer as comfortable as possible when on the march and when in action and to give greater freedom of movement generally. In these 1938 tests comparisons were made between these two new uniforms.

The denim version of the four-pocket Field Service uniform differed very little from the original 1932–34 experimental serge uniform. In place of the crested, bronze finished buttons and

Right: Five years elapsed
between the appearance of the
original experimental serge
uniform (see page 181) and the
further experimental designs of
clothing for active service and
training, introduced on 1 March
1938. In the photograph on the
left is shown the uniform
originally referred to as 'Overalls' but which subsequently
became the British Army
Battle-Dress. A denim version
of the 1932–34 experimental
serge uniform is shown at right
in the same photograph. The
denim garment was eventually
adopted but long after the war
in the 1960s when it re-
appeared in a modified version
as the Khaki No. 2 Dress for
other ranks of the Army. The
far right photograph provides a
different view of the same uniforms. Both photographs were
taken at the Central London
Recruiting Depot in Great
Scotland Yard, Whitehall, on 1
March 1938.

collar badges only plastic buttons were used, and the collar badges were done away with. Brass shoulder titles were also used.

The main features of the 'overall' style uniform were as follows.

Head-dress. The uniform was worn with the newly introduced khaki Field Service cap (see also page 134).

Blouse. The blouse was of a design similar to that introduced in 1936 and already being worn by members of the Royal Tank Corps, and it had a collar which could be worn either open or closed. Experiments were carried out with 'zip' fasteners on ten per cent of these blouses whilst the rest had buttons in order to test the merits of both.

Trousers. These were described as being designed similar to ski-ing trousers, being loose-fitting and buckled at the ankles.

Shirt. This had a collar attached and could be worn inside the collar of the blouse when the latter was closed, or alternatively outside when the blouse collar was left open.

Gaiters. No longer referred to as leggings and intended to replace the puttees, these were of the same canvas type already tested during the 1932–34 experiments. They were intended mainly for infantry use as a protection against wet conditions underfoot.

By the summer of 1938 the lack of newspaper reports concerning the original 1932–34 pattern Field Service uniform would seem to indicate that this item had lost favour to the 'overalls' pattern uniform which was already by this time being referred to as 'Battle-Dress'. On 9 July 1938 *The Times* reported that six soldiers and two officers had been inspected the previous day in the gardens

of Buckingham Palace by King George VI accompanied by the Adjutant-General to the Forces, Lieutenant-General C. G. Liddell. All the troops wore suits of Battle-Dress made up in different shades of serge: the uniforms varied from pale khaki to almost dark brown and the experiment was carried out to determine which shade would prove the most suitable.

A few days later, on 26 July, His Majesty once again inspected a party of troops, all wearing specimens of Army uniforms suitable for walking-out and ceremonial occasions in the event of the Battle-Dress being adopted. They were exhibited side by side with the existing Service Dress which was then being worn for all purposes.

On 20 April 1939 *The Times* reported that the final changes had been approved for the British Army's new Battle-Dress. It was hoped that the troops would have received the new uniform by the summer of 1939. The various Army commands had decided against the use of the experimental denim outfits that had previously been under review and came down in favour of drab serge material. The blouse of the new uniform was not as loose fitting as that of the experimental model, and it was fastened by dull coloured buttons. There were ventilation holes under the arms of the improved pattern of blouse and the waist buckle was lighter and flatter. The trousers were not cut so full and had a larger pocket positioned on the left leg. A field dressing pocket was provided at the top of the right leg. The ankle fastenings were buttoned instead of having a buckle and short strap.

All badges of rank to be worn on the new Battle-Dress were to be of worsted embroidery. Collar badges were not to be worn on the blouse, and the shirt with collar attached was not worn with the Battle-Dress, the existing collarless pattern of shirt being retained instead.

The article went on to state that the then current Service Dress was to be used for walking-out purposes and for most ceremonies. Officers and warrant officers were to wear the same pattern of Battle-Dress as that worn by other ranks and their garments were to be drawn on payment from the RAOC. There was no objection to an officer's uniform being made up with the material then being used for officers' Service Dress uniform. It was intended that the wearing of Battle-Dress was to be for service in time of war.

Denim overalls (1939 universal pattern).

As part of the report concerning the final changes that had been approved in March 1939 by the Army Council for the British Army's new Battle-Dress (Public Record Office file WO-32 11010), a decision was made regarding the denim overalls. These were to be of the same pattern as the Battle-Dress and were designed for wear over normal underclothing; they could, however, also be worn over the serge outfit in very cold weather, if required. Existing stocks of the then present material, No. 4 brown drill or denim, were to be made up into overalls of the new design. Meanwhile the question of the most serviceable and

economical material for overalls, such as denim, drill, etc., was under investigation and future stocks of the chosen material were to be provided accordingly. (For further details about denim overalls, see page 206.)

It was also decided that there was to be one universal pattern and colour of overalls for all arms, including the Royal Tank Corps, to replace the existing one-piece and two-piece overalls and RTC black suits. As large stocks of the Royal Tank Corps black suits still existed in 1939, the adoption of the universal pattern overalls by personnel of this corps was delayed, the intended change-over period being of two or three years' duration (see page 208).

Battle-Dress for Commissioned Officers and the Rank and File of the British Army, 1939–45

Blouse. This was cut on very easy fitting lines. The back was cut with a raised centre seam and the seam was raised well up on top of the shoulders; there were no side seams. The fronts fastened to the neck, which was finished with a panteen collar. The collars of the blouse were intended to be loose fitting, and the fit of the blouse was not wrong if the collar appeared to be large since it was designed that way.

The left forepart terminated directly down the centre of the front, and fastenings consisted of five

Below: The new patterns of clothing, November 1939. Denim 'Overalls' (left), worn with the drab field service cap; and (right) the new Battle-Dress with 1937 Pattern web equipment and khaki drab field service cap.

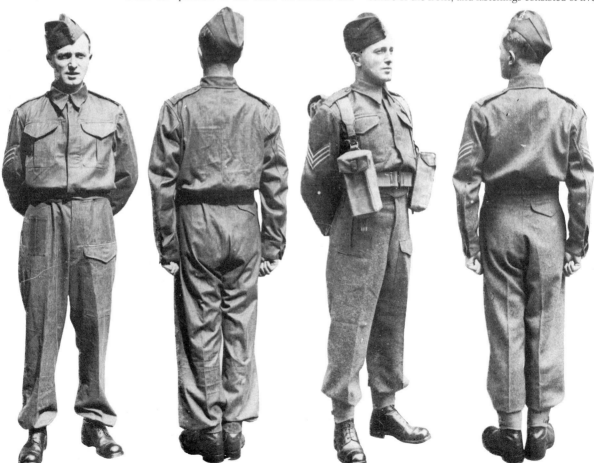

brass four-holed dish buttons, later changed to khaki drab vegetable composition or plastic buttons. All were originally concealed in a fly. Later pattern Battle-Dress blouses, known as '1940 Pattern Utility Battle-Dress', did away with the fly front, and all buttons down the front of the blouse and on the two unpleated breast pockets were exposed. There were two hooks and eyes for fastening the front of the collar on the stand.

The shoulder straps of the blouse were of the usual width. In the case of officers of the Household Cavalry and the Foot Guards, they carried metal rank badges of the authorized pattern, and in the case of all other Army officers embroidered worsted badges of rank (see also page 105 for 1943 introduction of coloured backing for officers' rank badges).

The waist section was gathered into a 3in wide belt. Extending from the latter on the left side was a 9in long strap which fastened with a metal buckle at the side of the waist that provided for adjustment.

Patch pockets were placed on each breast, the average size of these being 6in wide by 7in deep, with a 1¼in wide box pleat in the centre of both; these were done away with in the utility pattern Battle-Dress blouse. The flaps that covered these pockets were made 3in in depth at the centre tapering to 2in at their sides. The pocket was closed by means of a button-hole and button, a concealed inner flap originally taking the button-hole.

The sleeves were cut moderately full and were finished with a 3in deep cuff band into which the upper part was tucked. There was a small vent in the hindarm, with a button and button-hole in the fly of the cuff.

Trousers. These were cut moderately wide in the leg with plain bottoms. A strap was inserted ½in up in the leg seam at the bottom of both legs. This strap was 1½in wide and was long enough to reach to the front of the trouser crease where it was attached to a button when the trousers were worn without gaiters. Before the gaiters were put on, the strap on each leg was drawn over the front of each leg to fasten on a button placed at the side seam for that purpose. This strap and button arrangement was abolished in June 1941 as being unnecessary.

Further instructions were issued that emphasized that care had to be taken to ensure that the trouser legs ends were folded over the boots by holding the trouser bottom by the front and back seam and folding both creases to the outside of the leg. This prevented the insides of the trouser legs from rubbing together and also avoided undue wear with consequent premature repair and possible replacement.

Premature fraying of the bottom edge of the trouser leg cuffs also had to be avoided. This was achieved by reinforcing the trousers with tape. The drab tape, ⅞in wide, was sewn on to the inside of the trouser cuffs, the bottom edge of the tape being flush with the bottom of the trouser leg.

On the left leg a deep patch pocket with flap was placed. The position of the top of this pocket was about 9in from the waist and 1½in away from the trouser fly. The pocket was 7in wide by 11in deep and had a flap of similar shape to that used on the outside breast pocket. This was fastened with a button-hole, initially concealed in the lining but later exposed. The flap was placed 1in above the top edge of the patch pocket.

Placed high up on the right leg was a small patch pocket, 4½in wide by 6in deep, which had a flat pleat in the centre. The position of this pocket, designed to take the wearer's field dressing packet, was 6in from the top of the trousers and 1in from the trouser fly.

Ordinary side pockets were inserted, and there was a single hip pocket with flap at the back on the right side. This had a button-hole in the lining to conceal the button. The brace buttons were placed inside the tops for concealment. There were three button-holes inserted in the lining of the trousers which enabled the blouse to be fastened to the back of the trousers and thus kept them secure.

The use of Battle-Dress with the British Expeditionary Force, 1940.

Contrary to popular belief, the use of Battle-Dress by personnel of the British Expeditionary Force in France and Belgium in 1939–40 was not as widespread as fading memories would have one believe. During April 1940 two separate Army Council Instructions were published, which dealt with the wearing of Battle-Dress by officers joining

Below: The new Battle-Dress on view for the first time during Mechanized Army demonstrations at Aldershot, 22 February 1939.

the BEF (ACI 323 for w/e 10 April 1940) and the issue of Battle-Dress to other ranks prior to embarkation for the BEF (ACI 391 for w/e 24 April 1940).

The first set of instructions was published for the guidance of officers proceeding to join the BEF. They stated that:

1. Battle-Dress was seldom worn at GHQ or at HQs in the Lines of Communication area, officers who were proceeding to take up appointments at these headquarters being required to be in possession of Service Dress. Battle-Dress was only taken if already in the possession of the individual officer.

2. Officers proceeding to take up appointments other than at GHQ or in the L of C area, and also regimental officers who were proceeding overseas individually as reinforcements, were required to take Battle-Dress in those cases where it was regulation wear for their regiment or corps. Service Dress was allowed to be taken as an optional item.

3. Regimental officers who were proceeding with units for which the Battle-Dress was regulation

Right: Two versions of the Battle Dress uniform: the original style with fly-fronted blouse and pocket flaps, worn by Maj.-Gen. R. E. Urqhart (right), and the 1940 Pattern Utility Battle-Dress with exposed buttons, worn by Brig. J. W. Hackett.

wear were required to be similarly dressed. Service Dress was allowed to be taken.

4. Stocks of Battle-Dress were available with the BEF, and officers were able to obtain their requirements from these stocks on payment.

The second set of instructions (ACI 391 of 1940) stated that Battle-Dress was to be worn by all other ranks (except horsed personnel, who continued to wear other ranks' Service Dress) who were in future proceeding to the BEF. Where personnel who had been placed under orders for embarkation to the BEF were not in possession of Battle-Dress the officer commanding the unit in which the men were serving had to take immediate steps to issue all suits of Battle-Dress required. The Service Dress garments replaced by this issue had to be withdrawn before embarkation, and all those articles fit for reissue, or which were made fit for reissue after cleaning, were returned to the RAOC.

The AV Battle-Dress

In 1942, as part of the precautions taken by the British Army to protect its troops against the horrors of gas warfare, specially treated suits of Battle-Dress that had been impregnated with dichlorophenylbenzol chloroinide (AV) began to be issued to the forces in 1942 (ACI 1320 of 1942). This impregnated or AV Battle-Dress when first issued tended to feel stiff and slightly sticky to the touch, although this stiffness and tackiness wore off after a few days of use. White patches ('blooming') were unavoidable, but these could nearly always be brushed off or would wear off with use. When first issued the impregnated garments gave off a slight smell. This was supposed to be dispelled if the Battle-Dress were brushed and either worn or hung out in the open for a time.

Although it was not a very popular garment to have to wear since it smelt, felt and looked offensive, the underlying purpose of such treatment was to provide the wearer with some protection against mustard gas vapour. It was not capable of giving protection against spray, as large drops penetrated almost to the same extent as with normal Battle-Dress, and whilst small drops were to some extent destroyed this was not a reliable safeguard against their effects. Any form of misuse of the Battle-Dress gravely decreased the protection it afforded.

The AV Battle-Dress was eventually issued to all troops stationed in the United Kingdom and Northern Ireland on the scale of two suits per man; it was also provided as an initial issue to all recruits as well as in replacement for garments which had become unserviceable. It was not intended to issue the impregnated Battle-Dress for use in other theatres of war, except in the case of certain garrisons where stocks of AV Battle-Dress were held in bulk for use should the need arise.

In the case of officers, the AV Battle-Dress was only issued to those who were stationed in the United Kingdom and Northern Ireland. An initial issue was made to them free provided that the officers exchanged a non-AV suit of Battle-Dress of either WD or superfine pattern. These free issues were made for a period of three months from June to September 1942, after which date issues to officers were made only on repayment of the full vocabulary rate plus purchase tax; a free issue was also allowed for up to three months after the date an officer had disembarked on returning from abroad. Newly commissioned officers, as well as those officers who were not desirous of handing in Battle-Dress already in their possession, were issued with AV suits on repayment at full vocabulary rate plus purchase tax.

Dry-cleaning AV garments was the responsibility of the appropriate RAOC returned clothing depot and was not permitted to be undertaken by dry-cleaning contractors.

AV Battle-Dress was in no way antagonistic to vermin or infection and as such required disinfection or disinfestation with the same frequency as normal Battle-Dress. The following methods of dealing with infected and infested AV Battle-Dress were adopted.

1. Infected AV Battle-Dress was disinfected in a steam disinfector and then returned to the RAOC locally for disposal as salvage.
2. Infested AV Battle-Dress was disinfested by hot air. If this was not possible then the garments were disinfested with steam and after treatment by either method the Battle-Dress was returned to the RAOC locally and disposed of as salvage.

Modifications to the Battle-Dress and Overalls

Modification to the collar of the Battle-Dress blouse and to the collar of the Service Dress jacket.

The use of the Battle-Dress under field conditions very quickly brought to light that the rough collar of the blouse was causing problems to those individuals who had sensitive skin. Approval was given for the collars of their garments to be lined with Khaki Drill or other similar material when this was considered necessary by the wearer. As the collar of the blouse was designed to be worn open in hot weather the fabric chosen as lining for the collar had to be a reasonable match with the material of the blouse itself (ACI 306 dated w/e 3 April 1940). It is obvious that this was the beginning of the practice enjoyed by officers – and later with the introduction of the collar-attached shirt and tie by other ranks (see page 196) – whereby the neck openings of Battle-Dress blouses were lined with materials that seemed to range right across the spectrum of greens and browns. There is an example of a privately produced officer's Battle-Dress blouse on display at the regimental museum of the Royal Green Jackets at Winchester, Hampshire, where the collar and the 'lapels' of the blouse are lined with dark bottle green cloth. It is claimed that this style of blouse was worn by officers of the Rifle Brigade from 1941 onwards. What started out as a compassionate measure for some wound up as a fashion whim for all.

ACI 513 dated 25 May 1940 instructed that these modifications were allowed to be carried out at public expense in the case of other ranks, but no expense to the public was allowed in the case of officers. The provisions of ACI 306 of 1940 were extended to cover similar modifications to the collars of the Service Dress jacket when this was considered necessary.

A further ACI, No. 665 dated 6 June 1945, forbade the alteration to the collar of the Battle-Dress blouse by other ranks which prevented it from being buttoned up to the top when the tie was not worn. The cost of remodelling Battle-Dress blouses that had been altered in this way was charged to the individual responsible.

Modification of design of the Battle-Dress and Battle-Dress denim overalls.

In July 1940, as a result of the recommendations submitted by Army commands, the following improvements in the design of the Battle-Dress and denim overalls were approved.

The blouse. A new type of buckle, with teeth and fitted at the waist, was introduced to help prevent the belt of the blouse from slipping. Smaller button-holes at the waist were provided in order to prevent the buttons which fastened the blouse to the trousers from releasing themselves. In the case of the serge blouse, a stronger fly was introduced, and finally the collar of the serge blouse was lined with drab coloured drill material.

The trousers. A revolving shank button and button-hole were fitted to the field dressing pocket. The width of the leg was reduced at the knee and at the bottom of the leg to give a better fit when the trousers were worn with anklets, and the serge trousers were lined with drill over the loins at the back to give additional warmth.

Garments of the improved design were introduced as supplies became available and stocks of

Right: Paratroopers wearing the specially modified Battle-Dress trousers for Airborne Forces personnel; September 1944.

the obsolescent patterns were used up (ACI 788 dated 20 July 1940).

Modification to denim trousers – the provision of slits to side pockets.

On 17 January 1945 it was announced (ACI 51 of 1945) that the future production of the trousers of the denim overalls would have a modification in the design that would include a side slit to allow for easy access to the pockets of the Battle-Dress trousers when these were worn under the overalls. Authority was given for existing stocks of the overalls to be modified where the commanding officer of a unit considered it desirable. This work was carried out either by the unit tailor or under local contract arranged by the ADOS of the command concerned.

The specially modified Battle-Dress trousers worn by Airborne Forces personnel.

Members of the Airborne Forces were issued with a modified pattern of the Battle-Dress trousers to be worn when on operational duties. The leg pocket on the left leg of the BD trousers had been replaced on these modified trousers with a large expanding map pocket. The square letter-box pocket flap had a central button-hole which fastened to a button near the top of the map pocket and the two corners of the pocket flap were provided with snap fasteners. This expanding map pocket and the two (normal) side pockets were all lined with chamois leather.

There was a pleated patch pocket, without flap but secured by a single button, positioned on the right groin of the trousers and intended to house the first field dressing packet; two very similar pleated patch pockets were placed on the backside of the trousers at the hips. There was a small concealed pocket set into the outer leg seam of the right leg in which was carried the issue fighting knife in its scabbard. The slit opening was fastened by two press-stud fasteners and had the addition of a single button but without any corresponding button-hole. This button secured through the slit on the fob of the scabbard. All the trouser buttons, the fly fronted opening and the buttons on the waist-band on to which were fastened the trouser braces were in metal and were all concealed; only the three pleated patch pockets and the expanding map pocket had visible buttons, and these were in brown composition material.

The use of condemned Battle-Dress and head-dress.

Those Army personnel whose work was of an exceptionally oily or dirty nature could, at the discretion of the officers commanding units, be given permission for condemned Battle-Dress and head-dress to be retained by the wearers for wear on their dirty or oily duties. Such items of clothing had to be marked with the 'condemned' stamp by the individual's unit. On the subsequent replacement of Battle Dress or head dress, the condemned articles that were already in possession were withdrawn for disposal and those items that were newly condemned were retained for wear on dirty or oily duties.

10. KILTS AND KILT COVERS

Kilts

A correctly made kilt is the product of highly skilled craftsmanship. The pleated garment is worn on a wide waist-band with the pleating across the back and on the sides. The front – or upper apron – of the kilt is flat, overlapping the under apron and being fastened on the right side. At the waist it is fastened by two buckles and straps, a third strap coming through on the left-hand side to fasten the under apron in position. The blanket pin, brooch, rosette or ribboned bow that secures the flat portion of the kilt is correctly positioned 1in in from the edge of the double fringe that borders the edge of the upper apron and 2in up from the selvedge edge. There are two loops at the back of the waist-band and two at the front for the chain that secures the sporran.

A kilt for an average size soldier takes between seven and eight yards of full-width material. It should be hand-stitched throughout and the bottom edge should have a selvedge edge, never a hem. To obtain the correct length of kilt for each individual the wearer-to-be is required to kneel for the fitting. In this position the kilt should be 2in off the ground – or more if it is required for walking or working.

A soldier with a 30in waist and a 40in hip will have 15in of pleats at the waist and 20in at the hips. The aprons will likewise be 15in and 20in wide, both the under and upper apron measuring exactly the same. The number of pleats varies with the width of the tartan check. A large squared tartan will have fewer than one with smaller squares, which may well have as many as 32. The depth of the pleat varies with the size of the check in order that the continuity and proportions of the design are maintained. The pleats are stitched down a third of the way and then the spare material is cut away to eliminate bulk before this third is lined. A descriptive table of tartan patterns can be found on page 192.

For those of a curious disposition, nothing was worn under the kilt, the Army considering that the garment worn on its own was sufficient protection for the soldier. In order to enforce this ruling some guardrooms of kilted regiments had a plate glass mirror set into the floor which allowed the regimental police or guard commander to inspect at a glance those soldiers who were walking out wearing the kilt. It was also forbidden for a soldier wearing the kilt to travel on the upper deck of an omnibus, the act of climbing the stairs presenting problems which were best avoided. If there was no room on the lower deck then he was expected not to board the bus.

The Suspension and Gradual Reintroduction of the Kilt in the British Army, 1939–45

Files exist at the Public Records Office, Kew, that give a fascinating insight into the whole subject regarding the suspension of the kilt at the beginning of hostilities and the eventual reintroduction of this item for certain privileged troops.

In September 1939, Scottish regiments of the first contingent of the British Expeditionary Force had proceeded overseas from the United Kingdom wearing kilts. The Army Council were of the opinion not only that the kilt was unsuitable for modern warfare, but that the increase in the numbers of personnel in Scottish regiments being called to the colours was causing production problems, for each garment required a large amount of woollen cloth and was both expensive and time-consuming to manufacture.

It was decided that the active service dress for kilted personnel was to be the Battle-Dress and not the kilt. War Office Urgent Postal Telegram No. 54/General/7874 (PRO file WO32–11010), dated 25 September 1939, was directed to the BEF and to all commands and districts at home. Kilted personnel who were to proceed in future to any theatre of war in which Battle-Dress was worn by other arms were required to be clothed in the same uniform if time allowed, and stocks of Battle-Dress for kilted units which had proceeded to France before 30 September 1939 were sent to that country for issue to them under arrangements made by the GO Commanding-in-Chief BEF.

The reasons given for the above decision were:
1. The impossibility of maintaining a sufficient supply of kilts.
2. Agreement that the kilt was unsuitable for modern war.

Further and more precise details were promulgated by War Office Letter 54/General/8640 (MGO 7b) dated 30 October 1939, which set out for the guidance of all those concerned the future dress of all kilted personnel.

Dress for all ranks for active service and during training.
1. Battle-Dress in those theatres in which this uniform was worn. Kilted personnel at stations abroad, other than those with the BEF, had to wear Service Dress as prescribed for other dismounted units until Battle-Dress was available.
2. The dress prescribed for other dismounted units was worn abroad in hot weather.

Dress worn on other occasions.
Officers.
1. Service Dress jacket with trews or Service Dress trousers.
2. At stations abroad in hot weather, the Khaki Drill jacket with trews, or Khaki Drill trousers or shorts.
Other ranks.
1. Home:
   (a) Except for pipers and drummers, Battle-Dress; (b) Pipers and drummers, Service Dress jacket and kilt.
2. Abroad:
   (a) Battle-Dress at those stations where Service Dress was then being worn; (b) In hot weather, the dress as prescribed for other dismounted units.

Service Dress, including the kilt, that was already in the possession of officers and other ranks was permitted to continue being worn for walking-out at home and abroad until it became unserviceable. When this happened no further

issues were made except to pipers and drummers at home. The kilt from this time was not included in the clothing scale of personnel proceeding to stations abroad. Newly appointed officers were required to provide themselves with one suit of Service Dress, with trews or Service Dress trousers for wear outside a theatre of operations and, when required, one suit of Battle-Dress. The letter concluded by giving the same reasons for the discontinuation of the kilt as have previously been stated.

It is of interest to note that this letter, signed by G. W. Lambert, was circulated to the following officers and establishments: the General Officers Commanding-in-Chief and General Officers Commanding, Commands and Districts at Home and Abroad and Burma; the General Officer Commanding-in-Chief, British Expeditionary Force; His Excellency the Commander-in-Chief in India (GS Branch); colonels of regiments concerned; Army auditors; the commanders of the Staff College, the Imperial Defence College, the Equitation School, the School of Artillery, the Coast Artillery School, the School of Anti-Aircraft Defence, the Military College of Science, the School of Military Engineering, the Senior Officers' School, the School of Electric Lighting, the Royal Military College, the Royal Military Academy, the Signals Training Centre, the RASC Training Centre, the RAOC School of Instruction, the RAV School and the Army School of Hygiene; the Under-Secretary of State, Air Ministry; the Secretary, the Admiralty; the Adjutant-General, Royal Marines; the Military Secretary, India Office; the Under-Secretary of State, Burma Office; POO (P5); CIC Branston; and COO Branston.

Reasons for the suspension.
The two reasons given in 1939 for the suspension of the kilt warrant further examination.
1. The maintaining of supplies of kilts. In April 1940 the Ministry of Supply claimed that it could produce the requisite number of kilts but only at the possible expense of the production of greatcoat cloth. At that time the position with regard to greatcoats was considered satisfactory and it was felt that, if necessary, a proportion could be given up in order to satisfy the proposed kilt production.

In 1940 the cost of the kilt and appurtenances was approximately £4, whereas the cost of Battle-Dress trousers was only 11s. 4d.; the amounts of wool required were, respectively, 4lb 6½oz and 1lb 14oz. It was estimated that if kilts were issued for home use only as a second suit, at least 17,500 would be required as initial issue plus about a further 5,000 a year for maintenance. Thus the extra cost to the country was calculated at about £60,000 initially plus a further £17,000 per annum, whilst the additional amount of wool required to produce this number of kilts was put at about 44,000lb initially plus a further 12,500lb per annum. If the one suit of Battle-Dress in the possession of kilted personnel required cleaning or repair, the kilt would then have had to be worn on training unless a second suit of Battle-Dress was provided, all of which was added expenditure.

2. The unsuitability of the kilt in modern war. The arguments against the wearing of the kilt under the conditions of modern warfare were threefold. First, the kilt was considered to afford very poor protection against gas as compared to the trousers of the Battle-Dress, and the kilt itself was difficult to impregnate against gas spray. Second, experiences gained during the First World War proved that the kilt was an unsuitable garment for trench warfare and it certainly did not lend itself to modern mechanical warfare. Last, the kilt was perhaps the worst of all military garments for breeding and harbouring body vermin. Whilst this was in no way a reflection of the personal habits of the wearer, troops who were forced to live, fight and sleep in their clothing for long periods at a time under field conditions were easy prey to lice and other minor horrors of war. Delousing a kilt in the field took time, and there was hardly any point in the wearer washing and putting on clean underclothing only to have to put back on a partially deloused but still infested kilt.

There was a further objection, raised in 1940, against the retention of the kilt in the British Army under wartime conditions, and this concerned 'esprit de corps'. Although the Army on the whole had put on dowdy Battle-Dress, it was felt that its esprit de corps had not suffered; therefore, it was reasoned, if the Highland regiments were to be deprived of their kilts theirs would not suffer either. In any case, few soldiers in Highland regiments had ever worn a kilt before enlistment into the Army. The issue of kilts to men at home would result in Highland Regiments being placed in a privileged position with regard to other less fortunate regiments in that the former would have a smart walking-out dress whilst the latter, which included the Brigade of Guards, would have to walk out in Battle-Dress.

The Quarter-Master General of the time is on record as stating that he felt that if kilts were allowed for walking out at home, pressure would be set up for walking-out uniforms to be worn as an alternative to Battle-Dress for units other than Scottish units at home, and any modification of the rules as already laid down with regard to the use of the kilt at home would ultimately, in his opinion, lead to a demand for its use overseas. He pointed out that the kilt and its appurtenances cost seven times as much as Battle-Dress trousers and used three times as much wool to produce.

The reintroduction of the kilt.
In March 1942 strong representations were made to the Army Council by the General Officer Commanding-in-Chief Scottish Command for the official reintroduction of the kilt for wear by officers of ex-kilted regiments. In his letter to the War Office, Lieutenant-General Andrew Thorne requested that consideration be given to two proposals:
1. That the list of uniform required by officers during the current emergency should be amended to read 'Trews in the case of Scottish regiments or kilt in the case of ex-kilted regiments'.
2. That authority should be given for the release of other ranks' kilts then being held in depots and

stores for purchase at their listed price by officers of kilted battalions.

He went on to say that he had been strongly pressed by the colonels of the Scottish regiments and by the GOC the 51st (H) Division that he should urge the adoption of these proposals in the interests of prestige and morale and in deference to Scottish national feeling, which was very intense when it came to the matter of the kilt.

Up to the present time (March 1942) officers had, at some considerable cost to themselves, been able to purchase kilts and this had been the general practice. He drew attention to the publication of the official list of articles permitted to be supplied ('Amended Regulations as from 1st March 1942') which did not include the kilt; in practice, therefore, officers would in future be unable to obtain the kilt. He stated that it was only a matter

of time before the kilt would virtually disappear, and that younger officers upon joining Highland regiments would be debarred from wearing the item of dress in which these regiments took such pride and which it was normally their unique privilege to wear. He concluded by saying that he felt the loss of the comparatively small amount of cloth involved in the wearing of kilts by officers would be far outweighed by the general feeling of satisfaction that would be created should the Army Council see their way to acceding to his proposals.

This letter was the means by which the officers of the Army Council discovered that it had been the general practice in these Scottish regiments, despite the abolition of the kilt in 1939, that officers were able to purchase kilts of other ranks' pattern for their own use.

Table 43. Scottish Tartans[1]

Designation	Description	Worn by
Royal Stuart tartan	Scarlet groundwork intersected by broad black, blue and green stripes and narrow white, black and yellow stripes	Pipers of Scots Guards, The Royal Scots,[2] The King's Own Scottish Borderers (except 4th Bn), The Black Watch, 9th (Glasgow Highland) Bn The Highland Light Infantry[3]
42nd (Government) tartan	Alternate dark green and blue stripes about 2¼in wide separated by black stripes about 1in wide each way as groundwork; green stripes intersected by narrow black stripes and blue stripes intersected by double narrow black stripes	The Black Watch (except pipers); The Argyll and Sutherland Highlanders; The Royal Scots Fusiliers (except pipers); 9th (Glasgow Highland) Bn The Highland Light Infantry (except pipers)
Mackenzie tartan	Alternate blue and green stripes about 2in wide separated by black stripes about ¾in wide each way as groundwork; green stripes intersected by narrow white stripes edged with black 5½in apart, and alternate blue stripes intersected by narrow scarlet stripes edged with black 11in apart; blue stripes not intersected by scarlet intersected by four narrow black stripes	The Seaforth Highlanders
Gordon tartan	Groundwork as 42nd (Government) tartan; green stripes intersected by narrow yellow stripes about 6½in square; blue stripes intersected by narrow black stripes	Gordon Highlanders
79th (Cameron of Erracht) tartan	Alternate blue stripes about 3¼in wide and green stripes about 3½in wide separated by black stripes about 1in wide each way as groundwork; green stripes intersected by four scarlet stripes and blue stripes intersected by two scarlet stripes and one yellow stripe; scarlet stripe also divides blue and black stripes; yellow stripes form squares about 9in in size	The Queen's Own Cameron Highlanders[4]
Mackenzie tartan	Alternate dark green and blue stripes about 2½in wide separated by black stripes about 1in wide each way as groundwork; green stripes intersected by white stripes 7in apart and alternated blue stripes intersected by scarlet stripes 14in apart; blue stripes not intersected by scarlet intersected by four narrow black stripes; scarlet and white stripes edged by narrow black stripes	The Highland Light Infantry (except 9th (Glasgow Highland) Bn) and 6th Bn HLI
Douglas tartan	Alternate green stripes about 3in wide and blue stripes about 2½in wide each way as groundwork; green stripes intersected by light blue stripes about ¾in wide, latter divided by narrow black stripe; blue stripes intersected by narrow white stripes about 5½in apart each way	The Cameronians (Scottish Rifles)
Leslie tartan	Alternate dark green stripes about 3in wide and blue stripes about 3in wide divided by black stripe about 1¼in wide each way as groundwork; blue stripes intersected by narrow scarlet stripe and green stripes	The King's Own Scottish Borderers (except pipers)

From the correspondence on file at the Public Records Office (File WO 32–11011), it would seem that the initial reaction of the Army Council, and in particular of the Quarter-Master General, was that this practice was indefensible and that no modification of the existing position – that further issues of kilts should not be made other than for pipers and drummers – should be allowed. They feared that by granting the proposed concession for officers officially to purchase kilts they, the Army Council, would find it difficult to refuse an extension of this concession to other ranks, and this, they felt, the wool situation would not permit.

Moderation seems to have prevailed. The Queen raised the matter with a member of the Army Council (which suggests that someone must have made representations to Her Majesty con-

cerning this matter); the Prime Minister was involved, the Adjutant-General was known to be anxious to preserve regimental traditions, and in May 1942 the Army Council gave in.

An Army Council Instruction, No. 1515, was issued on 18 July 1942 which allowed kilts of other ranks' pattern to be issued on repayment to officers and warrant officers who were actually serving with Highland (formerly kilted) regiments, whilst stocks existed. The kilt remained a purely optional garment, and no coupon or allowance was considered in respect of issues under this instruction. Priority for the reissue of the kilt under the terms laid down by ACI 1515 of 1942 was given to the Seaforth Highlanders, the Queen's Own Cameron Highlanders, The Black Watch, the Gordon Highlanders and the Argyll and Sutherland Highlanders.

Designation	Description	Worn by
	by narrow black stripe; black and green stripes intersected by narrow white stripes about 5½in apart, with overcheck of white about 3in distant on each side	
Hunting Stuart tartan	Dark green stripe about 2in wide, blue stripe about 3½in wide and black stripe about 3¼in wide each way as groundwork; green stripes intersected by narrow red and yellow stripes alternately, about 5½in apart; in alternate squares green stripe divides blue and three green stripes intersect black	The Royal Scots (except pipers)
Hunting Stuart tartan	Dark green stripe about 2in wide, blue stripe about 3in wide and black stripe about 3in wide each way as groundwork; green stripes intersected by narrow yellow and red stripes alternately, about 4½in apart; in alternate squares green stripe divides blue and three green stripes intersect black	7th/9th Bn The Royal Scots (except pipers) and Queen Victoria School
Forbes tartan	Alternate dark green and blue stripes about 2¼in wide separated by black stripes about 1in wide each way as groundwork; green stripes intersected by narrow white stripe and blue stripes intersected by double narrow black stripes; white stripes edged by narrow black stripes	Liverpool Scottish[5]
Buccleuch tartan	Groundwork of black and white checks about 5/16in each way with overcheck of light blue every 5⅛in across in width by 6⅛in in length; black is omitted where light blue occurs	Pipers of 4th Bn The King's Own Scottish Borderers
Erskine (red) tartan	Alternate green and red stripes about 2⅜in wide each way as groundwork; green stripes intersected by two narrow red stripes each way and red stripes intersected by two narrow green stripes each way; whole forms repeat of pattern in check of about 4¾in square	Pipers of The Royal Scots Fusiliers[6]

[1]This table of Scottish tartans (based on information published in the *Vocabulary of Clothing and Necessaries, 1936, Part I*), applied to the period from 1936 to 1939. After the outbreak of hostilities in September 1939 Full Dress was no longer worn, and the use of tartan was therefore restricted; it was even more restricted with the suspension of the kilt (see page 189). Wartime alterations or introductions to the use of particular patterns of tartan have been noted on the table and are given as footnotes. I have not included in this table the Elcho or Hodden-Grey material that was worn by members of the London Scottish. This material was without pattern but was classed as a tartan.

[2]In 1933 the pipers of the Royal Scots were afforded the privilege of wearing Royal Stuart tartan on the wishes of King George V to mark the occasion of the regiment's tercentenary.

[3]In 1939 the title of the 9th (Glasgow Highland)

Battalion the Highland Light Infantry was changed to 'The 1st Battalion, The Glasgow Highlanders'.

[4]In 1943, pipers of the Queen's Own Cameron Highlanders were permitted the distinction of wearing Royal Stuart tartan in place of the Cameron of Erracht tartan. This distinction was granted to them by His Majesty King George VI to mark the regiment's 150th anniversary as well as its fine service record during the first four years of the Second World War.

[5]Members of the Liverpool Scottish who formed part of No. 5 Troop No. 2 Commando received special permission from the Prime Minister Winston Churchill in the summer of 1940 to re-adopt the wearing of the Forbes tartan kilt (see text).

[6]The use of Erskine (red) tartan (Dress Erskine) was adopted at the wishes of His Majesty King George V by the pipers of the Royal Scots Fusiliers in 1928 to mark the regiment's 250th anniversary.

Right: Three stretcher bearers, believed to be Gordon Highlanders, each wearing a kilt cover, an item of protective clothing that was used extensively during the 1914–18 War. Its wear was not so widespread in the Second World War, being restricted to Scottish regiments serving with the BEF in France and Flanders in 1939–40.

Members of the Liverpool Scottish who on their return from Norway in July 1940 were formed as part of No. 5 Troop No. 2 Commando received special permission from Winston Churchill, the Prime Minister, to re-adopt the wearing of the Forbes tartan kilt. They are said to have been the last Scottish troops operating as a kilted unit to wear the kilt in battle, when in March 1942 they went ashore from HMS *Campbeltown* wearing their Forbes kilts with covers as part of the raiding force that attacked the docks at St. Nazaire.

In June 1941 the CO of the 3rd Battalion the London Scottish (97th Heavy Anti-Aircraft Regiment, Royal Artillery) was refused permission for members of his unit to wear the kilt.

In August 1942 the officer in command of the Shetland Defence Rifle Company at Lerwick, an ex-kilted unit originally part of the Defence Battalion of the Argyll and Sutherland Highlanders, applied for, and in September received, permission to wear the kilt.

In August 1942 Canadian troops, warrant officers and officers, sought permission to wear the kilt. This was authorized on 14 September 1942 whilst stocks existed. Officers and warrant officers of the Canadian Army serving in the United Kingdom were permitted to obtain kilts of other ranks' pattern on repayment provided that such officers and warrant officers were actually serving with regiments 'formerly kilted'.

Kilt Covers

The ochre-coloured kilt cover, or 'kilt-apron' as it was sometimes called, was introduced for Highland regiments serving in the South African War as a camouflage measure. The cover was also used during the 1914–18 War and with the BEF in France and Flanders in 1939–40. It was said not to have been a very popular item, many Highlanders being of the opinion that the light-coloured apron was more conspicuous than the tartan cloth of the kilt that it was meant to conceal, but it did keep the kilt clean.

The cover, produced from a single piece of material, had six wide pleats which covered the rear of the kilt. The flat portion of the cover, which was worn over the front of the kilt, had the addition of a pocket with pocket flap fastened by a single brown button. The cover was secured around the wide waist-band of the kilt by being tied in position on the right-hand side by a series of three pairs of tapes, the upper tape being set inside a waist-band tunnel thus allowing this tape to be drawn in tight.

11. PERSONAL CLOTHING

Shirts, Trouser Braces, Underwear, Handkerchiefs and Towels

Shirts. Shirts issued to troops both before and during the 1939–45 war were manufactured from khaki angola material; they were plain fronted, without the breast pockets which were a feature of postwar Army shirts. They were long in the tails, especially at the back, and had long sleeves fastened at the wrist with a single small button. They were collarless, reinforced with a narrow neck-band of pale tan coloured cotton material. The neck opening reached to the upper level of the wearer's stomach and was secured by a vertical line of three small buttons, which in most cases were of gun-metal.

Because of the roughness of the angola shirting material individual soldiers sought to obtain Canadian or US Army khaki shirts to wear. These

Right: A squad of the Depot Essex Regiment on parade at Warley Barracks, Brentwood, attempt to keep cool on a hot summer's day by wearing, instead of tunics, collarless, open-necked shirts with sleeves rolled up; 18 August 1936. *Below right:* Men of 10th Field Hygiene Section, RAMC, 12 Corps, filling up from a water bowser; 12 June 1944. The Army issue braces are clearly shown here.

were of superior quality material and gave a more 'fashionable' appearance, especially those with a collar attached (which were considered a definite improvement on the British Army collar-attached shirt when that was introduced in late 1944 (see this page).

Troops stationed in India prior to the introduction of the collarless khaki shirt wore collarless shirts of grey material. These shirts gave rise to the appellation for the British soldiery in India of 'Grey backs'.

Officers wore shirts of a quality superior to that of shirts issued to the rank and file. They also wore collar-attached shirts with Service Dress and, once Battle-Dress had become commonplace, with the Battle-Dress blouse.

Trouser braces. These were required to be worn with all types of khaki trousers, Service Dress and Battle-Dress. The braces were of strong manufacture, with 1½in wide elasticated and adjustable drab coloured straps, brown leather tabs and metal fittings.

Underwear. Underwear for male troops consisted of vests, underpants and long-johns. All these items were produced in white cotton as well as khaki dyed materials, khaki coloured underwear being considered necessary for reasons of camouflage (underwear that had been washed and hung out to dry by troops bivouacked in a war zone was more conspicuous if it were white than if it were khaki green in colour).

Handkerchiefs. Handkerchiefs were also produced in khaki linen; white handkerchiefs were permitted to be used, but these had to be plain, without colour or design.

Towels. Towels issued to troops were both white and, during the war, khaki; the latter for the same reasons explained for khaki underwear. They were of 'hand towel' size.

Shirts for helpless patients.

On 6 November 1935 it was announced (ACI 288) that a new pattern of open-backed shirt made of blue angola material had been approved for use by helpless patients in military hospitals both at home and abroad. These replaced the white flannel vests in use at that time.

The introduction of the collar-attached shirt and tie for wear by other ranks.

In November 1944 it was announced that a shirt with a collar attached was being introduced into service in place of the existing collarless shirt; a khaki coloured tie was also intended to be provided for wear with the new shirt when sufficient stocks became available. The scale of issue for the new shirt was the same as for the former pattern of shirt, and the tie was issued on the scale of one item per man.

Ties were allowed to be worn when on duty in barracks, when on leave or for walking out, when working in offices or when attending lectures or similar indoor instruction; they were not permitted to be worn on other occasions, and the use of ties other than those of the regulation pattern was forbidden. Tie or collar pins were not allowed to be worn. When the tie was worn the Battle-Dress blouse was opened at the neck to the second button from the top, but when the tie was not worn the blouse had to be buttoned up to the top (ACI 1516 dated 15 November 1944).

Woollen Jerseys and Cardigans

Jerseys were worn by other ranks and cardigans by officers, although cardigans tended to be a prewar item of wear. Both garments were of plain khaki wool, the jersey having a 'V' neck opening with long sleeves and the cardigan fastening down the length of its front.

Right: A Warrant Officer, Class II, of the Scots Guards displays for the first time the recently introduced collar and tie to be worn with Battle Dress by other ranks.
Far right: The style of pullover favoured by Gen. Montgomery.

12. PERSONAL ACCOUTREMENTS

The Wearing of Bugle and Trumpet 'Strings' or Cords
Before the Second World War bugle and trumpet cords, as authorized by units, were allowed to be worn by buglers and trumpeters as 'body lines' when walking out in Service Dress uniform.

Whistles and Whistle Lanyards
Before the war, and in all probability during the war years, there was no sealed pattern for whistles or their lanyards. However, if worn by officers all whistles and lanyards had to be of the same pattern and colouring when worn within a single unit.

The method of wearing the lanyard, the carriage of the whistle and the colouring of the whistle lanyard was left to the discretion of officers commanding units, provided that all officers of a unit were dressed alike in this respect.

Before the war whistles and lanyards were carried in mounted service when officers were on duty with troops and in dismounted service when in marching or in drill order.

Right: A detachment from the 2nd Bn., West Yorkshire Regiment changing the guard at Windsor Castle, 15 August 1936. This was the first occasion since the Great War that a Line Regiment carried out guard duty at Windsor Castle. It was also the first time since 1759 that the West Yorkshires (then the 14th Foot) had been stationed in Windsor, having been sent there on their return from foreign service. The bugler leading the detachment is wearing bugle cords on his tunic. (See also the photograph on page 198)

Below right: Field Marshal Alexander talking in turn to an officer of the Royal Marines (far left), a member of the Highland Light Infantry (second from left) and two officers of No. 2 Commando Bde., both of whom are wearing whistle lanyards of twisted black and white cording.

Right: Band Serjeant, Serjeant Ashman from Bridgwater, Somerset, at a commemorative service for the 2nd Bn., The Devonshire Regiment; 27 May 1945. He wears the Baldrick, a colour sash and bugle cords.

Sashes worn by Warrant Officers and NCOs

Sashes, worsted or silk and scarlet in colour, were worn with uniform by those for whom it was authorized, on ceremonial parades, barrack duties and when walking out. They were not worn in marching order nor on training parades.

The sashes were worn over the right shoulder, under the shoulder strap of the Service Dress or Khaki Drill jacket, Battle-Dress blouse or greatcoat with the tassel end resting on the bayonet (when worn) on the left side. Sashes worn in the Somerset Light Infantry were taken over the left shoulder and hung down against the right hip.

Regimental warrant officers Class I did not wear sashes with Service Dress when the Sam Browne equipment was worn.

The Sam Browne Belt

Worn by officers of all branches of the service, this belt, when complete, consisted of a waist-belt, two shoulder-belts, a sword frog with steadying straps, an ammunition-pouch and a pistol-case, the whole being made of brown bridle leather.

The waist-belt was 2⅛in wide and of sufficient length to suit the wearer. It was fitted with a double-tongued brass buckle and had four 'D' rings secured to the upper edge for the attachment of the shoulder-belts (two at the back and one at each side), a running loop for the free end of the belt, two brass rings for attachment of the frog, and a hook for hooking it up. The waist-belt was lined with faced basil (a roughly tanned, undressed sheepskin). The shoulder-belts were plain straps, crossed at the back through a loop. They were 1¼in tapering to ⅞in, 6¾in from the points. The patterns were about 35in long overall, without chapes, although the lengths were varied to suit the wearer. They were fitted with studs for attachment to the 'Ds' at the back of the waist-belt. A chape, with stud and an oval buckle, was provided

Above right: The Sam Browne harness worn with two shoulder belts. Maj. John Frost of the Cameronians (Scottish Rifles), an early leader of the Parachute forces, leaves Buckingham Palace after receiving the Military Cross on 30 June 1942.

Right: Maj. Robert Cain of the Royal Northumberland Fusiliers was awarded the Victoria Cross for his gallantry in the Battle of Arnhem. Armed with a PIAT, Major Cain had at one time during the battle gone out alone, to deal with an approaching German Tiger tank. Despite being wounded, he had continued to fire on the vehicle which eventually he demobilized. Maj. Cain is shown here wearing the Sam Browne belt with single cross-strap, the configuration normally encountered, but which has the addition of a whistle and its holder; 4 December 1944.

for each, for attachment to the 'D' rings at the side of the belt.

The strap over the left shoulder was optional, except when it was required to support the revolver. The frog was fitted with two adjustable suspending straps, which were intended to pass through the rectangular 'D' rings on the lower edge of the waist-belt. The frog had a small brass 'D' ring on the top, to go over the hook on the belt when 'hooking up'. A stud was fitted on the front of the frog upon which a tab of the scabbard supporter was fastened.

The ammunition-pouch and pistol-case were fitted with loops on the back for attachment to the waist-belt, also with stud and tab fastenings. The loop on the pistol-case was furnished with a small brass hook, which passed through a hole to be made for the purpose in the belt to suit the wearer, in order that the case was secure and kept in position. The dimensions of the pistol-case varied in order to suit the size of the particular pattern of pistol carried.

The 'furniture' — the metal fittings — for the Sam Browne was in best yellow brass for all officers except for officers of rifle regiments, who had their fittings in white metal.

Swords and Scabbards

Before the war instructions relating to the carrying of swords and their scabbards were as set out in *Dress Regulations for the Army, 1934*; the patterns of the swords were those as laid down for the arms of the service. There were separate specifications for swords carried by field-marshals and general officers; Cavalry of the Line and RAVC officers; officers of the Royal Artillery and the RASC; officers of the Royal Engineers, R Signals, Infantry of the Line (excluding rifle and Scottish regiments), RTC, RAMC, RAOC, RAPC, AE Corps and AD Corps; officers of rifle regiments; and finally officers of Scottish regiments (their swords being incorrectly referred to as the 'Claymore, Officer's, Highland Pattern' but more correctly termed a 'Broadsword').

Swords were carried on prewar active service and when in 'marching order' by officers serving in cavalry regiments only; subject to this proviso, swords were carried on parades and duties unless otherwise directed. They were not worn on board ship, at stables or at mess other than in the Worcestershire Regiment, where the orderly officer and the captain of the week wore swords with mess dress. Swords when carried with a mounted 'order of dress' were carried on the saddle.

Universal pattern sword knot.

The sword-knot that was used with the 'Sam Browne' belt was the universal pattern of brown leather, except in English regiments of light infantry, when it was of black leather. It had a plain strap ⅝in wide made of pig-skin, best bridle leather or calf, its length in the double being 15in. The ends of the strap were secured into an 'acorn' having a plaited leather covering and 2½in in length. The strap was furnished with a plaited leather sliding keeper.

PART IV
Specialist and Protective Clothing

1. AIRBORNE FORCES

The design and subsequent manufacture of the basic items of clothing and equipment adopted by the embryonic British Airborne Forces were, in their initial stage, based largely on ideas gleaned from captured equipment and specialist clothing used by the German Airborne Troops. A damaged parachute and a Fallschirmjäger steel helmet captured from the Germans were amongst the few items available to the technical experts at the Central Landing School, Ringway; however, they could evaluate their properties and adapt their design for the production of similar British items. Much hard work, trial and error went into this important field of development, carried out in the main by Major John Rock of the Royal Engineers. He had been attached to the original Airborne Forces training centre established at Ringway, Manchester, during the summer of 1940 almost from the beginning.

Over a period of time many modifications were made to the basic items of prototype protective head-dress, clothing and equipment until eventually they were perfected and became standard issue to all ranks throughout the British Airborne Forces. Some of these items are described in this book.

British parachute clothing and equipment, although seemingly complicated, was in fact simple to wear and designed to give the wearer the maximum warmth in the air and the maximum freedom of movement once on the ground.

The 1942 Pattern Gabardine Jump Jacket
The design of this garment was almost directly copied from an item in use at the beginning of the war with the German Parachute Forces. Made from khaki-green gabardine material, this fly-fronted smock or 'jump jacket' was intended to be

worn by personnel of the British Airborne Forces both for training and for active service.

In order to avoid the possibility of the wearer's equipment or weapons, which were either attached to or lodged in his webbing equipment, becoming entangled with his parachute harness or being caught up on any projecting part of an aircraft's interior, the jump jacket was normally worn over the Battle-Dress and personal equipment, and it was normally discarded upon landing.

The jacket had two short, 'step-in' legs, a long frontal heavy-duty zip fastener concealed in a wide fly-fronted panel, and a series of heavy-duty snap fasteners which fastened the flaps securely. There were two slit-pocket openings, one at each side of the jacket, which allowed the wearer to reach through into his Battle-Dress trouser pockets; these were closed by short zip fasteners.

The jacket had long sleeves with outer and inner cuffs, the latter fastened by a single snap fastener adjustable to two positions. The inner

cuffs were short lengths of sleeves which were elasticated at the wrist and were fastened to make a windproof closure with a single snap fastener, also adjustable to one of two positions. The short 'step-in' legs of the jacket were adjustable on the side of the thigh by a single male and female snap fastener.

The full length zip, approximately 20in long, ran from just above the wearer's lower abdomen to the top of his breast. Three sets of snap fasteners on the upper part of the chest and another set at the neck opening closed the top of the jacket. The stand and fall collar was usually worn open.

The Denison Smock

The Denison Smock, named after its designer Major Denison and first introduced for use by the personnel of the Airborne Forces in 1941, was a camouflaged garment made from heavy-duty, windproof material. It was designed to be worn over a soldier's Battle-Dress suit and under his jump smock. Webbing equipment for training or active service was normally worn over the smock.

There were two internal pockets placed on the chest at the front with slit openings on either side of the neck and four external pockets all of the same size, two on the chest and two on the skirt; the latter had single-pointed pocket flaps secured by concealed, heavy-duty, brass-covered snap fasteners.

The smock was put on by being pulled over the head. On the original garments the neck opening had a short fly-fronted zip fastener which reached down to the base of the chest, stopping just above the line of the bottom edge of the breast pockets.

Attached to the lower edge at the rear of the smock was a 'tailpiece', a flap of the camouflaged material which when used was drawn up between the wearer's legs under the crutch and fastened in position on the inside of the front of the smock to one of a series of three pairs of snap fastener studs; fastening the tailpiece in this position formed the lower edge of the smock into very short 'legs' and at the same time held the edge of the smock firmly against the wearer's thighs.

The smock had shoulder straps produced from the same material as that used for the garment itself, and these were secured close to the short stand collar by a drab coloured plastic button. The collar was lined with khaki drab woollen angola shirting material. The ends of the sleeve were plain and could be worn closed around the wearer's wrists by means of a short button-hole tab and two plastic drab buttons. The bottom edge of the skirt likewise had a tab and snap fasteners on each side that when used gathered in the sides of the skirt around the wearer's thighs.

The camouflage patterning consisted of a light green base over which were printed large ragged areas of dark green and chocolate brown, the brown usually being overlaid on the dark green. Parts of the patterning were given the effect of having been applied with a wide brush stroke, as fine lines of brown or green showed up clearly at

intervals over the pale green base as well as over either of the other two colours.

Although the Denison Smock was intended to be a practical garment for use in the field – and in many respects it proved to be so – it did have certain disadvantages. Although it was windproof it was only showerproof, and it rapidly became soaked when worn in heavy rain. The original garment had to be pulled on over the wearer's head. This was overcome by individuals and some units opening up the smock right down the front and putting in a full-length zip fastener, usually taken from an unserviceable over-smock (see page 203). This modification, which allowed the smock

Right: Denison Smocks being worn by the men of the Army Film and Photographic Unit who took the pictures of the 1st Airborne Division at Arnhem: left to right, Sjt. D. M. Smith, Sjt. G. Walker and Sjt. C. M. Lewis, photographed at the A.F.&P. Centre, Pinewood on the day they arrived back in the United Kingdom, 28 September 1944.
Below right: The Airborne Forces' sleeveless over-smock, worn here by British paratroopers who are chatting with crew members of the US Army Air Corps Troop Carrier Command.

to be put on in the same manner as a normal jacket and made for its much more rapid removal, eventually became part of the official design of late war and postwar Denison smocks. The cuffs on the original garment were large and open-ended; even when they were gathered in around the wearer's wrists and buttoned to one of two positions the ends of the cuffs were not windproof.

Improvised windproof cuffs were created from footless socks sewn inside the cuff ends. This helped to close the gap between the wrist and the cuff, and again, as with the frontal full-length zip, this modification became a standard production feature in late-war and postwar garments.

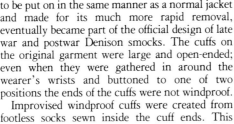

Right: Maj.-Gen. F. A. M. Browning wearing a modified form of Denison Smock for Officers.

Right: The sleeveless over-smock was worn over all personal equipment which in turn was worn over the Denison Smock. The over-smock was discarded once the soldier had safely landed.
Far right: The 1945 modification of the Denison Smock for use by snipers.

1945 modification for use by snipers.

It had been found that for the purposes of sniping the Denison smock could be made more efficient by the addition of a large patch pocket on its left side. Authority was given on 24 February 1945 by ACI 213 for airborne smocks held by snipers to be modified locally by unit repairers, where desired, as shown in the accompanying diagram. Such modifications were entirely optional and were only carried out at the discretion of the OC unit; smocks for normal airborne requirements were not modified.

The Airborne Forces (sleeveless) over-smock.

This garment, known officially as 'Jacket, Parachutists, 1942 Pattern', was an improvement on the previous gabardine jump jacket (see page 200). It was of a much simpler design in that it was sleeveless and had the distinct advantage of a full-length heavy-duty brass zip fastener down the front of the smock which enabled it to be taken off in an instant.

There was a tailpiece attached to the rear of the smock which when used was drawn up between the wearer's legs and fastened in position on the outside of the front of the smock to one of a series of three pairs of heavy duty snap fastener studs. There were two small expanding pockets positioned on the front of the smock, one on each side of the zip fastener and just above the edge of the smock. These had elasticated openings to the pocket. Hand grenades were sometimes carried in these pockets, ready for instant use.

The collar was of the short stand variety lined with angola shirt material. There were no shoulder straps to this smock. The garment was produced from hard wearing green denim material of the same sort as used for denim overalls. Despite this item being known as a '1942 Pattern' garment it did not begin to see general service throughout the Airborne Forces until just before D-Day on 6 June 1944.

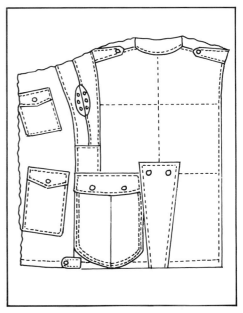

The SOE Camouflage Operational Suit and Protective Helmet.

Allied agents who were parachuted into German wartime occupied territory were issued with a special camouflage protective suit. This, together with its protective helmet, is a comparatively rare item in this country, although I know that there are more examples of the suit in private collections.

The suit, which was donned only for the purpose of making the one parachute descent into enemy territory, was worn over the agent's clothing of whatever sort that was. On landing undetected the agent removed the suit and buried it along with his parachute, and he was then ready to make his way to his objective dressed as a Frenchman, a Belgian, a Dutchman or even a German. This 'one-use-only' explains why the suit is difficult to obtain. There cannot have been many made and their life span was short.

The garment was manufactured from heavy-duty windproof material, very similar to, but slightly stiffer than, the material used for the Denison Smock. It was printed with a camouflage pattern of a type not found on any other British military garment. The pattern was not very distinct and was mostly green, although two shades of brown were also used, and the design was very irregular, it being difficult to distinguish a 'repeat' in the patterning.

The suit had two very noticeable features: the two full-length zips running down the entire garment from either side of the neck opening to the end of the ankle on each leg; and the large pouch at the back. The full-length zips allowed the garment to be put on and rapidly taken off again with the minimum of effort. The pouch built into the back of the suit was provided to accommodate a small parcel, suit case or attaché case. Entry to this compartment was from inside the suit, the internal opening being secured with a press-studded flap. Carrying a case or parcel inside the suit in this manner did not impede the movement of the parachuting agent – it guaranteed that the case or parcel descended with the agent and, most importantly, it left his hands free.

There were a number of purpose-made pockets, both internal and external. On the outside of the left arm, set on the cuff of the sleeve, was a narrow pocket 8½in deep by 2¾in wide which took a knife attached to an approximately 3ft long camouflaged parachute cord which in turn was sewn into the bottom of the pocket. This knife was provided in the event that the agent became caught up in a tree, and with it he would have been able to have cut himself free. Unfortunately, on the example of this suit that I have in my collection, the knife is missing, and I am therefore not able to describe the knife that was used. The opening to the knife pocket was secured by a short length of canvas strap which was press-studded to the outside of the pocket top. On the outside of the left thigh was a pocket with a flap shaped in such a way as to accommodate a revolver. The flap was secured by a single snap fastener.

Internal pockets were as follows. On the inside of the suit on the left side, directly behind the external revolver pocket, was a pocket lined throughout with carpet felt and large enough and shaped to accommodate the blade of a small shovel. Next to this was a second pocket, very narrow and 10¼in in length, that was meant to take the handle for the shovel blade. Both were closed by a flap of the canvas material and secured by a single snap fastener. The flap for the handle pocket was lined on its underside with a patch of carpet felt.

On the inside of the right leg at thigh level, directly opposite the shovel pocket, was another arrangement of pockets – two superimposed on one large pocket, all three being secured by two sets of two canvas straps each with its press-stud fasteners. These pockets are thought to have been provided for maps and/or documents. There were two breast pockets with slit openings on either side of two full-length zips, and these were identical to the internal breast pockets found in the Denison Smock.

On the narrow length of material flanked on either side by the two full-length frontal zips was one more zip fastened opening. The zip was 6½in in length and its purpose was to allow male agents to answer the call of nature once they were encased in their special protective suit and parachute harness.

At the back of the collarless neck was stitched a short leather tab to which was secured a small metal buckle; through this buckle was fastened the short leather strap that was stitched to the back of the special protective helmet worn by operational agents as part of the complete suit.

Of the two protective helmets I have in my collection, one is in green and brown camouflage that matches the camouflaged suit and the other is white. This suggests that there must have been an all-white snow camouflage suit for those agents who were parachuted into snow covered terrain. The shape of the protective helmet was not dissimilar to the crash helmets that used to be worn by racing cyclists. It had a rounded ridge of rubber padding around the circumference of the helmet, and a further rubber padded, rounded ridge ran across the length of the crown from front to back. The whole was covered in camouflage fabric that matched that used for the suit.

The helmet also incorporated a neck flap which extended over the ears and around the brow. The edge of this neck and the ear flaps and brow band were finished and reinforced with green binding. The chin-strap was a separate item that was fastened to the lower ends of the ear flaps by a press-stud fastener. The chin-strap was produced from fine brown leather with the chin cup in chamois leather.

Special agent helmets were also provided with very simple celluloid eye goggles. These had a cheap elasticated strap which was fixed to the helmet by being sewn to the back of the padded ridge. Directly below this position at the back of the neck flap was sewn a short length of leather strap, this being used to attach the helmet to the buckle sewn to the back of the collar of the suit. In this way the helmet remained attached to the suit even it were not actually being worn and thus could not be mislaid or lost.

2. PHYSICAL TRAINING INSTRUCTORS

The scale of issue of PT clothing to Army physical training instructors authorized for the United Kingdom was as follows.

One pair of canvas shoes to each APTC instructor if he did not already possess them

Two pairs of PT shorts

Two PT smocks (to each APTC instructor)

Two pairs of PT trousers (to each APTC instructor)

Two APTC gymnasium cotton vests

One striped (red and black) jersey to each assistant instructor and temporary assistant instructor in PT. 'Vests and Shorts, PT Kit', were issued as authorized for the unit in which the above instructors were serving or to which they were attached.

ACI 1020 dated 29 August 1945 authorized the above kit to be extended to all stations (other than tropical stations) overseas.

3. HOSPITAL CLOTHING

Hospital 'Blues'

Military personnel undergoing medical treatment as in-patients at military hospitals or recovering from operations, wounds or sickness, either at military hospitals or at places of convalescence, were issued, in lieu of their military uniform, with hospital 'blues'.

A complete set of 'blues' consisted of a royal blue, single-breasted serge jacket and matching serge trousers (hence the name), and a white shirt and collar worn with bright red tie. For walking-out purposes the soldier's cloth head-dress was worn and during inclement weather the Army greatcoat with blue armlet.

The quality of the serge was poor, the colour of the trousers and jacket did not always match and there was often quite a variance in the colour of hospital blues worn within any one establishment. I am not aware that there were any tailoring facilities available to make these somewhat shapeless garments more attractive, especially those worn by long-stay patients. Generally speaking, the 'uniform' was considered by those who were required to wear it as being ghastly; so unflattering in fact that many walking-out patients preferred to remain indoors rather than be seen out wearing it.

Tropical climates.

Hospital clothing made of blue drill, which was considered more suitable for wear in tropical climates than the then existing serge garments, was approved, as announced by ACI 117 dated week ending 14 February 1940, for use by certain stations abroad and in troopships and freighters carrying hospital cases. The new type of hospital clothing consisted of a blue drill jacket and a pair of blue drill trousers. No waistcoat was provided with this outfit.

The instructions went on to add that in future, from February 1940, only drill hospital clothing would be held on charge in Aden, Ceylon, Jamaica, Malaya and in the Sudan, Sierra Leone being added to this list a few weeks later. Serge hospital garments no longer required by these stations were, if fit for reissue, to be returned to Egypt or the United Kingdom. In Egypt, Palestine, Hong Kong and Mauritius (Bermuda being added later), both the serge and the new drill clothing was to be held on charge and either quality could be worn during the appropriate periods of the year as decided on by the local medical authorities.

On transports and freighters that proceeded beyond the Mediterranean the drill hospital clothing was held in addition to the serge hospital clothing, the type worn being decided by the senior medical officer on board.

Wearing of uniform by officers.

Army officers who had relinquished their commissions or who were relegated to unemployment whilst undergoing treatment in hospital as in-patients on account of sickness, wounds, etc. were permitted, at their option, to continue wearing uniform until they were discharged from hospital by the medical authorities.

Officers who, after relinquishing their commissions or being relegated to unemployment, elected to continue to wear uniform until discharged did not retain their AFs B 2606 (Revised), which were withdrawn from them, but they were furnished with a certificate by the officer commanding or military registrar of the hospital concerned which stated that the officer was wearing uniform under the terms of Army Council Instruction 390 dated 11 April 1945. This certificate was withdrawn when the officer was discharged from hospital.

The wearing of uniform by these officers did not confer on them any powers of command over military personnel, neither did it render them eligible for the grant of outfit allowance, tax concessions or medical, travelling or other facilities available on an entitlement or privilege basis to military personnel on the active list. Any existing entitlement to disability awards was not affected by their wearing uniform, however, but these officers did not acquire any additional entitlement through continuing such wear.

4. WORK CLOTHING

Officers' Prewar Two-piece Work Clothing

Jacket. This was produced from brown drill material and was single-breasted, similar in shape to a lounge coat. There was no opening at the back but just a back seam. Four small gilding metal buttons with rings and four eyelet holes were positioned down the front of the jacket.

The jacket had shoulder straps of the same material, 2¾in wide at the base and rounded at the top. There was a step roll collar, made and lined with body material, which had a depth of stand at the back of 1¼in and a depth of fall at the back of 1⅞in. The collar had a tab underneath with one button-hole that allowed the collar to be buttoned across at the front. The sleeves had wrist-bands 2½in deep, with one button-hole and three eyelet-holes; 1in wide box pleats were built into the top of the centre of the wrist-bands. There were 4½in deep vents at the lower end of the fore-arm at the hindarm.

Trousers. These were of matching brown drill material. They were fly-fronted, with two side pockets, and had an adjustable strap with buckle at the back of the waist. There were three belt loops around the waist-band and there were permanent turn-ups at the ends of the legs.

Officers' Prewar Combination Work Overalls

The whole garment was made from brown drill material. The combinations had a seam down the centre of the back and around the waist. They were fly-fronted and were fastened with four-hole bone buttons of medium size in a colour that matched the material of the overalls. There was a short cloth strap with a prongless buckle at both hips which allowed for a certain amount of adjustment for the wearer's waist or girth. The ends of the trouser legs had permanent turn-ups, and there were four eyelet ventilation holes in the foreparts under the arms.

There were shoulder straps of the same material as the body material, 2¾in wide at the base and rounded at the top. The matching step roll collar had a depth of stand at the back of the neck of 1¼in with a depth of fall of 1⅞in. There was a cloth tab underneath the collar with one button-hole which allowed the collar to be buttoned up across the neck.

The sleeves had 2½in deep cuffs with one button-hole and button in the hindpart; each cuff had a built-in 1in wide box pleat in the centre of the cuff at the top edge. There were 4½in deep vents at the lower end of the hind arms. The two cross-patch breast pockets, 6¼in wide and 7in deep at the top of the flap, had a box pleat in the centre of each, 2¼in wide; the pocket flaps were 6¼in wide and 2½in deep, with one button-hole. There were two side pockets and one patch hip pocket 6½in wide and 7in deep on the right side of the trouser portion of the overalls.

The wearing of combination overalls in certain mechanized units.

Army Council Instruction No. 165, published during the week ending 11 May 1938, announced that pending a final decision regarding active service and training dress for officers and other ranks of all arms to meet the needs of mechaniza-tion, combination overalls were to be used for training purposes by all other ranks of mechanized divisional cavalry units, cavalry light tank regiments, armoured car regiments, mechanized Royal Artillery units and the Royal Artillery Depot, and Royal Corps of Signals units. A free initial issue of one suit was made to all other ranks of these units, and further issues required to complete to the scale of two suits for each man were made on repayment.

Denim Overalls authorized as Work Clothing for All Services

Denim overalls were supposed to be supplied only in cases where such an issue was considered essential for the preservation of serge or drill garments, such as to personnel whose duties entailed undue soiling of such clothing. During the summer months denim overalls were normally used for training at stations in the United Kingdom in lieu of Battle-Dress. They were issued for wear in all areas except active service areas on the scale of two suits for each other rank. Overalls were not normally regarded as necessary in the case of the following personnel:

1. All ranks of RAPC, AEC, Garrison Staff, APTC, MPSC.
2. Lance-serjeants and high ranks of horsed cavalry, Foot Guards, infantry, RAMC, AD Corps, CMP and RAVC (other than pioneer-serjeants and those whose permanent duties included the maintenance of mechanical vehicles or of machine-guns).
3. Bands (other than band boys) of RA (Aldershot and Woolwich), RE, Foot Guards, RTR and RMC.
4. Survey personnel, RA and RE (other than those whose permanent duties included maintenance of mechanical vehicles).
5. RASC bakers and butchers.
6. Clerks and assistant clerks (other than corporals and lower rank serving as regimental clerks of cavalry, Foot Guards and infantry; as battery clerks, RA; and as engineer clerks not on the Establishment for Engineer Services).
7. Draughtsmen and assistant draughtsmen (other than corporals and lower ranks serving with RE).
8. Tradesmen of all ranks of trades not quoted above in which protection of serge clothing was not required, such as computers, dispensers, opticians, pharmacists, traffic operators, tailors and assistant tailors.

Personnel of the RAC and the REME serving at home and on foreign service overseas were issued with two suits of denim overalls except for clerks, storemen, postmen, officers' mess stewards and orderlies for whom one suit for each man was allowed if considered essential by the commanding officer of the unit.

Two-piece denim overalls and blue dungaree suits.

Two-piece denim overalls and blue working dungaree suits were issued in the following scale to personnel of the following units in lieu of denim overalls.

Two-piece overalls. One each to other rank of Motor Boat Companies, Royal Army Service Corps. Two each to fitter, fitter's mate, boilermaker, boilermaker's mate, blacksmith, blacksmith's striker, carpenter, coppersmith, tinsmith, C and W repairer, C and W repairer's mate, motor mechanic, stoker, SE, boilerwasher, brick archman, coalman, steam raiser and driver TP of transportation units Royal Engineers.

The overalls were also available for 90 per cent of the strength of Mechanical Equipment Training Company for the training of operators of excavators and tractors; for 80 per cent of the strength of Mechanical Equipment Workshop and Park Company, for workshop personnel, breakdown gangs, etc., and also for Mechanical Equipment Company, for operators of excavators and tractors; and for 80 per cent of the strength of General Workshop Unit, Canadian Forestry Company.

Blue dungaree suits, jacket and trousers. Two of each item to each engine driver (steam and diesel) and fireman (engine) of transportation units Royal Engineers.

5. TANK SUITS

The Prewar Black Two-Piece Working Dress
Introduced during 1935 (ACI 120 for the week ending 1 May 1935) for crew members of the Royal Tank Corps, this black two-piece working suit made from strong, hard-wearing drill material incorporated many of the features that were later to be used in the design of the Battle-Dress clothing. Indeed, it was the introduction of the Battle-Dress in 1939 that brought about the demise of the RTC black working dress. The brown drill overalls that were worn as working dress by tank crew members prior to the issue of the new two-piece black working suit continued to be worn until they became unserviceable; they were then replaced by the black drill garments when stocks of these became available.

The blouse of the suit had a short stand collar closed at the neck by two brass hooks and eyes. No buttons were visible anywhere on either the blouse or the trousers of this garment. The blouse was fly-fronted with six concealed, dish-shaped brass buttons. The 3in deep waist-band was extended on the left side to form a 9in long belt. This had a series of small reinforced holes, any of which allowed the belt to be adjusted and engaged with the single prong of the squared brass buckle which

was anchored on the right side of the waist-band.

The blouse also had two box pleated patch pockets on each breast. The pocket flaps, which were slightly rounded at the corners, were fly fastened. The shoulder straps, with their narrow, rounded ends, were fastened to the shoulder of the blouse nearest the neck by a concealed button. The cuffs to the sleeves were finished with a 3in deep cuff band, and there was a vent in the hind-arm which was fastened by a button through a button-hole concealed in the fly of the cuff.

The trousers were moderately wide as well as long in the leg. The cuffs of the trouser legs each had a short length of cloth strap attached to the trouser ends which was adjustable to and was fastened with a single-pronged rectangular brass buckle. This allowed the ends of the black trousers to be fastened tight around the wearer's ankles and to be 'bagged' over the top of the black leather ankle boots.

There was a large patch pocket sewn to the upper portion of the left trouser leg together with a plain pocket flap, also fastened with a concealed button. The trousers had ordinary side pockets and a single hip pocket on the right at the back with a flap fastened by a concealed brass button.

Below: The oversuit for tank crews.

For reasons of wartime economy both the denim Battle-Dress and the serge Battle-Dress suit were issued to new recruits undergoing training with the Royal Tank Regiment, and for maintenance work on and general wear in tanks. The black, two-piece tank suit continued to be used by those persons who possessed it, and it was worn until their units were fully equipped with denim BD and serge BD. The black working suits may have had to be handed into unit stores when no longer required, but enquiries have established that some prewar members of the RTR retained, even if they did not actually wear for other purposes, their two-piece black garment for maintenance work only for the duration of the war.

The Oversuit

Commonly known as the 'tank suit' and sometimes referred to as a 'pixie suit', the oversuit for tank crews was introduced in July 1943. The design of this new form of protective clothing had evolved from the numerous attempts the Army had made in its effort to produce a functional garment that was easy to wear within the close confines of an armoured fighting vehicle and at the same time was warm, waterproof and comfortable. It was intended, along with the 'Tank Suits, Jungle' and the denim tank suits, which were

introduced at a later date, to replace all earlier forms of protective clothing, such as oilskin clothing. However, this intention was not completely carried out as oilskin clothing was still being issued to certain personnel as late as January 1945 (see page 211).

The oversuit was manufactured from a heavy cotton fabric of a light khaki colour, which tended to vary from a pink hue to a buff colouring. The garment was completely lined with khaki coloured woollen angola shirting material. It was cut to generous measurements to allow it to be worn over the normal serge or Battle-Dress uniforms if required. The oversuit had thirteen pockets, it was reinforced at the knees, elbows and seat, it had a detachable hood (which was the probable reason for it being known as a 'pixie suit'), and it had specially strengthened shoulder straps. These last were so constructed that in an emergency the wearer of the oversuit could be hauled out of his vehicle by these straps, the straps being strong enough to take the dead weight of the man's body. When the hood was not being worn, the collar of the suit was usually turned down. The collar itself was faced with the same khaki coloured woollen angola shirting as used for the lining of the suit.

The oversuit for tank crews continued in service long after the end of the Second World War, its

Below: The RTR black two-piece working dress.
Below right: The hood to the oversuit for tank crews.

Right: The denim tank suit worn here by Tpr. E. (Mack) MacGuinness from Liverpool, a member of The King's Own Royal Regiment and the turret gunner of a Churchill tank. *Below:* The oversuit for tank crews.

use being extended to personnel of vehicles other than tanks.

The Jungle Tank Suit

The oversuit for tank crews operating in jungle or heavily wooded areas was a camouflaged garment. It was designed and constructed on exactly the same lines as the 'pixie suit' but was produced from a camouflaged fabric; it was intended for wear over drawers and shorts in summer and serge clothing in winter.

Denim Tank Suits

The 'Tank Suit, Denim' was introduced into the Army from 23 September 1944 (ACI 1278 of 1944). It replaced the former pattern of denim overalls and was designed to be worn over drawers and shirt in summer and over Battle-Dress in winter or during cold weather conditions. At the time of its introduction it was specifically produced to be worn by:

1. Personnel of the Royal Armoured Corps and Royal Engineers who operated in armoured fighting vehicles.

2. Personnel of the Royal Artillery who operated in armoured fighting vehicles, including crews of self-propelled equipment and tank observation posts, but excluding crews of carriers and armoured observation posts.

On 14 February 1945 ACI 168 of 1945 announced that the issue of the denim tank suit was to be extended to include certain Infantry personnel who operated scout cars.

The issue of the denim tank suit was made on the scale of two suits per man as detailed above, and requirements for officers were met on repayment. Denim tank suits were also issued, at the discretion of the officer commanding the unit, to clerks, storemen, postmen, officers' mess stewards and orderlies in the RAC and RE if they were engaged in work which fulfilled the necessary conditions as set out above. These other ranks personnel were issued one suit per man.

The denim tank suit was produced in khaki green denim and was fastened down the front from the neck to the crutch by a series of fly-fronted buttons. The suit was fitted with a built-in internal set of cloth braces which were stitched into position on the waist-band at the back and passed over the wearer's shoulders to be secured to the buckles stitched to the front waist seam. This gave additional support to the garment when most of the pockets on the front of the garment were full and tending to drag the suit down.

There were eight pockets to the suit: two fairly large breast pockets, two side pockets, two knee pockets, a hip pocket at the rear on the right hip and a field dressing pocket on the right upper leg. The breast, knee and rear hip pockets had pocket flaps, all of which were secured by a concealed button. A very noticeable feature of the left-hand breast pocket was the addition of two sets of pencil or pen holders, with six compartments in one and eight compartments to the other.

The tank suit was provided with a cloth belt sewn to the back and fastened at the front with a dull metal buckle. The ends of the trouser legs had a cloth strap and button fastening. Individuals were allowed to wear web anklets and webbing waist-belts with this garment, and the sleeves could be worn down or rolled up; the collar could be open at the neck or closed, fastened by two neck hooks and eyes. There were cloth shoulder straps fastened by a small khaki coloured dish button.

Oilskin Clothing for Crews of Armoured OPs and 20mm Weapons

In view of the exposed nature of his work, protective clothing, consisting of one oilskin jacket and one pair of oilskin trousers, was issued for each member of the crews of armoured observation posts and 20mm weapons serving in Europe and the United Kingdom or in other theatres where the theatre commander considered special protection was essential in especially exposed conditions. The clothing was held on unit charge for issue as required and was withdrawn from personnel when they ceased to be crew members of armoured OPs and 20mm weapons (ACI 18 dated 6 January 1945).

6. MOTOR-CYCLISTS' CLOTHING

The Rubber-Proofed Coat, Pattern 1942

The rubber-proofed coat for wear by motor-cyclists was made in such a way that the tail could be brought up through the crutch and buttoned over the wearer's stomach and around each leg, strong press-studs being provided for this purpose.

This coat was introduced in March 1942 to replace the existing motor-cyclists' protective clothing, which consisted of rubber-proofed jackets and leggings and which had been found to be unsuitable. The new coat underwent stringent testing under a variety of weather conditions before it was introduced.

The coat gradually replaced the rubber-proofed jacket and leggings as and when the latter became unserviceable. Both types of clothing were worn within a unit for a time until the new coat became the standard issue garment (ACI 610 dated 21 March 1942).

Below: Army despatch riders wearing the newly introduced rubber-proofed protective coat for motor-cyclists. The skirt of the coat fastened around the wearer's legs (as shown) and proved to be a vast improvement on the jacket and leggings previously worn.

7. PROTECTIVE COATS

The 'Tropal' Full Length Guard Coat

This coat was one of the few purpose-made cold weather items available to British troops at the beginning of the 1939–45 war. The coat was a full-length garment reaching down to just above the wearer's anklets, about 12in from the ground. It was produced from a stiff, hard-wearing, heavy-duty canvas material, the colour of which was orange-brown. The coat was single-breasted and fastened down its length at the front by a series of five bronze coloured metal loops and catches. It was lined with a waterproof material and around the trunk and chest was lined with sheepskin fleece (later patterns had the sheepskin lining replaced by quilted kapok lining[1]). The arms were

[1] I have in my collection two examples of the Tropal coat. One, which is sheepskin (fleeced) lined, has the official ordnance factory label sewn inside the coat flap which gives the information that it was known as a 'Coat, Sheepskin' and was manufactured by Wareings (Northampton) Ltd., dated May 1939. The other coat has quilted kapok lining in place of the sheepskin fleece lining, and its factory label continues to call it a 'Coat, Sheepskin'. This too was manufactured by Wareings (Northampton) Ltd., and is dated January 1940. A third example of this coat that I have seen (dated 1941) was referred to as a 'Coat, Kapok Lined'.

lined with khaki serge material, whilst the collar was faced with thick khaki serge material of about the same weight as used for the greatcoat. There were two side pockets with flaps, but the garment had no inner pockets. The deep collar, which could be worn turned up during cold weather when it practically covered the wearer's face and neck, could be fastened across the throat by a short strap and button and the inner lining of the sleeves was elasticated around the cuffs.

Because of its bulk, stiffness and length it would have proved almost impossible to fight wearing this coat, and it was too large for equipment to be worn over it, the exception being the anti-gas service respirator. Because of these factors and because it was actually designed as a guard coat it was used in the main by sentries and gun crews who were required to remain in the open in cold or freezing weather in a static or exposed position. The Tropal coat continued in use throughout the war and was still being worn during the 1950s.

Animal Skin Coats (including the 'Hebron' Coat)

Animal skins, usually those with a warm fleece, were made up into both jerkins and coats of varying lengths, usually at the expense of the individual but sometimes by unit tailors. Any

Right: An unofficial jerkin made from animal skin being worn by Corporal E. Roberts of Chester, a member of the Welsh Guards, dug in on the edge of a German garden in Hassum, north-west of Goch, February 1945.
Far right: The leather jerkin worn by Pte. G. Mills, 2nd Bn, Gloucestershire Regiment on 6 March 1945.

such coats were of an unofficial nature, and although there was no official acknowledgement that they existed, let alone instructions laid down for their use, they were frequently encountered being worn on active service overseas, usually by officers. They were particularly popular in the North African desert, where the temperatures of the night air could prove to be very cold. The 'Hebron' was a full length, sheepskin fleece lined coat that found favour with individual officers.

'Jon', the *Daily Express* cartoonist who drew the wartime desert characters 'The Two Types', depicted one of the two seasoned campaigners habitually wearing a sheepskin jerkin (amongst other dress irregularities).

The Leather Jerkin
This very popular item had its origins in the First World War. It proved to be a practical and comfortable garment for wear in the trenches and continued to be so during the Second World War. Because it was manufactured from stout, dark brown leather it was hard-wearing, and, being lined with khaki drab blanket material, it was also warm. It was sleeveless and collarless and was buttoned down the front by four large, flat, brown buttons. Shorter in length than the greatcoat and not having sleeves, it was a convenient garment to fight in, to work in and to wear when driving during cold or inclement weather.

8. SNOW CAMOUFLAGE AND COLD CLIMATE CLOTHING

Snow Suits and Snow Camouflage
Snow camouflage suits were being used by the British Expeditionary Force in the winter of 1939−40 at the time of the 'phoney war'. They consisted of a white smock, a pair of white over-trousers and a white cloth helmet cover. Rubber gum boots were sometimes worn with this outfit in place of leather ankle boots, depending on the state of the ground.

The clothing worn under this camouflage suit was the normal Army issue uniform, supplemented by the wearing of jerseys, long underwear, the Balaclava helmet and woollen gloves.

An improvement in materials available to the Army together with the innovation of the 'layering system' brought about a whole range of cold climate clothing together with an improved design of snow camouflage clothing.

Special Cold Climate Clothing and Personal Equipment
According to the *War Clothing Regulations, 1943*, Appendix V, page 138, special clothing and personal equipment were available for wear by troops operating in cold climate conditions. If a complete set of the items listed below were worn, the coldest of climatic conditions were met with comfort; varying degrees of cold could be dealt with by the deletion of various garments. Certain spare items were also issued, to be immediately available to replace items damaged or lost or which required drying out.

The garments were designed to allow for the maximum of warmth with the least possible increase in weight, thereby not being unduly cumbersome to wear nor impeding movement. The service greatcoat was not included in the scale owing to its weight; the smock and drab trousers were made in a windproof material and these took the place of the greatcoat.

The string vest. The whole system of clothing called the 'layering system' had been built up around the string vest, which was made of thick cotton strands knitted into a wide mesh. During cold climatic conditions one string vest had always to be worn next to the skin under the ordinary pattern Army wool vest. Because of the string vest's weave, it remained in close contact with the body, thereby trapping a layer of air between the wool vest and the body. This layer of air enabled the moisture vapour given off by the wearer during exercise to remain in vapour form instead of becoming liquid sweat, and to evaporate gradually. Moisture is a conductor, and clothes wet with sweat will conduct cold to the body and heat away from it. Sweat is also liable to freeze. Air is a good insulator, and the layers of air held in the string vest and between the hairs of woollen clothing kept the body warm. Experience showed that the string vest was an extremely comfortable garment to wear and a great success.

The neck square. This item was needed as an auxiliary in the proper use of the string vest system of clothing. It was tied around the neck (like a sweat rag) to seal off the stable layer of air held by the string vest and to prevent ventilating action when that was not required.

Woollen half-sleeved vests and long woollen drawers. These were the ordinary pattern Army vest and drawers and were required to be worn under all cold conditions.

The drab angola shirt. This was the ordinary pattern Army shirt and could be worn according to the prevailing temperature.

Heavy wool jersey. This garment was for use in really cold conditions and was not always found necessary when on the move. It was, however, of great value when not on the move, for example when resting or in camp.

Snow camouflage smock and trousers. These garments were made of a white coloured light cotton material and were only to be worn as the outer garment when snow was the predominant background.

Windproof smock and trousers. These garments were made of light cotton windproofed material and, being camouflaged, were worn as the outer garment under all snowless conditions. Their purpose was to prevent the air held in the layers of clothing from being blown away by cold, piercing winds. The smock had to be issued large enough to enable several layers of clothing, including the duffle coat, to be worn under it as necessary (see page 216).

Battle-Dress trousers. These were the ordinary Battle-Dress trousers and were required to be worn under the drab windproof trousers as conditions demanded.

The peaked cap with ear flaps. This item provided all-weather cover for the head, ears and cheeks. In warmer weather the earflaps were carefully tucked up under the lining. The black material that faced the underside of the peak was intended to provide additional protection against snow glare.

Woollen or Balaclava helmet. This was purposely made to a simple design that enabled it to be worn in a number of different ways, according to the needs of the individual.

The fur cap. Worn only under extreme cold weather conditions.

Heavy wool socks. These were specially made, thick wool socks, and it was considered that when worn in conjunction with other footwear, two or even three pairs of these socks worn together at the same time were sufficient to provide adequate insulation in all conditions. Two pairs of ordinary issue Army socks provided the same insulation as one pair of the special socks.

The 'FP boots' with grooved heel. These boots had been specially designed for wear in cold conditions. A slight groove or channel was cut into the back of the heel so that the boot could be used in an emergency for ski-ing. The boots, which proved comfortable to wear in temperatures as low as $-10°F$ ($42°$ of frost), were worn with an insole and two pairs of socks, and because of this boots one size larger than was normally worn were required to be fitted by the individual.

Snow toe-covers. These were worn for additional warmth in snowy conditions only, when sub-zero temperatures were encountered but when a change from hard to soft footwear such as moccasins would not have been practicable. They were made of blanket cloth, and were pulled on over the toe and instep of the boot and secured with a lace round the ankle.

Ski boots for marching. These were for use under the same conditions as the 'FP boots' by ski-ing personnel only.

Felt insoles. Provided for wear inside the 'FP boot' with grooved heel, these acted as an extra insulating protection.

Leather gauntlets. These gauntlets could be worn in all cold conditions and were also suitable for use when ski-ing. They could not be used for firing since, for the sake of warmth, the fingers were all accommodated in one compartment. The gauntlets were joined together in pairs by a long tape the average length of which was 4ft 6in and which was passed round the neck of the wearer over or under his clothing, thus allowing the gauntlets to be taken off and replaced quickly without the risk of losing them whenever he needed to use his fingers.

Triple compartmented woollen gloves. These were hard-wearing gloves which replaced the woollen gloves worn in normal conditions and were designed as three-compartment articles so that they could be used for firing. However, in cold conditions all four fingers were kept in the same compartment (unless firing), and the compartment which normally held three fingers was made specially large so that four fingers could be accommodated.

Three-compartment special woollen gloves. These were a warmer, but less hard-wearing version of the previous item. They were worn only inside leather gauntlets.

Long woollen wrist mittens. Useful items which insulated a man's wrist against cold.

Snow goggles. These were ordinary pattern goggles which had been used successfully in Russia and Iceland as a protection against snow blindness.

Duffle coat. Provided for wear in the coldest of conditions only and intended to be worn underneath the drab smock, this was issued only to certain personnel, for example sentries and vehicle drivers.

Moccasins. These were used in temperatures which for long periods were lower than 10°F, when it was found that hard leather boots were not comfortable.

Duffle slippers. These were for wear inside moccasins only. They were produced from soft blanket type material.

Boucheron boots. These boots replaced the rubber knee boots and were for use in wet snow and slush.

The correct order of putting on these garments was as follows.

On the body.
1. String vest (always worn next to the skin).
2. Wool vest.
3. Angola shirt.
4. Wool jersey (one or two as necessary).
5. Duffle coat (if worn).
6. Windproof smock.
7. Snow-camouflage smock.

On the legs.
1. Long woollen drawers.
2. Battle-Dress trousers.
3. Windproof trousers.
4. Snow camouflage trousers.

The Two-Piece Camouflage Windproof Suit
Produced from lightweight, windproof cotton material, these garments – the smock and the trousers – were intended to be worn as outer clothing during cold but snowless weather conditions (see also page 215). The smock was intended to be worn over the woollen jersey, the angola shirt, the wool vest and the string vest and was even worn over the duffle coat if the weather was cold enough and this item was donned. The windproof trousers were worn over Battle-Dress trousers and the long woollen drawers.

The smock was put on by being pulled over the wearer's head, there only being a short neck opening at the front which was closed by means of a short metal zip fastener. The smock had a built-in hood which when in place was gathered in around the wearer's face by an integral draw string tied under the chin. There were two medium size breast pockets, each with a box pleat and each with a pocket flap with a single point fastened by a single composition button. Two somewhat larger pockets were placed at waist level on either side of the smock. These had letter-box pocket flaps also secured by a single button. The bottom edge of the smock, which was in line with the wearer's hips, also had a draw string threaded through a built-in tunnel. The cord used both for

the hood and for the bottom edge of the smock was a woven braiding in dark brown. The elbows of the smock were reinforced by having an additional piece of the windproof material sewn to them as a large patch.

The trousers were of simple construction and without a front opening. They had two side slit pockets at each hip. The waist-band was gathered in by a length of braiding which ran through the tunnel around the waist and was tied in front. There was a large pocket positioned on the front of the left leg above the knee. The ends of the trouser legs were provided with a short tab and button which allowed them to be gathered in around the ankles and fastened in position. Like the elbows of the smock, the knees of the trousers had reinforcing panels, whilst the seat was also double reinforced.

The colouring and patterning of the camouflage was quite distinctive and there was nothing else like it in use by the Army during the 1939–45 war. It was predominantly chocolate brown, mid-brown and khaki green overlaid on a light brown base. The patterning was large, irregular and with edging that was sharp in places and in others appeared as though applied with a wide house-painting brush and thus showed up as a ragged patterning of fine lines.

Because of the nature and type of operations undertaken by the Special Air Service, this windproof outfit often needed to be worn. Doubtless this has given rise to the misconceived idea that it was a special SAS garment. It was not. Indeed, after the war this item was issued to members of the WRAC.

Right: The windproof camouflage jacket with attached hood, part of the Army's special cold climate clothing that was issued to drivers and infantrymen.

9. GROUNDSHEETS AND WATERPROOFS

The standard article for the protection of the individual soldier against wet weather was the British Army groundsheet. The anti-gas cape was permitted to be worn as protection against rain (see page 243), but the intended purpose of the anti-gas cape was to protect against liquid gas droplets.

The groundsheet was a rubberized waterproof sheet which, although intended primarily for lying on and for wrapping around bedding rolls and the like, could be worn as a garment. However, it was not very efficient as a waterproof cape: the rubberized material, whilst keeping out rainwater, also held in the wearer's body sweat, with the result that after only a short period of exertion by the wearer, the cape was as wet on the inside as it was on the outside. The neck arrangement was basic and did not stop persistent rain from running down the wearer's neck into his clothing, no matter how tightly the collar was buttoned. The bottom edge of the skirt to the groundsheet usually trailed over the back of the wearer's legs, and these rapidly became soaked with rainwater running off the cape.

Only a very crude form of bivouac shelter could be made with a couple of groundsheets. The anti-gas oilskin cape, although used in all theatres of war as a raincoat, was not regarded as an efficient military waterproof, especially in jungle theatres. It was too fragile and it tore too easily, and thus it suffered a high wastage. Both its design and its material made it unsuitable as a waterproof, and it was also useless as a half-tent shelter.

Above right: The Army issue groundsheet.
Right: A party of OTC boys marching out to manoeuvres in the Tidworth district; 30 July 1930. All are wearing their groundsheet over their rifles.

PART V
Equipment

1. PROTECTIVE HEADWEAR

Steel Helmets

Mark I.

At the outbreak of the 1939–45 war the standard pattern of steel helmet in use with the British Army (and, for that matter, with all other British armed forces) was the Mark I, the same pattern that had been in service at the end of the Great War. This circular shaped helmet had been designed, in the main, to protect men in trenches against missiles falling from above, particularly shrapnel. It was satisfactory for this purpose but shrapnel was, even in 1918, going out of use. With the onset of modern types of missiles, many of which were designed to travel horizontally, greater protection was required for the vulnerable areas of the head, such as the temples, the ear regions and the base of the skull at the rear, all of which were left unprotected with the Mark I.

Mark III.

The lining of the Mark I helmet was considered to be the most satisfactory amongst the steel helmets then in use with other nations, and early in 1941 the Medical Research Council examined the possibility of designing a new helmet around the old liner. The result of their deliberations was a new design of helmet known as the Mark III. Compared to the Mark I the total area of head protection was increased by 12 per cent, whilst protection against horizontally travelling missiles was increased by 15 per cent and against missiles falling from overhead by 11 per cent; the increase in coverage of the vulnerable areas of the head was 38 per cent. Questions concerning field of vision, ventilation, hearing, balance, protection against gas (i.e. the ability to adjust the anti-gas service respirator) and of its carriage all received attention when considering the new design.

Samples of the Mark III helmet became available for trials in the autumn of 1941, and in the opinion of the Home Forces and those in the Middle East it afforded greater protection, it had better balance, and although a little heavier than the Mark I model it was less tiring to wear.[1] It also had an improved chin-strap.

For various reasons the Mark III was not suitable for use by Royal Armoured Corps personnel, airborne troops or despatch riders, for whom a special helmet was designed (see below, pages 221 and 223). However, both General Headquarters Home Forces and initially Middle East Forces did not recommend the introduction of the new helmet, claiming that it bore a certain similarity to the shape of other foreign helmets, a feature they felt might have caused confusion in battle between friend and foe, but in the light of the increased protection afforded by the new helmet these objections were overruled and in the case of the Middle East forces eventually revised.

Production of the Mark III steel helmet involved a deep draw process and its manufacture was dependent on the allocation of the required grade of manganese steel necessary. Supplies of this new helmet therefore began to be introduced late in 1943. The change over from the Mark I to the Mark III was gradual and was made in the normal course of maintenance issues, priority being given to troops in operational theatres. The superiority of the Mark III helmet over the Mark I was not considered sufficient reason to justify a wholesale change-over, even if Britain's manpower and material resources would have allowed it; the only exception to this policy was that the assault formations of the 21st Army Group were completely re-equipped with the new helmet.

Mark IV.

In the spring of 1944 the question of suitability of design for the steel helmet rose again, this time in connection with the Far East war against Japan. The authorities proposed that the lining of the helmet be made detachable in order that its steel shell could be used as a basin or bucket. In September 1944 a method was adopted by which the liner was attached to the shell of the helmet by means of a simple 'lift-the-dot' fastener placed centrally on the roof of the helmet.

This helmet with its detachable liner was introduced as the Mark IV steel helmet. It was intended

---

[1] The Mark I steel helmet weighed 2lb 5½oz including liner, and the Mark III weighed 2lb 9½oz including the liner. For comparison, the US steel helmet, including the detachable liner, weighed 2lb 15oz.

Right: The Mark I steel helmet worn by a Gunner holding a 25pdr shell. (See also the photographs on pages 41 and 225 for a comparison with the early Mark I helmet worn with a leather chin strap.)
Below right: The Mark III steel helmet undergoing evaluation on Army manoeuvres, August 1941.

to supersede the Mark III on a maintenance basis and to equip the troops sent to the Far East on conclusion of the war in Europe.

The Mark IV was considered a satisfactory helmet, but it had one weakness in that the liner was held insufficiently rigidly. This fault was not corrected before hostilities ceased.

Carrying of steel helmets.

The subject of a practical method of personnel carriage for the steel helmet as well as the carrying of the steel helmet on specified occasions was dealt with in a number of wartime Army Council Instructions. The first ACI published on the subject was No. 35 dated 8 January 1941. It stated that wherever the steel helmet was carried by troops walking out, its position was to be on the respirator; it was not to be carried in any other position. Although this simple instruction was obvious to all concerned at the time it did in fact mean that the method employed to carry the steel helmet on the anti-gas respirator haversack was to pass the carrying strap of the haversack through the chin-strap of the helmet. This enabled the underside of the helmet to lie flat against the outer surface of the haversack when the latter was carried from the shoulder in the 'slung' position (see also page 240).

Seventeen days later a far more comprehensive ACI was published (No. 124 dated 25 January 1941) that covered the subject of carrying arms, ammunition, steel helmets and respirators. Under para. 4, steel helmets were to be carried by all ranks when in uniform, including personnel of women's organizations, if in their possession, whenever they left the vicinity of their quarters or places of duty, whether on leave or on duty.

On 2 July 1941 ACI 1118 was published, which issued instructions for the removal of the steel helmet from the respirator haversack at night. This ensured that the respirator facepiece could be adjusted with the minimum of delay in the event of a gas attack. The steel helmet had to be removed from the respirator haversack by the individual soldier before going to sleep.

On 1 October 1941 a further ACI was published (ACI 1900 of 1941) on the subject of carrying steel helmets. In this instruction it was stated that as the only practicable means of carrying a steel helmet at that time was by slinging

Above: Military Police formed to operate with armoured units practise firing on a rifle range in the Newmarket area. Both men are wearing the despatch riders' 'pulp helmet'. (See also the photograph on page 44.)
Above right: The despatch riders' Mark I steel helmet.

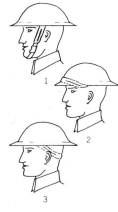

Above: Methods of wearing the Mark I steel helmet. 1, normal manner, chin-strap under chin; 2, with strap over front rim of helmet; 3, with strap around back of wearer's head.

it around the respirator haversack, which resulted in damage to the haversack and to the steel helmet chin-strap, it was decided that steel helmets would not in future be carried except when necessary. They were, however, to be carried on the following occasions.

1. When absent from quarters or places of duty for periods that exceeded 24 hours.
2. On training or operations.

Steel helmets were to be carried at any time on the instructions of the unit commander, who issued orders to this effect if he considered that they were operationally necessary. Individuals were required to take it upon themselves to wear a helmet when it appeared to them to be a reasonable precaution in view of hostile activity.

Whenever the steel helmet was carried it was either worn on the head (see accompanying sketch) or carried on the point of the shoulder, the method of carrying it slung around the anti-gas service respirator haversack being discontinued. The method employed in carrying the steel helmet on the point of the shoulder, usually the left shoulder, was achieved by passing the left arm through the chin-strap of the helmet and then pushing the helmet well up the arm to rest high on the back of the shoulder. It could rest there comfortably without restricting the movement of the individual.

The provisions of this ACI applied only to formations and units at home. Commanders abroad were required to issue orders, based on these instructions, to suit their peculiar circumstances.

ACI 603 dated 10 April 1943 touched on the subject of the carrying of steel helmets only to state that the instructions were as laid down by the previous ACI No. 1900 of 1941. However, the last wartime ACI on the subject, No. 816 dated 11 July 1945 and entitled 'Equipment – Carrying of Arms and Equipment by Military Personnel (including the ATS)', stated that the existing instructions regarding the carrying of arms, ammunition and equipment by personnel proceeding on leave and stationed in the United Kingdom had been revised and that steel helmets

were no longer required to be taken. The carrying of arms and equipment by personnel travelling on drafts, transfers, courses of instruction, etc. was in no way affected by this instruction.

Use of Crash Helmets

Periodic warnings were issued to motor-cyclists about the need both to wear their protective headgear correctly and to ensure that it was in sound condition. A typical instruction to this effect was one issued as ACI 545 dated 14 March 1942. It called attention to the fact that both the life and the continued efficiency of a motor-cyclist depended upon his crash helmet. It was important that the helmet was worn properly and that regular inspections were carried out to ensure that it was in good order.

Motor-cyclists were never permitted to ride with the chin-strap of their helmet unfastened. These instructions pointed out that most head injuries occurred after the rider had been thrown from his machine, and that if the chin-strap was not fastened the helmet was almost always thrown off at the very moment when it was most needed.

The protective value of the crash helmet, which in March 1942 was still the original pulp type, depended on the following points.

1. The integrity of the outer shell. Helmets that showed cracks in the outer shell were required to be returned to stores. The most common place on the helmet for a crack to develop was at the rim, which was the weakest part of the helmet.
2. The firmness of the inner sling. The loops of the inner sling had to be free from tears and all the stitching of the slings was required to be firm.
3. The lacing or cord which held the loops of the inner sling on the crown of the head had to be firmly tied, and in such a way that when the helmet was fitted the inner sling kept the wearer's head well away from the outer shell of the helmet.
4. The cord which passed around the rim of the helmet was on some types of DR crash helmet responsible for connecting the inner sling to the outer shell. If this was broken all the protective value of the inner sling was lost. Therefore, the ACI concluded, the outer cord of the helmet was

Above: The special non-crash helmet for tank crews.
Above right: The improved version of the non-crash helmet for crews of armoured fighting vehicles, worn here by a crewman being extracted by Royal Army Medical Corps personnel.

not allowed to be frayed and the knot had to be firmly tied.

Painted Surface.

Prior to June 1941 the pulp type despatch rider's crash helmet in use with the British Army was manufactured with a shiny khaki green surface, but after June 1941, by order of ACI 997 dated 14 June 1941, all future supplies of the crash helmets were provided with a matt surface and instructions were given for all the shiny helmets to be painted matt khaki green.

Despatch Riders' Crash Helmet (First Pattern)

The 'pulp helmet', so named as it was produced from lightweight but toughened papier-mâché, was the standard pattern crash helmet for use by despatch riders in the British armed forces before the war and up to July 1943, when it began gradually to be replaced by the despatch riders' Mark I steel helmet. Because of its internal construction, its external profile was higher than was the case with the DR's steel helmet: this was the result of the inner sling which, when the helmet was worn, rested on the crown of the wearer's head. The loops of this inner sling had to be tied tight enough to leave a space between the underside of the crown of the helmet and the crown of the wearer's head, the space being the safety margin afforded to the wearer in the event of an accident or collision. The inner sling was held in position by a cord laced in and out of a series of eyelet holes that pierced the rim of the helmet. The helmet had a leather neck flap that also formed the chin-strap.

Despatch Riders' Mark I Steel Helmet

In July 1943 approval was given for the issue of the 'Steel Helmet, DR Mark I' on the scale of one helmet for each officer and other rank, later to include personnel of the ATS, to whom a motor-cycle or side-car combination was specifically allotted in War Establishments.

With the issue of the despatch rider's steel helmet, the Mark I steel helmet, together with the

pulp crash helmet previously worn by motor-cyclists and despatch riders, was withdrawn from use. A pool of DR crash helmets was kept in unit stores in sufficient numbers to meet the requirements of pillion riders, side-car passengers and other users, including those undergoing motor-cycle training.

A very high proportion of injuries resulting from motor-cycle accidents were fractured skulls or other head injuries. The wearing of the DR Mark I steel helmet or the DR crash helmet was made compulsory for all officers, other ranks and auxiliaries who travelled on duty by motor-cycle, whether driving or riding as pillion or as a passenger in side-cars. The only exceptions made to this ruling were for operational, training or other conditions that made it necessary for other forms of headgear to be worn. These were as follows.

1. The Mark I steel helmet, during active operations, during operational training or in air raids, by occasional riders, pillion riders and side-car passengers.
2. Soft caps, where these were specially ordered by higher authority for the purpose of distinguishing opposing sides during training.
3. In other circumstances when authorized by the War Office, C-in-Cs or GOs C-in-C.

The RAC Mark I steel helmet that was issued to personnel of the Royal Armoured Corps was valueless as a crash helmet for motor-cyclists, since although it was of similar shape it had insufficient anchorage to make it stable enough; because of this it was not permitted to be worn by motor-cyclists.

The former DR crash helmet (the pulp helmet) continued in use with the Home Guard.

The Special Non-Crash Helmet for Tank Crews

Before the introduction of the Royal Armoured Corps Mark I steel helmet, crew members of tanks and AFVs were afforded a limited amount of head protection by wearing the special non-crash tank helmet. Strikingly similar in appearance and in quality of material to the protective helmet worn

Top, far left: Sjt. W. A. Morris, RE, from Freshford, Somerset, a member of the Army's Film and Photographic Unit, wearing the RAC Mark I Steel helmet.

Top left: The first model Airborne Forces' steel helmet with hard rubber rim, worn by Airborne troops undergoing training on the Dorset coast in preparation for their raid on the German radar installation at Bruneval; February 1942.

Centre row: A comparison of the second model Airborne Forces' steel helmet with flat rim (left) and the final model (middle).

Centre right: The sorbo rubber training helmet was an early attempt at providing Airborne troops with some form of protective head-gear.

Below, far left: A 'rubber bungy', the final form of protective training helmet for Airborne Forces; October 1941.

Below left: Members of the Glider Pilot Regiment, two of whom are wearing over their flying helmet the protective helmet.

by coal miners at that time, the non-crash helmet was made from very hard, but light, composition black material. The helmet was formed from a single length of this black material cut to shape and moulded to form the oval body; the open crown was covered with an oval patch made of the same hard material, shaped and riveted to, but slightly thicker than that used for, the body of the helmet. The rim of the helmet was moulded to form a narrow lip running completely around the perimeter. On the front of the helmet, approximately ½in above this moulded rim, was a padded ridge approximately 8in in length, 1¼in in depth and standing out from the front of the helmet to a distance of about 1in. The ridge was covered in black painted cloth and was held on to the front of the helmet by a pair of rivets at each end of the pad. It is also likely that the pad was also glued into position along its length. The inner lining consisted of a semi-ridged, leather-covered band held to the body of the helmet by a lace threaded in and out through a series of small holes punched through the shell of the helmet around and just above the moulded rim. The head-sling consisted of four lengths of canvas tape riveted to eight points on the inside of the helmet body in such a way as to form four loops. These were tied together with a short length of string and this formed the cushion that rested on the wearer's head. Three ventilation holes were cut into the body of the helmet.

There was an improved version of this non-crash helmet, produced from materials similar to those used in the construction of the despatch rider's pulp helmet. The surface of the helmet was covered with six panels of stitched canvas. It had a rounded ridge on the front and was provided with 'ear-flaps' which would seem to have been capable of accommodating RT ear phones. The adjustable chin-strap was a length of canvas webbing extending from the lower edge of the left 'ear-flap'. The three ventilation holes were very prominent on this version in that they were fitted with small rubber rings and stood proud from the surface of the helmet.

Royal Armoured Corps Pattern Steel Helmet

The steel helmet introduced for wear by crews of armoured fighting vehicles and intended to supersede the non-crash protective helmets in use with these forces both before and during the first years of the 1939–45 war had the same outer manganese steel shell as the steel helmet for airborne troops and the Mark I despatch rider's steel helmet.

The differences between these three helmets lay in the liners, all of which were adapted to suit the requirements of the respective users. The RAC steel helmet had the same pattern of lining as that used in the ordinary Mark I and Mark III steel helmet, but the chin-strap was simpler than that used on the ordinary steel helmet in that it consisted of an elasticated flat strap.

Steel Helmet, Pattern for Airborne Troops

Of the three similar patterns of steel helmet (the RAC helmet and the steel helmet for despatch riders being the other two), the steel helmet for British Airborne troops was the first to be brought into service. Early models of the Airborne Forces' helmet differed slightly in the construction of the liner and the appearance of the steel shell; later models were distinguished by having web straps instead of leather straps. Taken in order of development the steel helmets were as follows.

1. The first model had a hard rubber rim fitted to the edge of the manganese steel shell, giving the helmet the appearance of having a 'lip' around the edge which extended further out at the back of the helmet. The purpose of this rim escapes me, unless it was intended to direct rainwater away from the back of the wearer's neck. The hard rubber rim was short lived.
2. The second model had a 1in deep flat, hard rubber or composition material band fitted to the rim.
3. The third model had a plain manganese steel shell and is the type often encountered today in private hands or museum collections.

Models 1, 2 and 3 all had neck-straps, chin-straps and chin cups in black leather. The neck-straps were anchored to the inside of the steel shell at three positions. This arrangement, together with the chin cup, helped to ensure that when properly adjusted the helmet was held firmly on the wearer's head. The leather straps used as the helmet harness had one disadvantage in that when wet, through either rain or perspiration, it was difficult to thread the chin-strap through the brass rings. Leather too was expensive and in short supply, so that eventually Airborne steel helmets were produced with the head-harness manufactured from webbing straps. I have an example of this type in my collection dated 1944. Although considerable numbers of these helmets with the webbing harness were produced before the end of hostilities, very few seem to have been worn by British Airborne troops. Polish Airborne Forces appear to have been re-equipped with this type, at least in time for their part in the Arnhem air drop.

All helmets, regardless of their outer appearance or the type of head-harness used, were heavily padded on the inside of the shell.

Glider Pilot's Protective Helmet

Glider pilots were issued with two helmets: all received an Airborne pattern steel helmet for when they were required to fight as infantry once they were on the ground, whilst for wear in the cockpits of their gliders pilots wore a protective helmet which incorporated earphones and a mouthpiece for RT communication. The latter helmet was quite distinctive in that it had a flatter profile than was usually the case with other protective helmets and the rim of the helmet had a conspicuous band.

Airborne Forces Parachute Training Helmets (Early Patterns and Standard Pattern)

The earliest form of head-gear used by Airborne troops during periods of parachute training was a close fitting leather helmet, not unlike a flying helmet in general appearance. Although it

This page, right: A corporal of the Scots Guards whose helmet bears on both sides a transfer marking similar in size and colour to the cap band worn (also by the Scots Guards) on the coloured forage cap; see also the photograph on page 237.

This page, far right: Sjt. E. J. Allen of Luton about to climb into the cab of an Army Fire Service tender stationed at Caen, France, in August 1944. (See also photographs on pages 52 and 55.)

Opposite page, left: Royal Engineers from the 42nd (East Lancashire) Division undergoing instruction in mine detection, July 1942. The lead man sweeps the ground with the mine detector, listening for a buzz which will warn him of a mine. The short length of wire carried in his left hand will detect the presence of trip wires attached to mines. The man following will mark the positions of the detected mines. On the helmet of each man can be seen a small white square with red edging set on its point, the formation sign of the 42nd Division.

Opposite page, right: Men of the Manchester Regiment manning a Vickers water-cooled machine gun. The soldier in the foreground has a transfer of the regiment's cap badge, a yellow fleur-de-lys, on the right side of the steel helmet.

Opposite page, below: A 3in mortar detachment from 1st Bn, South Staffordshire Regiment in action during a display of modern infantry weapons and equipment held at Mytchett, Aldershot, on 21 January 1938. A transfer of the regiment's cap badge is worn on the front of the steel helmet.

afforded a certain amount of head warmth, it was unsatisfactory as a protective helmet.

Initial efforts to provide the Airborne troops with a protective training helmet resulted in a fairly crude prototype helmet formed from slabs of thick sorbo rubber cut and bonded together to form a head covering. It was tied under the wearer's chin by two short lengths of tape or cord. This prototype training helmet eventually evolved into the standard pattern training helmet that was used throughout the Airborne Forces for the duration of the war, and indeed for a considerable time after the war. Known colloquially as a 'rubber bungy', it was a linen-covered helmet thickly padded around the perimeter with heavy duty sorbo rubber. The short neck flap, which also covered the ears and ended in an adjustable chin-strap, was produced from the linen. The crown of the training helmet, surprisingly, was unprotected and consisted of only a thickness of the linen used.

Steel Helmet Markings

The marking of steel helmets had been a common practice before the war, when regimental badges or unit devices were frequently painted or transferred on to the helmets, usually on the left side. Marking was permitted to continue during the war, provided that the painting was carried out under unit arrangements. Markings included regimental and units flashes, lettering and or bands of colour for various distinguishing purposes. Some examples of different types of markings are given below.

Distinguishing marks worn by the Corps of Military Police.

In order that members of the CMP could be easily distinguished when wearing steel helmets instead of the Service Dress cap with its red cloth cover, it was decided as of November 1940 that

their steel helmets were to bear, in addition to the regimental badge of the white letters 'MP' set on a square blue background, a bright red band ¾in wide, the lower edge of which was ¾in above the dent in the helmet where the crown and the brim joined. The ¾in gap was necessary in order for the red painted band to be visible above the anti-gas curtain when worn. The square blue background for the letters 'MP' was positioned in the centre of the band at the front of the helmet (ACI 1339 dated 6 November 1940).

By April 1944 separate coloured bands painted on helmets worn by the three wings of the CMP had been introduced. The same ¾in wide band was used, as was the position on the helmet. Red painted bands were worn by personnel of the CMP (Provost Wing), white bands by members of the CMP (Traffic Control) and Oxford blue was used for the helmets worn by personnel of the CMP (Vulnerable Points Wing). The regimental badge 'MP', stencilled (or painted) on a square blue background, continued to be placed in the centre of the respective bands at the front of the helmet (ACI 494 dated 5 April 1944).

The Gloucestershire Regiment steel helmet back badge.

The unique distinction held by the Gloucestershire Regiment of having two cap badges, one full size worn at the front of the head-dress and the other a small size badge at the back, is explained on page 76. During the 1939–45 war this distinction was extended to the steel helmet. All personnel of the regiment were issued with a silver transfer (a representation of the small back badge) which was affixed to the back of the steel helmet. The design was of a size and outline similar to the metal version of the back badge but it was all silver without detail. An example of this steel helmet marking can be seen at the regimental museum of The Gloucestershire Regiment.

Steel Helmet Coverings and Painted Surfaces

The purpose of covering a steel helmet was to provide camouflage. Covering the helmet obviated any possible reflection from smooth or shiny surfaces, even from areas of the steel helmet where the metal was exposed, due to rubbing or abrasions. If the cover used on the helmet was sufficiently rough then the hard outline was broken, which in itself was an aid to personal concealment. Covers also helped to deaden the noise if the metal helmet was struck, which was vital in circumstances where stealth was required.

During the early stages of the war it was almost a fashion to cover the Mark I steel helmet in special sacking covers, which were usually made up in the unit's tailoring shop from sandbags. They were stitched in position on the steel helmet around a wire ring – usually a stiffener taken from a Service Dress cap – and once in position on the helmet they were not removable. The panels of the cover had loops of sacking stitched to them, their purpose being to provide the means whereby tufts of grass or foliage could be held on the helmet to further camouflage its shape. The fact that these sacking covers could not be removed was a grave disadvantage and a definite hazard in the event of a gas attack, for with them affixed to the helmet the latter could not be properly washed, and it was for this reason that the sacking covers were eventually dropped from use. Dark green helmet netting and helmet scrim began to be used on all patterns of infantry and airborne steel helmets when the possibility of gas attacks receded.

Painting steel helmets was a fairly simple means of camouflage, the paint used obviously being selected to match the colour of the countryside in which the wearer was to operate. A rough, non-reflective surface could be achieved by painting the helmet and whilst the paint was still wet covering it with a thin layer of clean, dry sand. The sand stuck to the wet surface and when dry generally took on the colour of the paint used. This method was particularly successful in North Africa and other desert areas. The use of the anti-gas helmet curtain (see page 240) should not be confused with attempts at helmet camouflage by the use of covers: this was quite a different item of equipment.

Snow camouflage was achieved by the use of white cloth covers, but I have yet to come across an example of a white painted British helmet intended as snow camouflage.

Top: Green helmet netting worn with (right) the parachutists helmet and (far right) the steel helmet. The bottle of beer Parachutist Fred Swinford is about to enjoy constituted his beer ration for the week.
Below: The green helmet netting allowed for scrim (short lengths of sacking material, usually dark in colour) to be attached to it (right) which further helped break up the hard outline of the helmet. It also allowed for a first field dressing to be carried in a convenient position (far right).

Steel Helmet Visors

Seventy-five per cent of all blindness suffered by soldiers during the Great War was due not to eye disease but to injuries caused by shell, bomb and grenade explosions. The great majority of these injuries were the result of fragments of metal which penetrated no deeper than the eye itself and which, had they struck elsewhere on the body, would have caused only trivial harm.

The question of some form of eye protection designed to reduce the incidence of eye injury and blindness was therefore raised immediately on the outbreak of the Second World War by Sir Richard Cruise, an eminent opthalmic surgeon. Captain Cruise, as he then was, had in 1917 designed a form of chain visor which could be attached to the rim of the British Mark I steel helmet. Although it was intended to help reduce or prevent injuries to the eyes, in practice it proved to be unpopular with the troops. A modified and improved version was developed in 1918 but this, too, failed to find acceptance and eventually it was withdrawn.

In 1939 samples of a further modified 'Cruise' visor were sent over to the British Expeditionary Force in France. This version was so designed that when not in use it could lie under the rim of the steel helmet. However, the reports of its use in the BEF were so inconclusive that 5,000 visors were manufactured to allow for a large scale trial to take place; unfortunately, military events overtook their production, and before they could be despatched Dunkirk had fallen to the Germans and the survivors from the BEF were back in Britain.

Trials were carried out instead by troops of the Home Forces in the autumn of 1940, but reports submitted by the troops trying out the Cruise visor and the advice of the Medical Research Council were against the adoption of any form of metal visor. It was found that rain made it difficult for the wearer to see through the visor, and the drops of water could not be shaken off easily. Stereoscopic vision was impaired, the wearer's field of view was reduced, and his ability to see in the dark whilst wearing the visor was markedly affected. In the light of these adverse reports the Army Council decided against any form of protective metal visor being adopted, and although work on perspex visors was being undertaken no satisfactory type was developed, and in 1941, on the advice of the Medical Research Council, the whole matter was dropped.

Below: Gracie Fields, the famous entertainer, surrounded by British troops of the BEF. This unidentified unit seems to have adopted the practice of painting their helmets with a camouflage pattern.
Below right: Steel helmets with sacking covers.
Bottom: The 'Cruise' visor worn with the Mark I steel helmet; October 1939.

2. WEB EQUIPMENT

The 1937 Pattern Web Equipment

The 1937 pattern equipment was designed to meet the conditions of warfare that prevailed at that time. The mechanization of the British Army, together with the introduction of the 'Bren' light machine gun and the 'Boys' anti-tank rifle necessitated changes in the personal equipment of the British soldier. Mobility as well as the ease of carriage of ammunition, grenades, food and water and other items necessary for survival in the field were all taken into consideration when designing the equipment.

The equipment was actually a development of the 1908 pattern web equipment. However, the new design was considerably lighter in weight than the 1908 pattern and it had the basic principle that its construction enabled it to be adapted for use to suit all arms. It was considered easy to assemble and to adjust, and it also possessed the important feature that, with the exception of the bayonet and the officer's haversack, no articles were suspended below the wearer's waist-line to impede his movement.

Although the 1908 pattern pack and supporting straps were included in and were attached to the 1937 equipment for the purpose of changing stations, there was normally no pack used in the 1937 pattern equipment as the kit accommodated in that article was carried in regimental transport. A haversack, sometimes referred to as 'the small pack', was therefore carried on the back and contained rations, water-bottle and other necessaries. The principle of carrying the haversack 'rucksack fashion' allowed this article to be easily discarded in order to permit access to its contents without disturbing the remainder of the equipment.

The rucksack method of carrying the haversack was both comfortable and self-balancing. The shoulder straps used for the carriage of the haversack were provided with hooks for attachment to the equipment in front in order to prevent pressure on the wearer's armpits, and these same shoulder straps were also used for carrying the 1908 pack when desired, the 1937 pattern haversack then being transferred to the wearer's left side and the equipment attached to the ends of the braces. The water-bottle in its carrier was then taken out of the haversack and attached to the ends of the braces at the right side of the equipment.

The 1937 pattern equipment was made throughout of strong and durable webbing, which was both waterproofed and dyed in the yarn before being woven. The result of the waterproofing treatment was (so it was thought) to render the fabric practically impervious to the weather, which might otherwise have caused it to become hard, to stretch or to shrink.

The webbing was thoroughly shrunk before being cut and made into articles of equipment and, where practicable and necessary, selvedged webbings woven to the correct width were employed to give added strength. Likewise, certain parts of the equipment were integrally woven: for example, the braces were woven with expanded parts to give a good bearing surface on the shoulders and the waist-belt had loops woven inside to receive the brass hooks for adjustment to its length as well as the hooks on certain articles carried on the waist-belt to keep them in position. Cartridge carriers, pockets and pistol-cases were also woven as separate units, thereby eliminating unnecessary sewing which, consequently, added to the strength and durability of the finished articles. All the buckles were stamped from sheet brass and were of the tongueless or self-locking variety,

Left: 1937 Pattern web equipment.
Right: Two men of the Black Watch from the 51st Highland Division putting on their 1937 Pattern web equipment.
Far right: Paratroopers in battle order ready for inspection. The soldier on the left is wearing an item of webbing equipment designed to accommodate extra magazines of 9mm Sten gun ammunition.

which allowed for adjustment to any desired position.

When the equipment had once been properly fitted it was kept assembled as far as possible. It was found convenient, once a correct fit had been achieved, to make a light mark on the underside of various parts of the equipment to show where each future adjustment should always come. This saved time and trouble for the individual in those cases where the equipment had to be taken apart and later re-assembled.

In the event of the equipment becoming dirty or greasy, it has to be washed in warm water using soap and a sponge, rinsed with clear water to remove all traces of soap, and then allowed to dry out thoroughly. Dust and dried mud had to be removed from the webbing with an ordinary clothes brush. A scrubbing brush was not allowed to be used on the equipment on any account. No cleaner was applied to the webbing equipment without first having been approved by the War Office (see page 237).

During peacetime the metal work on the equipment was polished but under active service conditions it was allowed to become dull to avoid catching the rays of the sun.

Despite all its considered advantages and improvements, the 1937 pattern equipment had its critics. It was claimed by some to be clumsy, noisy, cramping and uncomfortable, but the most severe criticism arose out of its use in jungle warfare. It was found that when the 1937 pattern was worn over thin Tropical clothing in sweaty jungle conditions such as in New Guinea and Burma a common complaint was that the braces chafed the collar-bone and armpits, and that the haversack was always dragging down from the shoulders and pulling the waist-belt up from the chest. The webbing material, despite its being waterproofed at the manufacturing stage, was found under these conditions readily to soak up rainwater. It was difficult to dry out in the normally humid atmosphere and because of this it attracted mould, and proving in use to be neither waterproof nor water repellent, it let through both wet and sweat. It was heavy when dry and heavier still when wet, and the press-studs were not reliable and the buckles slipped.

The 1944 Pattern Web Equipment

The 1944 Pattern equipment was developed to overcome the disadvantages inherent in the former 1937 pattern equipment, and incorporated a new principle of design which enabled the load to be carried to be evenly distributed and well balanced. It was first designed for use in the tropics, but it proved equally suitable for all conditions of modern warfare in other theatres. The main object had been to reduce the weight of the equipment and at the same time to maintain adequate strength in its construction to carry everything needed, and this was achieved by the use of fine yarn which effectively reduced the thickness of the various types of webbing whilst at the same time making it more pliable. The metal fittings were made of an anodized light alloy, which was specially darkened, required no

cleaning, and was much lighter than the former brass fittings.

The yarn used for the webbing was dyed and treated in its manufacture to make it both rotproof and water repellent. It proved impracticable to make it waterproof, however, as water would have in any case seeped through the interstices between the threads. It was hoped that the material would retain its water repellency for its normal life and thus obviate the necessity for the application of a renovator, but it was found that its water repellent properties deteriorated with age and that the use of a cleaner was found necessary to restore them. Scrubbing, bleaching and the use of blanco on this new equipment was forbidden.

There were three principle features in the design of the 1944 equipment.
1. A method of supporting the heavy contents of the large basic pouches that prevented down-drag of the equipment in front without counter-balance by weight on the back. This was achieved by the braces forming a sling: they were joined at the back where they crossed and were fixed to the waist-belt immediately at the rear of the basic pouches.
2. An increase in the carrying capacity of the haversack and its additional fittings, and also an increase in the size of the basic pouches.
3. The fact that, if necessary, and when operating in tropical areas, the waist-belt could be worn loose without affecting the carriage of the equipment. This was a particular advantage, especially in jungle warfare.

Although large quantities of the 1944 pattern equipment were manufactured towards the end of the war with the object of issuing it to the troops who were earmarked to proceed to the Far East on conclusion of the war in Europe, it was in fact never issued. The Japanese surrendered before this could take place and it was decided instead to adopt the 1944 pattern for universal issue in place of the 1937 pattern web equipment.

The Web Waist-Belt

1937 pattern.
This was issued in three sizes, extra large, large and small, the overall lengths of the webbing being 56, 50 and 44in respectively; the width of all belts was 2¼in. It was fitted with a clasp buckle (hook and loop pattern), two brass runners or slides, and two end pieces with hooks for adjustment at each end. Centrally at the back, on the outer surface, were two brass buckles fitted at an angle inclining inwards for attachment of the braces.

1944 pattern.
This was issued in two sizes, large and normal, having maximum adjustments of 48in and 40in respectively. The normal size was capable of fitting 95 per cent of all troops. The waist-belt was made in three parts, two side pieces and an adjustment strap, and the webbing used was 2in wide. The equipment could be worn with the central back portion of the belt completely removed without the equipment 'flopping about'. Thus, constriction of the waist was avoided and the equipment

Opposite page: The 1944
Pattern webbing equipment;
top right, haversack and water
bottle with cover; centre top,
brace attachments and basic
pouches; top, far right,
haversack with pick attached,
waist belt, bayonet frog,
machete and sheath, and left
side basic pouch with bayonet;
bottom right, webbing shoulder-
straps, waist belt, bayonet and
frog, and water bottle with
cover; bottom, centre, the
haversack with shovel, bedding
roll covered by a groundsheet,
and water bottle with cover;
bottom, far right, the shovel
with blade covered, and the
bedding roll flattened out and
wound round the haversack (an
alternative method of carriage).

was able to be worn by men with minor waist injuries.

A closing buckle of the hook and loop type was fitted to the front ends of the side pieces and a double hook on each rear end; a 1in link with gap was fitted diagonally to each side piece for attachment of the braces, and loops were provided for the spare ends of the adjustment strap. Two 1in, three-bar buckles were fitted to the back piece for attachment of the inner braces.

Grommets (eyelet holes with spur tooth washers) were fitted in the lower edge of the belt, four in each side piece and six centrally spaced in the adjustment strap, for the attachment by hooks of items such as the water-bottle cover. A 1in strap with a snap fastener was fitted to the right-hand side to secure the rifle when slung on the shoulder.

Webbing Braces

1937 pattern.
These were made in pairs, left and right, the left brace having a loop to receive the right brace. They were both integrally woven with a wide portion for the shoulders. They were issued in two sizes, 'normal' being 47in and 'long' 55in in length.

1944 pattern.
These had shoulder sections made of webbing 3in wide, with 1in wide front straps to connect to the basic pouches. Two 1in wide straps were sewn to the rear ends of the shoulder sections of the braces and stitched where they crossed. When correctly fitted these were attached to the diagonals on the side pieces of the waist-belt and were adjustable by the three-bar buckles. The other two inner 1in straps, which were not sewn where they crossed, were for attachment to the buckles on the back central portion of the belt, thereby taking the weight of anything on the back of the equipment.

The Basic Pouches

1937 pattern.
These were interchangeable and were rectangular in shape in order to contain two Bren gun ammunition magazines each, a number of grenades, small arms ammunition, or whatever was required by the wearer. A buckle was provided at the rear of the top of each pouch for attachment of the brace. This buckle had a loop at the top which served for connecting the hook on the shoulder strap. Two double hooks were fitted to the back of each pouch for attachment to the waist-belt.

Modified 1937 pattern. On 15 June 1940 it was announced by ACI 604 of 1940 that the 1937 pattern basic pouches could, if it were considered necessary, be modified by removing the web patch securing the two brass hooks on the back of the pouches and replacing them in a similar position but 1in lower. The object of this modification was to raise the pouch to a slightly higher carrying position.

When the modification had been carried out, the nomenclature of the pouch became 'Pouch, Basic, Web Equipment Pattern 1937, Mark II', the unmodified pattern being referred to as the Mark I version.

1944 pattern.
Left side. The internal dimensions were approximately 4½in by 3in by 9½in deep. On the back there were two wire hooks, provided for connecting the pouch to the waist-belt, a tapered chape with a 1in, four-bar buckle for the braces and two vertical webbing loops for the haversack straps. The hooded flap was fitted with the staple portion of a quick-release fastener which could be fitted to either of the two links on the front of the pouch. The normal method of closure was to use the bottom link; the alternative method was for use when longer items were carried in the pouch. The left-hand side had loops as an alternative method of carrying the No. 4, 5 and 7 bayonet.

Right Side. This was exactly the same as the left-hand pouch except that the bayonet loops were not fitted on the side.

In place of the former snap fasteners used on the 1937 pattern pouch to secure the lids, a quick-release type of fastener was used on the 1944 basic pouch. This consisted of a staple and link with a web tongue and tab for securing and release. Similar fasteners were provided to close the pockets on the sides of the 1944 haversack.

Basic Pouch for MT Drivers. This item was similar in size and construction to the 1944 pattern left basic pouch except that, in place of the attachments on the back, a 2in wide web loop was provided to enable it to be carried on the waist-belt to the rear of the brace attachment.

The Binocular Case

1937 pattern.
This was stiffened with vulcanized fibre and was provided with a box like lid closed by a snap fastener. It had two double-hooks provided on the back for attachment to the waist-belt and a similar hook was fitted horizontally at the top for connecting to the bottom edge of the compass pocket.

1944 pattern.
This was made of a double 'shell' of webbing interlined with felt, with a fibre stiffening fitted into the base. The hooded lid was provided with a quick-release fastener and on the back of the case two double hooks and a 'hanger' hook were fitted, similar to those on the pistol case.

The 1908 Pattern Web Supporting Straps
Used as part of the 1937 pattern web equipment, these were interchangeable, and each consisted of a strip of 1in wide webbing, fitted with a buckle at one end and an eyeletted tip at the other end.

The 1937 Pattern Two-Pocket Cartridge Carriers
They were designed to be interchangeable, and each comprised two pockets which were woven integrally. The interior of each pocket was divided

by a partition into two compartments, each capable of holding one clip of five rounds of .303in rifle ammunition. The flaps, with their beaded edges, were secured by means of snap fasteners, the lower studs being used when the pockets contained only one clip or were empty. An extension piece of webbing was fitted centrally to the back of each carrier to carry a buckle for connection to the braces. A brass link was also provided below the buckle to enable the end of the brace to be passed through behind the carrier. There were two double hooks fitted to the back of the carrier to connect it to the waist-belt.

Webbing Shoulder Straps

1937 pattern.

These were made in pairs, left and right. Each strap consisted of wide webbing, tapered at the front end, to which was sewn a hook having a side loop which carried a narrow strap, set obliquely. A removable buckle was provided on the wide portion for connection to the webbing tabs on the back of the haversack.

1944 pattern.

These were made as a left and right strap, each consisting of an integrally woven shoulder section 2in wide tapering to 1in, to carry a quick-release buckle through which a strap with a hook was adjustable. To the 'ear' on the side of the hook was sewn a narrow side supporting (or diagonal) strap, which was adjustable through a quick-release buckle on a short strap having a tip on the end for attachment to the corresponding buckle positioned on the base of the haversack.

Intrenching Tool and Carrier

1908 pattern tool and 1937 pattern carrier.

ACI 2339 dated 26 November 1941 announced that it had been decided to reintroduce the 1908 pattern intrenching tool previously rendered obsolete by Army Order 267 of 1923.

The head and helve were identical to the 1908 pattern implement but the web carrier had been modified to carry the implement helve as well. The carrier was secured to the ends of the left and right braces of the Pattern 1937 web equipment at the back of the waist-belt by means of the two brass 'Ds' on chapes provided; the side of the carrier, holding the helve, was placed outwards. Care had to be taken when placing the implement head in the carrier to ensure that the slight curve of the head conformed to the soldier at the point of contact.

Modified 1937 pattern helve.

The head and helve of the intrenching tool — sometimes described as an 'entrenching tool' — had remained unaltered since first being introduced in 1908. Both were reintroduced to be used as part of the 1937 pattern web equipment on the authority of ACI 2339 dated 26 November 1941. However, sometime during the 1939–45 war, on a date I have yet to establish, a modified version of the intrenching tool helve began to be issued.

On the end of the wooden helve, opposite the end that retained the head of the tool, a bayonet fitting, very similar to that on the .303in rifle, was attached. This was capable of receiving the 'pig-sticker' bayonet and turned the helve into a very useful instrument that could be employed when probing for hidden mines.

1944 pattern carrier.

This was a simple cover with a quick-release buckle. It was attached to the equipment by means of a 'hanger' hook.

The Water-Bottle Carrier

1937 pattern.

This consisted of a framework of narrow webbing straps with tabs at the top fitted with a snap fastener for securing the water-bottle. There was a buckle on each side of the webbing framework for attachment to the ends of the braces, if the water-bottle and carrier were carried in the slung position.

1944 pattern.

This was in the form of a 'bag' and was officially referred to as a 'water-bottle cover'. It was designed to take the new style aluminium water-bottle and drinking cup. A pocket was provided inside on the back wall of the bag for the filter bag; it also had a small flap which prevented the bottle catching the top of the pocket, and a web loop was fitted inside to take a tube of water sterilizing tablets. The bottle was retained in the cover by flaps which passed over the 'shoulders' of the bottle and were secured by snap fasteners. On the back of the cover there was a 'hanger' hook which was fitted to allow for attachment to the grommets in the right side of the waist-belt.

The Bayonet Frog

1937 pattern.

This was made of narrow webbing with a loop for suspending from the waist-belt, and it had two horizontal loops for securing the scabbard. The scabbard was inserted and pushed through until the stud on the outside came out between the two loops.

1944 pattern.

This was provided with a woven hole in the upper scabbard loop that enabled the No. 4, No. 5 or No. 7 bayonet to be carried by inserting the stud through the hole. The No. 1 bayonet was held in the frog in the usual way by the stud on the scabbard being inserted between the web loops. The narrow web loop was provided to slip over the hilt of the No. 1 or the No. 5 bayonet to prevent swinging.

Officers' Haversack

1937 pattern.

This was a rectangular bag approximately 12in by 9in by 2in which had a flap secured by one small strap and buckle. The interior of the haversack was longitudinally divided by a partition, and on the face (under the flap) two pockets were provided, both of which were closed by small snap fasteners, for the stowage of pencils, protractors, dividers, etc. A small buckle was fitted each side for attachment to the ends of the braces at the side of the equipment, and a loop was provided on the back of the haversack to enable it to be carried by hand when desired.

1944 pattern.

This was a rectangular bag approximately 13in by 2in by 9in deep, with a flap secured by a single strap and buckle. The interior was lined with a light waterproof material. Two buckles were provided on the back for attachment to the brace ends, and a loop at the top, acting by way of a handle, enabled the haversack to be carried by hand when desired.

Brace Attachments

1937 pattern.

These were interchangeable and were used only for sets of web equipment adapted for officers, certain warrant officers, NCOs and those personnel armed with a pistol, or ranks not carrying arms. They consisted of a 'gate' slide for attachment to the waist-belt, with narrow webbing fitted at the top to carry a buckle for the brace, below which a link was provided to receive the free end of the brace.

1944 pattern.

These too were interchangeable. Each brace attachment consisted of 1in wide webbing doubled and sewn to give rigidity, two 2in wire double hooks for attachment to the waist-belt and a four-bar buckle for the brace at the top, below which was a link to receive the free end of the brace.

The Pistol Case for RAC Personnel

1937 pattern.

This was a woven article finished to accommodate the 0.38in revolver. It was lined with smooth material and had a narrow strap with snap fastener for securing the revolver in the case. Positioned vertically down the front of the case was a narrow tube to take the metal cleaning rod, whilst stitched diagonally across the face of the pistol case was a strip of webbing fashioned to form six raised loops each designed to take one round of 0.38in pistol ammunition. There was a wide supporting strap fixed to the back of the case which had a narrow end which engaged a buckle fitted to the supporting strap; this formed a loop for suspending the case from the waist-belt. At the barrel end of the pistol case there was a detachable strap, fitted horizontally, which when tied around the wearer's right leg retained the case close to the latter.

1942 modification to the 1937 pattern case.

On 19 December 1942, Army Council Instruction No. 2662 of 1942 announced that the RAC web pistol cases had been found unsuitable for wear by RAC personnel. A decision had been made whereby all RAC pistol cases in the possession of RAC personnel were to be modified under unit arrangements as described below, in order to permit the pistol to be carried in its case on the waist-belt.

The two top rows of stitching where the 3in wide suspending strap was fixed to the back of the case had to be carefully removed. The strap was cut through ½in above the mouth, turned under, and the top row re-sewn by hand with strong thread. This produced a fair-way for the belt.

The Compass Pocket

1937 pattern.

This was similar in all respects to the ammunition pouch for 0.38in pistol ammunition except that it was lined with felt to protect the compass.

1944 pattern.

Similar in all respects to the 1944 pattern pistol ammunition pouch except that it was lined with felt and had a fibre stiffening in order to protect the compass.

The Pistol Ammunition Pouch

1937 pattern.

This was a woven article designed to accommodate the 0.38in pistol ammunition; it was provided with a box like lid secured by a snap fastener. Two double hooks were provided for attachment to the waist-belt, and on the back of the pouch there was a narrow webbing loop positioned at the top and a loop of thin webbing at the bottom. These were provided to enable the pouch to be worn in an assembly rather than just being fitted on to the waist-belt.

1944 pattern.

This was a woven article designed to carry pistol ammunition. It was provided with a box type lid secured by a quick-release fastener. In the flange at the bottom of the pouch were fitted two grommets for attachment to the pistol case, and on the back of the pouch there were also two vertical web loops for carrying the pouch on the belt as an alternative position. It had a horizontal loop fitted to pass over the brace attachment.

The 1937 Pattern Web Utility Pouches

These were rectangular in shape and were each of a size large enough to accommodate three Bren gun magazines, or two anti-tank rifle magazines, or a number of grenades, or three 2in mortar bombs, or a water-bottle, or small arms ammunition. One pouch of each pair was carried in front of the wearer and was provided with a narrow strap with buckle which passed through a loop on the back of the other pouch. This served as a retaining strap to be fastened round the soldier's waist. Each pouch was provided with a 'box' lid, closed by a snap fastener. At the top of each pouch there was a buckle fitted for attachment of the yoke for carrying over one shoulder.

The 1908 Large Pack

This pack, used as part of the 1937 pattern web equipment, consisted of a rectangular sack, the dimensions of which were approximately 15in by 13in by 4½in. It was open at the top and was closed by a cover secured by two narrow straps and buckles. Weather flaps were provided which were folded down under the cover. Two web loops were fitted to the underside of the bottom of the pack, through which the supporting straps were passed, and a short, 2in tab was fixed to each of the upper corners on the side nearest the wearer's back, together with small buckles to which the upper ends of the supporting straps were secured.

The 1944 Pattern Machete Sheath

This was made entirely of selvedged webbings and was constructed to give adequate reinforcement. An internal 'channel' was formed down one side to enable the machete to be easily inserted. The sheath had a sheradized brass mouthpiece fitted, and on the back there was a 'hanger' hook for attachment to the grommets in the waist-belt or, when desired, to the flap of the haversack.

The 1937 Pattern Yoke

This item was an integrally woven strap which had a wide portion for the shoulder and was reversible fore and aft.

The Webbing Haversack

1937 pattern.

This consisted of a rectangular bag approximately 11in by 9½in by 4in and had a flap secured by two small straps and buckles. The interior was longitudinally divided by means of a partition, which was in turn connected to the front of the bag by another small partition to form two front compartments of equal size; these compartments were intended to contain the water-bottle in its carrier and the rectangular mess tins. On the back of the haversack, near the top, were fitted two tabs for attachment to the shoulder straps, and on the base two small buckles were fitted for attachment to the diagonal portion of the straps. Weather flaps were provided which folded in underneath the flaps.

1944 pattern.

The dimensions of the 1944 pattern haversack were approximately 8in by 6in by 10in deep, and it had a flap secured by two small straps and quick-release buckles. Side weather flaps were provided, and in each of these an eyelet was fitted to enable the flaps to be secured, if necessary, by a piece of string or cord. On each side was fitted a pocket approximately 6in by 2in by 8½in deep, with a flap secured by a quick-release fastener; one pocket was designed large enough to take the mess tin and the other pocket rations or small kit.

A three-bar buckle was fitted to each side of the haversack, for attachment to the ends of the braces when it was necessary for the haversack to be carried on the side. On the back were fitted two 2in tabs for attachment to the shoulder straps, and two loops were provided to tuck away the spare ends of the straps. On the base were two three-bar buckles for securing the ¾in diagonal straps forming part of the shoulder straps. For carrying the bedding roll or blanket two long, ¾in wide straps with quick-release buckles were fitted to the base; sleeves were provided to enable these straps to be stowed away when not in use.

A chape with two grommets was provided, together with a horizontal strap (a portion of which was reinforced) which was fitted with a quick-release buckle; both were attached to the flap, and a small buckle chape and tabs, fixed to the bottom edge, could be used for the carriage of tools. When carrying the shovel the strap with the quick-release buckle was wound twice around the shaft, and when carrying a pick the reinforced portion of the strap was passed first round the head of the pick then round the shaft. At each bottom back corner of the haversack a strap was sewn, one strap having a three-bar buckle and the other a tip; these were passed through one or both of the web loops on the back of the basic pouches and connected round the body in front, and were particularly useful when troops were required to crawl. They prevented the sagging of heavily laden pouches, or they retained the haversack in position when quick action was anticipated.

The back and base of the haversack were lined with waterproof cloth in order to prevent penetration of moisture from the wearer's body.

The 1944 Pattern Rucksack

The 1944 pattern rucksack was a substitute for the 1908 pattern large pack used as part of the 1937 pattern equipment. It was made of lightweight duck and measured approximately 14in by 6in by 18in deep fully open. The main compartment had a kit bag type of fastening. Large eyelets were equally spaced in the top hem and a draw cord was provided. It had a large closing flap with a flat pocket on the underside 8in deep and was fitted with two partitions and a flap secured by quick-release fasteners. The large flap was closed by two ¾in web straps and quick-release buckles. A large pocket about 10in by 3in by 12in deep was provided on the front of the rucksack, and there were pockets 6in by 3in by 12in deep on each side. All three pockets had 'hooded' flaps with quick-release fasteners. The inner faces of the main closing flap and the centre pocket, as well as the inside of the hooded flap of this pocket, were all lined with a lightweight waterproof material which allowed clean and dirty articles to be kept separate. The rucksack was made large enough to hold the complete field scale of clothing and necessaries, including a spare pair of boots and a suit of Battle-Dress. It was intended that the rucksack should normally be carried in unit transport.

Webbing tabs and loops were fitted to the back and buckles on the base for the attachment of the shoulder straps previously described. Straps for an entrenching tool, similar to those on the 1944 pattern haversack, were provided. On each side of the back wall of the rucksack three 1in 'D' rings were fitted, equally spaced, to enable the rucksack to be secured to the 'Manpack Carrier, GS' when required; a waterproof bag was also provided

Blanco webbing cleaner in powder form (top) and cake form (bottom).

Right: A 1908 Pattern haversack worn by troops from the 5th Bde., 2nd Infantry Division, marching to Salisbury Plain for exercises; 30 August 1933. This was the first occasion that the Army adopted the 'revolutionary' formation of marching in three columns, which was introduced in response to the increase in the volume of traffic. *Far right:* A Scots Guardsman in battle order.

which was primarily designed to keep articles carried in the rucksack (or haversack) dry. By rolling over and fastening the opening, the bag could also be used as a piece of flotation equipment.

Cotton Bandoliers

As an additional means of carrying .303in rifle ammunition, bandoliers manufactured from drab coloured cotton material capable of containing 50 rounds were issued to troops requiring them. They were cheap to produce and were issued, factory filled, already containing the ammunition. When empty they were either discarded or, time permitting, returned to unit stores.

Authorized Cleaner for Use on Web Equipment

War Office approved cleaners for use on web equipment were supplied in two types: (a) powder for use on web equipment, web anklets and the service respirator haversack, and (b) block cleaner for use on web equipment and web anklets only. The cleaner, in blocks, conformed to the War Office standard colour and test, but its waterproofing quality was inferior to the powder; for this reason its use on the respirator haversack was prohibited. Neither form of cleaner was allowed to

be applied to the chin-straps of steel helmets, which, if they became dirty, had to be washed in warm, soapy water, rinsed in clear water and allowed to dry naturally.

The cleaner was made available to units and troops through the NAAFI. This was necessary in order to ensure that only those products of the correct shade which had passed the War Office performance test were available for use by the troops, and the control was also essential for regulating under war emergency conditions the supply of raw materials and their packaging.

The NAAFI supplied the cleaning powder in 56lb containers at the cost of 9d. per lb, so as to economize in the use of small containers. This enabled the requirements of units to be obtained in bulk for refilling the individual sprinkler containers available to the soldier from his initial purchase. The cost of such bulk supply was recovered from the soldiers under regimental arrangements.

Officers commanding units were ordered to prohibit the use of cleaners from other sources of supply as well as other unauthorized practices such as scrubbing webbing and using bleach or chlorine powder, which rotted the webbing fabric, or any other colouring mediums, such as service colour paints, camouflage emulsions and such like.

3. ANTI-GAS EQUIPMENT

War Gases

Gas is a chemical weapon relying on its poisonous effects and, like other weapons of war, its object is to kill or incapacitate. The Germans did not use gas during the 1939–45 war, but on their surrender it was found that they held large stocks of both old and new gases and some of these were ready for use in bombs and shells. The fact that the Germans did not resort to gas warfare nevertheless did not diminish the fear the Allies held that, despite the Geneva Convention, gas could have been used at any moment.

To counter the possible effects of a gas attack all troops of the British Army (as well as the other armed forces, the police and civil defence forces and the civilian population) were issued with a service respirator (in the case of civilians with a civilian respirator), as well as other items of anti-gas equipment which are dealt with elsewhere.

Based on the experiences suffered and gained during the Great War and the subsequent experimentation undertaken, the following facts concerning war gases and gas warfare formed the basis for the British Army's anti-gas measures.

The term 'gas' used during the Second World War, and especially during the Great War, was applied to any chemical substance, whether solid, liquid or vapour, which when released produced poisonous or irritant effects on the human body. Such substances were generally liberated into the air as vapour or irritant smokes. They mixed with the air and produced their harmful effects upon any unprotected persons (or animals) who were exposed to this atmosphere. In the case of certain of the chemical substances, such as mustard gas, a serious effect was also caused by direct contact of the human body with the liquid itself or with objects which had become contaminated by the liquid.

It was usual to divide war gases into two main groups, 'non-persistent' and 'persistent'. When liberated into the air, non-persistent gases formed clouds which drifted along with the wind, gradually mixing with larger quantities of air and so becoming less dangerous. Examples of such substances were chlorine, phosgene and the irritant smokes produced from certain compounds of arsenic. Persistent gases, for example mustard gas and many of the tear gases were usually liquids which evaporated slowly, giving off dangerous vapour. The ground and any other objects on which the liquid fell continued to give off vapour until the liquid had entirely evaporated or until steps had been taken to render it ineffective. In the case of mustard gas or other blister gases, contact with the contaminated ground or objects caused

skin burns until decontamination had been effected; even walking over contaminated ground was dangerous and was to be avoided.

The essential difference between the non-persistent gases and the persistent gases that could have been used as gas-bombs during an air raid or as gas shells fired by artillery was that the non-persistent gas would have produced a cloud which would be carried away by the wind, whereas bombs or shells containing persistent gases would explode and splatter liquid around the point of burst, the affected ground requiring special treatment ('decontamination') to render it safe.

The division of gases into two main groups was convenient because, as soon as the class of a gas had been determined, it was possible to decide whether or not the area in which the gas had been liberated required special treatment. Gases could also be classified according to the effects which they produced on the human body. These groups were designated by the following names.

Tear gas. Any eye irritant which even in very small amounts had an immediate effect upon the eyes, causing intense smarting, a profuse flow of tears and spasms of the eyelids (which generally made it very difficult to see) was described as a tear gas. In pure air the effects of the vapour soon wore off and no damage was caused to the eyes, though the liquid of a persistent tear gas could cause permanent injury. These gases were often called 'lachrymators'.

Nose irritant gas. Irritant smokes produced from certain arsenical compounds were in this class, but though they produced intense pain in the nose, throat and breathing passages during exposure to the gas these effects soon passed off in fresh air.

Lung irritant gas. An irritant gas which attacked the breathing passages and lungs. Chlorine and phosgene were examples of this type, and produced death if breathed in sufficiently large quantities. These gases were sometimes called 'choking gases'.

Blister gases. These substances, of which mustard gas was a typical example, caused intense irritation or burning of the skin according to the amount of gas which had come into contact with the affected part; in severe cases deep and extensive blisters were caused. These gases were known also as 'vesicants'.

No immediate pain was felt on contact with mustard gas in the solid, liquid or vapour form, but the effects became apparent a few hours later. Mustard gas also attacked the eyes and lungs, but in these cases also there was considerable delay before the symptoms were noticed, and it was this absence of immediate effect which constituted one of the greatest dangers of mustard gas. The need for protection was very often not appreciated until too late.

The effects produced by any war gas depended on the amount of gas involved and the length of time a person was exposed to it, and the stronger the gas the greater was the possible injury produced in a given time. It was not, however, to be assumed that small quantities of gas would always cause injury. In the case of gases which injured the lungs, a certain quantity had to be breathed in before any harm was effected. A person working hard breathed a much greater volume of air than a person sitting still, so that, if both were exposed to the same concentration of gas, the person working would suffer the greater injury. Only under exceptional conditions was there likely to have been sufficient gas present in the air to render one or two breaths dangerous.

The respirators which were produced before and during the Second World War, of which the service respirator as described here was the type issued to the British armed forces, were designed to give protection against all types of gas which were likely to be used as war gases. They were not, however, intended to afford protection against other gases which may have been encountered in industrial processes or in everyday life (they did not, for example, protect against carbon monoxide which is present in coal gas, exhaust gases from motor cars and gases from sewers, ammonia or similar toxic and noxious gases and vapours), and were therefore not to be relied upon for protection in the presence of peacetime dangers. In any event, they were incapable of rendering the wearer safe in situations where the danger arose from a deficiency of oxygen. Care had always to be taken in order not to damage the respirators by careless handling, or their efficiency would have been impaired.

The Service Respirator

The service respirator was the pattern of respirator issued to the fighting services. The protection it afforded was of the same kind as in the case of the civilian and civilian duty respirators, but the duration of its efficiency against gas was longer. It was designed to allow the wearer the greatest possible freedom of movement and the maximum use of his faculties. The weight of the container, for instance, was carried on the chest and not on the facepiece, and special attention was paid to the prevention of dimming of the eyepieces.

The service respirator was carried in a waterproof canvas haversack, the main part of which was divided into two compartments, one for the container and the other for the facepiece and anti-dimming outfit. The haversack had a canvas sling and a length of whipcord attached.

The facepiece was made of rubber, sometimes covered on the outside with khaki coloured stockinet, and was moulded to fit closely to the face; the gas-tightness of the respirator was dependent upon the closeness of this fit. It was held in position by elasticated bands attached to the rubber facepiece which passed round the back of the wearer's head.

The elasticated straps were provided with buckles so that the lengths could be adjusted to suit each individual. As the facepiece was made in five sizes − extra large, large, normal, small and extra small − few difficulties were experienced in obtaining a satisfactory fit for an adult soldier. Specially moulded facepieces were designed for those troops with abnormally hollow cheeks and temples and were issued to those who wore spectacles.

Left: A trooper from the 3rd Hussars wearing a gas mask and manning the new Bren light machine gun. The gas alarm rattle was used to simulate the noise of gunfire to save on ammunition. This soldier was one of 50,000 who took part in the biggest-ever Army manoeuvres, which were held in parts of Hampshire, Wiltshire and Sussex over a four-day period in September 1935.

The separate eyepieces were made of splinterless glass. In the later patterns of respirator these glasses were removed by unscrewing to allow decontamination of the facepiece by boiling, which would otherwise have damaged the glass.

A valve holder (a metal mount fixed in the front of the facepiece) connected the facepiece to the flexible tube and contained the outlet valve. Air was drawn in from the container, where all traces of war gases were removed, through the valve holder and along passages in the rubber wall of the facepiece to an inlet between the eyepieces. As a result of this arrangement the cool, dry air that entered the facepiece passed across the eyepieces and so reduced the dimming caused by condensation from expired air. As the wearer stopped breathing in, the small metal inlet valve in the neck of the container shut and locked a column of clean fresh air in the connecting tube. The air breathed out passed directly through the outlet valve to the outer atmosphere. This valve was designed to allow for clear and audible speech.

The flexible tube was made of rubber covered with stockinet. It was corrugated to give flexibility and to prevent its collapsing when bent. The ends were wired on to the valve holder at one end and to the neck of the container at the other. The container was a tinned iron box which contained activated charcoal for the absorption of gases such as phosgene and mustard gas, and a particular filter to prevent the passage of finely divided smokes like the arsenical gases.

An anti-dimming outfit was provided which consisted of a cylindrical metal box containing anti-dimming compound and a piece of cloth. When properly applied this compound caused the moisture condensed on the eyepieces to form a clear film which did not interfere with the wearer's vision.

The 'Alert' and 'Slung' Positions.

The haversack could be carried in either the 'slung' or the 'alert' position. When in the 'slung' position the haversack rested against the left side of the body with the canvas sling over the right shoulder. There were two methods of attaining the 'alert' position. In the standard method the sling was fastened behind the wearer's shoulders by means of the whipcord which was attached to one corner of the haversack, with the haversack resting on the front of the wearer's chest. In the alternative 'alert' position the sling was shortened by engaging the tab on the sling with the 'S' hook. The haversack then remained well up on the wearer's chest, supported from the neck, and was secured to the body by means of the whipcord.

Carrying the respirator.

The carrying of the anti-gas service respirator during the 1939–45 war was closely linked with the carrying of arms, ammunition and the steel helmet, all of which are dealt with in other places in this book (see pages 255 and 219).

On 3 July 1940 ACI 669 announced that officers and other ranks were to carry respirators on all occasions when on parade wearing equip-ment and whenever they were not in the vicinity of their quarters or place of duty. Respirators had always to be taken by all ranks when they were absent from their normal station, either when on leave or when on duty. The anti-gas service respirator had to be worn for inspection and for training purposes at least once a week.

The following year (ACI 124 dated 25 January 1941) instructions were still being published with regard to the respirator. They still had to be carried by all ranks, including personnel of the women's organizations, when (a) on parade wearing equipment, (b) whenever they left the vicinity of their quarters or place of duty, whether on leave or otherwise or (c) whether in uniform or in plain clothes, and the respirators were still required to be worn once a week for both inspection and training purposes.

In 1942 it was announced that in future the anti-gas service respirator was to be carried by officers, soldiers and ATS auxiliaries on the following occasions.

1. At all times when wearing field service marching order (FSMO), unless otherwise ordered by the commander. A commander was allowed to decide, after due consideration of the local military situation, whether the improvement in fighting efficiency obtained by the men under him by their not carrying the respirator outweighed the risk this action involved.

2. At any time when ordered by the CO to do so.

3. On piquets and guards, other than ceremonial ones.

4. After orders notifying that a state of emergency had been issued.

All officers, soldiers or auxiliaries absent from their stations had to take their respirators with them, but they were not required to carry them except on those occasions detailed above.

By mid-1945 (ACI 816 dated 11 July 1945) the need by those personnel stationed in the United Kingdom and proceeding on leave to carry the respirator no longer existed. However, these instructions did not affect the carrying of the respirator, or arms, ammunition or other equipment, by military personnel who were travelling on drafts, being transferred or on courses of instruction, etc.

Sandbag covers.

On 25 April 1942, two and a half years into the war, instructions were issued (ACI 893 of 1942) ordering the construction, under unit arrangements, of hessian covers made from sandbags for wear over the service respirator haversack. These covers were to be worn over the haversack in an effort to reduce the amount of wear and tear inflicted on it and were to be worn at all times other than on ceremonial parades and when walking out. The method of manufacture for these covers was given as follows.

1. Cut across one side of the bag at a point 19in from the bottom.

2. Cut across the other side of the bag at a point 13in from the bottom.

3. Sever the edges of the bag between the two cuts.

Each portion provided one cover with a 6in flap. The cover which was open at both ends was required to be stitched up at the end opposite the flap. No buttons were attached, but slits had to be made for the small 'Ds' on either side of the Mark VI haversack, or for the large button and whipcord on the Mark VII haversack. Five months later further instructions were issued (ACI 1877 dated 5 September 1942) stating that only unproofed sandbags were to be used for the purpose of providing covers for the respirator haversack.

Head-harness.

The head-harness of the anti-gas service respirator was a series of ¾in wide elastic webbing straps. The head-harness of respirators which had been in constant use for some considerable time became insufficiently strong to ensure a gas-tight fit of the respirator facepiece, and commanding officers were required to ensure that periodical inspections of anti-gas respirators were carried out to ensure that all head-harness straps were functioning correctly. Replacement of the elasticated webbing straps was regarded as a unit repair.

Marking the haversack.

Army Council Instruction No. 1279 dated 23 October 1940 ordered that all markings on anti-gas respirator haversacks which denoted the name of the owner's regiment or corps had to be barred out (obliterated). For this purpose haversacks that had been stencilled with black paint were barred out with PFU black marking paint, and any markings made with printer's ink had to be barred out with printer's ink. Although not mentioned in this ACI, the user's regimental number, his name and his rank were presumably allowed to remain.

ACI 338 dated 12 March 1941 and ACI 1667 dated 12 August 1942 both reiterated the security aspect of only showing the user's regimental number (or personal number in the case of officers) and his or her rank and name stencilled in black PFU paint inside the flap of the

facepiece and container compartment of the haversack. The fibre identity disc attached to the connecting tube of the respirator also bore similar particulars of identification.

In the case of the Home Guard, personal markings were made on the inside of the respirator haversack and were limited to the member's name and initials only.

The 1943 Light Pattern Anti-Gas Respirator and Haversack Carrier

On 27 March 1943 Army Council Instruction No. 520 announced that a new anti-gas respirator of a self-contained type with the filter container screwed into the left side of the facepiece was being gradually introduced throughout the Army to replace the existing general service anti-gas respirator. The new respirator was known as 'Respirator, Anti-Gas, Light'.

Like the general service respirator, the light respirator afforded complete protection against existing war gases, but the filter container, being of smaller dimensions, did not have quite so long a life when used continuously in gas as did the previous Type E container. However, the filter container of the new respirator was easily replaced when necessary.

The facepiece was made of black rubber which was moulded to fit closely to the wearer's face. The fit of the respirator was all-important and this was achieved by the use of six elasticated and adjustable head-bands which were attached to the edges of the rubber facepiece, passed round the back of the wearer's head and were sewn to the four corners of a small canvas 'pad'. The six elasticated head straps were each provided with prongless, self-gripping metal buckles and metal runners. This allowed for straps to be adjusted to fit the head of the individual and thus provide a gas-tight fit of the rubber facepiece.

The separate eyepieces were made of splinterless glass and, being screwed into position, were also removable. An anti-dimming outfit (Mark VI) was provided together with a packet of six anti-gas eyeshields (Mark III), three clear and three tinted. The anti-dimming outfit, which consisted of a small, circular, flat tin with a screw-on lid containing a specially treated piece of cloth, was housed inside the haversack carrier at the base inside a small pocket. The anti-gas eyeshields, separated by a sheet of folded white paper and held inside a thick strong cardboard wallet, were lodged inside the carrier in an internal pocket built on to the back wall of the haversack.

In order to prevent seepage into the filter container when there was a risk of the respirator being immersed in water, two cork sealing plugs joined by a short length of tape were provided with each respirator. When the respirator was carried with the filter container screwed into the facepiece, the cork plugs were normally fitted, the smaller one into the outer opening of the metal container and the other into the inside of the container mount within the facepiece. When not in use the plugs were carried in the haversack carrier and secured by passing the tape joining them under the flap of the canvas pocket provided for the anti-dim outfit (in early issues of haversack) or under the loop provided to house the haversack sling (in later issues). These cork plugs were not provided in the early issues of the light respirator.

As the container fitted to the left side of the facepiece interfered with the use of a rifle by personnel who were accustomed to fire from the left shoulder, all such personnel were required to retain the former general service respirator until such time as special light respirators in three sizes with the filter container fitted on the right-hand side became available.

The light respirator was marked by the attachment of an identification disc to a length of whipcord passed round the container mount on the facepiece. This disc was marked in the same manner as those used on the general service respirator.

The drab green canvas haversack carrier was 9¾in high, 5¼in across the front and 5in deep. It had a canvas 'lid' secured by a quick-release fastener and a metal ring attached to each side positioned just above a small canvas pocket. The soft woven carrying strap, which passed through these rings, was adjustable, its overall length being approximately 53in.

ACI 520 carried a warning that the haversack was not to be scrubbed with soap and water or treated with khaki equipment cleaner as both had a deleterious effect on the special finish of the cloth. Mud on the haversack had to be removed with a dry brush.

The process of equipping all Army personnel with the new 'light' type of anti-gas respirator in place of the general service respirator was a gradual one, and issues were carried out in accordance with a system of priorities. Units that were low on the priority list for the issue of the light respirator had to retain their general service respirators for as long as they were able to be maintained from the items that had been returned to stores by units which had received the light respirator at high priority.

Goggles and Anti-Gas Eye Shields

Goggles issued to MT drivers before the war were on the scale of one pair with case (a small oblong cardboard box) for each driver of 15cwt or 8cwt trucks with 'half' type windscreens. These goggles were originally fitted with plain glass but were eventually replaced by stocks of goggles with splinterless glass.

A modified type of anti-gas eyeshield that served the dual purpose of excluding dust and protecting against gas spray was approved for issue to crews of armoured fighting vehicles (ACI 1199 dated 6 September 1944). Designated 'Eyeshields, Anti-Dust and Anti-Gas, Mark I', they took the place of the anti-gas eyeshields previously worn by personnel composing the crews of armoured fighting vehicles. The scale of issue for the new eyeshields was the same as for the previous type except that the cardboard wallets for the anti-gas and anti-dust eyeshields contained four untinted and two tinted eyeshields.

Consequent upon the issue of the new pattern eyeshields, MT goggles were no longer required by personnel of crews of AFVs; these goggles were withdrawn and returned to the RAOC immediately the replacement of all former anti-gas eyeshields had been completed.

By June 1945 the general use of these anti-gas, anti-dust eyeshields was freely permitted for motor-cyclists and MT drivers (ACI 749 dated 27 June 1945). It was suggested that the tinted variety be worn to protect against glare, but they were not to be used for looking directly into the sun or for use against glare reflected from snow.

Camouflage Patterned Anti-Gas Capes

The subject of the adoption of certain items of camouflage equipment by the British Army for use in the field had been raised as early as 21 April 1939.[1] On 19 June 1940 notification was made (ACI 617 of 1940) that stocks of camouflaged anti-gas capes had become available. The official designation of this new pattern of cape was 'Cape, Anti-Gas, No. 1, Camouflaged'.

Until sufficient supplies of the camouflaged cape were obtained to permit its general issue, priority was given to formations in the United Kingdom prior to their joining expeditionary forces and, within such formations, to infantry units. They were to be equipped first with the new pattern cape, but both the old type and the camouflaged pattern were worn side by side within formations, although efforts were made to equip whole units with one pattern only as far as possible. In expeditionary forces, overseas garrisons and other theatres the camouflage capes were taken into use as and when stocks became available.

Quick-release attachment.

In September 1940 it was decided to adopt a quick-release attachment to enable the anti-gas cape to be brought from the 'rolled' to the 'worn' position as speedily as possible in order to afford protection against an air spray gas attack.

[1]Reference War Office letter 43/Training/2579 (SD2) of that date.

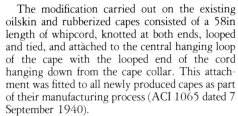

The modification carried out on the existing oilskin and rubberized capes consisted of a 58in length of whipcord, knotted at both ends, looped and tied, and attached to the central hanging loop of the cape with the looped end of the cord hanging down from the cape collar. This attachment was fitted to all newly produced capes as part of their manufacturing process (ACI 1065 dated 7 September 1940).

Wearing of anti-gas capes.

On 12 March 1941 ACI 336 of 1941 announced that anti-gas capes could in future be worn not only for protection against gas but also as rainproofs· at the discretion of local commanders, subject to the following conditions.

1. Precautions had to be taken to ensure that capes were not damaged by unduly rough wear; for example, they were not to be worn by troops loading or unloading heavy stores, or when digging, nor should they be worn by men driving or travelling in mechanical vehicles.

2. Capes were repaired when torn in the manner as laid down in *Equipment Regulations, Part I, 1932*, Appendix 37A.

3. Capes were not to be rolled when wet: they had to be dried in a natural temperature and not in front of fires or near stoves.

4. When not in use the capes were, whenever possible, left hanging up.

These instructions were reiterated on 27 May 1942 by ACI 1131 of 1942. This added the information that in order to conserve rubber the anti-gas capes were to be worn as far as possible in lieu of groundsheets. However, by 1943 the situation with regard to the stocks of groundsheets had improved to the point where the use of anti-gas capes as rainproofs was no longer necessary. ACI 867 of 1943, para. 4, withdrew from local commanders the authority to permit these capes being used as rainproofs.

ACI 204 dated 9 February 1944 and headed 'Clothing – Use of Capes, Anti-Gas, as Rainproofs during Training', reversed the situation, albeit in a modified fashion. These instructions drew attention to the fact that in assault operations certain personnel, or in some cases complete units, did not carry both anti-gas capes and groundsheets. In order that training for assault operations could be performed in the most realistic conditions, authority was given for the use during such training of anti-gas capes as rainproofs. This authority, which was exercised by local commanders, extended only to such units or personnel who did not carry groundsheets in assault operations, and it was limited to actual periods of training for such operations only. A rejoinder was added reminding the troops that anti-gas capes were easily damaged and that every effort had to be made to prevent undue wear and tear. The general use of anti-gas capes as rainproofs was not permitted since groundsheets at that time were readily available for that purpose.

Carrying and use.

On 25 March 1942 Army Council Instruction No. 627 of 1942 announced that in future the

Top right: Haversack Carrier for the 1943 Light Pattern Anti-Gas Respirator is shown here worn over the left hip of this paratrooper.
Centre right: The 1943 Light Pattern Anti-Gas Respirator, which was about half the weight and bulk of the former pattern. Troops earmarked for service overseas were the first to be issued with this new item.
Below: MT goggles worn by the driver of a Bren Carrier.
Below right: Clear anti-gas goggles worn by a member of the East Yorkshire Regiment.

anti-gas cape could be carried in any one of the following four positions as ordered by the local commander, having regard to the then existing circumstances and in accordance with the items of equipment which were being worn at the time, such as battle order, marching order etc.

1. The 'worn' position as then taught.

2. The 'rolled quick release' position as in use at that time. This was considered a convenient method of carrying the cape when equipment was not worn.

3. Rolled and carried inside the equipment haversack in place either of the water bottle, which was then required to be worn on the soldier's right side, or of the groundsheet if room could be found for this item in unit motor transport. If the latter course were adopted, the gas cape was allowed to be worn to give protection against rain except in the case of men digging, loading or unloading heavy stores or riding in mechanical vehicles. The cape had to be folded to a width of 11in, with tapes and whipcord inside, and then rolled, and it had to be placed in the haversack on top of all other items.

4. Rolled and attached to the back of the equipment belt by means of the tapes. This was a convenient method of carrying the cape when the haversack was not worn. When fitted in this way the cape had to be rolled in the manner in use at that time.

Painting of badges of rank.

The wearing of anti-gas capes obscured all forms of rank insignia, and as a move to overcome this problem instructions were issued on 28 March 1942 (ACI 647 of 1942) to the effect that in future all anti-gas capes were to be marked with the appropriate badges of rank of the individuals to whom the capes had been issued. The badges had to be neatly painted with detector paint No. 1 (green colour) on both sleeves of the cape, over a portion of the area previously treated with detector paint No. 2 (khaki colour). In the case of an officer the appropriate badges were painted on each shoulder and in the case of warrant officers or NCOs on the upper portion of each sleeve. The badges of a warrant officer Class I or II were not used but were represented by the appropriate letters of rank, e.g. RSM or BSM.

The painting of these badges was carried out under unit arrangements. No stencils were issued for the painting on of stars, chevrons or letters, which therefore had to be executed freehand, but stencils were supplied on demand for the painting on of crowns. In April 1943 further instructions were issued which replaced the use of detector paint No. 2 (khaki colour) with bituminous emulsion paint, SCC (Standard Colour Code) No. 14, which was the quality of paint then in use on 'A' and 'B' vehicles as a gas detector.

Gas detection painted sleeves.

War Office letter 57/General/133 (S.D.9(c)), dated 21 February 1940, gave instructions for all units to paint a portion of each sleeve of all anti-gas capes with gas detector paint No. 2. This khaki paint changed colour when it came in contact with

various types of war gases and because of this property was ideally suited for use on military vehicles and on special detector panels erected in the grounds of military, police and government establishments, and also for individual use on anti-gas clothing.

By April 1943 the threat of a gas attack had receded somewhat, and the War Office issued instructions (ACI 670 dated 24 April 1943) that in order to conserve stocks of detector paint the practice of painting portions of the sleeves of anti-gas capes was to be held in abeyance, presumably for the duration of the war.

Anti-gas capes for stretcher-bearers.

In 1942 the existing design of anti-gas cape was modified for use by all personnel included in the War Establishment as stretcher-bearers. This modification consisted of a number of press-studs which were attached to the hem of the skirt in such a manner that when they were fastened between the wearer's legs a divided skirt was formed. This modification was adopted primarily for the following reasons.

1. It prevented the skirt of the bearer's cape, if contaminated, from becoming draped over the head of the patient when the stretcher was lifted.

2. It provided protection both for the seat of the bearer against the heel of his boot when kneeling or squatting and for his knees.

To identify these modified capes from the existing anti-gas capes, the modified patterns were marked STRETCHER-BEARER immediately beneath the three five-pointed stars normally placed on all anti-gas capes.

Anti-Gas Hoods

The issuing of anti-gas hoods, designed to protect the wearer against blister-gas vapour and part of the issue anti-gas protective clothing, was discontinued in 1942 by authority of ACI 2695 of 1942. In place of the protection afforded by these hoods, anti-gas ointments of all types later than the No. 1 type were issued to be applied to the face and neck. These ointments were able to be applied without injury or irritation to the wearer's skin and were supposed to afford the same protection as the anti-gas hood. However, it was stated that after several applications of the No. 2 ointment irritation to the skin was likely to occur, and this ointment was not to be used in this way more frequently than was necessary.

Anti-gas hoods at the time of this ACI that were held by units had to be returned to the RAOC where they were reissued for waterproof purposes, such as in lieu of sou'westers, until existing stocks were exhausted. Stocks of anti-gas hoods held by stations abroad and not required for this purpose were utilized or disposed of under local arrangements. Units and drafts that were awaiting embarkation and which had already been completed to the authorized scale of hoods retained these items until arrival at the destination, when they were withdrawn.

Anti-Gas Gloves

In order to economize in the use of rubber, the

production of rubber anti-gas gloves was superseded by the introduction in September 1942 (ACI 1907 dated 9 September 1942) of oil-skin anti-gas gloves. Canvas overmittens were worn with both the old type rubber gloves and the new oil-skin type by those personnel engaged on all types of work except intricate work which would have been impossible to perform if overmittens were worn.

Anti-Gas Overboots

In September 1942 (ACI 1907 dated 9 September 1942), it was announced that the production of the 'Overboot, Anti-Gas, Rubber, No. 1' was to cease. In an effort to economize in the use of rubber, overboots No. 2, made from oil-skin, were introduced in their place.

Anti-Gas Curtains

As part of the scale of issue to all ranks of personal anti-gas equipment, it was decided on 10 August 1940 (ACI 891 of 1940) to include an improved version of the anti-gas curtain for wear with the steel helmet.

The original No. 1 pattern anti-gas curtain, which was manufactured from plain green oilskin cloth and fitted only around the brim of the steel helmet to hang down around the wearer's neck, was superseded by an improved design. Known as 'Curtain, Anti-Gas, No. 2', this new pattern was made in camouflaged oilskin fabric and covered the whole of the steel helmet whilst also affording protection to the back of the neck. Stocks of the former, obsolescent pattern curtains were required to be used up before the issue of the new pattern could take place, but where available the camouflaged pattern (No. 2) was issued to operational units in preference to the No. 1 pattern. As in the case of anti-gas capes, the curtains were issued to individuals if it were considered necessary; otherwise they were held in unit charge for issue when required. In order to save on wear and tear the helmet curtains were only worn when required for anti-gas purposes.

4. MISCELLANEOUS EQUIPMENT

Body Armour

In addition to the prewar and wartime efforts made to protect the personnel of the British Armed Forces against the possible use of war gases, protection against gun fire, shrapnel and fragmentation wounds by the use of body armour came under serious consideration during the Second World War. The possibility of the British Army adopting some form of body armour for the personal protection of certain categories of troops, namely those exposed to high risk, had been under consideration by the Medical Research Council as early as October 1940. It was felt that a lightweight 'suit' of armour of not more than 4lb was required for general use by infantry, air crews, etc. and a heavier 'suit' of up to 10lb for use by certain static troops such as anti-aircraft and naval gun crews.

In February 1941, on the recommendation of the Body Protection Committee of the Medical Research Council, and in preparation for its general use, trials were begun on a set of body armour. This set or 'suit' of armour consisted of three specially shaped, 1mm manganese steel plates (the same material as that used for the British Mark I steel helmet) and which together weighed 2¾lb. The first plate, worn over the front of the chest to protect the heart, the great blood vessel and lung roots, measured 9in wide by 8in deep; the second plate, 14in wide by 4in deep, was worn horizontally over the lower part of back of the chest below the shoulder blades in order to protect the base of the lungs, the liver and, by way

of the stemlike portion projecting upwards for 5in, part of the spinal column; and the third plate, 8in wide by 6in deep, hung from the lower edge of the first and covered the central and upper parts of the wearer's belly. All the plates were slightly rounded to fit the curve of the body, and they were attached to each other by a system of interconnecting webbing straps and metal buckles.

In order to overcome the problem of sweat building up between the inner surface of the steel plates and the wearer's body, the original production model had a spongy rubber beading affixed round the edge of each plate, the idea being that this beading held the plates away from direct contact with the wearer's body. However, a shortage of rubber forced subsequent plates to be produced with felt pads, the plates and pads being completely encased in canvas. The total weight of the armour suit, which also included the canvas covering, the straps and buckles, was 3½lb.

The size of the body armour was governed by the limitations placed on its design by its required weight. These factors, combined with the findings that the armour was likely to create worse wounds when high-penetration missiles,[1] on passing through the armour were caused to be retained inside the wearer's body instead of passing clean through an unprotected body, led to the suit being

[1]High-penetration projectiles were such items as rifle and machine gun bullets; low-penetration missiles were fine metal fragments from exploding bombs, shells and grenades.

designed in the way it was. It only covered those regions of the body where practically all wounds would have proved fatal, and it was therefore considered worthwhile to stop at least low-penetration missiles.

Five thousand sets of this armour were manufactured and put out for evaluation trials with units of the Home Forces and troops in the Middle East; almost unanimously it was recommended that it should be adopted. It was considered to be reasonably comfortable to wear, with no appreciable effect on the wearer's energy nor restrictions on his mobility, and the weight of the armour did not impair efficiency except on very long route marches. The chief objection was, however, that the clothing worn under the armour became very wet and sweaty, thus causing discomfort.

In April 1942 approval was given for the introduction of body armour into the British Army. Two months later production of the canvas covered pattern with felt pads, a substitute for and improvement on the original rubber edged pattern, was put in hand, once final confirmation trials, which were then being staged at the various infantry schools, had been concluded. It was found that, in the case of leading troops in close contact, complete freedom of movement when crawling or surmounting obstacles and rapid movement made in gaining cover were to some extent impaired, although these disadvantages were considered to be outweighed by the advantages gained in personal protection.

Towards the end of 1942 it was realized that the production of body armour would have been competing with the metal required for the manufacture

of steel helmets, and this resulted in priority being given to the latter. The estimate for the number of sets of body armour required by the forward troops of the British Army was given as 2½ million. The Royal Navy and the Royal Air Force and Combined Operations also had their requirements, and pending finalization of demands by all services an order for 500,000 sets was placed in hand by the War Office in September 1943 with the Ministry of Supply.

Early in 1944, as a result of growing indifference on the part of military theatres and army commanders together with the very small demands placed by them for these suits of armour, the initial order for half a million sets was reduced to 300,000. Eventually production was stopped at 200,000 sets, of which some 79,000 only were issued, 65,000 to the RAF and 15,000 to the Army in all theatres, the majority going to the 21st Army Group where the major portion was allocated to the Airborne Division.[2] The Army in Italy had no requirements except for some 300 sets for Royal Engineers personnel on special duties. The remaining stocks were held in War Office depots and were never issued.

The 3½lb suit of armour introduced during the war was never used in action. The trials showed it to be less efficient than had been expected, and although it could have been produced in large quantities in the last year of the war there was no demand for it.

[2] A complete set of 3½lb body armour can be seen on display at the Museum of the Airborne Forces, Aldershot, England.

Below: A series of photographs showing troops wearing and putting on sets of body armour; HQ of the 56th Infantry Division, 11th Corps area, Eastern Command, 21 March 1942. The correct method of wear was under the Battle-Dress (far left)

The Battle Jerkin (Assault Jerkin)

The original design for the battle jerkin, also known as the assault jerkin, was devised in April 1943 by Colonel Rivers-MacPherson of the Royal Army Ordnance Corps. The battle jerkin was an attempt to get away from the system in use from 1937 whereby the equipment worn and carried by a soldier consisted of a tight fitting waist-belt, supported by braces and straps to which were attached various containers, all of which pulled away from the centre of gravity of the wearer's body, thereby imposing unnatural strains on the fighting soldier.

The jerkin, an item of field service equipment, was devised along the lines of a poacher's jacket. It took the form of an armless, canvas garment on and within which were a number of pockets of varying size, including a small haversack type pocket across the back of the shoulders. It was constructed from stiffened and waterproofed cotton duck, dyed to suit the general background of the terrain in the theatre of war in which it was intended to be used. Examples of the jerkin I have seen range in colour from dark chocolate brown, which would seem to be the standard colour used in Europe, to a light sand coloured example in my own collection clearly marked with the black stencilled lettering FOR TRAINING ONLY.

There were a number of fundamental objections to the jerkin. Although it was manufactured in at least three basic sizes – 'small', 'medium' and 'large' – too many sizes were required to satisfy large-scale distribution, and this caused replacement difficulties when in the field. Moreover, because all the pockets were sewn-on fixtures of the jerkin, it was not capable of being adapted to enable the soldier to fight 'light'. It could not be fitted over the greatcoat, it was liable to chafe the wearer (especially on the side of the shoulders) and it was also found to be too hot for general use. All

these disadvantages led to it being abandoned as an item of universal issue field service equipment and instead was relegated for occasional use by special troops such as airborne forces, commandos or assault troops. Some attempts were made to redesign the jerkin on a skeleton principle in order to make it lighter and cooler to wear.

Altogether some 19,000 jerkins were made available to the 21st Army Group for use by the assault troops taking part in the landings in Normandy, but it was not used to any large extent, the main problem being that having stormed ashore and moved inland the assault troops were expected to discard the jerkin and revert to wearing their normal web equipment which had to be brought up the line to them. This presented too many logistical problems to be acceptable. Of the troops that did actually wear the battle jerkin, the majority found it to be both efficient and comfortable and that it could hold all the immediate personal and fighting gear they required for a short assault period.

The Skeleton Assault Jerkin

As has already been mentioned, the assault jerkin redesigned in skeleton form had been produced in order to make it lighter and cooler to wear. It was reduced to the simplest possible construction consisting as it did of only the two 'Bren' magazine pockets positioned on the front of the canvas frame which itself formed a Y-shaped arrangement attached at the back and below the two 'Bren' pockets at the front to a simple waist 'belt'.

The waist 'belt' was fastened at the front of the wearer's body by a simple webbing strap and brass buckle, with a canvas loop stitched on to the 'belt' on the left side designed to take the bayonet. There was a short, narrow webbing strap with a small brass buckle attached to the frame at the front in line with the top of the 'Bren' pockets which was

Below: Component parts of the battle jerkin. 1, Universal ammunition pockets; 2, Pack containing gas cape, 48-hour iron rations, cutlery and 100 rounds SAA if required; 3, Intrenching tool head carrier or 2 trench mortar bombs; 4, Right bomb pocket for 4 hand grenades, 2 two-inch trench mortar bombs or 2 slabs gun cotton; 5, Left bomb pocket for waterbottle (if not carried in pack) or 6 hand grenades or 2 two-inch trench mortar bombs or 2 slabs gun cotton; 6, Pocket on side of pack for securing machete or barrel of two-inch trench mortar; 7, Pocket for No. 4 bayonet; 8, Slot for carriage of SMLE bayonet or commando knife; 9, Pocket for intrenching tool helve; 10, Whipcord loops; 11, Tab for revolver holster; 12, Shoulder stops for rifle slings, etc.

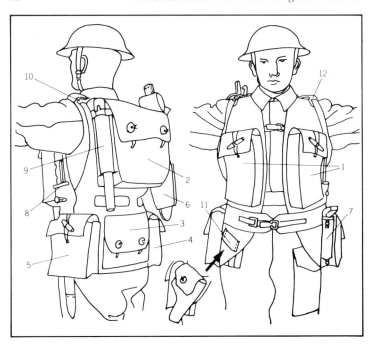

intended to help to retain the jerkin correctly on the wearer's chest. The 'Bren' magazine curved pockets, which were also capable of carrying rifle ammunition and possibly grenades (although the latter may have proved too bulky as the maximum depth of the fully extended pockets was only 1¾in), were provided with simple pocket flaps secured by a string loop and wooden toggle system.

The skeleton version of the assault jerkin was produced in the same dark brown stiffened and waterproofed cotton duck as was its bigger relative, the assault (or battle) jerkin.

The General Service Manpack Carrier

With the coming of mechanization the emphasis within the British Army had been to move away from the methods employed for load carrying by individuals towards carriage by motor transport. Even in the difficult and dangerous conditions of warfare on the North-West Frontier in India, the carrying of heavy loads was usually achieved by mule transport where motor transport was unable to go. The manhandling of loads was limited to very short hauls and there was no need for special equipment for porterage by the individual soldier.

The war in the Far East was responsible for reversing this emphasis on motor transport, upon which jungle and swamp country placed severe limitations. Animal transport, of which during the 1939–45 war there was a world-wide shortage, also had its limitations: if it was difficult to supply the troops it was just as difficult to supply and maintain the needs of the animal transport units serving them. In some theatres of the Pacific the only practical means of transport was man porterage. All this then led to the necessity for a suitable type of universal manpack carrier capable of the convenient carriage of all types of military stores and equipment.

Left and right: An officer from the 54th (East Anglian) Division (possibly Col. Rivers-MacPherson, RAOC) demonstrating the new battle jerkin during an exercise held in the Dunwich area, Eastern Command, an occasion when many secret weapons were demonstrated to the C-in-C Home Forces, General Sir Bernard C. T. Paget, and other high ranking officers; 14 April 1943.

Before 1944 certain special harnesses and carriers had been developed for individual items of awkward equipment such as the 3in mortar. The carriage of such items as artillery ammunition and general loads was achieved by the use of a frame type device known as the Everest carrier. A pack board type – the Yukon Pack Board – was also in existence and was favoured by the United States Army; weighing about 6½lb, it consisted of a plywood board fixed to a timber frame over which was stretched a canvas back-rest.

Experiments undertaken over a period of time at the Mountaineering Wing of the Middle East Mountain Warfare Training Centre in the Lebanon, in Syria, and at Army Operational Research Groups both in the United Kingdom and in India established that the pack board type of carrier was the most satisfactory. Frame type carriers, such as the Everest, concentrated the weight of the load on the area of the kidneys, and loads that exceeded 45lb could not be carried owing to the pain their weight caused. They also needed very careful adjustment to the individual to obtain the best results. With the pack type of carrier, in which the weight was well balanced up on the shoulders, loads up to 80 or 100lb could be carried after practice or by men of exceptional physique, although 45–50lb was the normal recognized load limit for long distance and continuous use.

In October 1944 a prototype general purpose manpack carrier was produced that did away with the need for an individual carrying harness for special stores and which could be used with any type of 'awkward' load. As ultimately introduced into the Service, after the inclusion of certain modifications resulting from trials, it consisted of a rigid, light aluminium alloy frame, painted dark green, with a shelf of the same alloy for use with certain square-edged loads. It weighed just 3lb 9oz or 4lb 1oz when the shelf was included, and was the lightest type of pack board carrier developed by any nation at that time. It was attached to the body by a set of quick-release webbing straps, with similar straps used for fitting the load. It was also provided with a tump line and a brow band or head-strap for use when carrying heavy loads. There was a total of thirteen dark green webbing straps, all with lightweight buckles.

The 'Carrier, Manpack, GS, 1945', to give it its official title, was simple to use and easy to adjust to suit the individual soldier. It was capable of being worn over the web equipment and without discomfort daily for long periods, and by means of the quick-release straps it was rapidly and easily jettisoned. The hands were left free for other purposes, and its method of attachment to the body was such that it did not become displaced when surmounting obstacles, nor was the height of the load above the shoulder line such as to catch in trees and undergrowth.

The maximum load a man could take on or off his back unaided was approximately 50lb; the normal load for an average man was set at 40lb provided the width was approximately 12in and the depth 6in normal or 12in maximum (the height was unrestricted). With practice or when

Right: The face veil worn by two members of No. 2 Platoon, 'C' Company, 46th West Riding (Doncaster) Bn, Home Guard fording a river during a demonstration assault exercise on 20 July 1942. (See also the photographs on pages 201 and 243.)

carried by soldiers with exceptional physique, weights of up to 70–80lb or more could be carried. Appendix A of the official War Office handbook on the 'Carrier, Manpack, GS, 1945' gave the following loads that were capable of being carried on the carrier.

Loads classed as easy to pack and carry were two large packs, total 30lb; seven blankets, 30lb; two 1-gallon water containers, full, 36½lb; three large packs loaded one above another, 45lb; one day's ration for 10 men, field service scale (tea, sugar, milk, margarine, tinned sausage, jam, potatoes, tinned vegetables, rice, bread, bacon, corned beef, cheese), 45lb; one sack of potatoes, 45lb; and one case of 48 tins of milk, 56lb.

Heavier and more bulky loads that were feasible to carry but over short distances were two 4.2in mortar bombs, loaded horizontally, 50lb; 960 carton packed .303in Mark VII ammunition in metal container, 60lb; one 14-man composite ration pack, large wooden box, 62lb; one case of 2 tins of biscuits (a day's ration for 112 men), 78lb; and two jerricans filled with petrol or water, 80–100lb.

Full-scale production of the GS carrier started in March 1945, but with the end of the war in Europe (May 1945) and the sudden end of the Japanese war (2 September 1945), little if any operational experience was gained in its use. A number of the carriers were made available for the crossing of the Rhine and received favourable reports.

The manpack carrier had not been designed for use in conditions of snow warfare and it did not ride well over cold weather clothing; furthermore, trials held in India and elsewhere shortly after the war brought to light certain faults in the GS carrier: when used by men under 5ft 7in in height

it tended to press down on the base of the spine, which led to discomfort and even minor injury; the quick-release straps were found to slip after continuous use; and there was found to be room for improvement in the point of balance and the positioning of the load and head-strap.

The Camouflage Face Veil

The veil consisted of a dark coloured net curtain 3ft by 3ft 6in, although veils were also produced with an irregular patterning of dark brown and grass green dyed into the net. It was intended to be worn over the steel helmet to cover the face, the respirator and the anti-gas cape, the object being to afford a measure of personal concealment to the wearer, from both ground observation and observation from low-flying aircraft; the use of the veil facilitated this by the elimination of light reflection from the helmet and face, and by enabling the wearer to merge himself more effectively into any natural background. The veil could be worn loose or attached to shoulder straps by tapes, at the discretion of the unit commanders.

The veil was considered an important item of equipment, and unit commanders had to ensure that wear and tear were kept as low as possible. Veils were not carried by troops except during exercises or operations.

In April 1942 approval was given for the issue of the camouflage face veil on the following scale to the following units.

1. Anti-tank artillery: three veils for each gun.
2. Light anti-aircraft units: one for each officer and man.
3. Reconnaissance units: one for each officer and man.
4. Infantry units (including Home Defence battalions, young soldier battalions, motor and support group battalions, machine gun battalions and commandos): one for each officer and man.
5. The Home Guard: one for each officer and man.
6. Field army artillery (less anti-tank): six for each regimental headquarters; twelve for each battery. Later on the veil became a standard issue of equipment to personnel of the Airborne Divisions.

Camouflage Cream

Dark brown camouflage cream for skin colouration was issued to certain field force troops and training establishments; green and black coloured creams also existed. For use by day the cream was only required to be applied to the forehead and cheeks; for use by night the face and neck needed to be well covered. The backs of hands also required attention. One application usually lasted up to 12 hours if necessary, and the cream was easily washed off, ½lb being considered sufficient for one application by 200 men for daytime use or by 100 men for night use.

Prior to the introduction of camouflage creams certain forms of skin coloration used by troops had proved unsafe and possibly dangerous: relatively safe substitutes for creams were burnt cork, soot, graphite and lamp black, but other substances had to be avoided (ACI 1323 dated 4 September 1943).

5. MISCELLANEOUS PERSONAL EQUIPMENT

Kit Bags

Use of kit bags by the BEF.

ACI 259 for the week ending 20 March 1940 stated that the universal kit bag was not authorized in the scale of necessaries for active service and that therefore this item had to be withdrawn from other ranks before they embarked for service in France with the British Expeditionary Force.

The only kit bag that was allowed in the personal active service scale in France at that time was the sea kit bag for use by personnel of the Auxiliary Military Pioneer Corps who were not issued with a pack. The universal kit bag used for containing greatcoats carried in unit transport was also authorized as unit public clothing for the BEF, but as such was part of the unit's equipment and not a personal issue.

Those kit bags that were withdrawn were returned to stores for reissue when necessary to recruits etc.

Embarkation.

Because of their conspicuousness from the air it was decided in April 1944 that white kit bags were to be used as little as possible. This safeguard was especially necessary at dock sides. In future, kit bags in the possession of troops mobilizing or being drafted for service overseas were to be of the dark variety. This was effected, as far as possible, by the exchange of kit bags within units. When this was not possible, arrangements had to be made within the command to obtain stocks by exchange. If, in turn, this proved impracticable then the Deputy Director of Ordnance Supplies) (DDOS) arranged for stocks of the white kit bags to be dyed drab green by local contractors. After April 1944 future production of kit bags was confined to those of dark colours.

Wartime marking of kit bags.

On the initial issue in the United Kingdom of the kit bag, the item was marked, under unit arrangement, with the soldier's name and regimental number. This was painted on the top half of the bag in a distinctive coloured paint, i.e. white paint for black or khaki coloured bags and black paint for white kit bags. For security reasons, no other markings that referred to the owner's battalion, regiment, corps, etc. were permitted.

Air travel bags for officers.

For the convenience of officers ordered to travel by air, a lightweight travelling bag made of equipment webbing and designed to accommodate the 44lb of personal luggage they were allowed to carry was introduced by the authority of ACI 1169 dated 30 August 1944. The bags were issued to officers on repayment on submission of a certificate to the effect that a bag had not previously been issued and quoting the authority for their journey.

Travel bags were obtainable at RAOC shops in overseas theatres of war and at home from either the London District Assembly Centre at the Great Eastern Hotel in the Marylebone Road or at the Central Ordnance Sub-Depot at Olympia, Hammersmith, London.

Ear Protectors

As early as September 1940 the War Office decided to introduce ear protectors to all military personnel on the scale of four protectors to each officer, other rank and member of the ATS in the United Kingdom. Designed to protect the eardrum against blast and, as it was somewhat quaintly put, 'screaming bombs', these rubber 'plugs' were intended to be inserted into the ear passage when needed. They were worn in pairs on the uniform, each plug being attached by a thin cord or string which was worn around the shoulders and under the shoulder straps with the plug ends tucked into the breast pockets of the SD or BD (ACI 1116 dated 18 September 1940).

The shortage of rubber seems to have brought about the use of cotton wool as a suitable replacement for the rubber ear protectors or 'plugs'. ACI 947 dated 23 June 1943 advocated the use of dry cotton wool to be used as ear protection during

Below: A soldier with his kit. Gunner John Cox prepares for a sea trip.

training. It claimed that investigation had shown that modern weapons were causing considerable damage to the ears of personnel who continually refrained from wearing ear protectors, and instructions were therefore issued by commanders concerned to ensure that ear protectors were worn during firing by members of gun detachments of field, medium and heavy artillery, of light anti-aircraft, heavy anti-aircraft and coast artillery units and of Royal Artillery and Infantry Anti-Tank units, and by members of infantry squads for 'Projectors, Infantry, Anti-Tank' (PIAT) and mortars.

The ideal protector was that which prevented injury to the ear-drums, was readily available, enabled the wearer to hear, was easily inserted and was harmless. All these requirements were found to be fulfilled by the use of cotton wool.

Instructions for the use of rubber ear protectors were as follows.
1. The protector had to be slightly moistened.
2. It was held correctly between the thumb and forefinger and inserted into the ear canal on the same side with a gentle screwing movement. The ear canal could be opened by pulling the ear upwards and backwards with the opposite hand passed behind the head.
3. When the protectors were correctly placed, the ears felt definitely muffled.
4. The correct depth and direction of insertion varied with the individual. The protector could conveniently be shortened by cutting off one or more slices, each the thickness of a sixpenny piece.
5. When not in use, the protectors were supposed to be kept as clean as possible by washing them with soap and water.

By 1943 the shortage of rubber made it impossible for these ear protectors to be issued to units other than those listed above, and in view of this and the fact that the rubber ear plugs were easily lost or soiled and were unsuitable for use in hot climates, cotton wool was found to be more practical and satisfactory.

By May 1944 (ACI 732 dated 17 May 1944), rubber ear protectors were withdrawn altogether and only cotton wool was used for ear protection.

First Field Dressings
It was announced on 10 April 1943 (ACI 604 of 1943) that as a wartime economy measure certain modifications to the existing instructions concerning the carriage of first field dressings were to be applied to troops stationed at home. In future first field dressings were not to be carried by troops stationed in the United Kingdom, except by (a) non-commissioned officers, (b) drivers and motor-cyclists, and (c) personnel attending battle schools, camps or exercises in which live ammunition or explosives were used.

First field dressings, other than those in use as listed above, were held in battalion, company or equivalent stores on the scale of one for each officer or other rank. Formation commanders could, however, order the carriage of first field dressings by any personnel under their command on such occasions and in such circumstances as they considered necessary. These instructions

applied only to troops, including the ATS, stationed in the United Kingdom; they did not apply to those serving in, or proceeding to, stations overseas.

Personal Utensils
At the time of the new experimental uniform that underwent evaluation trials during 1933 (see page 181), a decision was made regarding certain items of clothing and equipment that had been in use with the British Army prior to 1933.

The cap comforter (see page 157), trouser braces, the 'Housewife' holdall and the identity discs (see page 254) all remained as they had been. The 'Jack' or clasp knife, however, was improved by having a better type of tin-opener, and the rifle bayonet was reduced in size.

Mess tins.

Mess tins were issued as a pair, and, better than tin plates, they provided the individual soldier with the means of holding food or liquid in a convenient container sufficiently deep to allow him to either heat or cook food or liquid for a meal and then to eat or drink the same with ease. The folding handle on each tin, when unfolded out, allowed the mess tin to be held in a rigid position and, because the handles were poor conductors of heat, without burning or scalding the user's fingers.

Original mess tins were manufactured from tin plated metal and had a bevelled edge; mess tins produced during the 1939–45 war were produced in an aluminium alloy, and because they were pressed out from a single piece of metal they had no joins or rim. They were rectangular in shape, one of the pair slightly smaller than the other, and when the carrying handles were folded into the inner space of the tin the smaller tin could be fitted into the larger. When not in use the mess tins were usually carried in the small haversack, although some individuals adopted a method of carrying the mess tins in a suitably adapted webbing frame normally used to carry the water-bottle.

A practice developed amongst the British troops fighting in the Pacific whereby in order to carry less weight – and every possible item of extraneous equipment was discarded – only the smaller of the mess tins was carried. Even this item was cut down in height to a minimum just sufficient to contain a small amount of food or liquid.

The water-bottle.

This was an upright angular metal bottle, slightly kidney-shaped and enamelled. The bottle had a short spout stoppered by a cork through which was passed a metal rod secured by a nut, the rod providing the method whereby the cork stopper was attached to the body of the bottle by a short length of corded string. The whole of the water-bottle was tightly sewn into a covering of khaki felt cloth, the purpose of which was to protect the bottle and at the same time deaden any possible noise the bottle may make by being struck by other items of equipment.

Above: Personal utensils and equipment. A set of aluminium mess tins shown open (top left) and stowed (bottom left); centre top, an enamel mug; far right, top and bottom, a torch manufactured by Lucas; below centre, clasp knives manufactured by (left) D.C.C. of Sheffield and (right) C. Johnson of Sheffield.

In view of all its inherent disadvantages it is something of a mystery how the standard issue enamelled water-bottle remained for so long in service with both the British and Indian Armies: the bottle was heavy when empty, weighing 15oz; the outer felt covering tended either to rot or tear away, which made the bottle noisy; its awkward angular shape and its small spout made it very difficult to clean; the nut and rod inserted through the cork stopper quickly rusted; the cork itself tended to rot and affected the taste of the contents; the corded string disintegrated; and when dented the enamelling invariably cracked or flaked off, resulting in an almost certain leak. Moreover, there was no means by which a number of bottles could be carried easily for refilling, and in addition to all this the soldier had to carry a separate enamel cup, attached either to his waist-belt or to the strap of his haversack, which was both insanitary and inconvenient.

Drinking vessels.

These were usually enamelled drinking mugs of 1pt or ½pt capacity. Before the war they were in white enamel, but later dark brown mugs were issued.

Cutlery.

These consisted of a separate, all-metal knife, fork and spoon, a set of which was issued to each

man on joining the Army. Some units took the precaution of stamping the last three digits of the owner's regimental number on the handle of these items.

'Jack' or clasp knives.

The clasp knife, introduced in November 1932 at the time when the new experimental Field Service uniform went on display (see page 181), was an improvement on the clasp knife in use during the 1914–18 war, being shorter in length and having an improved tin-opener. Extremely well made (by C. Johnson & Co. of Sheffield, England), it had a single steel blade, a marlin spike, a tin-opener combined with a bottle-opener and, set into one end of the knife, a short form of screwdriver. The knife grip was produced from a hard black material, diagonally patterned for extra grip, and had a strong, movable steel ring set into the end of the knife for attachment to a lanyard.

An inferior form of clasp knife was introduced during the last year of the 1939–45 war which was produced from stainless steel. It had no hand grips, only a single blade and a short combined tin- and bottle-opener; this too had a short screwdriver blade and a small, movable attachment ring. This clasp knife was produced by 'D.C.C.' of Sheffield, and the example in my collection is dated 1945 and marked with the War Department broad arrow sign.

The 'Housewife' holdall.

This item, issued to all troops, was the means whereby a soldier was able to carry out minor 'running repairs' to his clothing. It consisted of a small linen pouch containing two balls of grey darning wool for socks, a card wound with 50yds of fawn coloured linen thread, a packet of five needles (two No. 2 and two No. 3 sewing needles and one No. 2 darning needle), a black plastic thimble, and a stout paper twist containing six brass dish buttons for replacement on Battle-Dress garments and five small brown plastic buttons for shirts etc.

The underside of the flap to the 'Housewife' pouch had a strip of khaki shirting material sewn into it to act in the same way as a 'pin cushion' for spare needles. When not in use, the pouch was rolled up and fastened by being tied around by its attached tapes.

Identity Discs

Serving troops of all ranks were issued with a set of identity discs. These consisted of a red and a green disc together with a 38in length of thin cord. Both discs were worn suspended on the cord around the soldier's neck and beneath his uniform. The No. 1 green disc was tied to the suspension cord 6in apart from the No. 2 red disc, and an additional red disc was issued to mark the anti-gas service respirator.

These identity discs, with the exception of the disc used for marking the respirator, showed the soldier's Army number, his initials, his surname in full and his religious denomination. The following abbreviations were used for recording religious denominations.

CE	Church of England
CI	Church of Ireland
Pres	Church of Scotland and Presbyterian
RC	Roman Catholic
Meth	Methodist
Bapt	Baptist
Cong	Congregationalist
J	Jewish
SA	Salvation Army
CSci	Christian Scientist
U	Unitarian
PB	Plymouth Brethren
Q	Quaker

In the case of soldiers who declared themselves to have been members of a denomination for which there was no recognized abbreviation, including those who professed negative denominations (for example atheists), no entry in respect of religious denomination was stamped on the discs.

On being commissioned, officers were allocated a personal number, and this number was inscribed on the officer's identity discs in the same manner and with similar information as for the identity discs of other ranks.

The purpose of these identity discs was to help in the identification of the wearer's body or remains in the event of the soldier or officer being killed or severely wounded. *Field Service Regulations*, Vol. I of 1930, Appendix VI, Section I, para. 1, stated: 'Anyone concerned in a burial, or finding a body, will remove the red identity disc. The green identity disc will on no account be removed from the body . . . In cases where there is only one identity disc it will not be removed. Should there be no means of identifying the body any detail which may assist in identification such as a cap badge, shoulder title, or number marked on equipment, should be carefully noted as well as the exact spot on which the body was found and the apparent date of death.'

The identification of the dead, usually carried out by the Graves Registration Service, was made difficult by two factors recognized during the war and reported from the different war zones: one was the neglect of individuals to wear their identity discs and the other was the removal, in some cases, by burial parties of both discs from the body. A third factor became apparent towards the later part of the war. The Graves Registration Service operating in the Middle East and the Far East reported in 1943 that the green and red fibre discs lost their markings after preliminary interment in hot damp soil, owing to the acids and gases generated; that they peeled and became illegible under desert conditions; and that if exposed to intense heat, such as in a burning AFV, they were totally destroyed. The cotton string used with the fibre discs proved useless as a necklace. It was not fireproof, and on interment it became foul at once and rotted away in a few days.

All these advantages brought about the introduction for jungle scales of stainless steel identity discs in lieu of the fibre pattern. These were fireproof, rustless and non-irritant. Indian forces adopted aluminium discs. Ideally, a fine stainless steel ball chain similar to that used by American troops would have been preferred on which to carry the new pattern of stainless steel identity discs, but this was not possible since the machinery required to manufacture this type of chain was not available in the United Kingdom; moreover, chains of this nature were coveted by the Japanese for their own personal adornment, and they were none too particular how they removed them from the necks of the American wounded. Nylon cord dyed light tan was accepted as the carrying cord. Despite its chief disadvantage of not being fireproof, it was rotproof, less liable to become fouled and was not adversely affected by anti-gas ointment or mosquito repellent. It also had no tendency to rattle.

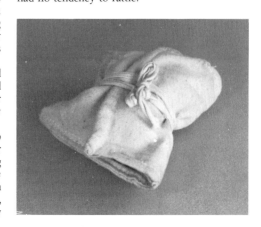

6. THE CARRYING OF ARMS AND AMMUNITION

The wartime carrying of arms and ammunition by military personnel was closely aligned with the carrying of personal equipment, the anti-gas service respirator and its haversack and the steel helmet (the last two subjects having been dealt with elsewhere in this book – see pages 240 and 219).

A number of wartime Army Council Instructions were issued on the subject of arms and ammunition, starting with ACI 669 dated 3 July 1940. This laid down that all officers in possession of revolvers, and all parties of troops and individual soldiers when on duty away from the vicinity of their quarters, were always required to carry arms and ammunition. All weapons when not with the individual had to be kept under lock and key or in the custody of a guard.

A much more comprehensive instruction, No. 124, was promulgated on 25 January 1941 under the heading 'The Carrying of Arms, Ammunition, Steel Helmets and Respirators'. This cancelled ACI 669 of 1940 and stated that the following instructions were applicable to forces stationed in the United Kingdom and Northern Ireland.

Arms and ammunition.
1. During periods of emergency. When orders that notified a state of emergency had been issued, all ranks, whether individuals or parties, when away from quarters or places of duty, were required to carry arms and ammunition, if the former were a personal issue.
2. Except during periods of emergency. At other times, commands issued their own orders regarding the carrying of arms and ammunition by all ranks when away from quarters on duty or proceeding on leave on short pass. These were framed to suit the particular conditions that prevailed in various localities such as country districts or town areas. The orders were based on the general principle that all ranks should be able to deal adequately with enemy parachutists or ill-disposed persons.
3. During leave exceeding 48 hours or at places of instruction. All ranks who proceeded on leave for periods over 48 hours or to places of instruction at military establishments or civil institutions were required to take arms if they were a personal

issue. Only officers took ammunition; other ranks did not do so.

Whilst on leave personnel were not required to carry arms, provided that they were able to make adequate arrangements for their security and could obtain possession of them within three hours. Personnel at places of instruction at military establishments or civil institutions, when they were not specifically required to carry arms for the purpose of instruction or when off duty, were not required to carry arms, provided that adequate arrangements could be made for their safe keeping and that they could be obtained within a period of three hours.

Officers commanding these military establishments issued orders regarding the carriage of arms and ammunition by personnel when they proceeded beyond the confines of the establishment which were in conformity with the instructions as laid down in paragraphs (1) and (2) above.

Personnel proceeding to Eire or Northern Ireland. Personnel proceeding on leave to destinations in Eire or Northern Ireland were not, under any circumstances, allowed to carry arms or ammunition. These had to be left with their units and not at ports of embarkation.

By 1943 the existing instructions regarding the carrying of arms, ammunition and equipment by military personnel on leave underwent a revision. The following instructions regarding arms and ammunition were published under ACI 603 dated 10 April 1943.

No arms or ammunition were to be carried by other ranks when on leave. Officers, on the other hand, were permitted to continue to carry arms and ammunition at their own discretion.

This ACI in no way affected the carrying of arms and equipment by personnel travelling on drafts, transfers, courses of instruction and the like, nor did it affect the carrying of arms by men who, on completion of their training at a training unit, normally proceeded on leave from which they then proceeded direct to join another units.

By 11 July 1945, ACI 816, in dealing with the subject of carrying arms and ammunition by personnel on leave and stationed in the United Kingdom, simply stated that no arms or ammunition were to be taken on leave.

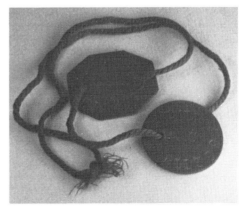

Left and right: The 'housewife' holdall and its contents.
Far right: Red and green identity discs.

PART VI
Local Defence Volunteers and the Home Guard

1. LOCAL DEFENCE VOLUNTEERS

The statutory authority for the formation of the Local Defence Volunteers (the LDV) was the Defence (Local Defence Volunteers) Regulations, 1940, which were made by Order in Council on 17 May 1940. The object of the force was to augment the local defences in Great Britain. The LDV was organized and administered by the War Office, and the Commander-in-Chief, Home Forces, exercised operational control over the force; he was responsible for the training and the volunteers of the LDV under the direction of the War Office. The Local Defence Volunteers in each military area were organized and commanded by area commanders under the direction of general officers commanding-in-chief Army commands. The area commander, in conjunction with the Civil Regional Commissioner, was responsible for the organization of each area into zones, each zone being sub-divided into battalions.

Each battalion in each area was in turn composed of companies which consisted of platoons and sections, according to local defence requirements. There was an honorary LDV organizer appointed for each area, whose task it was to assist military area commanders in all matters of raising, organizing and equipping LDV units within the area. These organizers did not hold LDV rank. The administration of the force was the responsibility of the Director General Weapons, Training, A (DGWTA) and was carried out locally through Territorial Army and AF Associations, each association having administrative charge of the units of the force raised within its area.

There was no fixed establishment for the LDV, the numbers enrolled depending upon the numbers eventually required. At the time of the formation of the LDV all suitable volunteers were accepted. Volunteers when enrolled were formed into sections, the normal approximate size of a section (which was the basic LDV unit) being 25 men although this rather depended upon local requirements. Sections were in turn grouped into platoons, companies and battalions on a general basis of four sections to a platoon, four platoons to a company and four companies to a battalion. All appointments in the LDV were acting and unpaid. Each battalion, company and platoon commander

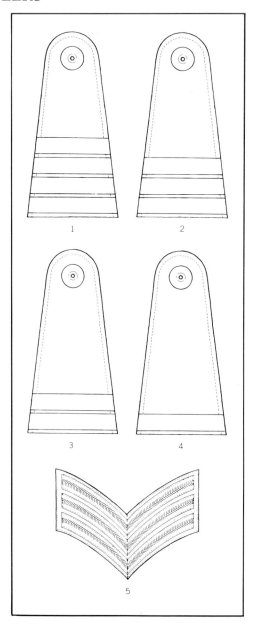

was permitted a second-in-command who was always one rank lower than his commander.

The LDV formed part of the armed forces of the Crown and as such an enrolled volunteer was, under Section 176 (8B) of the Army Act, subject to military law as a soldier, notwithstanding that he may have held a rank or a commission in any other of His Majesty's Forces. He was therefore obliged to obey all orders issued to him in accordance with instructions for the LDV as issued by the Army Council.

The basic qualifications required of volunteers for the LDV were that (a) they had to be men between the ages of 17 and 65 years of age; (b) they had to be British subjects; and (c) they had to be of reasonable physical fitness. Volunteers, subject to certain special conditions, normally undertook to engage for service in the LDV for a period that was not to exceed the duration of the war. There was no objection, however, to enrolment for any shorter period of time as stipulated by the volunteer. Enrolment did not exempt volunteers from liability to register and to be called up under the provisions of the National Service (Armed Forces) Acts.

Badges of Appointment

The first and only series of badges of appointment used by members of the LDV was introduced by ACI 653, published on the 24 June 1940. The badges consisted of stripes of dark blue cloth of varying numbers worn horizontally on both shoulder straps of the military garment being worn, as follows.

Zone commander: 4 stripes
Battalion commander: 3 stripes
Company commander: 2 stripes
Platoon commander: 1 stripe
Section commander: 3 worsted chevrons[1]

All members of the LDV were required to wear the LDV arm-band on the right upper arm (see page 263).

Proposed Issue of Uniform and Equipment

ACI 653 dated 24 June 1940 set out the intended scale of uniform and equipment that was proposed to be provided for each volunteer of the LDV as one suit of denim overalls, one service respirator, one steel helmet, one field dressing and one field service cap, but it is doubtful whether any of these items were universally issued before the LDV was absorbed into the Home Guard. It is of interest to note how the scale of issue increased somewhat when the Home Guard was established. The articles listed above were not available in any significant numbers in June 1940, especially as every spare item of clothing and equipment was required to replace items lost, damaged or abandoned by the British Expeditionary Force escaping from Dunkirk and other continental ports.

Until sufficient supplies of denim overalls were available, or on any other occasion when specially authorized to do so, members of the LDV were permitted to wear civilian clothing; when this was the case, and it must have been universally widespread, the LDV arm-band had to be worn, stitched securely to the right upper arm.

[1]Worn on left arm only.

Right: A member of the County of Essex Volunteers which, under the patronage of the Lord Lieutenant of Essex, was one of a number of similar volunteer formations that preceded the LDV.
Left: Local Defence Volunteers badges of appointment. 1, Zone cmdr.; 2, Battalion cmdr.; 3, Company cmdr.; 4, Platoon cmdr.; 5, Section cmdr.

2. THE HOME GUARD

Above: Cloth slip-on shoulder strap title for the Home Guard.

The statutory authority for the establishment of the Home Guard was the same as that for the Local Defence Volunteers, i.e. the Defence (Local Defence Volunteers) Regulations, 1940, of 17 May 1940 as amended by Order in Council of 31 July 1940. The object of the force was to augment the local defences of Great Britain by providing the static defence of localities and protection of vulnerable key points and by giving timely notice of enemy movements to superior military organizations. At the time of its establishment it was emphasized that the Home Guard had been assigned a definite role in the defence plans of the country, its value as a military force lying not in individual action by its members but in its proper co-ordination under the command of the appropriate military authorities.

The status of the Home Guard was that of a voluntary, unpaid, part-time force having its origin in the desire of patriotic citizens engaged in ordinary civil occupations to make some active and voluntary contribution to the defence of the realm, and especially to the defence of their own localities. Neither the Order in Council nor the terms of enrolment required full-time service, since it was realized that such full-time service would deprive many potential volunteers who were anxious to serve from doing so and would take others away from work of national importance. Where the need for continuous duty arose, the Home Guard adopted a shift system.

The Home Guard, like its predecessor the LDV, was organized and administered by the War Office. The Commander-in-Chief, Home Forces, continued to exercise operational control over this new force and he remained responsible for Home Guard training and for its volunteers under the direction of the War Office. The Home Guard in each area was organized and commanded by military area commanders through Home Guard area commanders, under the direction of GOs C-in-C Army commands. The military area commander was responsible for the organization of each area into zones, each zone being sub-divided into groups and each group into battalions. Each Home Guard battalion in each area was composed of companies which consisted of platoons and sections, according to local defence requirements, the authority to form a Home Guard unit or sub-unit being subject to the decision of the local military area commander. Like the LDV, the Home Guard possessed honorary organizers for each area. Their task was, as before, to assist military area commanders in all matters concerning the raising, organizing and equipping of units within their areas. These organizers, however, did not hold Home Guard rank.

Certain government departments – railways, public utility undertakings and factories of national importance – were permitted to form special Home Guard detachments in which their employees were enrolled for the protection of the undertakings concerned. These detachments normally formed units or sub-units of the local Home Guard organization, and their use in schemes for the defence of their factories etc. was

Right: Maj.-Gen. Sir Arthur, Smoth, GOC London District inspecting men of the Port of London Authority Home Guard, West India Docks on 25 July 1943.
Far right: Two members of the newly formed Home Guard getting the measure of a water-cooled Vickers machine gun at Brockham, near Dorking, Surrey. A Platoon Commander takes aim and non-existent ammunition is fed into the breech by a Company Commander. Both men are wearing the early Home Guard badges of appointment, which are sewn across the base of their Battle-Dress shoulder straps.

under the general supervision of the military authorities.

There was no fixed establishment for the Home Guard: the numbers enrolled, as with the LDV, depended upon the numbers eventually required. When enrolled, Home Guard volunteers were formed into sections which normally consisted of 25 men but depended on local requirements. The sections, the basic Home Guard units, were grouped into platoons, companies and battalions on a general basis of four sections to one platoon, four platoons to a company and four companies to a Home Guard battalion.

The Home Guard was a citizen force organized on the principles of equality of service and status; accordingly, there was no system of 'ranks', although there were 'appointments' suitably graded for the commanders of various formations. All appointments were acting and unpaid. Zone, group, battalion, company and platoon commanders were each permitted to appoint to themselves a second-in-command who was always one appointment lower than their own.

In the matter of discipline, the conditions governing the enrolled volunteers in the Home Guard were exactly the same as those already mentioned for those enrolled into the former Local Defence Volunteer force. Personnel of the Home Guard were subject to military law as set out under Section 176 (8B) of the Army Act. However, the basic qualifications required of volunteers attempting to join the Home Guard were somewhat more specific than was the case of potential LDV members. Potential volunteers (later referred to as 'members') of the Home Guard (a) had to be men between the ages of 17 and 65; (b) had to be of reasonable physical fitness; and (c) had normally to be British subjects. Exceptions were permitted with this last stipulation provided that the applicant had either served in His Majesty's Armed Forces in the Great War between 4 August 1914 and 11 November 1918 or had satisfactorily completed a period of no less than three years' service on full pay in His Majesty's Regular Forces. In no circumstances was an applicant allowed to be enrolled if in addition to British nationality he possessed German, Austrian or Italian nationality.

In 1941 the last set of conditions as listed above under (c) were enlarged upon so that the potential Home Guard member had to be (i) a British subject or (ii) a national, by birth, of an allied or neutral state who was vouched for by a Chief Constable of the county or borough in which he resided. However, neither a British subject nor a national of an allied or neutral state was eligible for Home Guard membership if he possessed German, Austrian or Italian nationality, except where the applicant had served with British forces during the First World War, when the case received special consideration if particulars had first been submitted to the Under-Secretary of State at the War Office. A national of an allied or neutral state was not eligible to enrol in the Home Guard if he was married to a woman of German, Austrian or Italian birth, unless he had served in the British forces during the Great War, although, again, special consideration could be sought in his case by submitting his details to the Under-Secretary of State at the War Office.

Right: Members of the
Southern Railway Home Guard
receiving instruction on the
Thompson sub-machine gun
from a Home Guard Warrant
Officer, Class II; 11 March
1942.

Right: The King, newly
appointed as Colonel-in-Chief of
the Home Guard, visiting a
battalion in the South-Eastern
Command, 12 July 1942. His
Majesty is shown here enjoying
a joke with a lance corporal,
the son of George Robey, the
famous comedian.

3. HOME GUARD RANKS AND INSIGNIA

Badges of Appointment, 1940

Two series of badges were introduced at different times, the first to indicate appointments bestowed on personnel of the Home Guard and the second to indicate ranks and appointments held by officers and other ranks of the Home Guard. Army Council Instruction No. 924 dated 15 August 1940 listed the following Home Guard badges of appointment.

Zone commander: 1 broad stripe 2in deep
Group commander: 4 stripes all ⅜in deep
Battalion commander: 3 stripes all ⅜in deep
Company commander: 2 stripes all ⅜in deep
Platoon commander: 1 stripe ⅜in deep
Section commander: 3 worsted chevrons
Squad commander: 2 worsted chevrons

The stripes were of dark blue cloth worn horizontally on both shoulder straps. No details were given as to the size of the gap between two or more of these stripes, but photographic evidence shows the gaps to be approximately ⅛in wide, sufficient to distinguish the individual stripes. The chevrons were of the usual Army worsted pattern and worn on the left upper arm only.

The Introduction of Warrant and Non-Commissioned Rank

On 3 March 1941 the War Office published details regarding the decision to introduce warrant and non-commissioned rank in the Home Guard (ACI 288 of 1941). There was no fixed establish-ment as exact numbers were dependent upon prevailing local requirements. The following scale was considered as a guide to the numbers of warrant officers and non-commissioned officers that were to be allocated to various Home Guard units. These numbers were not allowed to be exceeded.

For each battalion headquarters.
One warrant officer Class I (regimental serjeant-major)
One warrant officer Class II (regimental quarter-master-serjeant)
One colour serjeant (orderly-room serjeant)
Four serjeants
Four corporals

For each company headquarters.
One warrant officer Class II (company serjeant-major)
One colour serjeant (company quarter-master-serjeant)
One corporal

For each platoon headquarters.
One serjeant
One corporal

For each section headquarters.
One serjeant
One corporal

In each squad.
One corporal

Lance-corporals were appointed on a scale of one to each ten volunteers/members.

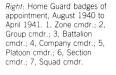

Right: Home Guard badges of appointment, August 1940 to April 1941. 1, Zone cmdr.; 2, Group cmdr.; 3, Battalion cmdr.; 4, Company cmdr.; 5, Platoon cmdr.; 6, Section cmdr.; 7, Squad cmdr.

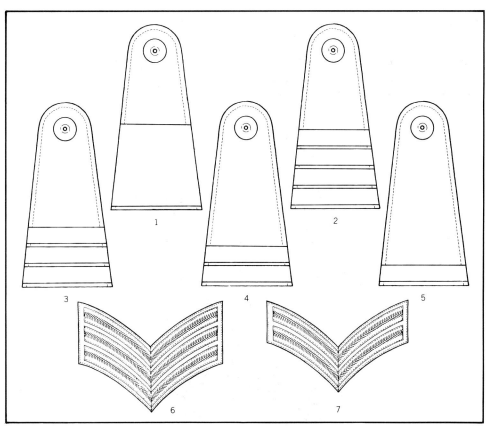

These ranks and appointments carried no financial benefits beyond those that were already then admissible for the Home Guard. Candidates for promotion to the rank of Warrant Officer Class I were recommended by officers commanding battalions and approved by zone commanders. Candidates for promotion and appointment to the non-commissioned rank of Serjeant and above, excluding Warrant Officer Class I, were appointed by officers commanding battalions; promotions and appointments below that of Serjeant were carried out by company commanders.

Warrant officers and NCOs could not be compelled to continue serving with the Home Guard should they wish to resign, but they were obliged to give fourteen days' notice in writing of their decision. Immediate discharge on compassionate grounds could be granted at the discretion of group commanders. A warrant officer or NCO could, with the consent of the authority that could appoint him to that rank, resign his appointment and revert to a lower rank.

Badges of Rank, 1941

On 24 April 1941 yet another ACI was published, No. 623 of 1941, which in its appendix gave instruction regarding the dress of officers of the Home Guard pending publication of an ACI on the subject. The badges of rank as worn by officers of the Home Guard, which cancelled out the previous system of cloth stripes, were to be in worsted material for wear on the Battle-Dress and in gilt metal for the greatcoat. These new badges of rank were the same as those in use by officers of the Regular Army.

The introduction of these 'new' badges of rank required that the Home Guard officers provide themselves at their own expense with the insignia they required. It is interesting to note in these days of inflation just how much these badges actually cost in 1941. It cost a Home Guard brigadier 17s. 3d. (approximately 86p) for two complete sets of insignia, each consisting of six stars and two crowns, one set in gilt metal and one in worsted, a total of 16 items which average out at a fraction over 5p per item. Home Guard colonels had to pay 13s. for their stars and crowns, lieutenant-colonels paid 8s. 9d. and majors 4s. 6d.; captains paid slightly more for their three stars per shoulder strap at 12s. 9d., lieutenants were charged 8s. 6d. and second lieutenants of the Home Guard managed to escape with the sum of 4s. 3d. for their four solitary 'pips'.

On 19 July 1941 ACI 1273 was published which dealt with the subject 'Dress and Badges for Officers and Members of the Home Guard'. From this and the previous interim instructions (see page 261) can be extracted a listing of ranks and insignia as set out in Table 44.

Table 44. Ranks and Insignia of the Home Guard, 1941

Rank	Badge[1]
Officers	
Brigadier	Three stars set in form of triangle surmounted by crown
Colonel	Crown above two stars
Lieutenant-Colonel	Crown above single star
Major	Single crown
Captain	Three stars in row
Lieutenant	Two stars one above other
Second Lieutenant	Single star
Members	
Warrant Officer Class I	Royal Arms in worsted[1]
Warrant Officer Class II	Crown set within wreath all in worsted[2]
Serjeant	Three worsted chevrons[3]
Corporal	Two worsted chevrons[3]
Lance-Corporal	One worsted chevron[3]

[1]The badges of rank and appointment as shown in this column for wear by officers and members of the Home Guard were of the same pattern and quality of material as those used by personnel of the Regular Army Infantry of the Line.
[2]These items were worn on both forearms of the Battle-Dress blouse and the greatcoat by warrant officers of the Home Guard.
[3]These items were worn on both upper arms of the Battle-Dress blouse and the greatcoat by NCOs of the Home Guard.

Gorget Patches
Home Guard officers with the rank of Colonel and above wore scarlet gorget patches on the collar of the Battle-Dress blouse as laid down for officers of corresponding rank in the Regular Army. Details of this type of gorget patch can be found on page 41 of this book.

Arm-Bands (LDV and Home Guard)
When the Local Defence Volunteer force was raised in May 1940 an intended scale of clothing had been drawn up and was actually published (see page 257). However, the War Office recognized that supplies of even the most basic uniform requirements were almost impossible to fulfil, at least in the immediate future, and civilian clothing was therefore permitted, all volunteers operating as members of the LDV being obliged to wear an arm-band bearing the letters L.D.V. This had to be

securely stitched to the right upper arm of the civilian garment midway between the shoulder and elbow.

With the establishment of the Home Guard in July 1940 a change-over took place, the existing LDV arm-bands being replaced with light khaki coloured bands bearing the words 'Home Guard'. All members of the Home Guard had to wear the new arm-band on the right upper arm when on duty. If volunteers/members of the new force had not been issued with a suit of denim overalls (see page 269 for scale of uniform and personal equipment normally provided for each volunteer in the Home Guard), they had when on duty to wear the Home Guard arm-band securely stitched to the right arm, midway between the shoulder and elbow of their civilian jacket or coat.

With the introduction of the Home Guard arm-band, the LDV band was withdrawn; the Home Guard arm-band in turn was withdrawn when the force received its Home Guard shoulder title and regimental flashes (see page 264). However, the arm-band did not disappear altogether, such bands as required for use with denim overalls held on charge by units for cleaning and decontamination purposes being retained and attached to them.

Those arm-bands that were withdrawn were returned to TA Associations, accompanied by a certificate from the Home Guard unit commander that stated the exact number of bands being returned. The TA Associations held approximately 20 per cent of these returned bands in case of the necessity for re-issue; all the rest were destroyed by burning. For reasons of security, every precaution was taken by all persons concerned to prevent arm-bands falling into the hands of unauthorized persons.

Distinguishing Marks
Shoulder titles − referred to within the Regular Army as 'regimental designations' − bearing the legend Home Guard, together with county and city distinguishing flashes indicating county and city names and battalion numbers, were first introduced in July 1941 to be worn on both sleeves of the Battle-Dress blouse and the greatcoat (ACI 1273 dated 19 July 1941). The shoulder titles were worn 1in below the seam of the shoulder and the distinguishing flashes were positioned 1/2in below the bottom edge of the shoulder titles. Both titles and flashes had to be sewn on garments under private arrangements, no expense to the public being permitted, and they were only issued simultaneously with the withdrawal of the Home Guard (or LDV) arm-bands.

Where Home Guard capes had been issued in lieu of greatcoats, all badges etc. were worn on the cape in the position corresponding to the position on the sleeves of the greatcoat.

County and city distinguishing flashes.
The list in Table 45 of Home Guard distinguishing flashes, the official name given to the initial letters and abbreviations worn as cloth insignia to indicate the wearer's particular county or city Home Guard affiliation, is as complete as I am able to make it. (It is possible that other

Above: Lapel badge for British Resistance Battalion 202. Members of this battalion (based in the north of England) and two other 'Auxiliary Unit' battalions, numbers 201 (based in Scotland) and 203 (based in the south of England), wore Home Guard uniforms. They did not, however, appear in any official list of Home Guard units.

Above: Typical Home Guard shoulder insignia, consisting of Home Guard shoulder title, Surrey Battalion and unit insignia.

distinguishing flashes existed and they may be known to others. It is sometimes possible to discover previously unknown Home Guard flashes from the study of contemporary wartime photographs, but unless there is correct information by way of a photograph caption only guesswork can arrive at an explanation.)

Table 45. *Home Guard Distinguishing Flashes*

Flash	Affiliation
A	Anglesey, Wales
AB	Aberdeen, city of, Scotland
ABK	Aberdeenshire, Kincardine, Scotland (3rd Bn)
ABN	Aberdeenshire, Scotland
ANG	Angus, Scotland
ARG	Argyllshire, Scotland
AYR	Ayrshire, Scotland
BDF	Bedfordshire, England
BHM	Birmingham, city of, Warwickshire, England
BNF	Banffshire, Scotland
BR	Brecknock, Wales
BRX	Berkshire, England
BUX	Buckinghamshire, England
CA	Caithness, Scotland
CAM	Cambridgeshire, England
CC	Caernarvonshire, Wales
CDN	Cardiganshire, Wales
CH	Cheshire, England
CLN	Clackmannanshire, Scotland
CO	Cornwall, England
COL	City of London
COV	Coventry, city of, Warwickshire, England
CRM	Carmarthenshire, Wales
CT	City of Lincoln, Lincolnshire, England
CUM	Cumberland, England
DBT	Dunbartonshire, Scotland
DDE	City of Dundee, Scotland
DEN	Denbighshire, Wales
DFS	Dumfriesshire, Scotland
DHM	Durham, England
DOR	Dorset, England
DVN	Devonshire, England
EHG	Edinburgh, city of, Scotland
EL	East Lancashire, England (28th to 32nd Bns)
ELY	Ely, Isle of, Cambridgeshire, England
ER	East Riding of Yorkshire, England
ESX	Essex, England
F	Fifeshire, Scotland
F&D	Denbighshire, Wales (7th 'Denflint' Bn)
FT	Flintshire, Wales
G	Glasgow, city of, Scotland
GLN	Glamorgan, Wales
GLS	Gloucestershire, England
H	Hampshire and the Isle of Wight, England
HD	Holland, Lincolnshire, England
HDS	Huntingdonshire, England
HFD	Herefordshire, England
HIS	University College Hospital, Medical School, London, England
HTS	Hertfordshire, England
IN	Inverness-shire and Nairnshire, Scotland (1st Bn)
INV	Inverness-shire and Nairnshire, Scotland (2nd Bn)
IOM	Isle of Man
K	Kesteven, Lincolnshire, England
KT	Kent, England
L	Lewis, Hebrides, Scotland
L	Lindsey, Lincolnshire, England
LEI	Leicestershire, England

Battalion and Unit Insignia

In addition to the wearing of shoulder titles and county or city distinguishing flashes and battalion numbers, a limited number of Home Guard units adopted the practice of wearing battalion and unit insignia. The practice was not, however, widespread.

Flash	Affiliation
LF	Lancaster, city of, England
LF	Lancaster, East Lancashire, England (21st, 22nd, 27th, 41st, 42nd, 43rd and 45th Bns)
LK	Lanarkshire, Scotland
LON	County of London, England
LR	Lancaster, East Lancashire, England (24th Bn)
M	Merionethshire, Wales
MAN	Manchester, city of, England
MAN	Manchester, East Lancashire, England (23rd, 25th, 26th, 44th, 46th, 47th, 48th, 49th, 50th, 51st and 56th Bns)
ML	Midlothian, Scotland
MON	Monmouthshire, Wales
MRY	Morayshire, Scotland
MRY	Montgomeryshire, Wales
MT	Motor Transport companies, Eastern Command, England
MX	Middlesex, England
ND	Northumberland, England
NK	Norfolk, England
NN	Northamptonshire, England
NRY	North Riding of Yorkshire, England
NS	North Staffordshire, England
NTS	Nottinghamshire, England
ORK	Orkney, Scotland
OXF	Oxfordshire, England
PEM	Pembrokeshire, Wales
R	Ross and Cromarty, Scotland
R&B	Renfrew and Bute, Scotland
REN	Renfrewshire, Scotland
R-L	Lewis, Hebrides, Scotland
RR	Radnorshire, Wales (Radnor Rifles)
RU	Rutland, England
SB	Scottish Border (Roxburghshire), Scotland
SF	Sherwood Foresters, Derbyshire, England
SFX	Suffolk, England
SHR	Shropshire, England
SKR	Stewarty of Kirkcudbright, Scotland
SOM	Somerset, England
SRY	Southern Railway Bns, England
SS	South Staffordshire, England
STG	Stirlingshire, Scotland
SU	Sutherland, Scotland
SX	Sussex, England
SY	Surrey, England
TAY	Tay Fencibles, Perthshire, Scotland
TWD	Tweed, Peebles-shire, Scotland
UTP	Upper Thames Patrol, England (12th Berkshire and 31st Middlesex)
W	Wiltshire, England
WAR	Warwickshire, England
WES	Westmorland, England
WL	West Lancashire, England
WL	West Lothian, Scotland
WNR	Wigtownshire, Scotland (1st Battalion)
WNM	Wigtownshire, Scotland (2nd Battalion)
WOR	Worcestershire, England
WR	West Riding of Yorkshire, England
Z	Zetland, Shetland, Scotland

Right: A member of the Home Guard's 'Upper Thames Patrol, Middlesex Flotilla', a unit which was formed as a 'Territorial Defence Force' before the formation of the LDV and patrolled the River Thames from Teddington to Staines. All craft in service with the UPT were owned and manned by members of the unit. They were the only Home Guard unit in the country to have the dress distinction of wearing the dark blue peaked cap of the Thames Conservancy with their own distinctive silver-embroidered cap badge and worsted arm flash.

Below right: Brig. Wade H. Hayes, Commanding Officer of the 1st American Squadron, Home Guard, accompanies the American Ambassador, John Winant, as he inspects the Squadron on 4 July 1942. Established on the 4 July 1940, the Squadron was officially incorporated into the Armed Forces of the Crown in September of the same year. It was based at the TA Head-quarters of the Queen's West-minsters in Buckingham Gate, London and was composed of American citizens living in London. All members of the unit wore an arm badge of a displayed American Bald Eagle bearing in its left talon a bundle of thunderbolts and in its right an olive branch. On its breast was a shield. The same emblem was worn as a cap badge and produced in gilding metal but had the addition of a ribbon on either side of the Eagle's head, bearing the legend 'e pluribus unum'.

Proficiency Badges

The War Office decided on 7 April 1941 to institute the award of a proficiency badge to members of the Home Guard (ACI 491 of 1941). The badge was of a universal pattern and took the form of a 1in square of red cloth which was worn with one corner uppermost sewn to the lower part of the right sleeve of the Battle-Dress blouse only; it was in fact positioned 5in from the bottom edge of the right sleeve measured from the lowest point of the square. It had to be affixed without cost to the public and was not worn on the greatcoat. A further ACI, No. 49 dated 8 January 1942, stipulated that these proficiency badges were only to be worn by members of the Home Guard below the rank of Serjeant.

The following were the qualifications and conditions for the award of the proficiency badge to personnel of the Home Guard.

General.

1. Candidates must have served in the Home Guard for a period of not less than three months.
2. The suitability of a candidate for the award of a proficiency badge was contingent upon the recommendation of his company commander and on the latter's affirmation that he was fit to undergo the requisite tests with a reasonable chance of success.

Tests. Candidates were required to pass the following tests:

1. General knowledge. They had to answer correctly four questions out of five based on Home Guard Instruction No. 14, Appendix A, para. 6.
2. A test of elementary training for rifle, as laid down in Home Guard Instruction No. 14, Appendix A, para. 2 (candidates were to meet the required standard on a miniature rifle range).
3. Elementary training in the automatic weapon with which the candidate's unit was armed. Alternatively, candidates were to have displayed a satisfactory knowledge of field works as laid down in Home Guard Instruction No. 14, Appendix A, para. 3; or to have displayed satisfactory knowledge of simple map reading, i.e. to have answered correctly three questions out of four based on Home Guard Instruction No. 14, Appendix A, para. 4; or to have been able to give satisfactory instruction in any one subject in Home Guard Instruction No. 14, para. 8, and to have been employed as an instructor; or to have been able to pass the signalling standard as laid down in Home Guard Instruction No. 42 if employed as a signaller; or finally to have been able to pass the first aid test as laid down in Instruction No. 42 if he was employed on medical duties.

The responsibility for the conduct of these tests as laid down rested with the area commander. This responsibility was allowed to be delegated to Home Guard officers holding appointments not lower than Home Guard company commander when the area commander was not desirous of conducting the tests under his own arrangements; in these circumstances the area commander had to arrange for periodic test inspections to ensure that the requisite standards were being adhered to.

Annual requalification examinations and tests for the retention of the Home Guard proficiency badge already awarded were introduced, presumably from 1942 onwards, and successful candidates were awarded a 'bar' or bars, one for each successive year of successful requalification,

Right: Men of the Lincolnshire Home Guard being inspected by Lt. Gen. T. R. Eastwood, CB, DSO, MC, in June 1941. All members are wearing the Lincoln Imp shoulder emblem.

to be worn with their existing proficiency badge. These bars were of red cloth, 1in long by ¼in deep, and were worn horizontally, directly below the lower point of the proficiency badge.

Skill-at-Arms Badges

The information published in *Regulations for the Home Guard, 1942*. Volume I, under Section IX ('Dress and Badges', on page 33) that dealt with the subject of dress and badges of rank, titles and flashes was amended on 15 May 1944 to include details regarding the wearing of skill-at-arms badges in the Home Guard.

The Home Guard proficiency badge, the 1in square red cloth badge previously detailed on page 266 of this book, was ordered to be worn 1in higher up on the right forearm so as to make room, for those persons who had become eligible, for the wearing of the rifle marksman's badge (crossed rifles) and the signaller's badge (crossed signals flags). These skill-at-arms badges were worn only by qualified Home Guard personnel up to and including the rank of Corporal.

The design, size and colouring of these badges were the same as those worn in the Regular Army (see page 57).

Wound Stripes and Service Chevrons

On 16 February 1944, with the publication of Army Council Instruction No. 234 of 1944, the War Office announced that His Majesty the King (George VI) had been graciously pleased to approve the institution of wound stripes and service chevrons in the Home Guard. These stripes and chevrons were distinctions worn in respect of service undertaken since the declaration of war and were not intended to be regarded in the nature of a reward. There were no posthumous awards.

The initial issues of wound stripes and service chevrons for wear on Home Guard clothing was made from WD sources. They were accounted for in the same manner as rank badges and chevrons, and free replacements were made when necessitated by fair wear and tear. They were not worn on the greatcoat. On discharge from the Home Guard, members were permitted, at their own option and expense, to continue to wear on their civilian clothing such wound stripes or service chevrons to which they had been entitled when serving with the Home Guard.

The wearing of wound stripes or service chevrons other than of the sealed pattern as issued from WD sources was strictly forbidden and was not in any circumstances permitted, neither were embroidered chevrons permitted to be worn.

The following instructions regarding the issue of wound stripes and service chevrons applied to all ranks of the Home Guard.

Wound stripes.

In respect of wounds or injuries sustained in the Second World War. These stripes were of narrow gold braid 1½in in length and were worn vertically on the left sleeve (forearm) of the Battle-Dress blouse. One wound stripe was issued in respect of each wound or injury sustained whilst on Home Guard duty as a direct consequence of enemy action, for example during an actual enemy attack, aerial or otherwise, and which, before general mustering of the Home Guard, had been reported in accordance with *Regulations for the Home Guard, 1942*, Volume 1, para. 27(a) and certified in the report as due to enemy action. After mustering, qualification was an injury or wound sustained while on Home Guard duty as a direct consequence of enemy action, which had been reported in accordance with *Regulations for the Home Guard, 1942*, Volume I, para. 28(b)(iii) and accepted by the War Office Casualty Branch. Self-inflicted wounds or injuries did not qualify for the award.

In the case of members who, before enrolment into the Home Guard, had served with the armed forces, each occasion on which such members were reported as wounded in the records of the casualty branch of the service concerned constituted the authority for wearing a stripe. Similarly, in the case of members who were enrolled for full- or part-time service in a qualifying service before their enrolment into the Home Guard, each occasion on which a wound or injury was sustained in circumstances which would have entitled the member to the issue of a wound stripe by the organization concerned, and which had to be proved to the satisfaction of the officer commanding the unit, entitled the Home Guard member to wear a stripe. The list of qualifying services with regard to the subject of Home Guard wound stripes is as shown on page 115 of this book for the Regular Army.

Claims by members of the Home Guard for the award of wound stripes had to be made to the officer commanding their unit. After verifying entitlement from documents in the possession of the member or from other reliable sources, a list was forwarded to the Territorial Army Association that administered the unit for record and issue purposes.

In respect of wounds sustained in wars other than the Second World War. A single wound stripe of red rayon (lustrous) braid was worn to denote wounds sustained in previous wars, irrespective of the number of wounds. The stripe was 1½in in length and was worn vertically on the left sleeve (forearm) of the Battle-Dress blouse.

Claims by a member of the Home Guard had to be made to the officer commanding his unit, who verified entitlement from discharge papers or other reliable documents that were in the member's possession. After verification had taken place the names of those entitled to wear the stripe were notified to the TA Association for record and issue purposes, cases of doubt being referred to Department HG2 of the War Office.

Wound stripes were worn vertically on the outer side of the sleeve midway between the two seams, the bottom of the stripes being 4in from the bottom edge of the sleeve. When more than one stripe was worn, they were spaced at ½in intervals. Members of the Home Guard entitled to wear both the gold stripe(s) and the red stripe wore the latter to the rear (i.e. on the right when facing the jacket) of the gold stripe(s).

Service chevrons.

Chevrons (printed in red on a khaki background) to denote length of service in the armed forces (including the Home Guard) and the qualifying services (see page 115) during the Second World War were worn on the right sleeve (forearm) of the Battle-Dress blouse. One chevron was issued in respect of each completed year of service. In computing the number of chevrons which a member was entitled to wear, broken periods of service were aggregated. Sentences of detention or imprisonment that exceeded 28 days did not count towards computing aggregate service.

Issues were made as single chevrons or in sets of two, three or four chevrons. When a member became entitled to an additional chevron the previous issue was withdrawn and a new set was issued; withdrawn sets, provided they were in serviceable condition, were put back into stock for reissue.

Officers commanding Home Guard units were required to verify the total length of service of all ranks under their command, and they authorized the issue of the appropriate sets of chevrons to each member, having reported the number of sets required to the TA Association. Previous service in the armed forces, full- or part-time, and during enrolment in a qualifying service, was aggregated when estimating the number of chevrons to which personnel were considered to be entitled, provided that they produced proof of such service. The earliest date from which service in the Home Guard (or the LDV) counted was 14 May 1940. Cases of doubt regarding service in the Home Guard were referred to the TA Association concerned for verification of service from the member's enrolment form.

The chevrons were worn with the apex uppermost, on the outer side of the right sleeve of the Battle-Dress blouse, midway between the two seams, the apex of the lowest chevron being 4in from the bottom edge of the sleeve.

Persons not serving with the Home Guard at the date of this ACI (16 February 1944).

Application from persons who were no longer serving with the Home Guard had to be made direct to the officer commanding the unit in which they originally served, who, if he were satisfied as to entitlement, granted an initial issue of one set of wound stripes and/or service chevrons in respect of qualifying service. No additional free issues were made if the applicant had already been supplied with wound stripes or service chevrons whilst serving with the Forces. In all cases replacement had to be made at the expense of the individual.

Cap Badges

Home Guard units were authorized from 3 August 1940 to wear the cap badges of the county regiments to which they were affiliated. In August 1940 supplies of these badges were not available in sufficient numbers to meet the then existing requirements, but this position eased as the war progressed.

In April 1941 the subject of cap badges for the Home Guard was again mentioned, in the Appendix to ACI 623 dated 24 April 1941. All ranks of the Home Guard below that of full Colonel were required to wear the cap badge of the regiment of the county to which they belonged unless otherwise authorized by the War Office; no other badges were permitted. Home Guard officers of the rank of Colonel and upwards wore the Royal Crest badge on either the drab Field Service cap or the coloured Field Service cap.

Three months later, on 19 July 1941, ACI 1273 was published. It dealt with the subject of dress and badges for officers and members of the Home Guard and specified further details regarding the wearing of cap badges. Officers of the rank of Colonel and above were permitted to wear the coloured Field Service cap in lieu of the drab Field Service cap. When this happened the cap badge worn was in gold embroidery and was the authorized Royal Crest pattern, and both the coloured FS cap and embroidered badge had to be provided at the officer's own expense. The cap badge for use on the drab FS cap and the officers' pattern SD cap was the Royal Crest in gilt metal.

Right: Members of the Home Guard drawn from the 1st County of London Bn mount guard at Buckingham Palace to mark the first anniversary of the formation of the Home Guard; 14 May 1941. Dark brown leather waist belts and black leather gaiters were a common feature of Home Guard uniforms in the early war years.

4. UNIFORMS AND PERSONAL EQUIPMENT

At the time of the formation of the Home Guard, the following scale of uniform and personal equipment was intended to be provided for each volunteer (member): one suit of denim overalls, one service respirator, two anti-gas eyeshields, one outfit of anti-gas ointment, one steel helmet, one field dressing, one greatcoat, one pair of boots, one pair of gaiters, one waist-belt, one haversack, and two Home Guard arm-bands; also provided were one blanket for every two men and one groundsheet for every four men.

It was hoped that these articles would have been provided as soon as possible. However, sufficient supplies were not always immediately available and their allocation depended on the priority of requirements. Until sufficient supplies of the denim overalls became available, or on those occasions when specially authorized to do so, Home Guard volunteers/members wore civilian clothing when on duty. In this event they had to wear the Home Guard arm-band securely stitched to the right arm, midway between the wearer's shoulder and elbow.

Some time between August 1940 and July 1941 members and officers of the Home Guard were issued with serge Battle-Dress. This must have been a distinct improvement on the denim overalls previously issued and worn by the Home Guard, if only for its thermal quality compared with that of the much thinner denim material. Officers were not permitted to wear any form of uniform other than that issued to them, except if they were already in possession of army Service Dress; however, they were permitted to wear this only when not actually on duty with troops, provided that the correct badges of rank held in the Home Guard and the Home Guard shoulder title were worn. In the interests of economy both of money and wool, new Service Dress uniforms were not allowed to be purchased under any circumstances.

Commanding Officers of Home Guard units were expressly forbidden to order the officers under their command to purchase articles of clothing such as khaki shirts, collars and ties, brown shoes and such like. These articles were permitted to be worn, but their use was entirely optional.

Members of the Home Guard wore the Battle-Dress as issued, together with the drab Field Service cap. The cap badge of the regiment of the county to which they belonged was worn, unless otherwise authorized by the War Office. Badges of rank – as described on page 263 – were worn by warrant and non-commissioned officers on both arms of the Battle-Dress blouse and greatcoat as laid down for the corresponding ranks of the Infantry.[1]

The Home Guard Cape

Towards the end of 1940 units of the Home Guard began to be issued with serge capes. It is understood that these capes were introduced to be worn in place of the Army greatcoat where these were in short supply. Made from khaki serge Battle-Dress material, a correctly fitted cape reached to its wearer's knees. It had a fairly deep collar closed at the neck with a hook and eye attachment and was buttoned down the front with five large, four-holed, flat khaki buttons; for additional warmth the cape was half-lined across the shoulders down to waist level with soft khaki shirting material. The cape was meant to be showerproof.

There were two internal, open-top pockets on either side of the cape at the front and it had a set of two built-in shoulder harness cloth straps through which the wearer passed his arms before adjusting it. These straps also allowed for the cape to be worn partially fastened and thrown back over the wearer's shoulders. On the inside of the bottom edge of the cape, on either side of the

[1]For badges of rank for officers of the Home Guard see page 263; for Home Guard officers' head-dress and cap badges see page 268; for gorget patches worn in the Home Guard see page 263; and for distinguishing marks worn by personnel, including officers, of the Home Guard see page 263.

wearer's body, were a small khaki horn button and a reinforced button-hole, their purpose being to allow for the edge of the cape to be buttoned together loosely around the wearer's wrist to form a simple 'sleeve'.

Where capes had been issued in lieu of the greatcoat, Home Guard badges etc. were to be worn in the position on the cape similar to that on the sleeve of the greatcoat.

I can find no information as to how long these Home Guard capes remained in service.

Clothing for Use by Mounted Patrols

Mounted Home Guard sub-units were authorized by the War Office to patrol certain sparsely populated stretches of the countryside. The formation of these horsed patrols was usually undertaken by members of the Home Guard who were owners of horses, but only sound horses fit for the duties they had to perform were allowed to be used. Maintenance allowances and forage rations were provided for these sub-units, and Home Guard personnel engaged on these patrols were issued with one pair of Bedford cord pantaloons and one pair of puttees to replace their Battle-Dress trousers and web or leather anklets, the items so replaced being withdrawn. The Battle-Dress blouse was worn with the pantaloons. The Service Dress jacket normally worn by horsed units (see page 179) was not issued to the Home Guard.

5. HOME GUARD AUXILIARIES

On 20 April 1943 it was announced in the House of Commons by the Secretary of State for War that a limited number of women were to be nominated for service with the Home Guard. They were to perform such non-combatant duties as cooking, driving and clerical work. The age limits were set at 18 years and 65 years, but owing to call-up for military and industrial services most of the nominated women were in the older age groups. Many of these women were in fact already undertaking work of a similar nature, being members of the civilian Women's Voluntary Service for Civil Defence (WVS).

On 26 July 1944 their designation was altered from 'Nominated Women' to 'Home Guard Auxiliaries', and four months later, on 1 November 1944, in common with the rest of the Second World War Home Guard, they were 'stood down'. In all there were over 30,000 auxiliaries.

Home Guard Auxiliaries had no authorized uniform but they did wear on their civilian clothing a special brooch-badge. This was of plastic composition in silver-grey finish and consisted of the letters H.G. surrounded by a laurel wreath edged with a fine line. The badge measured about $1\frac{1}{8}$in in diameter.

Below and below right: The Home Guard serge cape introduced in late 1940.

Appendices

1. GLOSSARY

A & SH Argyll and Sutherland Highlanders; known jokingly during the 1914-18 war as the 'Agile and Suffering Highlanders'

AA Anti-Aircraft

AAG Assistant Adjutant-General

AA & QMG Assistant Adjutant and Quarter-Master-General

AB Army Book

ACC Army Catering Corps; also called – unfairly – 'Aldershot Cement Company'

ACI Army Council Instruction

AD Corps The Army Dental Corps

AD MS Assistant Director of Medical Services

ADOS Assistant Director of Ordnance Services

ADS & T Assistant Director of Supplies and Transport

AEC Army Educational Corps

AEF Allied Expeditionary Force

AF Army Form

AFV Armoured Fighting Vehicle

AGRA Army Group Royal Artillery

AMS Assistant Military Secretary

AO/s Army Order/s

AOP Pilot/s Air Observation Post Pilot/s

APM Assistant Provost-Marshal

APTC Army Physical Training Corps

APTS Army Physical Training Staff

AQMG Assistant Quartermaster-General

ATS Army Technical School (boys) & Auxiliary Territorial Service (women)

AVO Administrative Veterinary Officer

BD Battle-Dress

BEF British Expeditionary Force, which was sent to France and Belgium in 1939; wags suggested that BEF stood for 'Back Every Friday' because the Force was so close to Britain.

BGS Brigadier, General Staff

BM Brigade Major

Bn Battalion

CBE Commander of the Order of the British Empire

CCMA Commander, Corps Medium Artillery

CCRA Commander, Corps Royal Artillery

CD and AA Coast Defence and Anti-Aircraft

CE Chief Engineer

CG Coldstream Guards

CGS Chief of the General Staff

CIC Chief Inspector of Clothing; see CISC

C-in-C Commander-in-Chief

CIA Chief Inspector of Armaments

CIGS Chief of the Imperial General Staff

CIRES Chief Inspector of Royal Engineer Stores

CISC Chief Inspector of Stores and Clothing (abbreviation superseded by CIC)

CIST Chief Inspector of Supplementary Transport

CMP Corps of Military Police

CO Commanding Officer

COO Chief Ordnance Officer

Coy Company

CRA Commander, Royal Artillery (of a division)

CRASC Commander, Royal Army Service Corps

CRE Commander, Royal Engineers

CSO Chief Signals Officer

CSRD Chief Superintendent, Research Department

D Director; eg DST, Director of Supplies and Transport

DAD Deputy Assistant Director

DADOS Deputy Assistant Director of Ordnance Services

DAG Deputy Adjutant-General

DAAG Deputy Assistant Adjutant-General

DAMS Deputy Assistant Military Secretary

DAQMG Deputy Assistant Quarter-Master-General

DA & QMG Deputy Adjutant and Quarter-Master-General

DCGS Deputy Chief of the General Staff

DCM Distinguished Conduct Medal

DD Deputy Director, eg DDMS Deputy Director of Medical Services

DDOS Deputy Director Ordnance Services

DDS&T Deputy Director Supplies and Transport

DEMS Defensively Equipped Merchant Ship

DFC Distinguished Flying Cross

DG Director-General, eg DGTn, Director-General of Transportation

DJAG Deputy Judge Advocate-General

DMO&P Department of Military Operations and Planning

DQMG Deputy Quarter-Master-General
DR Despatch Rider, also known as 'Don Rs'
DSO Distinguished Service Order
DW The Duke of Wellington's Regiment (West Riding); also known as 'The Duke of Boots'
EF Expeditionary Force
EFI Expeditionary Forces Institute (the name used by NAAFI when overseas)
ENSA Entertainments National Service Association, jokingly called 'Every Night Something Awful' or as Tommy Trinder, comedian and wartime member of ENSA, dubbed it 'Even NAAFI Stands Aghast'.
ER Equipment Regulations
FS Field Service
FSMO Field Service Marching Order; refers to webbing equipment
GCVO (Knight or Dame) Grand Cross of the Royal Victorian Order
GHQ General Headquarters
GM George Medal, Gilding metal
GO/s General Order/s
GOC General Officer Commanding
GS General Service
GSO General Staff Officer
HAA Heavy Anti-Aircraft
HT Horse Transport (obsolete)
i/c in charge
IC Internal combustion
KCVO Knight Commander of the Royal Victorian Order
KD Khaki Drill
KG Knight of the Garter
KR King's Regulations
LAA Light Anti-Aircraft
LRDG Long Range Desert Group
MBE Member of the Order of the British Empire
MC Motorcyclist
MC Military Cross (for officers)
MG Machine Gun
MM Military Medal (for other ranks)
MP Military Police
MPSC Military Provost Staff Corps
MT Mechanical Transport/Motor Transport
NAAFI Navy, Army and Air Force Institute, see also EFI
NCO Non-Commissioned Officer
OC Officer Commanding
OCTU Officer Cadet Training Unit
OO Ordnance Officer
ORs Other Ranks
PIAT Projectile Infantry Anti-Tank, an individual anti-tank weapon
(P)MLO (Principal) Military Landing Officer

PTI Physical Training Instructor
RA Royal Artillery
RAC Royal Armoured Corps
RAChD Royal Army Chaplains Department
RAMC Royal Army Medical Corps
RAOC Royal Army Ordnance Corps
RAP Regimental Aid Post
RAPC Royal Army Pay Corps
RASC Royal Army Service Corps. Humorously interpreted as 'Run Away Somebody's Coming' and, after the fighting in North Africa when a RASC supply column was rumoured to have been captured by the German Afrika Korps complete with all its stores of food, ammunition, POL and water, 'Rommel's Auxiliary Supply Column'.
RAVC Royal Army Veterinary Corps
RAV School Royal Army Veterinary School
RE Royal Engineers
REME Royal Electrical and Mechanical Engineers
RM Royal Marines
RMA Royal Military Academy
RMC Royal Military College
RP Regimental Police, Regimental Paymaster
RTO Railway Transport Officer
RWF Royal Welch Fusiliers ('Welsh' before 1920)
SAA Small Arms Ammunition
Sam Browne A leather belt and shoulder harness named after its inventor General Sir Samuel J. Browne (1824-1901), who devised this apparatus to help him draw his sword after he had lost his left arm. So practical was Browne's device of shoulder straps and pistol and sword supporting straps that the idea was utilized by many foreign armies.
SAS Special Air Service
SASC Small Arms School Corps
SC Staff Captain
SD Service Dress
Serjeant Commonly used in official publications before – and sometimes during – the 1939-45 War in preference to 'Sergeant', and adopted throughout this book.
SL Searchlight
SLO Searchlight operator
SOE Special Operations Executive
TA Territorial Army
TAF Tactical Air Force
THR Tower Hamlet Rifles
TP Trade pattern
WD War Department, Westminster Dragoons
WE/s War Establishment/s
WO War Office (the War House), Warrant officer

2. THE ARMY COUNCIL

The government of the Army was vested in the Crown. The command was placed in the hands of the Army Council, which was also responsible for the administration of the Regular Forces. The administration of the Territorial Army, and later the Home Guard, was in the hands of the County Associations at all times other than when called up before the war for annual training in camp, when embodied, or when on actual military service.

The Army Council was composed as follows:

The Secretary of State for War. This was a parliamentary appointment. He acted as President of the Army Council and was responsible to the King and Parliament for all the business of the Army Council.

Military Secretary to the Secretary of State. His was the responsibility of executive duties connected with the appointment, promotion and retirement of officers, with selections for staff and extra-regimental appointments, and with the grant of honours and rewards. He was the Secretary of the Selection Board attending meetings of Corps and Departmental Selection Boards, and he held interviews with officers on personal questions relating to appointments, promotions, etc.

Parliamentary Under-Secretary of State for War. This was a parliamentary appointment. He acted as Vice-President of the Army Council and was responsible to the Secretary of State for War for the administration of business affecting the Territorial Army Associations and the War Department Lands.

The Chief of the Imperial General Staff (1st Military Member). His duties covered all questions of military policy affecting the security of the Empire; advice as to the conduct of operations of war and orders in regard to military operations; aid to civil power; the collection and collation of military intelligence; censorship; international law; defence security intelligence; war organization, fighting efficiency and training of the military forces; the training of the Staff of the Army, and, in conjunction with the AG (Adjutant-General), the QMG (Quarter-Master-General) and the MGO (Master-General of the Ordnance), the selection of officers for staff appointments; the education of officers and the selection of candidates for commissions in the Cavalry, Royal Artillery, Royal Engineers, Royal Signals, Infantry, Royal Tank Regiment, Royal Army Service Corps and Army Education Corps; and educational training.

The Adjutant-General to the Forces (2nd Military Member). His duties consisted of the raising and organizing in peacetime of the personnel of the military forces, together with their mobilization, discharge and record offices; the peacetime distribution of military units; the administration of the Cavalry, RA, RE, R Signals, Infantry, RTR, RASC, RAMC, RAOC, AEC, AD Corps, QAIMNS, TANS, Corps of Military Police and MPSC; discipline; martial and military law; the selection of officers for staff appointments in conjunction with the GGS, QMG and MGO; appeals; administrative arrangements connected with training and education; medical, dental and hygiene services; prisoners of war; personal and ceremonial questions; medals; regimental honours and titles; vocational training; and the civilian employment of ex-soldiers.

The Quarter-Master-General to the Forces (3rd Military Member). His responsibilities and duties entailed the quartering of the Army; policy as to the provision of accommodation; the movement of troops, animals and stores by sea, land and air and the administration of technical transportation services, both railway and WD, with their personnel; the construction and maintenance of fortifications, barracks, ranges, hospitals and stores buildings; the administration of works services and personnel; the provision, custody, maintenance and issue of building stores; the technical examination of works services; the administration of supply, transport and barrack services and their civilian personnel; the custody and issue of barrack stores; the provision, inspection, storage, issue and repair of all MT vehicles on the establishment of RASC units or driven by RASC personnel and the provision and custody of reserves and spares for such vehicles; the impressment of vehicles on mobilization and subsidy schemes in respect of vehicles in peace; the administration of remount and veterinary services and their personnel; travelling, lodging, furniture, fuel and light, field, stable, ration and forage allowance and policy in regard thereto; questions relating to the training of cooks, the use of cooking apparatus in the field and in barracks, messing and regimental funds, the NAAFI and philanthropic institutes on WD land; the technical training of the RAVC, Royal Army Veterinary School and School of Farriers; postal services in war; salvage; and the selection of officers for staff appointments in conjunction with the CIGS, the AG and the MGO.

The Master-General of the Ordnance (4th Military Member). Duties included the scientific development of war material; research, design experiment, manufacture, proof and inspection of guns, carriages, tracked, semi-tracked, and wheeled vehicles, small arms, machine-guns, ammunition, grenades, bicycles, chemical defence appliances, position- and range-finders, optical instruments, technical stores connected with the RA, RE and R Signals, general stores and clothing; the inspection of all MT vehicles; the provision, storage, issue and repair (other than first line repair) of the above, with the exception of MT vehicles on the establishment of the RASC units or driven by RASC personnel; the administration of Army Ordnance Services and their civilian personnel and Royal Ordnance Factories; the administration of the Military College of Science, RAOC School of Instruction, Ordnance Committee, RA Committee, Small Arms Committee, Chemical Defence Committee, Mechanization Board, RE Board and Supply Board; the Technical Establishment, and personnel of the design, inspection, research, proof and experimental establishments pertaining thereto; questions regarding patents, royalties and inventions; and the selection of officers for staff appointments in conjunction with the CIGS, the AG and the QMG.

The Permanent Under-Secretary of State for War. He was Secretary of the Army Council, and responsible for the general control of War Office procedure and the conduct of official business; the editing and issue of Army Regulations; and the administration of the Royal Army Chaplains Department, the Royal Army Pay Corps, etc.

The Financial Secretary of the War Office. His duties consisted of financial policy, labour policy and contracts.

3. ARMY NUMBERS

A soldier, when posted to a corps, regiment, etc. upon enlistment, was assigned an Army number by the officer in charge of records; the Army numbers allocated to corps etc. are given in Table 46. A soldier, whether originally enlisted for service in the Regular Army, the SR (Supplementary Reserve) or the TA (Territorial Army), retained the Army number originally allocated to him throughout his service, irrespective of any subsequent posting or transfer, except that any man deemed to have been enlisted into the militia under the Military Training Act of 1939, who had previously been allocated an Army number, was given a fresh Army number in accordance with the instructions contained in *Regulations for the Militia (other than the Supplementary Reserve), 1939*, paras. 11–13, and the use of his previous Army number was discontinued. An ex-soldier who re-enlisted retained the Army number which he previously bore.

As the RASC was divided into two main branches, the prefixes S (Supply) and T (Transport) were added Army numbers to denote the branches in which the soldiers of that corps served. If a soldier of another corps re-enlisted into, or transferred to, the RASC, the officer i/c RASC records notified the soldier's CO of the prefix letter to be added to his Army number, but a soldier of the RASC who re-enlisted into, or transferred to, any other corps retained his Army number without the use of the prefix.

On conviction by court-martial (or on trial being dispensed with) on a charge of fraudulent enlistment, a soldier resumed using the Army number which was originally assigned to him.

In all documents relating to a soldier, his Army number preceded his name. If he was transferred, deserted, was discharged or died, the number was not given to any other soldier. Finally, a soldier promoted to warrant rank retained his number.

Table 46.   Army Numbers allocated to Corps etc.

Corps etc.	Allocation of blocks of numbers	
	From	To
Royal Army Service Corps	1	294,000
Household Cavalry:		
The Life Guards	294,001	304,000
Royal Horse Guards	304,001	309,000
Cavalry of the Line[1]	309,001	721,000
Royal Artillery		
Field Branch		
Coast Defence and Anti-Aircraft Branch	721,001	1,842,000
Royal Engineers	1,842,001	2,303,000
Royal Corps of Signals	2,303,001	2,604,000
Grenadier Guards	2,604,001	2,646,000
Coldstream Guards	2,646,001	2,688,000
Scots Guards	2,688,001	2,714,000
Irish Guards	2,714,001	2,730,000
Welsh Guards	2,730,001	2,744,000
The Black Watch	2,744,001	2,809,000
The Seaforth Highlanders	2,809,001	2,865,000
The Gordon Highlanders	2,865,001	2,921,000
The Cameron Highlanders	2,921,001	2,966,000
The Argyll and Sutherland Highlanders	2,966,001	3,044,000
The Royal Scots	3,044,001	3,122,000
The Royal Scots Fusiliers	3,122,001	3,178,000
The King's Own Scottish Borderers	3,178,001	3,233,000
The Cameronians	3,233,001	3,299,000
The Highland Light Infantry	3,299,001	3,377,000
The East Lancashire Regiment	3,377,001	3,433,000
The Lancashire Fusiliers	3,433,001	3,511,000
The Manchester Regiment	3,511,001	3,589,000
The Border Regiment	3,589,001	3,644,000
The Prince of Wales's Volunteers	3,644,001	3,701,000
The King's Own Royal Regiment	3,701,001	3,757,000
The King's Regiment	3,757,001	3,846,000
The Loyal Regiment	3,846,001	3,902,000
The South Wales Borderers	3,902,001	3,947,000
The Welch Regiment	3,947,001	4,025,000
The King's Shropshire Light Infantry	4,025,001	4,070,000
The Monmouthshire Regiment	4,070,001	4,103,000
The Herefordshire Regiment	4,103,001	4,114,000
The Cheshire Regiment	4,114,001	4,178,000
The Royal Welch Fusiliers	4,178,001	4,256,000
The Royal Northumberland Fusiliers	4,256,001	4,334,000

Corps etc.	Allocation of blocks of numbers	
	From	To
The East Yorkshire Regiment	4,334,001	4,379,000
The Green Howards	4,379,001	4,435,000
The Durham Light Infantry	4,435,001	4,523,000
The West Yorkshire Regiment	4,523,001	4,601,000
The Duke of Wellington's Regiment	4,601,001	4,680,000
The King's Own Yorkshire Light Infantry	4,680,001	4,736,000
The York and Lancaster Regiment	4,736,001	4,792,000
The Lincolnshire Regiment	4,792,001	4,848,000
The Leicestershire Regiment	4,848,001	4,904,000
The South Staffordshire Regiment	4,904,001	4,960,000
The Sherwood Foresters	4,960,001	5,038,000
The North Staffordshire Regiment	5,038,001	5,094,000
The Royal Warwickshire Regiment	5,094,001	5,172,000
The Gloucestershire Regiment	5,172,001	5,239,000
The Worcestershire Regiment	5,239,001	5,328,000
The Royal Berkshire Regiment	5,328,001	5,373,000
The Oxfordshire and Buckinghamshire Light Infantry	5,373,001	5,429,000
The Duke of Cornwall's Light Infantry	5,429,001	5,485,000
The Hampshire Regiment	5,485,001	5,562,000
The Wiltshire Regiment	5,562,001	5,608,000
The Devonshire Regiment	5,608,001	5,718,000
The Somerset Light Infantry	5,662,001	5,718,000
The Dorsetshire Regiment	5,718,001	5,763,000
The Royal Norfolk Regiment	5,763,001	5,819,000
The Suffolk Regiment	5,819,001	5,875,000
The Northamptonshire Regiment	5,875,001	5,931,000
The Cambridgeshire Regiment	5,931,001	5,942,000
The Bedfordshire and Hertfordshire Regiment	5,942,001	5,998,000
The Essex Regiment	5,998,001	6,076,000
The Queen's Royal Regiment	6,076,001	6,132,000
The East Surrey Regiment	6,132,001	6,188,000
The Middlesex Regiment	6,188,001	6,278,000
The Buffs	6,278,001	6,334,000
The Royal West Kent Regiment	6,334,001	6,390,000
The Royal Sussex Regiment	6,390,001	6,446,000
The Royal Fusiliers	6,446,001	6,515,000
The Inns of Court Regiment	6,802,501	6,814,000
Honourable Artillery Company (Infantry)	6,825,001	6,837,000
The King's Royal Rifle Corps	6,837,001	6,905,000

Corps etc.	Allocation of blocks of numbers	
	From	To
The Rifle Brigade	6,905,001	6,972,000
The Royal Inniskilling Fusiliers	6,972,001	7,006,000
The Royal Ulster Rifles	7,006,001	7,040,000
The Royal Irish Fusiliers	7,040,001	7,075,000
Royal Dublin Fusiliers[2]	7,075,001	7,109,000
Royal Irish Regiment	7,109,001	7,143,000
Connaught Rangers[2]	7,143,001	7,177,000
Leinster Regiment[2]	7,177,001	7,211,000
Royal Munster Fusiliers[2]	7,211,001	7,245,000
Royal Army Medical Corps	7,245,001	7,536,000
The Army Dental Corps[3]	7,536,001	7,539,000
Royal Guernsey Militia and Royal Alderney Artillery Militia[4]	7,539,001	7,560,000
Royal Militia of the Island of Jersey[4]	7,560,001	7,574,000
Royal Army Ordnance Corps	7,574,001	7,657,000
Royal Army Pay Corps	7,657,001	7,681,000
Corps of Military Police[5]	7,681,001	7,717,000
Military Provost Staff Corps	7,717,001	7,718,800
Small Arms School Corps	7,718,801	7,720,400
Army Education Corps[6]	7,720,401	7,732,400
Band of the Royal Military College	7,732,401	7,733,000
Corps of Military Accountants[2]	7,733,001	7,757,000
Royal Army Veterinary Corps	7,757,001	7,807,000
Machine Gun Corps[2]	7,807,001	7,868,000
Royal Tank Regiment	7,868,001	7,891,868
Royal Armoured Corps[7]	7,891,869	8,230,000

Corps etc.	Allocation of blocks of numbers	
	From	To
Militia[8]	10,000,001	10,350,000
Intelligence Corps	10,350,001	10,400,000
Royal Army Pay Corps[9,13]	10,400,001	10,500,000
Middle East 2nd Echelon (for issue to Allies locally enlisted)	10,500,001	10,508,000
The Army Dental Corps[10,13]	10,510,001	10,530,000
Royal Army Ordnance Corps[11,13]	10,530,001	10,600,000
Reconnaissance Corps	10,600,001	10,630,000
Army Catering Corps	10,630,001	10,655,000
Army Physical Training Corps[12]	10,655,001	10,660,000
Royal Army Service Corps[13]	10,660,001	11,000,000
Royal Artillery (Coast Defence and Anti-Aircraft Branch)[13,14]	11,000,001	11,500,000
Pioneer Corps[15]	13,000,001	14,000,000
The Lowland Regiment[16]	14,000,001	14,002,500
The Highland Regiment[16]	14,002,501	14,005,000
General Service Corps[16]	14,200,001	15,000,000
India (for local enlistments into British Corps and Regiments)[16]	15,000,001	15,005,000
Royal Electrical and Mechanical Engineers[16]	16,000,001	16,100,000
Non-Combatant Corps	97,000,001	97,100,000
The London Regiment (TA)[17]	—	—
The Auxiliary Territorial Service (Women)	W/1	W/500,000
Voluntary Aid Detachments[16]	W/500,001	W/1,000,000

[1]Included Army numbers from 558,471 to 558,761, allocated to personnel enlisted for the Royal Armoured Corps, outside the block of numbers allotted for that corps.

[2]Disbanded units.

[3]The Army Dental Corps became the Royal Army Dental Corps in 1946.

[4]The allocation of Army numbers to the Royal Guernsey Militia, Royal Alderney Artillery Militia and Royal Militia of the Island of Jersey was discontinued in 1929.

[5]The Corps of Military Police became the Royal Corps of Military Police in 1946.

[6]The Army Education Corps became The Royal Army Education Corps when the title 'Royal' was granted on 28 November 1946.

[7]See footnote 1.

[8]Army numbers for the Militia were allocated in accordance with *Regulations for the Militia (other than the Supplementary Reserve), 1939*, paras. 11–13.

[9]The title 'Royal' was conferred in 1920, shortly after the Corps was formed.

[10]See footnote 3.

[11]The Army Ordnance Corps received its 'Royal' title in 1918.

[12]The Army Gymnastic Staff (AGS) changed its title after the Great War to 'Army Physical Training Staff.' It received its title 'Army Physical Training Corps' on 16 September 1940.

[13]These numbers were additional to those previously allocated and shown at the beginning of this listing.

[14]These numbers were in addition to those already allotted.

[15]The Auxiliary Military Pioneer Corps was formed in October 1939 and adopted the cap badge and motto used by the Labour Corps of First World War fame. The Labour Corps was raised in 1917 and disbanded in 1922. The AMPC changed its title to 'Pioneer Corps' within a short time of its foundation in November 1940, and in 1946 it was honoured with the title 'Royal Pioneer Corps'.

[16]This unit was introduced from September 1943.

[17]Records were maintained by the record offices administering the corps to which these units belonged.

Right: Film actress Anna Lee with troops of the Queen's Royal Regiment (West Surrey) at Aldershot.

Bibliography

Army Council *Instructions*, issued between 1933 and 1945/46. Published by the War Office and circulated down to companies, batteries and equivalent units

Bain, Robert *The Clans and Tartans of Scotland*, 5th edition. Collins, London, 1977

Bloomer, W. H. and K. D. *Badges of the Highland and Lowland Regiments (including Volunteer and Territorial Battalions)*. Published in 1982 by the authors at 94 Melbourne Grove, East Dulwich, London SE22

— *Scottish Regimental Badges, 1793–1971.* Arms and Armour Press, London, 1973

The Bulletin; Journal of the Military Historical Society, London. Issues consulted: Aug 1960, Aug 1962, Feb 1968, May 1968, Aug 1968, Nov 1973, May 1979 and Aug 1979

Cabinet Office *Orders of Battle, 1939–1945.* 2 vols. HMSO, London, 1960

Campbell, D. Alastair *The Dress of the Royal Artillery.* Arms and Armour Press, London, 1971

Cole, Lieutenant-Colonel N. *Formation Badges of World War Two.* Arms and Armour Press, London, 1973

— *Heraldry in War: Formation Badges, 1939–45*, 3rd ed. Gale and Polden, Aldershot, 1950

Gaylor, John *Military Badge Collection.* Leo Cooper, London, 1983

Grimble, Ian *Scottish Clans and Tartans.* Hamlyn, London, 1973

India, Government of *Dress Regulations (India) 1931*; plus amendments up to No. 90 of Dec 1941 plus those of 1 May 1941, 1 Aug 1943, 18 March 1944, 7 July 1944 and 30 Dec 1944. Govt of India, Delhi, 1931

— *Clothing Regulations (India) 1939.* Govt of India, Delhi, November 1939

Kipling, Arthur L. and King, Hugh L. *Head-Dress Badges of the British Army.* 2 vols. Muller, London, 1979

May, Commander W., Carman, W. Y. and Tanner, J. *Badges and Insignia of the British Armed Services.* A. and C. Black, London, 1974

Parfitt, G. Archer *The Award of the Croix de Guerre (1914–18) to Units of the British Army.* Gale and Polden, Aldershot, 1975.

Regimental Badges and Service Caps. George Philip, London, 1941

Ripley, Howard *Buttons of the British Army, 1855–1970.* Arms and Armour Press, London, 1971

Swinson, Arthur (ed) *A Register of the Regiments and Corps of the British Army.* Archive Press through Arms and Armour Press, London, 1972

War Office *Dress Regulations for the Army, 1934*; plus amendments of June 1937, Oct 1938 and April 1940. HMSO, London, June 1934

— *Carrier Manpack GS, 1945.* HMSO, London, September 1945

— *King's Regulations for the Army and the Royal Army Reserve, 1940.* HMSO, London, July 1940; plus various amendments from Sept 1940 to Aug 1943

— *The Pattern 1937 Web Equipment.* HMSO, London, October 1939

— *Regulations for the Clothing of the Army, 1936*; plus amendments 1 to 7 (Jan 1937 to Oct 1939). HMSO, London, May 1936

— *Priced Vocabulary of Clothing and Necessaries, 1936*; plus amendments to 1939. HMSO, London, 1936

— *War Clothing Regulations, 1941.* HMSO, London, March 1941

— *War Clothing Regulations, 1943.* HMSO, London, 1943

Westlake, R. A. *Collecting Metal Shoulder Titles.* Warne, London, 1980

Wilkinson, F. J. *Badges of the British Army.* Arms and Armour Press, London, 1969; plus editions with Price Guide supplement